NEWFOUNDLAND AND

A History

Although the inclusion of Newfoundland and Labrador as part of Confederation is of national significance, it represents only a small portion of the province's past. Sean Cadigan has written a definitive history of one of North America's most distinct and beautiful regions. The site of the continent's first European settlement one thousand years ago and a former colony of England, this easternmost point of the continent has had a fascinating history in part because of its position as the gateway between North America and Europe. Examining the region from prehistoric times to the present, *Newfoundland and Labrador* is not only a comprehensive history of the province, but an illuminating portrait of the Atlantic world and of the European colonization of the Americas.

The book traces the major developments in the region's history, from the first European settlements, the extinction of the indigenous Beothuk by European settlers, the conflicts between settlers and the imperial government, to the Royal Newfoundland Regiment's near annihilation at the Battle of the Somme, the rise of Newfoundland nationalism, Joey Smallwood's case for confederation, and the economic disappointments that resulted after Confederation. Paying particular attention to the ways in which Newfoundland and Labrador's history has been shaped by its environment, this study considers how natural resources such as the Grand Banks, the cod fishery, and off-shore oil have affected the region and its inhabitants.

Written in an engaging and accessible style, *Newfoundland and Labrador* brings the rich and vibrant history of this remarkable region to life.

SEAN T. CADIGAN is an associate professor in the Department of History at Memorial University of Newfoundland.

Newfoundland and Labrador

A HISTORY

Sean T. Cadigan

UNIVERSITY OF TORONTO PRESS
Toronto Buffalo London

© University of Toronto Press 2009
Toronto Buffalo London
www.utppublishing.com
Printed in the U.S.A.

Reprinted 2013

Reprinted in Canada 150 Collection 2017

ISBN 978-1-4875-1660-4

Library and Archives Canada Cataloguing in Publication

Cadigan, Sean T. (Sean Thomas), 1962–
Newfoundland and Labrador : a history / Sean T. Cadigan.

Includes bibliographical references and index.
ISBN 978-1-4875-1660-4

1. Newfoundland and Labrador – History.   I. Title.

FC2161.C33 2009   971.8   C2008-906586-7

University of Toronto Press acknowledges the financial assistance to its publishing program of the Canada Council for the Arts and the Ontario Arts Council.

University of Toronto Press acknowledges the financial support for its publishing activities of the Government of Canada through the Book Publishing Industry Development Program (BPIDP).

The book has been published with the help of a grant from the Canadian Federation for the Humanities and Social Sciences, through the Aid to Scholarly Publications Program, using funds provided by the Social Sciences and Humanities Research Council of Canada.

Contents

Acknowledgments

Gerry Hallowell first approached me in 1997 on behalf of the University of Toronto Press to write this history of Newfoundland and Labrador. I agreed to do so just before I learned that I was expecting my first daughter, Elizabeth. This touched off a chain of events, which although very rewarding from the perspective of family, led to many delays in producing this work. I dedicate this book to Elizabeth, to her younger sister Margaret, and to their mother and my partner Bonnie Morgan, who also read and provided advice on an early version.

I thank the University of Toronto Press for its patience, and I am particularly grateful to Len Husband, editor of Canadian history, for his advice and encouragement.

A number of people helped me by giving freely of their time and advice. Alan Macpherson, professor emeritus in the department of geography, Memorial University, assisted my interpretation of the Norse in chapter two. Peter Sinclair, department of sociology, Memorial University, advised me on many aspects of the writing of this book and, more importantly, has been a steady source of friendship and collaboration. As always, Mark Leier, department of history, Simon Fraser University, has offered good-humoured counsel and camaraderie.

Most important has been the advice and support of Rosemary Ommer, now the director of special projects, Office of the Vice-President Research, University of Victoria, who has been a mentor to me since my days as a graduate student. Rosemary's direction of two major projects, the Eco-Research Project (based at Memorial University from 1993 to 1997) and Coasts Under Stress (a partnership between researchers at Memorial and the University of Victoria from 2000 to 2006), introduced me to the importance of ecology in history. Rosemary read an earlier version of this book and advised me through the rewriting of a number of chapters.

The responsibility for any error or omission in this work is solely my own.

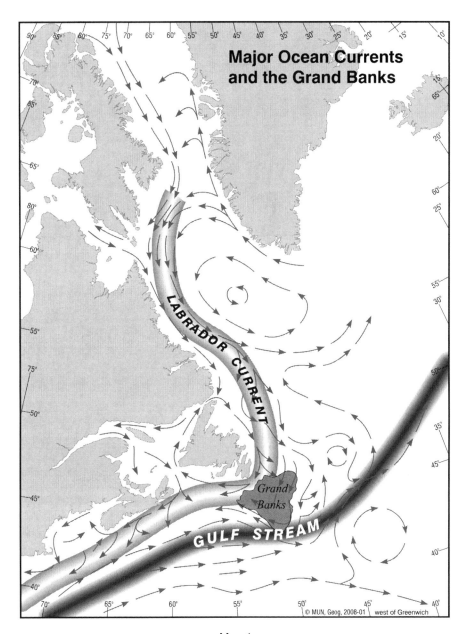

Map 1

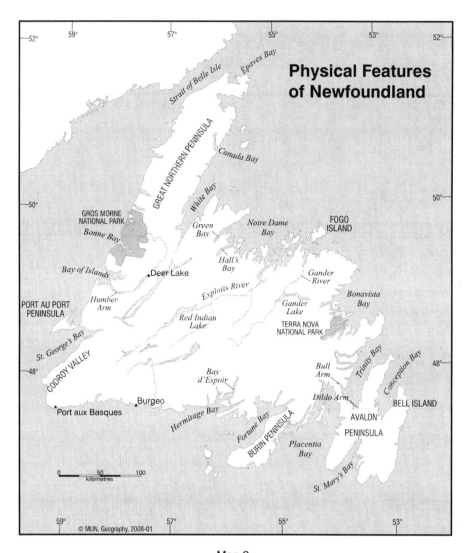

Physical Features of Newfoundland

Epaves Bay

Strait of Belle Isle

Canada Bay

GREAT NORTHERN PENINSULA

White Bay

GROS MORNE NATIONAL PARK

Green Bay

Notre Dame Bay

FOGO ISLAND

Bonne Bay

Hall's Bay

Bay of Islands

Deer Lake

Gander River

Exploits River

Gander Bay

Bonavista Bay

PORT AU PORT PENINSULA

Humber Arm

Red Indian Lake

Gander Lake

TERRA NOVA NATIONAL PARK

St. George's Bay

CODROY VALLEY

Bay d'Espoir

Bull Arm

Trinity Bay

Conception Bay

Burgeo

Dildo Arm

BELL ISLAND

Port aux Basques

Hermitage Bay

Fortune Bay

BURIN PENINSULA

AVALON PENINSULA

Placentia Bay

St. Mary's Bay

0   50   100
kilometres

© MUN, Geography, 2008-01

Map 2

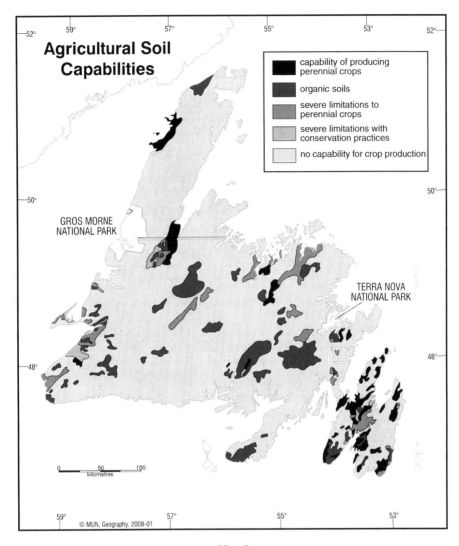

Agricultural Soil Capabilities

Legend:
- capability of producing perennial crops
- organic soils
- severe limitations to perennial crops
- severe limitations with conservation practices
- no capability for crop production

GROS MORNE NATIONAL PARK

TERRA NOVA NATIONAL PARK

0   50   100
kilometres

© MUN, Geography, 2008-01

Map 3

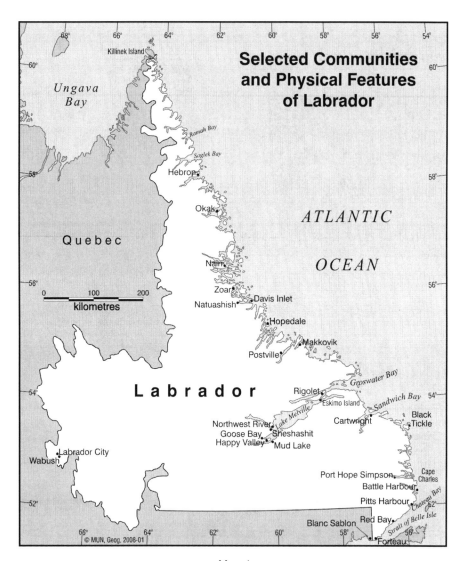

Selected Communities
and Physical Features
of Labrador

68° 66° 64° 62° 60° 58° 56° 54°

60°

Killinek Island

Ungava Bay

58°

Ramah Bay

Saglek Bay

Hebron

Okak

ATLANTIC

Quebec

Nain

OCEAN

56°

Zoar

Davis Inlet

Natuashish

0   100   200
kilometres

Hopedale

Makkovik

Postville

Labrador

Rigolet

Groswater Bay

Lake Melville

Eskimo Island

Sandwich Bay

54°

Cartwright

Black Tickle

Northwest River

Goose Bay   Sheshashit

Happy Valley   Mud Lake

Labrador City

Wabush

Port Hope Simpson

Cape Charles

Battle Harbour

Pitts Harbour

Chateau Bay

52°

Blanc Sablon   Red Bay

Strait of Belle Isle

Forteau

© MUN, Geog, 2008-01

66° 64° 62° 60° 58° 56°

Map 4

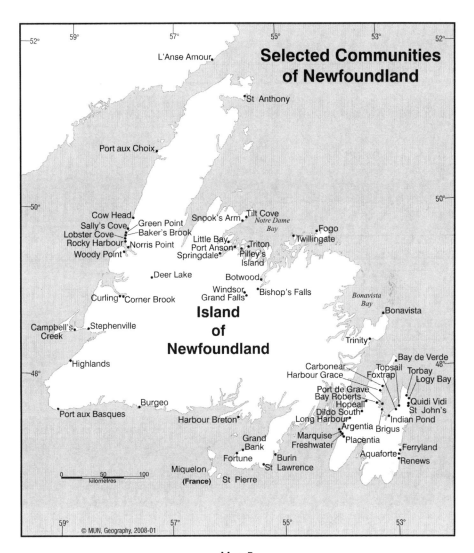

Selected Communities of Newfoundland

L'Anse Amour

St Anthony

Port aux Choix

Cow Head
Sally's Cove
Lobster Cove
Rocky Harbour
Woody Point
Green Point
Baker's Brook
Norris Point

Snook's Arm
Tilt Cove
Notre Dame Bay
Little Bay
Port Anson
Springdale
Triton
Pilley's Island

Fogo
Twillingate

Deer Lake

Botwood

Windsor
Grand Falls
Bishop's Falls

Bonavista Bay

Bonavista

Island of Newfoundland

Curling
Corner Brook

Campbell's Creek
Stephenville

Highlands

Trinity

Carbonear
Harbour Grace

Topsail
Foxtrap
Torbay
Logy Bay

Bay de Verde

Burgeo

Port aux Basques

Harbour Breton

Port de Grave
Bay Roberts
Hopeall
Dildo South
Long Harbour
Argentia
Marquise
Freshwater
Placentia
Brigus

Quidi Vidi
St John's
Indian Pond

Aquaforte
Ferryland
Renews

Grand Bank
Fortune
Burin
St Lawrence

Miquelon
(France)
St Pierre

0   50   100
kilometres

© MUN, Geography, 2008-01

Map 5

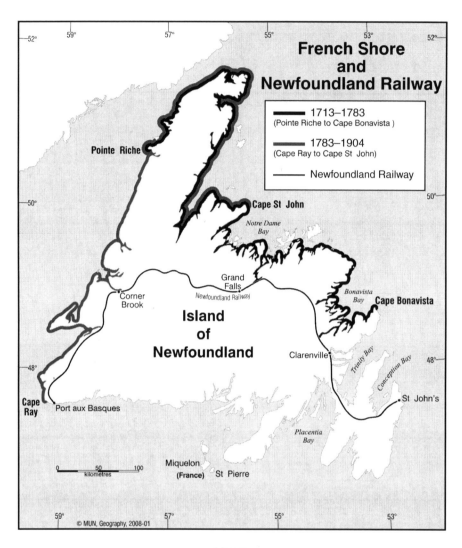

**French Shore
and
Newfoundland Railway**

	1713–1783
	(Pointe Riche to Cape Bonavista)
	1783–1904
	(Cape Ray to Cape St John)
	Newfoundland Railway

Pointe Riche

Cape St John

Notre Dame Bay

Grand Falls

Newfoundland Railway

Corner Brook

Bonavista Bay Cape Bonavista

**Island
of
Newfoundland**

Clarenville

Trinity Bay

Conception Bay

St John's

Cape Ray

Port aux Basques

Placentia Bay

0   50   100
kilometres

Miquelon
(France) St Pierre

© MUN, Geography, 2008-01

Map 6

NEWFOUNDLAND AND LABRADOR

A History

Introduction

Scarce Environmental Leeway, Nationalism, and the Long Term in Newfoundland and Labrador

'We are not a nation,' declared J.R. Smallwood in his motion to send a Newfoundland delegation to Canada to discuss the possibility of union in 1946. Smallwood was not commenting on Newfoundland and Labrador's unique cultures or identities. Instead, he insisted that its small population, the relative underdevelopment of its economy, the poverty of its people in comparison with Canada, Britain, or the United States, its domination by the largely mercantile elite in St John's, and the failure of independent liberal democratic government to address any of these problems meant that Newfoundland and Labrador could not sustain itself economically and politically.[1] Yet, while Smallwood acknowledged that Newfoundland and Labrador had not undergone the developments associated with successful economies elsewhere, he was unprepared to accept that the environmental circumstances of his country did not favour such a transformation. For thousands of years Newfoundland and Labrador's cold-ocean environment had supported relatively small-scale, local populations spread out along a vast littoral and heavily dependent on the harvest of marine animals such as cod, seals, and whales. There was little in this environment that could sustain the industrial and urban transformations that occurred elsewhere in North America and the British empire. Nonetheless, in their response to specific local, colonial, and imperial relationships that governed the exploitation of marine resources, colonial leaders, by the late nineteenth century, had embraced a landward, often nationalist, policy of industrial development which ignored the basic ecological constraints that had defined previous societies in Newfoundland

and Labrador. Smallwood's vision of economic development was another variety of this commitment to landward industrialization, which continued to neglect Newfoundland and Labrador's dependence on marine resources and the diverse needs of its many peoples. Like the policies of earlier colonial nationalists, Smallwood's efforts foundered on the stark reality of the province's fragile but unavoidable dependence on its maritime resources. While initially quite rich, these resources have provided scarce leeway in terms of how societies have used them in conjunction with landward resources. The story that follows is the story of those resources and the political, cultural, social, and economic responses of the people of Newfoundland and Labrador in a changing world.

Newfoundland and Labrador's rich maritime ecologies and comparatively impoverished land-based ones are the legacy of an ancient process which began over 500 million years ago. Tectonic forces in the Earth's crust began to split the primordial single land mass of the planet into continents and ocean floors. About 190 million years ago, land masses emerged with the basic shapes of the continents we know today, although they were much closer together. What became known as the Grand Banks was a massive continental shelf of what would become known as North America, as the land mass parted from what would become Europe and Africa (see map 1). Tectonic pressures constantly worked on this shelf, producing shelves adjacent to the land masses of Newfoundland and Labrador and sunken regions that, over about 50 million years, filled with sediments. Within these sediments formed large reserves of oil, making the basins we know as Jeanne D'Arc, Orphan, and Whale the basis for offshore oil industry exploration and development.

The formation of the Grand Banks was one of two determining factors in the development of the ecologies of Newfoundland and Labrador. About 65 to 75 million years ago, shifts in the earth's crust formed what we now call the Labrador Sea, a trench between the continental shelf of North America and the shelf that incorporates the islands from Ireland to Greenland. The same process widened the shelves around Labrador and Newfoundland and produced corridors of deeper waters throughout the shelves and banks, which would become important migratory routes for fish such as cod. After a fairly warm period, a cooling trend that extended from 40 to 50 million years ago made the waters around Newfoundland and Labrador 'a sparse and subarctic environment.' Although the area has experienced considerable variations, it has retained these essential characteristics to the present.[2]

Although the continents continued to drift apart, and the Grand Banks continued to sink while sea levels rose, the banks remained a shallow shelf with a well-defined edge. The banks formed a massive undersea barrier to the warm-water northerly flows of the Gulf Stream, turning them eastward away from Newfoundland and Labrador. The northern edge of the banks diverted the southward icy flow of the Labrador Current toward the southeast, where it runs into the Gulf Stream off the southeastern Grand Banks.

While the Grand Banks have profoundly influenced the ecological circumstances of Newfoundland and Labrador, so too has the Labrador Current. The current has two branches. The first is the counter-clockwise offshore flow of the West Greenland Current in the Labrador Sea. This gyre mixes with, and brings northward, waters from the North Atlantic Current of the Gulf Stream off the southeastern Grand Banks. The second is the inshore stream that originates in the polar waters of the Canadian Current. These waters flow from the Arctic Basin, picking up volumes from the freshwater drainage of Hudson and Ungava bays as well as the coast of Labrador. The inshore stream follows a longitudinal trough, which keeps it close to the shores of Labrador and the northeast, southeast, and southwest coasts of Newfoundland. Moderated by its southerly and westerly flows, the inshore flow of the Labrador Current nonetheless remains very cold, having a major impact on the climate of coastal Labrador and most of Newfoundland. Fresher Labrador coastal water from the inshore current flows westerly along the Labrador side of the Strait of Belle Isle.[3]

The mixture of waters from the Labrador Current and the Gulf Stream produces a rich blending of temperatures and salinity. The constant inputs of fresh water and solar warming in the surface waters of the inshore current result in shelf water. This shelf water mixes with the offshore current, modified by the warmer, deeper waters of the North Atlantic Current, called slope water. The counter-clockwise flow of the Labrador Sea, with its steep gradients, means that shelf and slope waters meet in a shelf-break front along the edges of the nearby banks. The mixing of the waters constantly brings to the surface more nutrient-rich waters. These nutrients foster the bloom of phytoplankton, microscopic plants that are the most elemental part of the food chains of the animals of the North Atlantic. The much shallower waters of the Grand Banks further allow sunlight to reach the ocean floor, permitting the photosynthesis required by phytoplankton to grow. At the same time, the cooler waters of the Labrador Current partially inhibit the growth of bacteria that would, in otherwise warmer waters, kill much of the phytoplankton. Microscopic animals known as zooplankton feed on the phytoplankton, serving in turn as the meals for larger fish and crustaceans, which, in their turn, become the prey for each other, seabirds, and marine mammals.[4]

The land masses of Labrador and Newfoundland are distinct from each other. Labrador is the most eastern extension of the Precambrian rock of the Canadian Shield. The Labrador portion of the Shield has four distinct geological provinces: Nain, Churchill, Grenfell, and Superior. The Churchill province has been historically significant for its huge reserves of iron ore. Newfoundland, on the other hand, is a geological orphan of the Appalachian mountain system to the southwest, although part of its westernmost zone, called the Humber, shares a geological ancestry with the Precambrian rock of Labrador. The Dunnage zone of central Newfoundland contains vast amounts of rock of volcanic origin, consisting of copper, gold, lead, silver, and zinc deposits that have served as the basis for mining on the island since the late nineteenth century. To the east are the gneisses and granite formations of the Gander zone. The easternmost Avalon zone has a separate geological origin from that of the other zones and consists of Precambrian volcanic and sedimentary rocks that have yielded, in various places, iron ore and other minerals for commercial extraction. Labrador and Newfoundland also have separate glacial histories. Although glacial periods have occurred as early as 800,000,000 years ago, the last glacial period began about 100,000 years ago and ended about 10,000 years ago. Subdivided into periods of differing ice sheets, those of the Late Wisconsin period appear to be responsible for many of the province's river valleys and coastal fjords. Labrador lay under the Laurentide Ice Sheet, although the eastern Mealy Mountains and portions of the Torngat Mountains probably remained uncovered. Most of Newfoundland was covered by local glaciers.[5]

While the combined impact of ancient geological processes and glaciations produced, in many areas, a coastline of daunting, fortress-like cliffs that loomed over the sea, most of the land masses of Newfoundland and Labrador remained subject to the impact of the Labrador Current. The current's constant flow of cold water, and the icebergs and pack ice it brings through Labrador waters into those of Newfoundland throughout the spring and early summer, produce very late, cool, and wet springs and cool summers throughout much of southern coastal Labrador and most of Newfoundland. The exceptions are those parts of the west coast from Bonne Bay south and the central lowlands of the Exploits and Humber River valleys, areas which are beyond the influence of the Labrador Current and which have longer, warmer summers (see map 2). Colder conditions and shorter summers characterize the subarctic climate of south and central Labrador and the arctic conditions of northern Labrador. Persistent high air pressure over the Labrador Sea in the spring makes easterly and northerly winds common. Newfoundland's climate is a maritime one, with plenty of precipitation in the form of rain, fog, or snow. Although the prevailing winds are westerly, tropical and continental cyclonic systems track over Newfoundland and southern Labrador, bringing highly unpredictable and stormy weather, with impressive volumes of precipitation. Along the south and east coasts of Newfoundland, inhabitants may expect a maximum of about 145 frost-free days each year, but the number of such days is much shorter to the north and in Labrador.[6]

Newfoundland and Labrador's maritime, subarctic, and arctic climates, and its great amounts of precipitation, aggravate the poor quality of its soils. The retreat of the Wisconsinan glaciation about 10,000 years ago scraped bare much of the land and contributed to a very rough terrain. As the ice withdrew, it left rocks and gravel covering much of the high ground, while the highest elevations had nothing but naked bedrock. Low-lying lands, especially along river valleys, retained a stratified mix of sand, silt, and gravel. About one-third of the land surface of the island of Newfoundland has almost no soil. There are only extremely small pockets of organic soils throughout the island, and larger areas of mineral soils, including relatively fertile deposits of mixtures of alluvial soils, river sediments, and marine sediments. These sparse areas permit limited agriculture, but the generally shallow and acidic soils usually contain much gravel and little humus. They retain little water, and frequent, often heavy precipitation and spring run-off make them vulnerable to erosion and leaching, a process whereby water drains nutrients from the soil. The vast bulk of Newfoundland's surface area may be said to have 'no capability for crops or permanent pasture use,' while much of the rest faces 'severe limits' that restrict what may be grown (see map 3). Nonetheless, the combination of relatively fertile glacial debris and warmer weather in the vicinity of the Humber and Grand Codroy rivers and their tributaries, on the west coast of Newfoundland, and in the watersheds of the Exploits, Gander, and Terra Nova rivers in central Newfoundland, give them a better agricultural capacity than most areas.[7]

Climate and geology have also shaped the nature of Newfoundland and Labrador's forests. The western and central regions of Newfoundland contain the island's best tracts of forest. Much of Labrador to the northwest of Groswater Bay is either treeless tundra, where permafrost may be found, or tundra mixed with patches of stunted forests, as is the coastal area to the southeast and the Strait of Belle Isle (see map 4). Much of western Labrador is peat land, a mixture of lakes, rivers, bogs, swamps, and muskeg, broken by higher land of either barrens or forest. Barrens dominate the southeastern interior of Labrador, composed of rocky, windswept stretches of mosses, lichens, and areas of stunted black spruce or balsam fir. The shores of Lake Melville and its tributaries, including the watershed of the Churchill River, are covered with boreal coniferous forest (the easternmost of which has been described as 'the finest coniferous forest of the Province'), dominated by black spruce and much smaller mixed stands of balsam fir, white spruce, white birch, and balsam poplar. Similar boreal forests cover much of central and western Newfoundland, although there is mixed forest and tundra at the tip of the Northern Peninsula and smaller areas of peat land on the western side of that peninsula as well as at the bottom of the Burin and Avalon peninsulas. Although absent from the Labrador boreal forest, white pine was an important species in central and western Newfoundland. Its maximum size there of eighty feet in height and three feet in diameter made it much smaller than the white pine of Canada and the United States, and therefore less desirable commercially, but the local white pine nevertheless became an important commercial staple of the lumber trade, so much so that Newfoundlanders had commercially annihilated it by the early years of the twentieth century. Large tracts of the interior of the Northern Peninsula, the south coast of Newfoundland, and a corridor of land running from the south coast through the base of the Baie Verte Peninsula and then northeast along the coast of Notre Dame Bay are barren.[8]

The boreal or tundra-like nature of Newfoundland and Labrador supports a limited flora. Arctic grasses and sedges are common throughout the tundra-dominated areas. Peat moss dominates the peat lands, while lichens are common throughout most areas. Feather mosses often cover the ground under the great tracts of conifers, as do a rich variety of mosses in wetter areas. Flowering plants include pondweeds, irises, and orchids, as well as the pitcher plant, an insect-trapping plant that is common in bogs and which is now the provincial flower. Perhaps the most delightful plants to be found throughout Newfoundland and Labrador are the flowering ones with edible berries. Local people are especially fond of three varieties of the rose family: bakeapples (*Rubus chamaemorus*), plumboys (*Rubus pubescens*), and raspberries (*Rubus idaeus*), among many others. Hardly less esteemed are members of the heather family, including the blueberry (*Vaccinium angustifolium*), marshberry (*V. oxycoccus*), cranberry (*V. macrocarpon*), and the highly prized ingredient of jams, jellies, pies, and other confections, the partridgeberry (*V. vitis-idaea*). While these berries are delicious additions to local diets, they have had limited commercial potential. Other plants include members of the honeysuckle family and a wide variety of woody shrubs, including the ubiquitous alders, which are common in forested regions and are important in enriching the soil with nitrogen. Finally, there are massive numbers of dicotyledonous herbs, mostly non-native plants that accompanied European migrants, including dandelion, thistles, and goldenrods.[9]

The restrictions of soil, climate, and flora that characterize Newfoundland and Labrador might best be appreciated when we consider the narrow range of fauna they supported. Labrador has had a greater variety of mammalian species than Newfoundland, twenty-two in comparison with twelve on the island. Before the local aboriginal people's first contact with Europeans, a small number of species lived in the interior of Newfoundland: caribou, American beaver, and arctic hare. These animals served as prey for a large number of predators besides humans, including the now-extinct Newfoundland wolf, bears, and lynx, and a variety of small animals such as marten, mink, weasels, otter, and red fox. Bats and meadow voles are also part of the native fauna, while polar bears and arctic foxes are occasionally sighted. With the exception of polar bears, Labrador had no other large mammals than did the island but had a greater variety of smaller ones, such as porcupines, wolverines, lemmings, moles, flying squirrels, foxes, and shrews. The last was introduced into the island of Newfoundland, as were snowshoe hares, red squirrels, eastern chipmunks, house mice, Norway rats, and mink. Moose were introduced to Newfoundland in 1878 and from Newfoundland to Labrador in 1953. While Labrador shares the insect varieties of the other areas of the Canadian Shield, the island of Newfoundland has a relatively small number of insects. Many of these are European migrants, but Newfoundland, like Labrador, has many black flies and mosquitoes. Overall, the far greater number of predators relative to prey species in the prehistoric period has led one historian to call Newfoundland 'a rather impoverished piece of the boreal forest in the mouth of the St. Lawrence.'[10]

The dominance of its marine environment meant that Newfoundland's and coastal Labrador's marine and aquatic fauna were much more bountiful and, to a much greater extent than land-based ones, sustained the areas' human populations. Although large cold-water marine ecosystems with fewer species in fairly simple food chains dominate the western North Atlantic, its marine fauna were exceptionally abundant. The profusion of zooplankton supported capelin, a pelagic fish of small size but great numbers and with a flesh rich in oil. Along with Atlantic herring, capelin became the main prey of the gadoids, or codlike fishes: Atlantic cod (including many sub-populations or sub-stocks, such as those that constitute the historically important northern cod groups), Greenland cod, haddock, pollock, and hake. In addition to the gadoids, capelin, and herring, the seas were home to many species, including smelt, flounder, mackerel, redfish, lobsters, and other shellfish. Coastal areas supported mussels, soft-shelled clams, and other small marine animals. Anadromous species that migrate to rivers from the sea to breed, such as Atlantic salmon, arctic char, lake trout, mud trout, and lake whitefish, returned to rivers from the waters off the Newfoundland and Labrador coastlines. Lake whitefish were introduced into Newfoundland in the 1880s, as were later pink salmon, brown trout, and rainbow trout. There are also a variety of eels, eel-shaped fishes, sharks, and rays in coastal waters. Many of the fish were the prey of the seabirds such as ducks, geese, murres, gannets, puffins, terns, gulls, loons, and the now-extinct flightless great auk and the Eskimo curlew.[11]

A variety of marine mammals lived off these aquatic species. Although a navigation hazard, the pack ice that dominates the Labrador shelf and the northern Grand Banks serves as the winter habitat for harp seals. For millennia, millions of harp seals migrated each year from their summer grounds in the Davis Strait along the Labrador coast. There the seals swam close enough to shore to be hunted from land with harpoons or nets. At the Strait of Belle Isle, the herd split in two as one group moved into the Gulf of St Lawrence and the far larger one moved down the northeastern coast of Newfoundland. In both areas the seals fed and mated in open water. In the spring, the females hauled up out of the water to bear and nurse their pups on the pack ice that had drifted south on the Labrador Current. Other seals swam regularly in coastal waters: harbour, ringed, bearded, grey, and hood as well as walrus. In addition to seals, a variety of whales and dolphins inhabit the waters off Newfoundland and Labrador, including pot head, minke, humpback, fin, and sei whales, and harbour porpoises, white-sided dolphins, and white-beaked dolphins.[12]

Several views have been proposed about how best to support human society in this cold-ocean environment. Since the early nineteenth century, this debate has been a defining element in the history of Newfoundland and Labrador.[13] The following twelve chapters explore the history of this debate in light of the strategies various societies developed to adapt and survive in such an environment. The book examines and interrogates the logic of a peripatetic Newfoundland nationalism that claims that the province can survive as a separate economic and political unit.

Chapter one considers the manner in which most prehistoric peoples depended on the exploitation of coastal marine resources. The nature of early European contact with the descendants of such peoples, the subject of chapter two, reflected the boreal, tundra, and cold-ocean coastal ecologies of Newfoundland and Labrador. The Norse abandoned the limited agricultural capacity of the area, while later Basque, French, and English adventurers found plenty of whales and fish to exploit, and the early Europeans were migratory hunters and fishers. Chapter three examines the manner in which the fishing industry and imperial rivalries fostered limited settlement, largely to the detriment of aboriginal peoples. Eventually, British hegemony in Newfoundland and Labrador resulted in the development of a naval government which failed to meet the more complex needs of a resident fishing industry and nascent colonial society. Chapter four therefore looks at the consequent transition from naval government to colonial government by 1824, showing how the societies and governments that existed in Newfoundland and Labrador before 1824 exhibited remarkable adaptations to the exigencies of life in a cold-ocean coastal environment.

Such adaptations were much less important in the struggle of colonial reformers for representative and responsible government, the subject of chapter five. Since they needed to obtain British imperial consent for constitutional change, but were faced with imperial indifference to the management needs of the Newfoundland fishery, Newfoundland governments turned to a ruinous program of landward economic diversification, which is examined in chapter six. Chapter seven considers the rise of colonial nationalism in Newfoundland by the early twentieth century. Local nationalist sentiments intensified with the participation of Newfoundlanders and Labradorians in the First World War, but war debt and postwar depression exacerbated the economic and social problems arising from the failures of Newfoundland's landward development, and merchants and politicians frustrated the efforts of the Fishermen's Protective Union to secure better management of the fishing industry.

The subsequent social and political crisis led to the suspension of responsible government in 1934, the subject of chapter eight. The collapse of responsible government, however, did not lead to more interest in how communities might develop successfully in an environment dominated by the sea, and chapter nine explores how a British-appointed Commission of Government embraced the previous trajectory of economic development policy in Newfoundland. This occurred despite early misguided experiments which sought to achieve the moral reform of Newfoundlanders and contrary to an interesting proposal for the cooperative revitalization of Newfoundland and Labrador outports. The massive public spending triggered by the Second World War convinced many Newfoundlanders and Labradorians that they could have the same type of modern, urban, and consumerist society as had been developing elsewhere in North America. Chapter ten examines how such convictions fuelled Smallwood's successful campaign to bring Newfoundland and Labrador into Confederation in 1949, but how his subsequent development policies followed the earlier failures in landward development of the late nineteenth and early twentieth centuries. The modernization of Newfoundland and Labrador continued nonetheless, supported by federal spending in Newfoundland. Chapter eleven considers the new generation of neo-nationalists in Newfoundland and Labrador who were the products of such modernization. The book concludes with a consideration of the ecological and social problems posed by recent neo-nationalism within a long-term perspective on the history of Newfoundland and Labrador.

1

The First Peoples by the Sea

The area from the northern coast of Labrador at Saglek Bay to the south coast of Newfoundland may seem cold, barren, and unforgiving, yet for almost seven millennia prehistoric peoples lived and travelled throughout the coastal regions of almost every part of what is now the province of Newfoundland and Labrador. The first peoples of Labrador consisted of two broad groups, referred to in the scholarly literature as 'Indians' and 'Palaeo-Eskimos,' divided somewhat in ways that parallel the modern-day divisions between the Innu and Inuit. Both colonized the island of Newfoundland in successive waves of immigration that spanned many thousands of years. Everything we know about these people comes from the work of modern-day archaeologists, who have uncovered evidence of pathways of cultural exchange, trade, and migration. Despite their many differences, one essential common trait defined those who made Newfoundland and Labrador their home: they lived by their own cunning and wits in using the riches of the sea.

The Maritime Archaic people were descendants of the great migration of 'Palaeo-Indians' from Eurasia across the Bering Strait into the northern reaches of the American continent. Around 7000 BC, in the wake of the receding glaciers, Palaeo-Indian hunters settled along the coast of southern Labrador. The acidic soils of the region have left little evidence of these people beyond some stone tools, particularly various forms of chert, a stone prized by prehistoric peoples for the ease with which it could be fashioned into tools. Archaeologists suggest that they moved into Labrador to harvest its rich marine resources; they call the Palaeo-Indians 'Maritime Archaic' because of their heavy reliance upon the sea. By about 5500 BC the Maritime Archaic people in southern Labrador had tools that were distinct from those of their relatives in other parts of eastern North America. Some began to move northward along the Labrador coast around 4500 BC, and by 3000 BC others had crossed the Strait of Belle Isle to settle the island of Newfoundland. The expanse of time in which they lived and migrated across the coastal areas of Labrador and Newfoundland is astonishing when we consider that the entire history of settlement by people of European descent in the same region is only about five hundred years.

Archaeologists have found evidence of the Maritime Archaic people as far north as Saglek Bay on the coast of Labrador, through Sandy Cove and Rattler's Bight in Hamilton Inlet to L'Anse Amour in the Strait of Belle Isle to the Beaches in Bonavista Bay on the northeastern coast of Newfoundland. The richest discoveries have been made at Port au Choix on the west coast of Newfoundland, where an ancient burial site has told us most about these first people (see map 5). Located just south of the Strait of Belle Isle, the region was likely the area of longest Maritime Archaic occupation and lay along the major migration route from Labrador to Newfoundland. Two peninsulas, Point Riche and Port au Choix proper, jut out into the sea, where the cold Labrador Current meets the warmer Gulf waters. Although Port au Choix contains no easily worked stone, its ideal location for hunting made it an attractive place to live, and it became a hub in the exchange of cherts from Cow Bay in the south to Ramah Bay in the north.[1]

It was the sea rather than the land that sustained the Maritime Archaic people. Caribou and a variety of smaller land mammals, in addition to berries and other plants, were important sources of food and material. However, Newfoundland and Labrador's boreal forests, bog lands, or subarctic terrains offered few sources of food as bountiful as those of the sea. The Maritime Archaic people hunted a variety of seabirds and ducks, including the great auk and the Eskimo curlew, for meat and eggs. More important to the Maritime Archaic people were the harp seals that arrived in the region each spring; these early people also hunted other types of seals, whales, and walruses. They fished for cod, various flatfish, salmon, trout, and shellfish.[2]

The Maritime Archaic people used slates and cherts to make spears and lances for hunting, developed barbed and toggling harpoons to take marine mammals, and appear to have made barbed bone tips with which to spear fish. They do not seem to have had the bow and arrow but may have hunted birds using small darts. Since migratory animals such as harp seals and caribou were available only on a seasonal basis, the Maritime Archaic people likely organized themselves into small kin groups, or bands, that could easily follow their prey. The elaborate burial ground at Port au Choix suggests that the Maritime Archaic people were not simply nomads. They likely saw the area surrounding their cemetery as the home from which they journeyed out to hunt and gather. During the fall and winter, the Maritime Archaic people may have followed caribou into interior upland areas, where they could also hunt bear, beaver, and arctic hare. The late winter and early spring would draw the Maritime Archaic out onto coastal headlands to take seals. The Maritime Archaic people may have used boats to hunt harp seals, but the drifting ice often came so close to shore that they could probably often hunt without such craft. The presence of so many toggling harpoons in Maritime Archaic sites suggests that they stayed on the coast throughout the spring and summer to hunt seabirds and other seals, and to fish.[3]

While we know something of their economy, it is more difficult to put a human face on the Maritime Archaic people. Much of the culture and values of these first people will remain unknown, but there is some evidence upon which we might speculate. Artefacts and DNA analysis from archaeological research at Port au Choix suggest a clear division of labour between the men and women, although there is little evidence about who took responsibility for childrearing. The people of highest status would have been the men who had the greatest hunting skills and who travelled to hunt migrating birds, caribou, and beaver, which provided hides, furs, bone, and sinews that were crucial for utensils, clothing, and tools. Wives of these men likely accompanied them on the hunt to assist and process the game. The people of this group ate more meat and were buried with many more goods, further suggesting their higher status. The best hunters would have been accepted as leaders of the hunt and accorded respect through burial rituals. But the number of goods buried with them indicates that the Maritime Archaic people valued sharing their wealth, not accumulating it. Younger, more inexperienced males who were not yet skilled hunters probably made unattractive mates for women. These men would have depended upon the game they could more easily hunt while perfecting their skills. Finally, those too old to travel or hunt, as well as young children, stayed with women who had not taken a spouse or who had borne children and stayed behind to care for them. The predominance of saw-toothed points and harpoons suitable for spearing fish in their graves suggests that these women fished to provide for those who could not do so for themselves. Although the infirmities of age may have made elderly adults less important in providing their people with sustenance, the knowledge they had accumulated, and could pass on, likely meant that older people continued to be valued. The Maritime Archaic people may have viewed the elderly as shamanistic due to their knowledge of animal behaviour, the weather, and the environment in general.[4]

The manner in which the Maritime Archaic people buried their dead also provides clues to their spiritual life. The condition of many skeletons suggests that they had been buried after flesh had decomposed from them and others had been buried in careful bundles. Both suggest that although Maritime Archaic people died throughout the year, their remains were only temporarily interred until an appropriate time for ritual burial arrived. The presence in the graves of exactly the same types of tools and weapons as adults would have used in their day-to-day lives suggests belief in an afterlife in which people would continue on as they had in life. In particular, the Maritime Archaic people likely assumed that infants and children would grow into adults even after death. As these goods required a great deal of skill and effort to manufacture, the act of placing them in the graves likely indicates the respect and affection held by the living for their deceased. The presence of amulets fashioned from bone, antler, and stone into the shape of various animals further suggests that the Maritime Archaic people believed they could acquire traits, powers, or characteristics of the creatures being emulated. Similarly, the presence of large numbers of claws, teeth, and bones from a variety of animals suggests that the first people hoped to gain the abilities of these animals by possessing some physical part of them: the teeth of a fox, for example, may have been thought to pass on its crafty hunting skills. The presence of an image of a killer whale carved from stone in the grave of one young adult male has led some archaeologists to speculate that the Maritime Archaic may have held some animals in special regard, perhaps even to the point of forming a cult around them. Surely, there is no better animal for sealers to emulate and placate than a killer whale, for these toothed sea mammals not only are themselves remarkably successful seal killers but also are reputed to attack small boats. Hence, they would present a constant source of anxiety to people hunting from dugouts or skin boats. Additionally, based on the manner in which beaks, bones, and carvings of birds appeared in specific graves, there may have been

some totemic association between individuals or families and specific species of birds.[5]

It is too easy to forget, when describing the Maritime Archaic people's society at one point in their history, that they were innovative
people whose culture changed over their three-thousand-year history. The social and community organization of the Maritime Archaic
peoples was not static; archaeological evidence of their dwellings
suggests that the earliest people lived in single-family pit dwellings
that would be typical of small hunting-and-gathering bands.[6] The
later development of large multi-family longhouses suggests that the
Maritime Archaic people came to congregate in larger communities
for a variety of political, economic, social, and ceremonial reasons.
Stone projectile points found by archaeologists at L'Anse Amour suggest that the Maritime Archaic people constantly refined their hunting technology. Furthermore, Maritime Archaic occupation patterns
shifted over time. About 4000 BC, these people began to expand northward up the Labrador coast, possibly in response to a gradual warming trend that would have expanded the range of territory suitable to
the pattern of Maritime Archaic hunting. Over the course of the next
one thousand years, Maritime Archaic people reached as far as Saglek
Bay, where they found Ramah chert, an almost translucent, beautiful grey silicate stone that flaked easily into sharp cutting edges. This
northward movement may have brought the Maritime Archaic people into contact with the Palaeo-Eskimos, a people whose way of life
reflected their arctic environment.

The early Palaeo-Eskimos arrived in northern Labrador from the
western arctic sea about 2000 BC. As the climate cooled again, forcing
the tree line southward, Palaeo-Eskimos moved from the high Arctic
southward as far as Hamilton Inlet during a period of several hundred years. Their archaeological remains contain many small cutting
blades and harpoon heads well suited to hunting marine animals. It
is likely that the Palaeo-Eskimos spent their lives on the coastal edge
of the pack ice, hunting the seals, walruses, small whales, and polar
bears that frequented blow holes and polynnas, small open bodies of
water in the spring ice. The Palaeo-Eskimos would retreat as the pack
ice did, turning to hunting harbour seals, seabirds and other fowl, and
perhaps even caribou that came out to the coast, as well as fishing for
salmon and arctic char. These animals would have provided enough
food to make trips to the interior unnecessary.

Although it appears that the Maritime Archaic people of Labrador
retreated along the Labrador coast and into the interior around Lake

Melville as the Palaeo-Eskimo advanced, there is little evidence to suggest conflict between the two peoples. The Maritime Archaic people continued to travel to the coast to hunt, and the two peoples may have traded and interacted with each other. The Palaeo-Eskimos appear to have acquired toggling harpoons from the Maritime Archaic people, possibly in exchange for teaching them about the bow and arrow. Although differences persisted in the styles of tools and housing of the Maritime Archaic and Palaeo-Eskimo peoples, both balanced seal hunting with caribou hunting along the coast.[7] Yet both cultures retained their integrity and appear to have avoided much intermingling.

We do not yet know what became of the Palaeo-Eskimo and Maritime Archaic peoples. Their populations appear to have moved and fluctuated with changes in climate and through cultural interaction. Studies of similarities in blades, tools, and other artefacts suggest that the Palaeo-Eskimo people may have developed into the Dorset peoples between 2000 BC and 1500 AD. Around 1000 BC, the Maritime Archaic people in Newfoundland disappeared, possibly because of changes in climate, a shift in the resource base upon which they depended, or the southward advance of the Dorset subgroup known as the Groswater, or Early Dorset people. In Labrador, the Maritime Archaic people appear to have relied more on hunting in the interior during a period of warming temperatures between 4500 and 2000 BC, and the later southward movement of the Dorset may have reinforced this trend. The archaeological evidence of the interior hunters has led them to be described as 'Intermediate Indians.'[8]

From approximately 1000 BC to 800 AD, a number of distinct subgroups of Dorset populations waxed and waned in Labrador and Newfoundland. In addition to the Groswater people, there were distinct Middle and Late Dorset cultures, although it is unclear whether groups developed one from the other or developed distinctly from common, possibly Palaeo-Eskimo ancestors. All of the Dorset developed tools that suggest the hunting of marine mammals remained the cornerstone of their lives. The remains of their early dwellings – small oval structures composed of bone, wood, and skins on top of irregular excavations – indicate that the Dorset initially investigated the hunting potential of an area through irregular seasonal visits. Once they learned of abundant, predictable, and accessible prey, such as the harp seals of the Gulf area, the Dorset established more permanent communities based on the construction of larger, rectangular, semi-subterranean houses. The Dorset people do not seem to have used boats in their hunting despite their reliance on marine animals. Particular subgroups, such as the Groswater people, may have disappeared because they did not adapt to adverse climatic change. However, as in the case of the later Middle Dorset people, cultures adapted by incorporating interior hunting, especially of caribou, into their seasonal round of activities.[9]

By about 500 BC a Late Dorset culture developed in the northern coastal areas of Labrador. The Late Dorset people differed from earlier peoples in a number of ways. Unlike the other Palaeo-Eskimos, the Late Dorset people were hunters of the *sina*, or seaward edge of the pack ice. Furthermore, while the other Palaeo-Eskimos usually combined hunting land animals with those of the coastal waters and lived near inner bays of river mouth sites, the late Dorset preferred to live on outer coastal areas. From there, hunting parties travelled out to the edge of the pack ice.[10]

Specialists in hunting marine animals in winter, the Late Dorset moved south from northern Labrador to Newfoundland and inhabited many of the sites previously occupied by earlier Palaeo-Eskimo peoples. Those who migrated to Newfoundland concentrated on the west coast, in Notre Dame Bay, and in Bonavista Bay, where they had access to the richest food source available: the harp seals of the Gulf and front herds. Some settled on the south coast and Trinity Bay and probably depended much more on harbour seals. Both areas also had caribou herds that migrated close to the coast. Such herds would have allowed the Late Dorset people to maintain their characteristic maritime way of life. Unlike their predecessors, the Late Dorset preferred Ramah chert, although those who eventually settled in Newfoundland used a wide variety of cherts and nephrite in the construction of tools, implements, and ornaments. The beautiful carvings and pendants made from ivory, bone, and antler found among their burial sites, although stylistically different from those of the Maritime Archaic people, suggest similar spiritual beliefs. The Dorset buried their dead in rock crevices with kits containing tools, weapons, amulets, and other objects. Around 800 AD, the Late Dorset population in Newfoundland disappeared. Although the reasons for this collapse are not clear, their dependence on maritime resources would have left them extremely vulnerable to fluctuations in the availability of seals. Adverse wind conditions, for example, if persistent for a few years, might have kept the pack ice offshore. This would have led to a subsistence crisis that could have, in turn, eventually led to the collapse of the Late Dorset population.[11]

The arrival of the Thule, the ancestors of the modern-day Inuit, spelled the end of the lineages of Dorset cultures. The Thule were sea-farers who swept across the Arctic from the western Alaskan coastline by about 1000 AD. They first arrived in Labrador about 1200 or 1300 AD. Living in a treeless world, they invented houses, dog sleds, and skin-covered boats that were framed with whale bones and driftwood. Their single-person kayaks and larger umiaks gave the Thule a tech-nological advantage in transportation in a coastal environment. Pad-dling these craft, the Thule harpooned small whales such as bowheads using toggling harpoons that would not come back out of the wound, attached to lines with floats that tired out wounded animals enough for them to be approached and killed. The Thule did not hesitate to use whatever resources they found as they ventured south during the fif-teenth century AD, eventually reaching the area around Nain. In doing so, the Thule had supplanted the Late Dorset people, whose material culture disappeared from the archaeological record. It remains unclear whether the Dorset were assimilated into Thule culture through inter-marriage and the adoption of the superior Thule technologies or met more violent ends. The similarity of some of their harpoon technology, and Inuit stories about earlier people, suggests that there might have been a cultural exchange between the two groups.

Initially, the Thule established very small settlements, probably liv-ing in kin groups of between one and three families. In the summer, the Thule fished and hunted caribou inland. They used the ground to shelter themselves, digging the foundations of their homes partially beneath the surface of the soil, then building a top structure using whatever materials might be at hand, from sod to whale bone. The Thule built these houses on outer islands to be close to ice-free polyn-nas, where the whales, walruses, and seals that were their favourite prey surfaced. Hunting and butchering whales and walruses required the Thule to congregate in large numbers. During the winter, some Thule might leave the main camp to move into the interior in search of game, building snow houses for shelter. Similarly, during the sum-mer the Thule might move around bays and headlands, camping in tents of boulders and hides. Thule dominance of the coastline may also have led the Intermediate Indians who met them to depend even more on interior resources such as caribou, and some Intermediate Indians appear to have moved across the Strait of Belle Isle, possibly evolving into the Beothuks.[12]

By about 200 AD an Amerindian cultural complex that likely con-tinued the Intermediate Indian tradition occupied the coast from just below Nain southward into the Strait of Belle Isle. Although some modifications in the style of tools and other artefacts have been found, there are enough similarities to suggest a broad relationship between them, the earlier Intermediate people, and the subsequent Point Revenge Indian people of the fifteenth century. Like the other people of prehistoric Labrador and Newfoundland, their material of choice for tools was Ramah chert, a stone found only at Ramah Bay, which lay in Dorset territory. Although there was little overlap between the areas where Dorset and prehistoric Indian people established their camps, and both designed their tools very differently, some sort of exchange relationship facilitated the prehistoric Indians' access to Ramah chert. The evidence of one group at the Daniel Rattle archaeological site, for example, suggests they maintained hunting camps along the coast in outer headland areas to hunt seals in the spring and fall, to hunt walruses during the winter, and to fish during the summer. They also used these camps as bases from which to trade with neighbouring Dorset people. Although they had access to a variety of cherts and other stones to make utensils, the people of the Daniel Rattle complex ritually burned Ramah chert, which suggests the stone may have had a spiritual significance for them. During the episodic disappearances of people, associated with the shift from Middle to Late Dorset people, the prehistoric Indians probably travelled to Ramah to procure its prized chert, but otherwise they appear to have gotten the stone from other people. The Point Revenge people appear to be the direct ancestors of the current-day Innu, formerly known as the Naskapi and Montagnais people of Labrador.[13] The Thule people who later occupied Northern Labrador provided the Point Revenge people with another trading partner in chert but also provided competition for access to marine resources.

Archaeological evidence suggests that a 'Recent Indian' people (so-called to distinguish them from the Maritime Archaic people) had become part of life on the island at about the time of Christ. There remains much to be learned about the relationship between the Point Revenge people of Labrador and Recent Indians of the island, but they may have had a common ancestor in the Intermediate Indians. Trade of materials, knowledge, and marriage partners from Labrador to the island would have been easy because the narrow Strait of Belle Isle serves as a highway as much as a barrier. The natural resource funnel of the Strait concentrated marine mammals such as seals and whales at specific times of the year, making it an ideal hunting location. The archaeological evidence suggests that the Recent Indians moved back and forth across the Strait and that they had some sort of exchange relationship with the Dorset people as well as Point Revenge people. Once on the island, the Recent Indians would have been able to follow the harp seals in a southeasterly direction along Newfoundland's northeast coast. The harp seals would have been particularly important prey as large numbers congregated close to shore on the arctic pack ice during the spring whelping season. Other Recent Indians moved to the island's south coast, where grey and harbour seals frequented its year-round, ice-free waters and near where the largest herds of caribou wintered.[14]

Although they shared much of their culture, there was variety among the Recent Indians. The 'Cow Head' tradition, for example, refers to the remains of people first identified at Cow Head on the west coast of the Great Northern Peninsula. There were also the 'Beaches' and the 'Little Passage' peoples. The earliest evidence suggests that these Recent Indians relied on hunting and gathering marine resources, although they likely hunted inland as well. Like the Point Revenge people, those of the Beaches (800–1200 AD) developed an economy based on the resources of the inner coastal areas. More important, the Beaches people used Ramah chert, which they would have had to get from Labrador through trade. The Little Passage people descended from the Beaches and were distinct in their greater use of bows and arrows rather than spear throwers and darts. It is possible that this technological shift made the Little Passage people more successful competitors for resources with the Dorset, perhaps even in warfare. Whatever the case, the rise of the Little Passage people has been associated with the disappearance of the Dorset in Newfoundland.[15]

The earliest sites of the Little Passage people, named after a site between Hermitage Bay and Bay d'Espoir, are dated to some time between 1100 and 1200 AD. These people ranged around the entire coast of Newfoundland and are the direct ancestors of the Beothuks. The Little Passage people depended on a delicate balancing of marine and land resources. From spring through early fall, they would have been on the coast hunting and gathering marine resources. In the fall, they established camps inland, from which they would hunt caribou and trap smaller game and fur-bearing animals. The abundance of the caribou may have even drawn some of the Little Passage people into a more interior-dependent lifestyle than their contemporaries.[16]

By the fifteenth century, the Little Passage people had evolved into what we know as the Beothuks. Although the Beothuks occupied a large area, the best guess of anthropologists is that there were as few as 500 people before European contact and no more than 1,600. While in popular imagination they were mysterious people of the forest, the sea dominated the life of the Beothuks, as is evident in the importance of canoes in their lives. Their ocean-going canoes allowed them to visit outer islands to hunt seals and gather eggs and to pursue small whales, which they killed with toggled harpoons, a technology they probably learned from the Dorset people. Unlike most canoes, those of the Beothuks had straight, deep sides narrowing to a V-shaped keel, which, when ballasted with rocks, were very stable, and were not easily blown off course.

In the fall the Beothuks travelled further inland but do not appear to have strayed far from the coast. Initially moving inland to pick berries, the Beothuks soon turned to the organization of their caribou hunt. This hunt was important; they needed to kill large numbers of caribou so that they could store meat and fat for the coming winter. They relied upon caribou skins, sinews, and bone to make clothes, tools, and even their homes. The Beothuks constructed fences of broken trees, which often extended for many miles, to herd the migrating caribou to particular places at river crossings or ponds where hunters lay in wait. Some caribou might be killed as they passed through the fences, and the Beothuks often took to the water in canoes to chase and kill the slow-swimming animals.

Since a successful caribou hunt required many hunters, the Beothuks divided tasks by gender. Many women were needed to butcher and process the animals into food, prepare skins, and make clothes. Men directed the hunt, but women and children may have helped pursue and kill the caribou. The large amount of work required for the hunt meant that the members of kin groups who otherwise spent the summer apart ranging along the coasts came together in the fall and winter. Away from the harsh winds of the exposed coastline, the interior must have been a more appealing place to spend the winter. Although the often deep snows of the interior could be daunting, the Beothuks' warm clothing and snowshoes allowed them to live and travel in comfort. They survived the dark and cold months by congregating in large groups and living off stores of food prepared in advance for the most brutal of seasons. To cope with the cold months, the Beothuks built more substantial houses, or mamateeks, that could accommodate about ten people. While the tops of the winter mamateeks were conical, the bottoms consisted of as many as eight walls made from tree trunks driven into the ground. The Beothuks banked earth against the outside of these walls to provide insulation and used layers of moss and bark to insulate their homes.

A band, or extended kin group, of between thirty-five and fifty-five people would winter together in a cluster of winter mamateeks. They held special ceremonies of feasting and dancing each year as they came together to cover themselves with red ochre; a coating would last usually for a year, and it was a source of shame to be asked by the band to remove it. Each person covered his or her body with ochre in particular ways to denote membership in the band. Winter was an important time in the formation of families, as young people would select their mates during the social times. Festivals and games also tightened the bonds within the band. Bands cooperated for specific labour-intensive subsistence activities such as the construction of fences by which the Beothuks channelled caribou and the preparation of the animals for use once they were slaughtered.[17] The Beothuks were monogamous, and the relationship between men and women within the family was fairly equal. There is little evidence to suggest that male authority, or patriarchy, was very important.

The scale of the caribou hunt, and its importance to the subsistence of the Beothuks, likely encouraged the recognition of some leadership among an otherwise egalitarian people. Preparations for the hunt required skill and coordination. The long fences would have to be built and maintained, and the hunters' actions coordinated, during the slaughter. They might have chosen a 'chief' for his hunting skills, knowledge of religious ceremonies, and ability to lead in emergencies. Male hunters with unusual prowess, or perhaps those with wisdom and generosity, would be recognized by the group. Therefore, leadership was consensual. Such leaders would bear some evidence of their status, such as wearing slightly different clothes, by having a somewhat larger mamateek, or bearing some emblem of authority. Such authority would only last, however, as the band consented to be led by that person. The esteem in which the Beothuks held their leaders is suggested by the special burial treatment the latter received. When a leader died, the members of his band would inter him in a lavish burial hut. They would later lay to rest members of this person's immediate family when they died. The Beothuks buried others by wrapping the deceased in birchbark, then laying them out on top of the ground covered with stones.

Men and women shared in the spiritual leadership of the Beothuks as shamans or healers. Healers knew the medicinal lore of local plants. While shamans could also be healers, they were much more. The shamans served as intermediaries between the Beothuks and the spiritual life they felt animated the world around them. There is not much evidence about the Beothuks' religious beliefs beyond their animism, a spiritual belief common to all of the First Nations of North America. The Beothuks further believed in a Great Spirit that had power over all things. They feared a 'devil,' or malign spirit, that punished the wicked. The Beothuks appear to have treated death as a form of sleep. In addition to ensuring that they buried the deceased with grave goods that would assist them later, the Beothuks preferred to inter their dead close to the sea.[18]

The Beothuks followed a seasonal round of resource exploitation dominated by life on the coastal fringe. In summer they frequented the sheltered inner shores and estuaries of the island's great bays as they fished and hunted small game. They lived in small family groups and fanned out over wide areas to increase the likelihood of finding enough resources to live on. Their housing reflected the seasonal pattern of their lives. The Beothuks' summer mamateeks could accommodate one to three families. These were covered with animal hides and bark, which could easily be put up and taken down and were well suited to travel along the coastline. The seashore was the place of plenty and warmth for the Beothuks. Although the company of friends and kin must have warmed them against icy winds and cold nights, the early spring was a welcome time. The Newfoundland interior supported very few fur-bearing animals, and there were no big-game animals to hunt besides the caribou. The spring brought sea ice and accompanying cold, wet weather with it, but the ice also brought an abundance of seals when the Beothuks' winter stores ran short. The Beothuks consequently welcomed the chance to move to outer coastal areas to hunt seals. It is likely that from such a coastal camp the Beothuks first saw the distant sails of European ships.

The sun rose and set over several distinct cultures over the seven millennia since people first set foot on the Labrador coast. From the receding of the last glacier to the arrival of European explorers, each of the first peoples by the sea had lived where they could combine the resources of the land with the abundance of food from the sea. Peoples with superior seafaring technologies such as the Inuit and the Beothuks inherited the edge of the continent and the island of Newfoundland, and thrived. They were our first peoples by the sea.

2

The European Encounter

The cultures and material lives of the Innu, Inuit, and Beothuk differed from one another, but these differences paled by comparison with those that existed between the First Nations and the European newcomers. The Norse explorers, who began to expand from Scandinavia from the eighth through eleventh centuries, were doughty seafarers. Familiar with the skills of latitude sailing, the Norse were expert in finding their way at sea by observing ocean currents, coastlines, and the migrations of fish and birds. The material basis of their lives was not, however, the sea. For all the romance and legend of the Vikings, by the tenth century AD, most Norse were Christian farmers rather than pagan warriors. Exploring for new land to farm, the Norse found little prospect in what is now Newfoundland and Labrador. While they came into conflict with the first peoples, the Norse had little impact on their way of life. Later European explorers and fishers came to catch fish and hunt whales but otherwise saw little reason to settle the area. English attempts to establish proprietary colonies found that some local farming and forestry were indispensable to profitable fisheries, but none of these landward activities supported settlements or colonies without the fisheries. Limited contact and seasonal trade meant that their early encounter with Europeans left the land beyond the western seas as the domain of the first peoples.

Norse expansion into the North Atlantic reflected the changing nature of medieval Scandinavian society and economy. The fundamental basis of Norse society was the *landnam*, or freehold farm or estate in a patriarchal social organization. Norse men expected to own farms or

practise crafts freely in animal husbandry and tillage that was suited
to the use of pastures at high latitudes and in mountainous surround-
ings. Such expectations did not mean that Norse society was egalitarian. A hierarchical order of kings and nobles, sometimes referred to
as magnates, provided freeholders with military protection and effective government in return for the control of larger estates and tribute.
The magnates employed servants and slaves to work their estates and
formed alliances with better-off neighbouring independent farmers.
By the eighth century AD, population in Scandinavia developed beyond the capacity of local resources for freehold farming. A warming
trend had made more land available for tillage, a process that benefited the kings and nobility, pushing the greater population to look for
new land to clear. As the population continued to grow, people found
less pasture land, and interest in the colonization of new areas grew.
Norse explorers, merchants, and plunderers developed vessels that
were able to venture out into the deeper oceans from coastal waters
and navigable rivers. These vessels increasingly carried members of
the elite and their retinues, who were leaving behind more powerful
rivals or the growing power of the Norwegian crown, or who were
banished because of crimes against such competitors.[1]

These Norse explorers established colonies in Iceland, supported
by professional traders and ships' crews who participated for a share
of any profits. The Norse of Iceland later explored Greenland. One of
the most important of these was Eirik raude Thorvaldson (Eric the
Red). He first explored Greenland from 982 to 985 AD, and, with his
son Leif (known as 'the Lucky'), established colonies there over the
next thirty years. They found some pasturage within the fjords of
Greenland as well as woodland that would provide construction materials and fuel. Its subarctic southern coasts could not support much
livestock; Norse settlers had to hunt the same seals and caribou as did
the Greenland Inuit. The hazards of navigation around the Greenland
coasts may have carried some Norse vessels to the coasts of Newfoundland. Such appears to be the case with Bjarni Herjolfsson, who
in 986 AD brought back reports of new lands that encouraged the 1001
AD explorations of Leif the Lucky. Leif claimed Leifsbudir, a location
close to the current-day L'Anse aux Meadows, as his *landnam*. The settlement he built at Leifsbudir served as the gateway to the southern
land he encountered, Vinland, the 'Land of Wine,' a vaguely defined
area that might have encompassed the coastlines from the Gulf of St
Lawrence to the Bay of Fundy. He first sighted Helluland, the 'Land
of Flat Rocks,' which may have been Baffin Island. The next area was

Markland, or the 'Land of Woods,' a part of the Labrador coast. This area held much promise for the Norse, as there was always a demand for good timber. Vinland, with its varied woodland, game, and reputed wild grapes, was by far the most attractive area.[2]

Over the next nine years, Leif and his family led expeditions to Vinland. These were more prospecting voyages than attempts at colonization; there were likely no more than ninety people at any time living on the coast. The Norse explorers brought few of their female kin. The base camp they built at L'Anse aux Meadows contained halls, servants' huts, and forges, but no barns or other structures for sheltering livestock. Additionally, the Norse built their dwellings at L'Anse aux Meadows close together in a way that would make them easy to defend, rather than in the dispersed fashion of Norse farming communities. Finally, most of the artefacts left by the Norse at L'Anse aux Meadows suggest a people busy with boat repair rather than farming. The large halls likely housed the leader of the expedition, along with his retinue, while labourers and slaves would have lived in the smaller huts.[3]

L'Anse aux Meadows was a staging area from which the Norse could explore the Labrador coast, the eastern and western shores of Newfoundland, and the north shore of Quebec. The Norse may well have met proto-Algonkian-speaking First Nations at Vinland and retreated back to the safety of L'Anse aux Meadows. The defensive nature of the L'Anse aux Meadows buildings suggests that the Norse used it as a retreat, possibly from clashes with First Nations. While it may have appeared to be a safe harbour, L'Anse aux Meadows was a risky choice. Long before the arrival of the Norse, Épaves Bay had been a favourite place for first peoples to hunt and gather, and they may have been uneasy about Norse settlements. Meanwhile the Norse may have been nervous about encountering strange new people who were unlike the Inuit they had encountered in Greenland. Leif's brother Thorvald led an expedition to claim Krossanes as his *landnam*, not far from Leifsbudir. He spent two summers and a winter in Newfoundland and had fought with people whom the Norse called Skraelings. Iron swords were not particularly superior to the stone-tipped spears and bows and arrows of the 'Skraelings,' resulting in the death of Leif's brother during a skirmish in which eight of the nine of the Norse's foes were killed.[4]

The Norse did not need Vinland, since Greenland still had plenty of land for settlement. It is possible that the Norse could cross the Davis Strait to cut timber without establishing any settlement. The trip was only a short one from the northern hunting grounds of Greenland. Such hunts might have led the Norse across the Strait in search of furs. All of this activity, however, depended on the Greenland colony's ability to sustain Norse exploration and resource exploitation further abroad. By the early fifteenth century, Norse Greenland was itself in grave trouble. A cooling trend appears to have undermined farming and trade with Europe. As the Norse colony at Greenland withered, the base necessary for further voyages to North America disappeared; although there is evidence that a ship from the Eastern Colony of the Norse in Greenland visited Markland in 1347. It would be about 150 years before Europeans would again visit Newfoundland and Labrador.[5]

The knowledge gained by the Norse about the island of Newfoundland and the coast of Labrador had little lasting effect on their European neighbours' consciousness about what lay beyond the Atlantic's western horizon. In the fifteenth century, Bristol merchants certainly knew about Iceland's fishing grounds, and there were reports in England that an English Minorite, or Franciscan friar, had recounted travels in the North Atlantic, possibly as far as Markland, to the court of the English King Edward III in 1360. However, Iceland likely represented the outer limit of Europe's western world. In 1477, for example, Christopher Columbus may have travelled to Iceland on board a Bristol ship, but probably heard little from the island's inhabitants about Greenland let alone lands further west. The Norse explorations played no obvious part in Columbus's or John Cabot's later explorations and landfalls in the Americas.[6]

From the Norse explorations through to Cabot's voyage and on to the fisheries and whaling enterprises of the sixteenth century, Europeans often came to exploit the marine resources in waters off Newfoundland and Labrador's coasts. They had little interest in colonization, or in 'taking possession' of the region. The migratory fishery to Newfoundland, well under way by 1502, was one of the earliest continuous European activities in North America, although it was only conducted during the summer months. Everyone involved with the migratory fishery, including the Spanish, French, English, and Portuguese, took a good look at Newfoundland and Labrador's coasts while fishing in the waters surrounding them. North America provided no treasure to be looted such as the Spanish had found in the Caribbean. Throughout North America, Europeans found, as had the Norse before, that the First Nations of the continent's eastern seaboard sometimes resisted intrusion on their lands but at other times were keen to trade. Fur trading, like whaling and fishing, did not require settlement in the hostile new lands.[7]

As long as the trade and resources of Europe provided enough opportunity, merchants had little reason to invest in expeditions to the New World. Merchants from Bristol, England, for example, probably invested in a few westward adventures shortly after 1480, but they had plenty of more secure investments in the trade of fish, wool, cloth, and wine between England, Iceland, and the Iberian peninsula. Bristol-based vessels fished in Icelandic waters, but as Iceland fell more into the orbit of the Hanseatic League, the main competitor of the English for trade in Europe, some Bristol merchants decided to search for fishing grounds to the west and likely funded the discovery of fishing grounds surrounding Newfoundland. While English mariners had fished in Icelandic waters, they lacked the navigational skills for great voyages of discovery to the west. Instead, Bristol backers turned to the Venetian citizen Zuan Caboto, called John Cabot by his investors. Cabot's own desire was to find a route to the riches of the Orient, or at least an equivalent of the gold Columbus found in South America. Cabot was one of a number of the fifteenth-century Mediterranean mariners who had become skilled in celestial navigation.[8] Bristol merchants did not put much money into developing the Newfoundland fishery, though, and did not invest a lot in his voyage.

It is impossible to say whether Cabot even landed in Newfoundland and Labrador during the 1497 voyage. Cabot left Bristol on 20 May and appears to have made for Ireland, from which he could have sailed west along the line of latitude. The difficulties of taking navigational readings in the period, combined with the lack of certainty about exactly what part of the Irish coast Cabot sailed from, make it impossible to determine where he landed in June of 1497. The sparse descriptions of this landfall made by Cabot, and his son Sebastian, as well as the rumours that circulated in Europe about Cabot's adventure, variously support a landfall in Cape Breton, Newfoundland, or southern Labrador. We must remember that geographical information about what was to Europeans a 'New World' was imperfect at best. While the most educated speculation places Cabot's landfall 'somewhere between Sandwich Bay, Labrador, and White Bay, Newfoundland,' no one can claim definitely that Cabot raised the royal standard and took possession of Newfoundland or Labrador for the English crown. It is more certain that, having explored the waters around Newfoundland, Cabot left from Cape Dégrat in the Strait of Belle Isle to sail east and collect his £10 reward and yearly £20 pension from King Henry.[9]

   Despite better financial support for his 1498 voyage, Cabot and his crew disappeared at sea. Although the explorer had found rich fishing grounds, they were located in a daunting climate without much else that was immediately lucrative and in waters that fishers from Portugal may have already been using. Bristol merchants continued to prefer to trade local cloth for French and Iberian wines, turning their attention to the western Atlantic only as wars in Europe increased their dependence on Spanish and Portuguese markets. Cod itself did not interest the Bristolians since England had enough fish for its own needs in closer waters, but they did wish to increase their import trade and identified Portugal and Spain as the likely sources. While Bristol merchants and shippers traded for high-priced, low-volume items such as sugars, spices, fruits, and wines, they had only cheaper high-volume items such as cloth to exchange. Although Bristolians eventually expanded into the trade with the West Indies and the Atlantic Islands such as the Madeiras, for much of the fifteenth and sixteenth centuries, they did not give up on the dream of finding a direct route to Asia's luxury goods. Bristol merchants backed John Cabot's son Sebastian, for example, in his expedition up the Labrador coast in 1508. Throughout the first half of the sixteenth century, the crowns of England and Spain sought Sebastian Cabot's skills as an explorer, navigator, and cartographer, meaning that his reputation and fame eclipsed that of his father. While precious metals, gems, spices, and cloths may have been on the minds of the Bristol merchants, the humble cod proved to be England's Atlantic treasure in the long term.[10]

   In the short term, Portugal claimed that England had no right to Newfoundland, which it claimed by right of the Treaty of Tordesillas in 1493. The Portuguese crown sponsored the exploratory voyages of the Corte-Real brothers, Gaspar and Miguel, in 1501 and 1502. To substantiate its claim, the crown gave Gaspar Corte-Real the captaincy over any territories he might discover. Gaspar followed in Cabot's wake in more ways than one, also perishing at sea during his voyages. The Portuguese concentrated on their trade routes to India around the Cape of Good Hope, but João Alvares Fagundes, a wealthy, retired military officer of Porto, had royal permission to explore and govern territories in Newfoundland and the offshore islands now known as St Pierre and Miquelon. Fagundes's claims led to no concerted efforts to colonize but provided a convenient way for the Portuguese crown to keep open the possibility of some day directing their imperial efforts northward into the Atlantic. However, the lucrative trade in Asia and South America meant that while the Portuguese explored and sometimes fished around Newfoundland, they were otherwise insignificant in European expansion there. Cod could be had from other nations' fishers in exchange for wine, silver, or gold. There was no need to catch it directly.[11]

The Portuguese involvement in what the English called the fisheries of the 'New found Isle landes' was small but still greater than that of the English in the first half of the sixteenth century. The Portuguese and English were adventurous dabblers by comparison with the French and Spanish. The Basques from the Bay of Biscay area in southern France and northern Spain, who might have sighted Newfoundland or Labrador before Cabot, had dominated the European cod fishery since medieval times because they had access to plentiful supplies of salt. With this salt, the Basques produced a better-quality preserved fish that could be traded over long distances. The Basques continued to bring cod to Europe from the west even after they stopped fishing in Icelandic waters, but before Cabot's voyage. The Basques came to these waters not only to fish for cod, but also to hunt whales. By 1530, they were well established as the premier fishers and whale hunters of the south coast of Labrador, which they called *la Provincia de Terranova*, and the island of Newfoundland, which they called *Ile de Baccaillau*. Although a few vessels from each of the western European nations were visiting Newfoundland, the Basques were most numerous.

Along the Labrador coast, the Basques hunted bowhead and right whales for their baleen and blubber. Baleen could be used to make items that needed to be strong and flexible, and the oil rendered from whale fat was the petrochemical of the early modern era. Europeans burned it in lamps for light and used it as an industrial lubricant. The major whaling centres on the southern Labrador coast were at Red Bay and Chateau Bay. Usually twenty to thirty Basque ships travelled to these areas to hunt throughout the summer and might stay until January, and even later if the arctic sea ice blocked their ships. Each Basque ship sailed with a crew of 130 and would take back at the end of the season about two thousand barrels of whale oil per ship, each barrel weighing about 181 kilograms.

Whale hunting was a dangerous business. Much of what we know about the hunt comes from the remains of tragedy in the industry, both actual and anticipated: the wills left by whale hunters fearful that they might not return home and the archaeological investigations of the remains of those buried far from family, friends, and home on the Labrador coast. The Basques hunted whales by chasing them in small boats, harpooning the huge animals, and then attaching floats to the line, or allowing their boats to be dragged, until the exhausted whale could be killed. The whalers could be capsized and drowned, but many others died of lack of provisions and exposure when ice forced them to overwinter on the Labrador coast. While there is evidence of Inuit and Innu exchange of material goods with the Basques, and perhaps even employment of the latter by the Basques, there is not much evidence of good relationships with local first peoples, which might have helped the whalers endure the winter.

A number of factors diminished the Basque presence in Newfoundland and Labrador. By 1600, the Basques had depleted the whales they hunted and shifted their effort to cod fishing on the south coast of Newfoundland. Spanish Basque merchants and shipowners found their fleet drafted and trade taxed to support the Spanish Armada, lost in the disastrous defeat by England in 1588. As a result, the Spanish Basque fishery was in ruins by the late sixteenth century, and French Basque merchants moved in to hire their crews, use their ports, and sell fish and oil to them. French Basque gentry and merchants, such as Adam de Chibau, moved into their Spanish counterparts' trade, often with the financial backing of Spanish merchants.[12]

The influence of the Basques reached beyond their own fishing industry. Basque pilots were like the Cabots; they were available for hire and appear to have guided the ships of many nations to the waters off the eastern North American seaboard. Throughout the sixteenth century the fishery did not consolidate in any particular western European port. Over fifty ports continued to send ships across the Atlantic at the century's end, although certain ports had already begun to emerge as especially important. Norman financiers who backed French fishers, for example, got most of the supplies for their fishing voyages from the ports of Bordeaux and La Rochelle. By the 1550s, fishers from French Basque ports joined the Bretons and were supplied in a similar manner. From the 1540s, Spanish Basque fishers were going as well. While fishing fleets from Portugal and Spain tended to be small, the French fishing fleet grew rapidly to several hundred vessels by the late sixteenth century.[13]

We must assume that many of these fishers went to waters close by Newfoundland and Labrador, but we cannot say for sure. Records of fishing enterprises of the period tend to be very general about the destinations of voyages. There are, nonetheless, records that suggest that the French were active in Newfoundland waters. In 1527 European visitors to St John's reported seeing many Breton, Norman, and Portuguese fishing vessels in the harbour. Jacques Cartier appears to have depended on the familiarity of fishers from Brittany with the northeastern and northwestern coasts of the island in his own voyage of exploration. As in the case of other fishers, the French voyages to Newfoundland in the 1530s and 1540s were to establish inshore fisheries. These ships left Europe early in the spring and returned later in the fall. Fishing would be done near a shore and the salted cod dried on the beaches during the brief summer. Only after 1545 did fishing ships appear to be able to carry all of the materials required for the fishery of the great banks off Newfoundland. When such bank fishing developed, it did not require land or time for the construction of shore facilities at Newfoundland. Crews on the banks did not dry cod but pickled it in brine on board the ship and could thus catch full cargoes more quickly. These ships could, consequently, return to Europe much faster than those involved in the shore fishery.[14]

Early European merchants, shipowners, and fishers organized their production for international markets in broadly similar ways, although there was much local variation in what might be termed 'vernacular' practices. French, Iberian, and English fishing voyages all tended to use ships in the range of 40 to 50 tons, although they might occasionally use ships as large as 200 tons. Shipowners and merchants spread risk by investing individually in a great number of ships, a way of not having too many eggs in one basket should one ship be lost at sea or have a bad voyage, as commonly occurred. The sixteenth-century fishery was not organized on a national basis. Merchants might provision their ships and engage crews from ports throughout northwestern Europe, making some cooperation between the fishing industries of individual countries a necessity. Merchants engaged crews by share agreements to begin work in April of each year. Once hired, crews pressured their masters to hurry through the process of provisioning their ships and sailing to western Atlantic fishing grounds. Any delay ate into the short fishing season, from June through August, in the waters around Newfoundland, and made likely a smaller overall catch. Upon arrival, fishing crews had to build cookhouses and shelters, stages for unloading and preparing cod, as well as flakes on which the fish could be dried.[15]

Crews did not fish from the large ships they sailed from Europe. They used small boats that they rowed or sailed from shore to the fishing grounds. Each small boat had a master, botswain, and an unskilled man. These men would use two or three handlines, each containing a couple of baited hooks. After a long day's work, the crew heaved their catch up onto the stage, where the shore crew took over.

Members of the crew, called headers and splitters, prepared the fish for salting. Under the watchful eye of a beach-master, unskilled crew members would pile the split fish with salt and, after a few days, spread it to dry on beaches or flakes. Crews always included a few young men who were apprenticed to learn the business of the cod fishery. Once the fishing was over in late August, crews often sailed their ships to the markets for cod, exchanged the cod for a paying cargo of foodstuffs and wine, and then sailed to another port where this might be sold. Back home, crew members received their pay according to skill, or at least a balancing of accounts as they might have taken an advance on their wages at the beginning of the voyage. Shares varied from the highest for beach-masters, ships' pilots, stewards, and surgeons through ships' carpenters, skilled fishers, and shore workers. The unskilled apprentices received the least, perhaps only a quarter of what the beach-master might earn. All received their pay by a share of the total share due to the ship's master. The precise nature of shares varied considerably by the region from which crews came. Crews from the Breton coast, for example, tended to accept less pay than their Norman counterparts because their masters provided them with wine or cider.

The provision of wine or cider might have lightened the hearts of crews who otherwise ate plainly. Without some light spirits, crews might have lived on little more than bread and water. Victuallers provided ships with biscuit, the staple of the crew's diet. In addition to their daily ration of biscuits, the crew ate smaller amounts of dried peas and beans, and some fat in the form of bacon or olive oil. These legumes might be cooked with a very small portion of salt meat or fish, and would be seasoned with garlic, mustard, or vinegar. The terms of their employment allowed each crew member some storage for their own freight, a right called portage. Those who wanted a better diet might well have used such space to bring along more diverse extra food such as cheese. While crews could not work on empty stomachs, merchants had to supply the voyage with all the other equipment required by fishing: boats, hooks, lines, and salt. All together, the supplies the merchants provided on credit represented a significant risk. If the fishing voyage failed there would be no return on the investment, and voyages would not succeed if inadequately equipped. On a successful voyage, merchants expected to receive a 20–40 per cent return on their loans.[16]

The increased European activity in the waters of the southern Labrador coast and Newfoundland attracted the attention of the first peoples of the region. At some point during the turn of the sixteenth century, the Inuit began to migrate south of Nain, establishing a community at what is now called Hopedale. Good hunting could be found in nearby waters, and the climate was slightly warmer than the northern parts of the Labrador coast. Other Inuit chose to settle at Eskimo Island, located between Hamilton Inlet and Groswater Bay, an area not frequented by whales and walrus, the basis of their economy and well within the territory of the Point Revenge people, who may not have welcomed such an incursion. The main advantage of Eskimo Island was that it served as a good base from which the Inuit could raid Basque whaling stations to the south. Basque whale hunting competed directly with the primary economic activity of the Inuit. There was little basis for trade between the Europeans and the Inuit, but the Europeans had boats that the Inuit could take, as well as spikes and nails that could only be secured by burning the whaling station structures. While Eskimo Island was close enough for the highly mobile Inuit to strike at the Basques, it was far enough away to make European reprisals unlikely.

Archaeological investigations suggest that the Inuit initially built homes much like those of their Thule predecessors but by the mid-seventeenth century had begun to use multi-family dwellings. The Inuit homes at Eskimo Island contained a great deal of European goods, including iron spikes they had fashioned into various hunting tools. They used European hardwoods in making floats and ground red roofing tiles the Basques had brought from Europe either for pigment or as whetstones for sharpening blades. Glass beads also seem to have been an object of Inuit desire, something that the Basques likely brought with them for trade. By the early seventeenth century, Inuit from other communities as far north as Killinek were acquiring smaller amounts of all these goods. The Inuit of Eskimo Island had become more than raiders by the end of the seventeenth century. They began to serve as 'middle man' traders between Inuit further north and the Innu of Labrador and European traders to the south. The size and complexity of the Inuit homes at Eskimo Island continued to grow, suggesting their success as traders.[17]

The Inuit's southern expansion profoundly affected the Innu of the central and southern Labrador coasts. The Basque whalers, as well as French and Dutch traders, encountered Innu hunters on the coast, suggesting that the prehistoric Indians' use of coastal resources had survived into the initial period of contact with Europeans. Archaeological investigations of Basque whaling sites have revealed projectile points associated with both Point Revenge and Little Passage people. These people may have come to Basque posts to trade food for European metals. Relations between the Innu and the Inuit may have worsened as a result of the presence of Europeans as trading partners. The Innu decision to turn away from the sea to rely on hunting caribou may have been related to violence at the hands of the Inuit, who wanted to monopolize access to Europeans, or to escape the growing hostility of Europeans to any people of the First Nations whom they may have blamed for the wintertime raids upon their property.

Dependence on the caribou hunt changed the Innu, who developed social strategies that allowed them to hunt caribou over the vast territory of the Labrador interior. To increase the chance of finding caribou, the Innu ranged throughout the interior in small family bands led by male hunters. The dispersed nature of this hunting pattern allowed the Innu to take advantage of local supplies of edible plants, small game, and fish that would not sustain a large community. By spreading out, the Innu did not break down into small, nomadic bands that had little to do with each other. On the contrary, the Innu remained in contact with each other as a nation. Each band looked for the great caribou herds, which, when found, would require the assistance of other families in killing and processing. Innu society might be thought of as a web spreading throughout the interior. People travelled from band to band, meeting at favoured locations at different times of the year to share information about hunting opportunities. In winter, the Innu family bands would choose a good location near a lake or river for fishing. During the spring, these bands would meet with others at places in the interior along which caribou were known to migrate to calving grounds in the high country. During the summer, the Innu would stay on barren land in the higher country. There the Innu would find porcupine, arctic hare, and fowl such as ducks, geese, and ptarmigan to hunt. When autumn approached the Innu would again rendezvous at points where they knew caribou herds would migrate back to wintering grounds.

In the fall, working in small groups of hunters and their families, but occasionally working in larger communities, the Innu would take 750 to 1000 caribou. While men killed the animals, women and children processed them into preserved meat, fat, and skins. As the success of the hunt became clear, a small group would leave to contact other hunting groups to advise them of their own good fortune. European observers often thought that the Innu were being wasteful in their apparent slaughter of the animals they encountered, but nothing went to waste as people came from all over the interior to share in the hunt. In addition, preserved caribou was used in the caches that made interior travel possible and served as the main component of the Innu's winter diet.[18]

The landward orientation of the Innu meant that chance contact with European fishers or explorers was unlikely. The situation was much different for the Inuit, and contact with Europeans foreshadowed greater difficulties to come. Some of the European goods found among the remains of the people of Eskimo Island may have come from contact between the Inuit of Baffin Island and the English explorer Martin Frobisher. Although the English lagged behind the French and the Basques in entering the Newfoundland fishery, they continued to have contact with the lands beyond the sea. Bristol merchants, for example, continued to fund searches for the Northwest Passage. They assisted Frobisher's second voyage and supported even more Humphrey Gilbert's voyage in 1583.[19] From the 1520s, the English continued to explore the western seas, and in the 1530s, English explorers had ventured to the Strait of Belle Isle to follow up on the work of Jacques Cartier. Frobisher had served with merchant ships in the trade routes to West Africa and, by the 1550s, had likely learned about the voyages of the Corte-Reals from Portuguese seafarers he had worked with. In three voyages undertaken in 1576, 1577, and 1578, Frobisher explored the northern Labrador coast, the bay that bears his name (which Frobisher thought to be a strait), and Baffin Island generally. Frobisher's tendency to kidnap Inuit for information and interpreters provoked hostile relationships with them, and later Dutch whalers' visits to the Davis Strait found the Inuit willing to trade but not otherwise welcoming of the Europeans.[20]

Basque whaling stations, such as those at Red Bay and Chateau Bay in the Strait of Belle Isle, continued to be a longer-lasting source of European goods. The archaeological evidence for the early seventeenth century suggests that access to European goods had little impact on Inuit life. When the Inuit moved south, it was most likely to search for better hunting and greater supplies of local wood provided by the more hospitable climes of the central Labrador coast. It may also be the case that early contact with Europeans, such as the Frobisher and Dutch expeditions, introduced diseases among the Inuit that disrupted their community life and made access to European goods for trade more important. Gradually, contact with Europeans led to changes in the life of the southern Inuit. Well into the eighteenth century, these Inuit began to build larger, multi-family dwellings, integrated more

European metals into their tool production, and dealt determinedly with any new Europeans they encountered, such as the French from New France. Among the Inuit, good hunters and shamans had always had a special status. Some of these began to use their skills to acquire European goods for trade with other Inuit. Combined with the better resources of the southern coast, the Inuit there began to develop a society and economy based on trade as well as subsistence activities. From the north, Inuit traders acquired ivory, baleen, sealskins, oil, and feathers that they could supply to Europeans. The Inuit traders then sent European goods north. The wealth generated by this trade allowed the southern Inuit to establish larger settlements. As trade grew, and community size increased, the southern Inuit may have found that they could no longer maintain, or did not have to engage in, seasonal settlement on outer islands for hunting. Instead, the southern Inuit could rely on those to the north to do so. The more centralized and larger Inuit communities of the south often did not enjoy good relationships with each other. It may be that rivalry grew as each community tried to support its trade with the north.[21]

To the south, the island of Newfoundland had been figuring more prominently in the European cod fisheries of the western Atlantic, particularly in the case of England. Merchants in Bristol found they could sell codfish to southern Europe in exchange for the products they were importing, thus easing the ongoing trade deficit problem of the late sixteenth century. The riches Portugal and Spain had plundered in South America and the Caribbean excited envy among their European neighbours, England included. The English and French did not have the financial resources or political stability to build similar empires, but such problems did not stop some English adventurers from dreaming. While Frobisher had hoped to find a direct trade route to Asia, his contemporary, Sir Humphrey Gilbert, thought about a different kind of approach. Gilbert, along with Frobisher and other adventurers such as Sir Francis Drake, spent some of their time in the 1560s plundering England's enemies as privateers. In 1566, Gilbert proposed that England should build a colonial empire of silver and gold as had the Iberians. By 1578 he had convinced Queen Elizabeth to allow him to establish, or 'plant' as Gilbert might have termed it, a colony in North America. Although Gilbert planned to plant somewhere to the south on the North American mainland, the familiar sailing routes in the fishery led him to Newfoundland in 1583. There he landed at St John's and boldly claimed the island for England despite the presence of ships from other nations in the harbour.

Gilbert's trip brought him a watery grave and little else. His contemporaries probably did not think much of his colonial adventure, but the wars of the late sixteenth century began to convince many English of the need for a greater colonial presence in the western North Atlantic. In 1578, for example, Anthony Parkhurst proposed that the first country to establish settlement at Newfoundland would gain control over the entire fishery. If England did not become that country, then some other such as France would beat it to the prize.

The English government did not have the financial resources to support colonization. Rather, it listened to the wild speculations of colonial promoters such as Parkhurst and fellow writer Edward Hayes (who had accompanied Gilbert on his earlier adventure), who dreamed of rich timber lands, shipbuilding yards, mines of precious metals and stones, fertile farms, and factories. Promoters argued that all these activities would supply the needs of colonial fishing people much more cheaply than they could be provided for from England. By lowering the costs of the fishery, the colonies would prove immensely profitable to anyone who would invest in them.[22]

By the mid-1570s the effort of ports such as Bristol in the fishery increased dramatically, and it looked as if there would be much support among the city's entrepreneurs for some colonial adventure. War with Spain between 1587 and 1604, however, forced the English to turn away from any interest in colonization. The defeat of the Spanish Armada in 1588 gave English merchants more confidence about fitting out ships for the cod fishery. A defeated Spain continued to try to exclude the cod of its enemy from its market, but through the 1590s Irish, Dutch, and French merchants were willing to buy English-caught fish for shipment to the Spanish market, where the price was high. The requirement of financing of the fishing ships and the dealing with foreign shippers encouraged patterns of investment that, in the long run, proved better than the chartered companies in underwriting the fishing industry. West Country merchants knitted together an interest in the Newfoundland fishery that would last centuries and built on the longer trading relationships between ports such as Bristol and the Portuguese to ensure access to salt.

A good example of the West Country merchants is the Newman family of the Devonshire port of Dartmouth. The family had a long history in the cloth and woollen trades and at the beginning of the sixteenth century began to trade in wine. Soon they started trading their wine for fish and salt for the local market. Once started, the Newmans' contact with the fish trade began to grow. By 1589 John Newman was trading fish and sending vessels to Newfoundland to acquire more. The Newmans invested heavily in shipping, and the fish trade gave them the opportunity to deploy their vessels in both the production and marketing of an important commodity. By the early seventeenth century, the family had assigned some ships to fishing, with catches being transferred to cargo ships that headed for Iberian and Mediterranean markets.[23]

Peace in 1604 led to more English interest in colonies and the expansion of industrial enterprises abroad. Through the end of the sixteenth century the number of ships sailing annually from Bristol increased, and by the 1620s between eight and sixteen vessels sailed for the fishery each year. The crown lacked the money or commitment to overseas enterprises and depended upon subjects to undertake the expenses of harassing the shipping of enemies (through privateers) and founding colonies. The king was willing to grant lands in the new world to private investors if they enforced English law and increased the trade of the kingdom. The renewed interest in an English fishery in Newfoundland did not mean that anyone rushed to undertake the expenses of forming a colony. Bristol investors were uninterested, but some wondered if a colony might supply the fishery itself without the cost of shipping in provisions. In 1610, for example, Bristol and London merchants founded the London and Bristol Newfoundland Company in an effort to lower some of the costs associated with the migratory fishery. King James I granted the company a royal charter for the entire island of Newfoundland. The investors hoped that their colony in Conception Bay, named Cuper's Cove (later Cupids), under the direction of John Guy, would make money. Colonists could fish earlier and later in the year than migratory fishermen and would not have to rebuild wharves and stages each spring. Colonists could also lay claim to the best fishing grounds and beaches for drying fish before the arrival of competing fishers in the early summer.[24]

Guy's colony at Cuper's Cove represented a first attempt at organized European settlement in Newfoundland, an attempt that likely did not profit the investors. The colony was more successful, however, in establishing the notion among some English adventurers that the island, or at least the Avalon Peninsula, was a 'new land' devoid of Christian inhabitants and thereby open to be claimed by the English as their own. Earlier proponents of settlement and people active in the migratory fishery, such as Anthony Parkhurst (who visited Newfoundland a number of times between 1575 and 1578) and Captain Richard Whitbourne (who visited Trinity Bay in 1579), gave no indication that they noticed the Beothuks at all or else felt that the Beothuks did not frequent the Avalon Peninsula. This was important, since the 1606 colony at Jamestown, Virginia, had met a hostile reception from local Amerindians. Since no 'Christian king' had sovereignty over the new land, the Europeans felt free to move in and establish their own laws. And since the indigenous peoples Europeans encountered had not 'improved' land by cutting its forests and fencing and planting fields, they had not made the land into private property. In their own minds, Europeans thought the land was free for them to take. First Nations who lived on the land might be suitable trade partners or maybe even souls to save though conversion to Christianity, but they were not subjects of a Christian king and therefore had no real rights. In other words, the supposed moral superiority of Christianity was seen by the English and other Europeans as giving them the right to subordinate first peoples in their own lands, especially if such subordination included the establishment of lucrative fur trades or other commercial activities.

Originally, John Guy's instructions had been to establish peaceful relations with the Beothuks; he had met with a few and exchanged a few European items for some furs. Rumours of Beothuks living in nearby Trinity Bay had reached Guy's colony by 1612, when he sent explorers across the arm of land separating Conception and Trinity bays. Although these explorers met no Beothuks, they discovered evidence of the extensive use the Beothuks made of the area extending from present-day Dildo Arm to Bull Arm. This discovery prompted Guy into mounting a larger expedition; in October he sent a barque and shallop with crews and trade goods into Trinity Bay. The crews of these vessels were to explore the resources of the south side of the bay and to contact the Beothuks. The explorers found Beothuk camps at what are now Hopeall and Dildo South and, when they ventured into the interior, found a canoe, evidence of a fire, and smoke on the shore of Dildo Pond. Guy's men left some trinkets and biscuit in exchange for taking some beaver meat and children's moccasins. Guy's party then ventured to the bottom of Trinity Bay, where, in the vicinity of what is now known as Bull Arm, they discovered a Beothuk path that crossed the narrow Isthmus of Avalon to Placentia Bay. Again discovering ample sign of the Beothuks' presence, the English sailed further, with Guy hoisting a white flag in the hope of establishing that he meant only trade, not harm. This tactic met with some success, as a group of Beothuks used a signal fire to draw the ships' attention. Eight Beothuk men met with Guy and his captains. They exchanged mutual signs of friendship, gave each other gifts, and shared a meal. Guy's party stayed in the area for a while to explore. While Guy established no commitment to trade with the Beothuks his group had met, the Bristol colonizer had reason to hope. On the explorers' return to Cupids, they passed the site of their original meeting with the Beothuks and found some furs and other goods hung, apparently left as gifts. Guy had not brought along much to trade, so he left a pair of scissors, some needles, a knife, and a hatchet in place of some of the skins.[25]

The Beothuks had little interest in trade and avoided the unpredictable and potentially dangerous fishers, although there is evidence that sixteenth-century European visitors had brought iron goods specifically for trade with them.[26] They did not need European allies in their own conflicts with other peoples as was often the case in North America. More important, European fishers left behind iron nails and many other items when they left each fall; the Beothuks could scavenge abandoned fishing premises for the metal goods that made their lives easier. Most hunter-gatherers did not have the same notion of private property as did the property-obsessed Europeans and would have viewed anything left behind when a people moved on as free for others to take and use.

By contrast, the Innu and Inuit of Labrador established fur trades with French, English, and Basque fishers, whalers, and explorers. The Innu, who visited the Great Northern Peninsula, may even have traded European manufactures for furs from the Beothuks, becoming 'middle men' in the trade. The opportunities for desirable European goods such as portable and durable copper kettles and iron knives, hatchets, and spear points may have prompted the Innu to shift their economy from a heavy reliance on marine resources to a more interior adaptation. Harvesting greater numbers of fur-bearing animals and spending less time on the coast likely prompted some cultural changes, but the low frequency of meeting with Europeans allowed the Innu to maintain many qualities of their society. Although the Inuit's relations with European fishers and whalers had been more strained, the Labrador coast's more daunting ecology was inimical to sustained, direct contact between the two peoples.

Little came from John Guy's hope for trade with the Beothuks, and the colony failed to live up to the expectations of its backers. Growing competition from London merchants, and the feeling that the investors at home had not supported the enterprise with sufficient funds, caused John Guy to withdraw from the adventure. Others, such as

John Mason and Henry Crout, continued to explore the island and attempt contact with the Beothuks, but little came of it. The French in Canada brought missionaries along to convert the First Nations, and these missionaries acted as intermediaries between the two peoples. The fledgling colonies in Newfoundland could not afford to support missions, and the English were more interested in making a profit from the fish trade than they were in the fate of the Beothuks' souls. More important, the far greater numbers of seasonal migratory fishermen who arrived from Europe each year overshadowed the settlers' efforts. For example, Guy had sent only two craft into Trinity Bay in 1610, but more than sixty ships in the migratory fishery carried English fishers into Trinity Bay in 1620. These migratory fishermen cared little for trade with the Beothuks and knew less about the first peoples than the settlers did. While the settlers were careful about the manner in which they tried to contact the Beothuks, the seasonal fishermen blundered ashore in great numbers looking after their own wants and worrying little about giving offence to anyone else. Fear and suspicion matched these fishermen's ignorance; they had a tendency to shoot first and ask questions later when approached by the Beothuks.[27]

Despite their efforts to establish good relations with the Beothuks, the French who became involved in a migratory fishery to Newfoundland developed a relationship as poor as the English one. Initially interested in fisheries as an outgrowth of their European trades, and in exploratory adventures in search of oriental riches, the occasional and seasonal visits by Europeans to the shores of Labrador and Newfoundland provided little reason for the development of good relationships with the first peoples. As in the case of Frobisher's relationship with the Inuit, intermittent contact with the first peoples could lead to hostility and conflict. The Basques may have inadvertently affected the trade and relations of the Labrador peoples. Overall, however, the impact of Europeans on the first peoples was minimal as even the first attempts at proprietary colonies proved disappointing. Growing European interest in settlement and colonization would change this, leading to conflict reminiscent of the Norse experience centuries before, but with more disastrous implications for the Amerindians of Newfoundland and Labrador.

3

Migrants and Settlers: The Development of a Fishing Society, 1610–1775

The Cupids colony failed as a profitable colonial adventure on the part of its Bristol investors, but it was the first blow against the dominion of Newfoundland by the first peoples. The Cupids colonists built a well-fortified and comfortable compound, sowed their crops, sawed lumber for boats and buildings, and began to fish in their first year. Over the long term, the colonists hoped they could locally supply the fishery more cheaply than migratory fishers and enjoy a longer fishing season by being freed from travelling to and from Europe each year. While profits from such a colonial strategy proved elusive, the Cupids settlers laid the basis for permanent European settlement in Newfoundland. Early colonization failed, but English interests came to accept settlement as necessary for the defence of their fish trade from European rivals and encroachments by locally competing aboriginal interests.

Europeans mistook the coastal lands used by the Beothuks as empty, and migratory fishers felt free to leave fishing premises unprotected at the end of the fishing season. From the Beothuk perspective, they could gather from abandoned fishing premises each winter the metal goods that made their lives easier. The Beothuks did not see the premises as private property but rather as something abandoned and therefore free to take without the risk of contact with potentially violent Europeans, although their scavenging eventually earned them a reputation as thieves. Thus, in the first century or so of sharing the island with European visitors, the Beothuks prospered from the iron tools that made their lives easier without altering their culture and communities.[1]

No lucrative fur trade with the Beothuks awaited the Cupids colony, which also found that its agricultural and other landward economic activities provided few opportunities for profit. The colonists' fishery faced persistent depredations by pirates such as Peter Easton. The Bristol and London Company began to sell rights to colonize parts of Newfoundland to investors such as the Welshman William Vaughan in 1617. Vaughan established a colony between Caplin Bay and Placentia Bay on the Avalon Peninsula. The colony's settlers benefited from the leadership of Captain Richard Whitbourne, but, despite a move to Renews in 1618, the colonial adventure was over by 1619. Vaughan and Whitbourne wrote books – *The Golden Fleece* and *Discourse and Discovery* respectively – promoting colonization, but both acknowledged that future colonization would have to depend on the fishery. Former partners of the Bristol and London Company established a more successful colony at Bristol's Hope (Harbour Grace), Conception Bay, in 1618, which lasted until 1631. Those who fished there likely prospered, but without much help from their governor. In 1623 Henry Cary, Viscount Falkland, established another colony between Ferryland and Aquafort on the north, and Renews in the south, but little is known of the colony as it too ceased to exist by 1628. While all of these colonies disappointed their backers, they brought out settlers who stayed and formed the basis of a permanent population of European descent in Newfoundland.[2]

These settlers learned that their well-being depended on the fishery just as the merchants who backed the migratory trade came to understand that they depended on settlers. West Country merchants were coming to dominate the English fishery; from 1610 the migratory trade from the ports of Plymouth, Dartmouth, and Bideford in Devonshire, as well as from Dorset and Hampshire, had thrived. The merchants of these ports used a share system to finance their industry, but it was expensive and risky to fit out vessels and crews for the annual trips to Newfoundland. Some settlers annoyed the West Country merchants by trying to exploit exclusively good shore facilities previously used by the migratory fishermen. Overall, the settlers were too few in number to be more than a nuisance, and many West Country merchants found that they could make money by supplying the settlers alongside the migratory trade. Settlers and migratory fishers probably saw little difference between themselves. There were few female settlers, meaning that most single males had little opportunity to establish their own households or accumulate much property on their own. The population of those who saw Newfoundland as their home consequently grew slowly. While many of the single men among the settlers may have hoped to return to England, or perhaps move on to another colony, in the meantime they hired migratory labourers to help in their fisheries and made money by cutting wood for the migratory operations. Some settlers might sell liquor and tobacco to the migratory fishermen from their homes. Providing a little comfort to migratory fishermen could be a lucrative supplement to the unpredictable fishery.[3]

Although migratory shipowners found that the handful of settlers in Conception Bay posed little threat to their voyage, the same could not be said for the colony of Avalon, established by George Calvert, who acquired William Vaughan's rights to the area. An investor in the Virginia and the East India Companies, Calvert was determined to succeed in Newfoundland. He sent artisans and builders to Ferryland, under the command of Edward Wynne, to construct a fortification, stone quay, forge, kitchen, mansion, and houses, all along a cobblestone street. By 1625, one hundred settlers were farming and fishing there, and Wynne brought out additional artisans, as well as women to bake bread and brew beer for them. Calvert was well connected in England, becoming Lord Baltimore for his role in English politics but, as a Roman Catholic, decided to make Avalon into a bulwark against Protestantism in the new world. He brought his family to Ferryland, with more Catholic settlers and a priest in 1628, and, although he tried to ensure that the colony would be guided by religious toleration, his 'Romish' sympathies antagonized the bulk of his Protestant colonists.[4]

Plagued by sectarian tensions, Baltimore's colony successfully fought off raids by French pirates under the command of Captain Raymond de la Ralde, but the colonists found it difficult to raise much besides root crops to supplement insufficient imported supplies, particularly during the cooling global climate of the early seventeenth century. In 1629, Baltimore moved to Maryland because of political harassment in London and the troubles of the colony, but he did not abandon the colony of Avalon, realizing that his settlers were engaged in a lucrative fishery. He left as his agent in charge of the plantation, a former soldier, emphasizing just how much attention had to be devoted to defence rather than productive enterprise.[5]

Official colonization had failed, but a settler population had been established that needed a mechanism to resolve disputes with migratory fishing interests. 'Fishing admirals' had customary legal authority for the migratory fishery since at least the beginning of the

seventeenth century. The first fishing captain to arrive in each Newfoundland harbour for the fishing season would become admiral, the
second vice admiral, and the third the rear admiral. Without court
officers or chambers, the fishing admirals were to keep law and order
in the fishery. A 1634 code issued by London's Court of Star Chamber,
the Western Charter, formalized the fishing admirals' legal authority
over the administration of the fishery, giving them legal jurisdiction
over all but capital crimes and theft of more than 40 shillings. Capital
crimes were to be tried in England – an unworkable system which required the accused and witnesses to be transported across the sea before justice could be done. Through to 1670, the English government
sought to buttress the migratory fishery by making fishing admirals
enforce laws against the transportation of passengers to Newfoundland or the assignment of legal rights to overwintering shore crews
since some migratory shipowners feared that if too many people became residents on the island, then all the best space on shore would be
lost to them. The fishing admirals did little to discourage settlement
and probably followed English common law in their judgments, usually confining themselves to settling disputes over the right to use
particular fishing rooms.[6]

In practice, fishing admirals reflected the ambivalence of English
state policy toward the growing interdependence of residents and migratory fishing interests. It was difficult to distinguish between the
two since settlers were often transient, moving from fishing station
to fishing station looking for work or better facilities for fishing. To
anyone living and working there, Newfoundland was simply part of
a 'Greater New England,' an integral part of the trade of the Atlantic world in which the people of the British Isles were accustomed to
moving about. 'By-boat keepers,' migratory boat owners who came
out yearly to fish, but who left their water craft in Newfoundland,
were becoming more important in the fishery and were becoming difficult to distinguish from residents by their conduct of business and
tendency to settle. Proponents of settlement pointed out that settlers
helped to keep Newfoundland out of the hands of the French and were
a profitable source of trade for many merchants and shipowners. The
Western Charter consequently recognized settlement, but protected
migratory fishers' use of land, timber, and shore facilities, and continued to allow the mayors of the West Country towns to oversee the
administration of justice at Newfoundland.

West Country shipowners and merchants had built the trade without state protection, monopolies, or subsidy, as had been the case in

other areas of imperial expansion, and did not want the government
to interfere in their trade. They were content that the charter of 1634
recognized their right to fish and trade at Newfoundland. Most West
Country merchants had begun to specialize in trade, carrying by-boat
keepers and passengers to Newfoundland, supplying them and resident fishers in return for their catches. Merchants crammed many
people and a lot of goods into their ships. Most ships were from 40
to 100 tons in size, but they could occasionally be as small as 15 or as
large as 200 tons. Provisions were stored below, and the passengers
and crew were quartered on the deck, although there was usually
only enough space for half of the people to sleep at once. Despite the
harsh nature of conditions, there was no shortage of people willing
to go fishing. Every winter, merchants and shipowners would spread
the word that they needed crews for the summer. In February, the
rural people of the West Country would attend fairs in market towns
such as Poole or Newton Abbott looking for work. Agents of the fish
merchants or their ships' captains would pay potential members of a
fishing crew a small sum in advance to seal a contract. New fishing
servants would then make their way to port and help prepare the
voyage. Sometime before February, West Country ships would sail
for the coast of Ireland, as had the Cabots so many years before. Here
they could run before prevailing easterly winds that carried them to
the Grand Banks. Once finished at Newfoundland, many ships sailed
for Mediterranean or West Indies markets first, while others left behind crew members to make room for fish. In such cases, it might be a
long time before crews saw their home ports again.[7]

Tensions between migratory shipowners and those who supported
settlement and the by-boat fishery continued, but the English Civil
War of 1642–8, the Restoration of the English crown in the 1650s, and
war with Spain from 1655 to 1660, all disrupted the migratory trade
but made the administration of Newfoundland a low priority in London. During the seventeenth century, the English did not dominate
the naval and mercantile affairs of the North Atlantic. By the 1630s,
Dutch traders were using more cost-effective cargo ships and better
access to Spanish ports to make serious inroads on the carrying trade
in English-caught fish. Many English merchants and shipowners
participated in the fishery by financing sack ships. These were cargo
vessels that carried provisions, equipment, and labour to the Newfoundland fishery in return for fish products to be sold in southern
European markets; their owners and backers made money solely in
freight rather than the production of fish. Preoccupied by war, the

English government had little energy to spare for protecting the sack trade and the cod fishery and relied on some settlement at Newfoundland to protect its claim to the island. The threat of Dutch mercantile hegemony in Europe, by 1656, prompted fierce maritime rivalry with England. Many of the English policies, such as the Acts of Trade and Navigation of the 1660s which required English merchants to use English-registered vessels, were acts of economic warfare against the Dutch. Twice the Dutch raided Newfoundland, first hitting St John's, Bay Bulls, and Ferryland, then, in 1673, Ferryland alone. The Dutch were not prepared to establish settlements that could compete with the English and French at Newfoundland and abandoned their interest in it. The French responded to the Dutch threat and the English presence in Newfoundland by building the settlement and military fortification of Plaisance in 1662, using it as a base to guard approaches to the Gulf of St Lawrence and New France as well.[8]

By comparison with the French, English settlement grew informally. Some West Country merchants left behind servants to maintain possession of shore facilities against competitors who might arrive first the next spring. These wintering servants could protect premises from pillaging and could begin fishing earlier in the spring. Merchants in the migratory trade found their overhead costs could be lowered by supplying residents or by-boat keepers. Many by-boat keepers also stayed year-round to guard their premises and take advantage of a longer fishing season. A few by-boat keepers and servants settled permanently, marrying into resident families established in the earlier colonial ventures of the seventeenth century. The permanent settlers who owned boats, gear, and shore premises became known as planters. They supplemented the potentially profitable but risky business of fishing with a little subsistence farming, cutting wood, building boats, trapping furs, and providing services and supplies to migratory fishers.

The balance between residents and migratory fishing interests could be upset. By 1638, for example, the English merchant and adventurer David Kirke had acquired rights to Baltimore's interests at Ferryland. Kirke established his own family there and began to trade with Baltimore's old settlers. Entrenching himself as the patron of local settlers, Kirke used his colonial charter to act as governor, taking the best fishing facilities for his colonists and taxing migratory fishers working within the boundaries of his colony by taking a portion of their catch. By 1652, Kirke, a royalist, was out of favour with the new Commonwealth government in London. It acted upon West

Country merchants' complaints about Kirke by sending a governor, John Treworgie, who quieted relations between settlers and the migratory shipowners. Kirke likely died in prison in 1654 awaiting trial for charges of interfering in the migratory fishery, but his wife, Lady Sarah Kirke, continued to manage the family's business at Ferryland through 1679, eventually building the largest and most successful plantation in Newfoundland. Three of the Kirke sons also became successful planters, continuing in the fishery until they were driven out by the French army in 1697. Charles II had recognized that amicable relations between settlers and migrants would be maintained if colonial authorities protected the latter. The Crown allowed the West Country adventurers new charters in 1661 and 1676, which protected the Western merchants from colonial interference such as that by Kirke.[9]

Although government remained hostile to colonization, persistent threats from the French over possession of the island served as a counterweight. The English government accepted some settlement as desirable, but without the expense of colonial government. The capitalist organization of the English fishery mixed with the varying social aspirations of its participants to produce a hybrid society. The interrelated resident and migratory fisheries depended on hired labour, with servants comprising about 90 per cent of the local population in summer and outnumbering planter families' members by two to one during the winter. The great merchant-planters such as the Kirkes assumed a gentry-like patron–client relationship with neighbouring smaller-scale planters. The Kirkes used their ability to extend credit to planters and market planters' fish to cultivate the loyalty and fish supplies of their neighbours. Their ownership of boats separated the planter gentry and planters from their hired servants, skilled and unskilled. Smaller planters, however, worked beside their servants, and both depended on the merchant capital of the planter-gentry to fish. The servants worked for shares and occasionally, if they were very skilled, for fixed wages. Cash was always in short supply, but servants were happy to take part of their pay in the tobacco, wine, and other beverages that merchants came by easily in the cod trade. Most servants were the young of West Country artisan, yeoman, and husbandman households who hoped to one day establish their own households either in England or in Newfoundland. Although planters and fishers alike did their best to farm as part of their seasonal round of work in Newfoundland, the local ecology would not support the type of commercial farming emerging among the gentry and producing classes in England, with its concomitant social and political respectability. For people of means, Newfoundland remained a nice place to visit for trading and fishing, but it was a disreputable place to settle.[10]

English fishers faced stiff competition from the French, especially from the port of Saint-Malo, and fierce rivalry between the English and French resulted in a regional division of the fishery by the 1650s. The English controlled the shore between Bonavista Bay and Saint Mary's Bay. The French fished off the coast north of Bonavista Bay (which they called the Petit Nord), and in Placentia and Saint Mary's bays. The French fisheries were lucrative, especially since they could be combined with excursions to Nova Scotia and the Labrador coast for a supplementary fur trade with Natives. Although there were never more than eight hundred or nine hundred people at Plaisance, the French base protected the French fishery. Between 1660 and 1680 greater numbers of Basque and Breton ships entered the bank fishery and expanded into England's markets in Spain and Italy, protected by tariffs against English competition at home.

The English government knew that some settlement helped hold Newfoundland against French territorial ambitions. West Country merchants favoured imperial spending on the navy rather than colonial fortifications to protect their commercial interests and feared the creation of colonial institutions such as courts, which would have to be paid for by a tax on fish rather than settlement. In 1675 the Board of Trade even asked convoy commander Sir John Berry to remove settlers from Newfoundland. Berry could not do so because residents had no means to pay for their return to the British Isles and were so intermingled with migratory fishing interests. As early as 1678, West Countrymen who had been long involved in the fishery, such as Nehemiah Troute, openly argued in favour of settlement as a means of protecting the property of the migratory fishers when they left at the end of the fishing season.[11]

English fishers likely feared the Beothuks more than the French. Each spring, the Beothuks came to the coast to hunt seals and gather birds' eggs at about the same time as the first fishers from Europe arrived. The Beothuks and the migratory fishermen became competitors for coastal resources, but without a fur trade to alleviate tensions between Natives and newcomers. Overwintering Newfoundland fishing servants trapped what furs were available from the small number of fur-bearing animals on the island, but the large number of seasonally abandoned fishing premises continued to supply iron for the Beothuks to take. They did so by burning premises to obtain the thousands of nails left behind that were holding together the migratory fishers' boats, stages, flakes, and other buildings. This raised the enmity of the migratory fishers, who found blackened rubble each spring instead of boats ready for the water and flakes ready for drying fish. The long-term result was that the migratory fishery came to depend on even more settlers to protect its boats and premises. While the English settled the Avalon and the French used the Petit Nord, the Beothuks were relatively unmolested in Notre Dame Bay until well into the eighteenth century.[12]

The strengthening of the French presence at Plaisance during the 1690s made it difficult for the Beothuks to harvest resources outside of a relatively small area increasingly pressured by the territorial expansion of many other peoples, both First Nations and Europeans. The Mi'kmaq of Nova Scotia were able seafarers who had become one of the most important fur trading partners and military allies of the French. It is possible that Mi'kmaq had been resorting to southwestern Newfoundland as part of a larger foraging territory since the sixteenth century. A few came to Newfoundland as allies of the French in their conflict with the English and soon began competing with English furriers on the Avalon Peninsula. By 1690 the English and French were at war again. Anxious to protect their fortified fishing port, the French encouraged more Mi'kmaq to come to the south coast, and many settled close by Plaisance. Over the next twenty years the Mi'kmaq and other Native allies assisted French military campaigns against the English Shore and took a role in raiding English settlements. The Beothuks lost access to much of the south coast of Newfoundland, not through Mi'kmaq hostility, but to overall European encroachments and conflict on the coastal areas that were so necessary to their economy. To the north, Innu began visiting the island to trap furs on the Great Northern Peninsula. While Innu may have traded with the Beothuks, there was little opportunity for such in the French and Mi'kmaq forays overland from Plaisance to St John's in the 1690s and 1700s, which used Beothuks' portage routes. The Beothuks retreated from such encroachments on their territory, thereby losing access to the Avalon Peninsula.[13]

The arrival of European fishers in Notre Dame Bay in the early eighteenth century changed the Beothuks' way of life. The Europeans explored the river systems that emptied into the bay, finding bountiful salmon populations to exploit and furs to trap during the winter. The European fishing effort not only brought colonists into the last refuge of the Beothuks near the coast, but also competed with them for the salmon upon which the Beothuks had increasingly relied. In the short term, the Beothuks desperately attempted to defend their territory by stealing or destroying Europeans' equipment and even molesting or killing European fishers, occasionally beheading their victims for ritualistic celebrations of their victories. Over time, as Europeans re-taliated, the Beothuks retreated further into the interior, where they came to rely almost exclusively on caribou for their sustenance, build-ing extensive fencing for the hunt. Their need to store more meat for longer periods of time also meant that they had to invest more effort in preserving and building storehouses. Settlements probably grew around such storage facilities, fostering Beothuk identity and solidar-ity against the Europeans. Archaeological evidence suggests that they began to engage in ceremonial feasting, and the accounts of later Be-othuks captured by settlers suggest that the indigenous people con-sidered cooperation with Europeans as traitorous. Thus, the Beothuks did not simply flee into the interior, but rather chose to retreat there to regroup and take a stand against the Europeans who encroached on their lives.[14]

The English government left their three thousand or so settlers in Newfoundland defenceless and without supplies when war with France broke out in 1690. The fishing fleet was not permitted to sail until 1694 because of the fear that the navy might be short of sailors. Then, during the winter of 1695–6, French and Native soldiers under the command of Pierre Le Moyne d'Iberville marched overland from Plaisance to attack English settlements, destroying houses, stores, and flakes, and expelling the settlers in every community except Bonavista in the north. Some settlers fortified Carbonear Island and successfully held off the French attack there. The poorly supplied French were un-able to hold on to the settlements they had taken when an English relief expedition arrived in 1697. Although English officials and mer-chants might have been satisfied that naval power rather than set-tlement held Newfoundland for them, this was small comfort to the settlers and merchant capitalists who had lost the labour and capital they had invested locally over a generation.[15]

The opportunity for a new policy toward Newfoundland came at the end of the seventeenth century. Many in England continued to believe that only the migratory fishery would train men for the navy and stimulate English West Country manufactures, while others ar-gued that English possession of the island depended upon settlement. King William's Act (10 and 11 William III, cap. 25) enacted a compromise between these contradictory ideas in 1699. The act restricted residents' attempts to engross all good shore facilities at the expense of the migratory fishery by reserving the areas they usually used. At the same time the act recognized that residents had the right to use property they had before 1685 as well as any land occupied between 1685 and 1698. King William's Act gave most land over to the purposes of residency, except long-time fishing ships' rooms.[16]

In effect, the act was a compromise between those who wanted settlement and those who feared such settlement might harm the migratory fishery. It also provided Newfoundland with its first official local court system, confirming fishing admirals in the informal administrative and limited judicial authority they had previously exercised, and now requiring that the commanders of the naval convoy that cruised Newfoundland waters each summer to become an appellant authority over that of the fishing admirals. In practice, naval commanders primarily used their judicial powers to govern the use of wages and credit in the fishery, but, although the fishing admirals remained by statute the most important civilian authorities, naval officers could regulate the sale of alcohol and the observance of Sunday services among the migratory fishing crews. Especially when the military threat of the French was strong, the highest-ranking post captain, or commodore, of the naval convoy's authority superseded the authority of the fishing admirals.[17]

The War of the Spanish Succession (1702–13) demonstrated that the limited English settlements were still vulnerable to attack from Plaisance. The French had captured St John's again in 1709, and the English used their naval superiority to blockade Plaisance. This time, however, the restoration of peace saw the French give up most of their territorial claims in Newfoundland. Although the fishery was important to Plaisance, privateering had been one of the most lucrative activities engaged in by the shipowning and mercantile members of the small colony's elite. Peace could secure access to the cod fishery, which remained crucial to the imperial economy, but local privateering would only threaten such access. The Treaty of Utrecht in 1713 established English possession of Newfoundland. France abandoned Plaisance, although a small number of French fishing families persisted on the southwest coast of Newfoundland until the 1740s. The French and Mi'kmaq moved to other colonies on Ile St-Jean (now Prince Edward Island), the Gaspé Peninsula, and Cape Breton. The French used Cape Breton to protect the maritime approaches to their St Lawrence colony and to serve as a base for their fishery, while private traders continued to visit Newfoundland to engage in illicit trade as well as to fish legally. More important, the Treaty of Utrecht allowed the French to continue in their migratory fishery. The French gained the right to fish and use shore facilities on the Newfoundland coast from Cape Bonavista to Point Riche during the fishing season (see map 6). Anglo-French rivalries on the American mainland meant that France would lose Cape Breton by the Treaty of Paris in 1763. While France regained the islands of St Pierre and Miquelon off the Newfoundland south coast as a base for its bank fishery, some of its former Mi'kmaq allies in Cape Breton began to leave for occasional visits to St Pierre and, eventually, settlement in Bay d'Espoir on the south coast and St Georges Bay on the west coast of Newfoundland.[18]

Treaty rights did not alone guarantee that English fishers would prevail over the French. War had sapped much of the labour used by the French in their fisheries. Even more important, France's loss of territory in North America had led to an important technological shift in its fishery. The French had been using the dry cure that was favoured by the Mediterranean and Iberian markets, but the war had eroded the French resident fishery and restricted access to coasts for dry curing. This meant that French merchants had to turn more to a 'green' cure, in which fish was pickled while ships were on the banks fishing. British merchants now had an advantage in supplying the Mediterranean, Spain, and Portugal with the dry-cured product. The old Basque ports and Bayonne continued to decline throughout the eighteenth century, although the ports of Saint-Malo and Granville recovered some of the former ports' business. The merchants of these ports, increasingly without markets elsewhere in southern Europe, supplied the protected French market through the port of Marseilles. The merchants of Saint-Malo and Granville continued to pursue the green fishery on the Grand Banks and the dry fishery in inshore Newfoundland waters that was protected by treaty rights.[19]

The fishery of the English West Country grew under the shelter of the English navy's strengthened position in the North Atlantic. The navy provided greater security in trade, which encouraged the merchants of Bristol and London to concentrate on other trades. The accumulated knowledge among West Country merchants allowed them to dominate the industry, but they depended more on the resident fishery at places such as Trinity, first settled in the seventeenth century by a small number of planters. There were still too few settlers to supply enough fish to merchants for export. As a result, a number of West Country merchants established capital and labour-intensive

fishing operations to facilitate their trade. The greater demand for labour led merchants to recruit Irish servants from the ports of Cork,
Youghal, and Waterford, where they purchased provisions. Irish merchants who supplied the ships kept an eye open for opportunities to
enter the trade; some turned to the fishery of Placentia, which had
been taken from the French. Since they were now recruiting from the
Irish labour market, the people who came to fish there were almost
exclusively Irish, and the area around the town became a great centre
of Irish settlement.[20]

With little political interference from London, West Country
merchants and their Irish partners prosecuted their trade without
distinguishing between residents and migrants. The Newmans of
Dartmouth, for example, saw their firm grow during the early eighteenth century through a thriving partnership with a local St John's
plantation operated by the Holdsworth family. The firm established
a house at Lisbon to oversee its fish marketing and later developed it
into a partnership with Poole and other Dartmouth merchants. Just as
important was the family's need to establish a St John's operation to
manage the Newfoundland side of the trade. The brothers Robert and
Richard operated a fleet of ten vessels from St John's. In 1757 Robert
Newman purchased a substantial plantation at the upper end of St
John's harbour. In addition to fishing premises, Newman acquired
meadows, gardens, and dwelling houses there. While merchants such
as the Newmans, whether from Dorset, Devon, or Waterford, tended
to go to St John's only for the summer fishing season, they had invested significant capital in Newfoundland and recognized the needs
of a resident community.[21]

The complexity of the fish trade allowed more Irish entrepreneurs
into the fish business and made St John's a centre of growing importance. The preference of some of the Irish and West Country partnerships to use St John's as a base indicates the growing importance of
that port as a mercantile centre. Other harbours of the Avalon Peninsula, such as Ferryland or Old Perlican, had much better shore
facilities and local fishing grounds, but St John's great advantage
was its location. The port lay roughly in the centre of the Old English
Shore, which stretched from Trepassey in the south to Greenspond
in the north. Furthermore, St John's fjord-like natural harbour and
small opening, the 'Narrows,' was an easily defended berth for naval and merchant vessels alike. Although a difficult passage for any
vessel, merchant ships and migratory fishing vessels often stopped
at St John's at the beginning of the season to gain news of where the

fishery seemed most likely to succeed. As war disrupted the English migratory fishery on the Grand Banks, many merchants established branches of their businesses in St John's. These merchants often stationed junior partners in the harbour to deal with planters who established resident fisheries along the coastline beyond the Narrows.

St John's central location, and the constant arrival and departure of merchant ships, made the port an ideal choice for Britain's unofficial capital in Newfoundland. From 1697 the English had a military garrison fortify the harbour. More important, throughout the eighteenth century, the naval squadron used St John's as its base of operations. The naval squadron rendezvoused at St John's in the spring before dispersing to patrol the coastline and the western waters of the North Atlantic. The navy brought with it rudimentary religious and government institutions. In 1697, the Reverend William John Jackson had been stationed in St John's as a chaplain with the naval squadron. Reports of the desire by St John's inhabitants to build a church led to his return in 1701 as a minister at the behest of the Bishop of London. The Church of England did not see Newfoundland as an important field of activity. While Jackson began to receive support from the Anglicans' missionary vehicle, the Society for the Propagation of the Gospel (SPG), it showed little interest in Newfoundland after Jackson left two years later. In 1711, Josias Crowe, the commodore of the English squadron, assembled St John's merchants and his other naval officers to develop laws for the better government of local people. Crowe ordered money collected from residents to support the town's new church and clergyman and to provide for local policing and protection of fishing rooms. As the non-fishing establishment grew, some planters turned from fishing to other economic areas such as keeping public houses or taverns. Against the background of a law which was intended to protect the migratory fishery, naval officials charged with enforcing King William's Act encouraged the development of government to serve the needs of residents.[22]

As settlement continued to grow, residents wanted a fuller administration of justice than provided by the legal regime designed for a migratory fishery. Merchants and planters faced problems of enforcing agreements over credit and punishing crime while both the fishing admirals and the naval squadron were home in England. Planters and merchants had invested significant capital in St John's and were concerned by the growing number of servants who overwintered in the town. In November 1723, a group of these prominent residents founded their own court and elected three magistrates. The gather-

ing cited the political philosophy of John Locke to justify the right to
create institutions to defend their property. These magistrates, Chaplain John Jago and merchants Samuel Rooke and Allyn Southmayd,
heard civil disputes about debt and property ownership, a variety of
petty criminal cases, disagreements between masters and servants,
and public nuisances. While most of the people who participated in
the court's proceedings, whether defendant or plaintiff, accepted its
legitimacy, English authorities did not. This particular court does not
appear to have met the next year, but merchants had begun to suggest
that the British government appoint magistrates to protect property,
and commanders of the naval convoys began to appoint justices of the
peace to supplement the fishing admirals.[23]

The earliest institutions of government in Newfoundland were judicial, but the naval character of government was much different than
that of the other English colonies in North America. Both law and custom prohibited taxation in the fishery, discouraging the British government from appointing a civil governor and administration which
would then have to be paid for out of the imperial treasury. With King
William's Act, naval commanders had the right to hear appeals of
decisions made by fishing admirals, and British authorities expected
them to counterbalance the authority of the fishing admirals. During
the War of the Spanish Succession, naval commanders had also assumed duties that might usually have been exercised by a civilian
governor, but their primary motivation was to prepare settlements on
the English Shore for French attacks. Gradually, after 1729, the English government included in the commanders' commission a vague
mandate to enforce British policy. Smuggling, property ownership,
and emigration all proved to be problems that demanded some greater presence of government authority at Newfoundland, and a 1729
order-in-council provided the convoy commander, Henry Osborne,
with full civil and military authority over Newfoundland. This recognized his right to delegate judicial authority to magistrates during the
winter and to subordinate naval officers as surrogates. Newfoundland naval governors, in effect, became the island's chief executive
and judicial authority during their presence on the summer station.
The fishing admirals were unhappy that the navy was assuming authority without parliamentary approval and tried to limit the jurisdiction of the naval governors' magistrates, but England's attorney
general confirmed the governors' and magistrates' authority.[24]

The growth of settlement meant that the naval governors wanted a
year-round legal establishment at Newfoundland to deal with crimi-

nal matters. In 1749, the naval governor George Rodney pressed for judicial reform, assuming the duties of a chief justice, a practice followed by future governors until 1781. In 1750, the British government established by order-in-council a Court of Oyer and Terminer at Newfoundland to hear criminal matters, and Rodney made his naval surrogate judges responsible for specific districts. By the 1760s, the naval state consisted of the executive authority resident within the office of the commander stationed at St John's for the summer. The commanders governed by decrees that were carried out by civil magistrates in nine districts, and by naval surrogates in five maritime districts which they patrolled in their capacity as commanders of naval ships. Slowly, this naval administration acquired the basic offices of day-to-day government that many settlers would have been familiar with in their home countries: constables, coroners, sheriffs, and grand juries that could make presentments on behalf of local people.[25]

While not a colonial administration, naval government was well suited to people spread out in settlements along an immense littoral. Most people abided by English common law, so a police force was unnecessary, and in the last resort the naval commanders could rely on their ships' guns, sailors, and marines to back up their orders and judgments on any part over the coast under their authority. Ships' officers used customary corporal punishment such as flogging aboard ship, and such might be used in sentencing for crimes in Newfoundland. The official culture of the British navy frowned on arbitrary discipline that might result in mutiny; officers were professional and disinterested in who won disputes over such things as the allocation of shore space; and the British government 'did not permit the indiscriminate use of military force' in the administration of justice. The ritual and the ceremony of the navy's presence in their harbours further gave settlers a sense of connection to an authority that was above the commercial interests of the fishing industry. For the first time, settlers could have their cases heard by judges who were committed to upholding the customary laws of their communities, as well as statutory law, but who were not the representatives of merchants who gave them credit, bought their fish, or paid their wages.

The justice of the officers was not ideal. The naval government's administration reflected the class divisions of the day. Court officers, for example, came from the ranks of the merchants, mercantile agents, and prominent planters who dominated every fishing community. The appellant authority of the naval surrogates and the naval governor meant, however, that final authority lay with naval officers drawn from the British gentry. These officers, in addition to having no direct interest in the fishery, had the status and social and political connections to allow them to face down any recalcitrant merchant.[26] The summary justice and administration of naval government thus gave some order to a settler society continually augmented by more migrant fishers. Only some of these fishers stayed permanently as residents, but even those who stayed the shortest contributed to the myriad needs of local society.

The population of Newfoundland was growing rapidly. In 1750, the total population of European descent on the island was less than ten thousand and by 1764 had grown to about sixteen thousand. During the summer the population swelled with the arrival of migrant servants, both English and Irish, and then settled back down to smaller numbers during the winter. While the fishery paid good wages in comparison with what they earned as labourers at home, working conditions were brutal. The dangers of the sea were many; servants undertook an arduous voyage simply to reach the fishery and then would often spend days at sea in small, open craft engaged in hauling baited lines laden with cod. Since masters did not like their servants sleeping while there were fish to be caught, servants might go for days without rest while working in the cold and wet. Buying liquor from their masters and merchants was sometimes the only comfort available and may have left servants indebted at the end of the fishing season, thereby forcing them to stay in Newfoundland during the winter to get by as best they could. Other servants may have decided to stay to trap furs to make extra money.[27]

The naval officers were alarmed more by the propertyless servants who stayed than by other settlers. Moreover, while estimates of their proportion of the resident population are unreliable, contemporary observers felt that the Irish were becoming the most numerous of the settlers, at least on the Avalon Peninsula. Growing numbers of Irish worried fishing masters and naval authorities. Many of the Irish servants spoke only Gaelic, and their mutterings about the conditions of employment and other complaints remained a mystery to masters and officials. Harsh work and poverty gave the Irish good reason to be dissatisfied, especially during Newfoundland's long winters. Not all of the Irish were impoverished, and increasing numbers of the resident planters and merchants were of Irish origin. The class differences that existed among the Irish were small comfort to local officials, however.[28]

Most of the Irish who migrated to Newfoundland were Roman

Catholics. They arrived at a time when English Protestant sentiments had been inflamed by the tensions with France that erupted in the Seven Years War (1756–63). Anxiety about war stirred up long-standing English fears about the influence of 'papacy' within its dominions. In the British Isles, such fears had led to anti-Roman Catholic 'penal' laws limiting property rights, citizenship, and freedom of worship. The pro-Stuart rebellions of 1715 and 1745 renewed anti–Roman Catholic sentiment, spreading even to Newfoundland in 1715, when the governor accused an Irish man at Placentia of hiding refugee rebels. Although the enforcement of the penal laws waxed and waned, the rise of the Hanover monarchs encouraged their vigorous application in England. To assure the loyalty of Roman Catholics who lived within the empire, the government designed an oath of allegiance which required repudiation of the leadership of the pope. After 1745, the governor noted that many of the Irish in Newfoundland refused to take the oath. The Catholic (Stuart) uprising against the Protestant monarchy in Britain failed in 1745 (allowing authorities to relax the application of their anti-Catholic laws) but popular anti-Catholicism increased both in Britain and in Newfoundland. Governors and surrogates feared that the complex class antagonisms of Ireland would accompany new migrants. In Ireland, wealth and land ownership rested in the hands of a Protestant oligarchy whose language (which the Irish associated with English rule, oppression, and exploitative rents) remained English. The vast majority of the Irish, especially in the areas from which people migrated to Newfoundland, were Roman Catholic, and their language of resistance was Gaelic.[29]

The history of the Irish within the British empire meant that imperial officials suspected disaffection wherever Irish settlement concentrated. Not only were an increasing number of the settlers around St John's Irish Catholics but so were many of the soldiers. The naval government's early trial of capital offences, through the court of Oyer and Terminer, concentrated on the discipline of Irish soldiers and fishing servants, although other people appeared before the court as well. The crimes were severe: manslaughter, murder, and gang rape. Usually the accused were Irish, but this was not a guarantee of conviction, and the court pardoned capital sentences in some cases. While spectacular cases might shock authorities, such as the 1754 robbery and murder of prominent St John's merchant and magistrate William Keen by a group of ten Irish men and women (Keen had a history of using his judicial office to harass the Irish), the Irish had become indispensable to the fishery and found ready defenders in West Country merchants, who did not feel that they seriously threatened the peace in Newfoundland.[30]

In both Ireland and Newfoundland, the labouring Irish turned to their clerics for leadership in the fight against exploitation. The disruption of the Irish Roman Catholic Church by the English penal laws meant that priests often served their parishes without the diocesan control of bishops, and a similar situation developed in Newfoundland, where a generation of itinerant priests claimed to serve their people without the need for permission by bishops to administer the sacraments and acknowledged no higher institutional authority.

The nature of the trade between Waterford and the West Country meant that Ireland played a great role in the formation of Newfoundland society despite the concerns of English authorities. Nevertheless, the West Country continued to dominate the Newfoundland trade and, although settlement increased, many people continued to identify with their English places of origin. Their links to home were constantly reinforced: most of the provisions and all of the capital goods required for the fishery came from Irish and West Country ports, although New England ports were becoming more important in the supply of provisions during the eighteenth century. Planters could only acquire labour, provisions, and capital goods by securing them on credit from the West Country merchants.

Class relationships in the fishery were complex, but ownership or control over the means of providing credit was clearly the great divide among residents. The fishery depended completely on Iberian, Mediterranean, and West Indies markets for the sale of its fish products. Fish sales resulted not in cash but in cargoes of other goods that fish merchants carried to Europe. Almost all of the Newfoundland trade took place on ships built and owned outside of the island, although boats used in the fishery might be built locally. The only people with access to enough capital to engage in the export trade were the West Country and a few Irish merchants. These merchants were the only ones who could provide credit to planters and therefore were at the apex of social and economic power. West Country merchants, such as Benjamin Lester of Poole, in Dorset, built thriving trades. Lester was active in the administration of Trinity, the Newfoundland headquarters of his trade. While willing to use his commission as a justice of the peace to augment his authority over local servants and settlers, Lester otherwise took little interest in Newfoundland. Like the naval governors, Lester usually returned to England each winter.[31]

Places such as Trinity were developing beyond the capacity of transatlantic mercantile and naval elites to govern effectively. In Trinity, merchants employed servants directly to catch and cure the fish they traded. In the 1753 summer fishing season, for example, Joseph White employed twelve fishing boats and ten sailing vessels worked by 213 servants. In winter, White kept on 30 caretaker servants. Even the planters who fished independently of merchants relied on hired labour. These smaller masters still hired on average about 25 servants each in the summer of 1753. The problem with a fishery that relied on a great deal of hired labour was its relatively high fixed overhead cost, in an industry marked by prices that fluctuated widely due to international factors beyond local control. Depressed conditions in the industry throughout the 1760s meant that most masters dismissed their servants, although no other industries existed to absorb the surplus. Until 1771, 'masterless servants' roamed Trinity, committing robberies and other crimes to survive. Newfoundland governors encouraged former masters to return some of the unemployed to Great Britain. The remaining surplus labour appears to have stimulated an offshore bank fishery. Despite depression, the number of boats employed in the inshore fishery continued to increase between 1750 and 1775. The inshore fishery averaged about 175–200 per year employing between 875 and 1,000 servants. This growing inshore fishery was probably the result of expanding household production by planters, who could rely on family labour and supplementary farming to lower overhead costs. By 1775, in other words, Trinity was unmistakably a place of settled society, and one of many such communities around the old English Shore.[32]

The naval government enjoyed a close relationship with the citizens of Atlantic commerce. Local administrative policy could vary considerably from one naval governor to the next, but in the main the governors tended to see themselves as the administrators of a British industry, not a settled society. Governor Sir Hugh Palliser, who first came as governor in 1764, was determined to restore the dominance of the migratory fishery over the resident fishery. He had previously commanded the squadron that took St John's back from a French occupation in 1762. His naval experience against the French undoubtedly made Palliser seem an excellent choice to British officials for governor of Newfoundland. While the Treaty of Paris in 1763 had restored to the French their fishing rights in Newfoundland waters between Cape Bonavista and Point Riche, there were modifications that required enforcement. The British government had further agreed to allow France the islands of St Pierre and Miquelon to serve as bases for its local fisheries. It was Palliser's duty to ensure that the French conformed to the treaty by not fortifying the islands or building any facilities other than those necessary for their migratory fishery. The governor also ensured that British migratory and resident fishers respected the right of the French to fish on the treaty shores. At the same time, Palliser defended British sovereignty by making clear to the French that they were subject to British authority while fishing and enjoined the French naval squadron to police smuggling between the French at St Pierre and Miquelon and residents of the south coast. Although the French complained about Palliser, their capable governor of St Pierre and Miquelon, François-Gabriel d'Angeac, successfully fended off the worst of Palliser's accusations about treaty violations and did his best to ensure that French colonists' fishing efforts did not provoke British hostilities.[33]

The residents of Newfoundland were unhappy that Palliser tried to revive the migratory fishery at their expense. Merchants complained that the governor had decided to protect the migratory fishery by stopping resident merchants' and fishers' encroachments on the ships' rooms in St John's for warehouses and stages. Palliser also wanted to stop merchants from advancing too much credit to planters and servants and stranding the latter in Newfoundland by seizing the catches of masters who could not repay their debts. Unpaid servants possessed no means by which they could return home, and imperial policy could not tolerate this threat to a well-trained supply of British seamen, who were also consumers of British-made goods. Palliser proposed that the British parliament should make it illegal for British ships to leave migratory servants behind in Newfoundland at the end of the fishing season. During his time as governor, the British did not enact such legislation, but this did not stop the governor from taking matters into his own hands by occasionally ordering masters to pay their abandoned servants' passage home.[34]

Palliser further found the development of a settled population disturbing because so many were Roman Catholic Irish. He disliked the fact that Irish Catholics seemed to outnumber English Protestants, and that the Catholics managed to 'have priests secreted among them, to the great disturbance of the peace and good government of the country in the winter season.' Palliser did not allow Roman Catholics to freely practise their religion.[35] He also strove to discourage Roman Catholic Mi'kmaq fur trappers from Cape Breton who had begun to settle in St George's Bay and Bay D'Espoir. Palliser feared that these former French allies, and perhaps Acadians who disguised themselves as Natives, could potentially aid France in resuming its territorial ambitions on the island.

Although Palliser was no friend of the development of Newfoundland, his policy on Labrador unintentionally ensured that it would be maintained as a resource frontier to be exploited by Newfoundland residents. The governor only wanted to make sure that the fisheries and seal hunt of the Labrador coast were preserved for the migratory fishery. When Palliser assumed the governorship in 1764, Montreal-based merchants such as Daniel Bayne and William Brymer dominated the trade of the Labrador coast west of the Strait of Belle Isle, while merchants from Jersey and England dominated the trade in the Strait. In 1765, Palliser declared that no colonial interest had a right to property in the valuable seal hunt on the Labrador coast to the detriment of British migratory interests. In 1767, the governor proclaimed that only the first three ships to arrive from Britain in the major harbours of the coast could leave behind sealing crews for the winter. Palliser had hoped that the British government would agree to his ambitious plans to fortify and defend the coast and subsidize British vessels on migratory fishing trips to Labrador. Unwilling to bear the expense, the British government did not agree to Palliser's administrative plans. The Quebec merchants demanded that the British government and courts recognize their property rights and sued Palliser for damages. The case dragged on until 1769, when the Privy Council found for the plaintiff but also declared that Palliser's actions were in keeping with the British government's policy and ordered the government to pay the damages rather than Palliser personally. Palliser had also tried to deny fishing ships from the American colonies access to the Labrador coast, but the British government would not support him.[36]

Palliser's attempt to limit colonial property rights on the Labrador coast ironically established the basis for settlement that would, in the long run, supersede the British migratory industry there. The governor's intervention against Quebec merchants helped Jersey merchants such as the DeQuetteville Brothers and West Country firms such as Thomas Bird of Poole and Noble and Pinson of Dartmouth, to establish posts for the salmon fishery and sealing along the Labrador coast of the Strait of Belle Isle from Blanc Sablon to Forteau. Palliser's 1765 regulations allowed the first of these merchants' vessels to reach any harbour the right to maintain crews over the winter to catch seals and whales. The second vessel gained the right of an exclusive salmon fishery in the harbour, while the third had the right to trade with local First Nations. The Jersey and West Country merchants

found that sealing, salmon fishing, and the fur trade required substantial premises maintained on a year-round basis. They petitioned
the Board of Trade for rights to property and year-round residence,
which the Board granted in 1773. Within a decade, these firms were
bringing hundreds of servants from Jersey, the Bay de Chaleurs, and
St John's to work in their industries. Many of these servants began
to work on their own account, but continued to trade with the Jersey
and West Country firms, so that the migratory and resident fisheries
on the coast co-existed.[37]

To make the coast safe for the migratory fishery also required improved relations with the Inuit. The Inuit sometimes raided the southern coastal fishing premises, taking boats, weapons, and any tools they
found useful. Palliser felt that trade was the key to better relationships;
it would give the Inuit the goods they wanted without violence and
provide a product for export. The governor turned to the Moravian
missionaries, who had long experience in missions among the Inuit of
Greenland and knew a similar dialect of the Inuit language. Some of
their members had even attempted to establish a mission to Labrador
in 1752 but had disappeared during the trip. One of the Moravian
brethren, Jens Haven, decided that the mission should try again and
secured Palliser's support in 1764. Palliser permitted Haven to issue
certificates guaranteeing the Inuit peaceable trade with English merchants and promised naval protection to English traders who chose to
deal with the Inuit under the auspices of the Moravians. The Moravians planned to establish missions and open trading posts nearby to
entice the Inuit to settle and convert. The missionaries further wanted
to keep the Inuit from trading with others who might abuse them
or give them alcohol. Palliser accompanied four missionaries to the
coast in 1765. There he issued a proclamation forbidding the crews
of French ships in the fishery at Newfoundland, whom Palliser believed encouraged hostility toward the English among Natives, from
visiting the Labrador coast to trade with the Inuit. Palliser promised
his government's peaceful intentions and goodwill to a council of
Inuit at Pitt's Harbour. The Moravians set about to mediate disputes
between the English fishing on the coast and nearby Inuit; however,
some plundering of premises by the latter continued. The governor
constructed a blockhouse at York Harbour from which such premises
would be guarded by a year-round garrison.

An attack by Inuit on the fishing post of London merchant Nicholas
Darby at Cape Charles in 1767 led to retaliation by the York Harbour
garrison. The garrison killed twenty men and captured nine women

and children who were sent to St John's as prisoners. Palliser sent most of the Inuit back to their people, but kept one woman, Mikak, her son, and one other boy. He sent the captives to England to impress Mikak with the magnitude of English power in the hope that she would communicate the futility of resistance to her people. Palliser and Haven successfully used Mikak, who was an object of great curiosity for the British aristocracy, to get more support for the Moravian Missions from the Board of Trade. In 1769, Mikak returned to her relatives on the coast, having promised Haven and Palliser she would encourage her people to trade with the English and cease travelling to the island of Newfoundland. Mikak soon became the second wife of her sister's husband, Tuglavina. Inuit society was polygamous, and marriages could be dissolved easily. Mikak used her influence to secure local Inuit acceptance of a Moravian mission at the site of what is now Nain and negotiated privileged access to the English for Tuglavina. Mikak eased the meeting of the two peoples and thus prevented a repeat of the sort of violence which had often accompanied earlier attempts.[38]

The Moravians established their first mission at Nain in 1771, paying the Inuit in fishing equipment and other tools. The Inuit were quick to adopt useful European technologies but retained the elements of their own technology when there was no better European item. They used wooden boats, which were superior to the multi-person, skin-covered boat, for example, while continuing to use the single-person kayak. This prompted economic change as the Inuit diverted hunting effort from food species to fur-bearing animals for trade. The missionaries mingled trade with preaching. Through the 1770s and 1780s the Moravians established successful missions at Okak and other bays. It was the beginning of the integration of the Labrador Inuit into the transatlantic economy and caused significant changes in their lives. Nain had been a seasonal camp before the Moravians established the mission, but now the missionaries encouraged the Inuit to abandon their nomadic economy and settle there so that they would be able to make it to church each Sunday. Those Inuit who did so had to trade for many of the necessities of life which they had previously provided for themselves. This required breaking with their extended families who lived together and shared resources, and Inuit European-style nuclear families started to live in single houses and to function as single economic units.[39] Over time this had far-reaching implications. The new diet that included European items was less healthful than their earlier diet, and increased contact with Europeans spread diseases such as smallpox. Sedentary Inuit families adopted Christianity and abandoned practices such as polygamy, although the changes were slow. For all of the cultural changes prompted by Moravian activity, their presence lessened the acts of inter-ethnic violence on which the Inuit had come to be the victims. South of the territory the Moravians were coming to dominate, British traders such as George Cartwright established their own premises partially by forming reciprocal relationships with local Inuit. Such relationships could end in tragedy, as when smallpox devastated the family of Cartwright's associate Attuiock in 1773. Through the activities of furriers, fishers, and seal harvesters such as Cartwright, people of European ancestry were becoming familiar with the coast of Labrador and how one might live there.[40]

Under Palliser, naval government had become a weapon in the defence of the migratory fishery and imperial interests. Although naval government provided rudimentary administration to settlers, it showed little interest in doing more to meet their needs. In the Moravians, Palliser found a church that appeared to advance the greater cause of the preservation of the British migratory fishery. The Church of England, like the Roman Catholic and dissenting churches, had taken little interest in Newfoundland. The development of British colonial populations through migration and subsequent natural increase forced the churches to pay more attention. The fishery had attracted people from the southeast of Ireland, the Channel Isles, and the English West Country. These migrants brought their Roman Catholic, Anglican, and dissenting faiths with them. In the absence of a clergy, settlers provided their own ministrations by performing sacraments, conducting everything from baptisms to funerals, and developing their own informal forms of worship. While the development of settlement drew the institutions and clergy of the churches to Newfoundland and Labrador, settlers were reluctant to give up their own forms of religious observance. Throughout the 1760s and 1770s, even as more clergy arrived, settlers insisted on performing their older religious services, challenging the clergy's sole right to perform and charge fees for the same.

The growth of popular support for lay leadership was a particular problem for the Anglican hierarchy. In towns throughout British North America, the tendency for respectable artisans, shopkeepers, and other members of the middling classes to choose preachers from among themselves fanned the flames of dissent. In St John's, the economic impact of the military establishment helped to foster an artisan and shopkeeping class that was not directly involved in the fishery.

Consequently, it is not surprising that local dissenters chose an army paymaster, John Jones, to lead them in prayer. Jones was a successful organizer and moulded his civilian and military followers into a recognizable congregation. Jones's success angered the Anglican missionaries Edward Langman and Walter Price, but to little avail. Jones returned to seek ordination on his own once he had established his prominence in the church life of the port town. As a result of SPG complaints about the laity's religious officiating, Governor Edwards, in 1779, ordered the justices of the peace to restrict the religious ministrations of the lay people. Anglican missions had opened at St John's and Harbour Grace, but the church was less than enthusiastic in its early ministry to the people.[41]

Neglected by the more established churches, people in outlying settlements such as on the north side of Conception Bay turned to the Methodists. They embraced Methodism's evangelical popular disillusionment with the older churches' conservatism. The Methodism of John Wesley rejected the aristocratic ritualism and hierarchy of the older Roman Catholic and Anglican churches in favour of a more individual and reasoned explication of faith. In Newfoundland, the Irish preacher Laurence Coughlan, although ostensibly carrying out an Anglican mission in Conception Bay at the request of local merchants in 1766, began to preach a more radical Methodism than that advocated by Wesley. Fishing people in Conception Bay, particularly young women, rallied to Coughlan's message that the individual experience of 'being born again' was more important to salvation than one's status in society or position within the more established churches. Coughlan's message was particularly appealing among people who had decided to settle and establish their own household fisheries. For the most part, the merchants upon whom these fishing people depended were Anglican and, occasionally, Roman Catholic. Coughlan preached against settlers' taking alcohol on credit and argued for a temperate and frugal life that would lessen dependence on merchants' credit. An itinerant minister, and able to preach in Gaelic, Coughlan eventually built a strong following among Irish settlers on the north shore of Conception Bay. In four years, Coughlan organized his followers through small meetings, often appointing 'common' people to hold services, and building a sense of community in opposition to the merchants and their clerical supporters in the more conservative churches. By 1770, merchants complained about Coughlan, who called his detractors 'the Children of Darkness,' 'the Enemy,' and 'the Children of Disobedience.' Coughlan left Newfoundland three years later because his failing health had made it impossible for him to bear the harsh climate. The force of his personality, his religious radicalism, and his affiliation with the SPG meant that Coughlan had established no organizational support for his version of Methodism. Subsequent itinerant preachers kept Methodism alive among the growing population of Conception Bay, but the influence of more moderate Wesleyanism gradually became dominant with the later evangelistic mission by William Black to Newfoundland on Wesley's behalf in 1791.[42]

Palliser had been determined to preserve Newfoundland and Labrador for the British migratory fishery. Nevertheless, a resident society of competing interests had developed, and, as the growth of Methodism suggested, its members were beginning to think about how best to pursue their own agendas. Palliser had feared that such a resident society might become as troublesome as the New Englanders, who in the aftermath of the Seven Years War bristled under the taxation and restrictions of the British crown. For about 165 years, the English had found that some settlement was necessary to protect the Newfoundland and Labrador fisheries from European rivals and aboriginal competitors. Although some English mercantile interests feared that settlers would compete with their migratory trade, and the crown feared the expense of governing settlers, settlement remained limited because of Newfoundland's comparatively poor landward resources. The American Revolution was about to change this and to make Palliser's last-ditch efforts to defend the migratory fishery come to naught.

4

Not Quite a Colony, 1775–1824

Tied as they were to British interests in the international fish trade, the residents of Newfoundland and Labrador did not join the Americans in their revolution in 1776. However, over the next half-century or so, the impact of the revolution and subsequent upheavals in the North Atlantic world laid the foundations for the triumph of resident interests and settlement over those of the migratory fishery. New England had been an important source of provisions for the fishing industry, but the revolution forced merchants in the fishery to find alternate supplies in Canada, Nova Scotia, and Europe, and to rely on residents' gardening and livestock for as much food as possible. Conflict disrupted the labour supply as well: servants faced the risks of enemy attacks on their vessels or impressment into naval service if they continued to work in the migratory fishery. Merchants who supplied the migratory trade and the larger vessels, which fished on the banks, thus found labour scarcer and more expensive. Merchants also found access to the best markets in Europe closed by the allies of the Americans in the early 1780s. Similar conditions prevailed during the wars with Napoleon and the War of 1812, although the market conditions of these wars inflated the price for salt fish. Postwar recessions led planters to retreat into smaller-scale household production, and merchants to rely on such households' supplementary economic activity to subsidize the fish trade.

The growth of the resident fishery fostered the development of a local capitalist class. In 1775 Newfoundland society had consisted of small communities of fishing people grouped around the premises of

West Country merchants. These communities were more closely tied to the merchants' home ports in Britain than to each other. The principal partners of these firms continued to reside in Britain but increasingly relied on local agents to manage their supply trade. Even the revival of the migratory fishery at the end of the American Revolution did not weaken West Country firms' relationships with residents. Many of the firms withdrew completely from the migratory fishery during a 1789 depression in the industry, concentrating exclusively on supplying residents with goods on credit while marketing their fish. As the resident fishery grew in importance, West Country merchants found it more difficult to control their agents, who often pursued business interests of their own in Newfoundland.[1]

Specific West Country areas, sometimes in association with Irish ports, became linked with particular areas of settlement in Newfoundland in the 1780s. Settlers from Trinity northward depended on the Poole firms of Benjamin Lester, John Slade, and Jeffrey and Street. A wider group of Poole, Dartmouth, and Topsham merchants, along with a sprinkling of London, Cork, and other West Country firms supplied the residents of St Mary's and Placentia bays in the south. Bristol merchants dominated the trade of Harbour Grace, while Poole firms were more important in Carbonear. The southern shore of the Avalon Peninsula between St John's and Trepassey was a South Devon preserve, while the merchants of Dartmouth were the most important in St John's. Together, the merchants of Dartmouth and Poole were the most important in the Newfoundland trade, while the two largest merchant houses were those of Benjamin Lester and Jeffrey and Street. On the Labrador shore of the Strait of Belle Isle, the Jersey firms of Nicolle and LeBoutillier and the West Country firm of Joseph Bird dominated. The agents, or junior partners, of firms who resided in Newfoundland were transatlantic capitalists whose social and political ambitions lay with their city of origin and Britain in general.[2]

British authorities were unhappy that the resident fishery grew at the expense of the migratory fishery during the American Revolution. Imperial officials had by now accepted limited settlement, but the migratory fishery had been important for the West Country, Jersey, and Irish economies. British officials feared that an expanded resident fishery would be a market for local capital and labour and would be conducted by potential sympathizers with American republicanism. The British Board of Trade decided to revitalize the migratory trade by taking the advice of former governor Sir Hugh Palliser. He argued that the growth of the resident fishery had been caused by merchants' truck practices, which left indebted migrant labourers stranded in Newfoundland at the end of a fishing season, unable to pay their passage home. Those servants who worked for resident planters or by-boat keepers might not be paid when fish merchants seized the catches of their masters for debts the latter owed before wages were paid. Either way, servants had to stay over in Newfoundland and over time (see chapter 3) established their own households, often through marrying into already resident planter families. To remedy this, Parliament passed 15 George III, cap. 31 in 1775, subsequently called Palliser's Act. The act required that any servants hired in England must have prearranged, fixed wage agreements, in writing, with their masters before commencing the fishing voyage. Further, no master could advance more than half the wages in provisions to a servant during the season. The remaining half wages had to be paid in good bills of exchange on the servants' return to England at the end of the season. Masters also had to guarantee return passage.

Palliser's Act, and subsequent Newfoundland judicature acts, also insisted that the law of current supply apply to all those working in the fishery. This law gave servants the first lien against an insolvent or bankrupt master's catch, ensuring they would be paid their wages if their employer died or became insolvent. The second lien went to merchants who had advanced the planter credit in the current fishing season. Previous creditors received subsequent liens in the order in which they had extended credit. This new law, known locally as the wage and lien system, strengthened the hand of fishing servants in dealing with their masters and merchants. Palliser's Act provided for the imprisonment, whipping, and forfeiture of wages by deserting or negligent servants. Such provisions were in keeping with the criminalization of servants' breach of contract in the Anglo-American law of master and servant, but by the late eighteenth century local courts ignored them in favour of obliging masters to pay wages. Courts in Harbour Grace (the administrative centre for much of the northeast-coast Newfoundland fishery), for example, did not imprison or whip negligent or deserting servants. Servants almost always won suits against masters who had denied them their wages, although they were less likely to win cases against masters who deducted wages for negligence. Surrogates and magistrates usually asked for smaller deductions by masters in favour of their employees even in cases lost by servants. While the Board of Trade intended Palliser's Act to ensure servants returned home, local courts' rigid enforcement of the wage guarantees transformed the act into a defence of servants' rights. The administration of wage law, later extended to the resident fishery, protected servants more than their masters, making Newfoundland a more attractive place for the propertyless to stay.[3]

Palliser's Act failed to discourage the resident fishery even as merchants involved in the fishery, especially in St John's, came to see themselves as Newfoundland residents. Despite its administrative and military importance, St John's had not yet become the local metropolis. Other centres, such as Trinity, Harbour Grace, Carbonear, Ferryland, and Placentia served as important merchant outposts of firms which operated a triangular trade, centred in Britain, between Newfoundland, the United Kingdom, and the overseas markets for salt fish. The limited civil expenditures of St John's were of little interest to the local mercantile community.[4]

The American Revolution changed this. Conscious of the military imbalance between themselves and the British on the open sea, the Americans harassed the empire wherever possible, including the Newfoundland fishery. Merchants worried about their investment in the bank fishery and feared that the garrison in St John's, a company of old men and boys in the Royal Highland Emigrants and a company of invalid artillerymen, could not defend the port. The naval squadron stationed at Newfoundland during the summers had also been reduced in size since 1769, and it faced a daunting task in trying to defend the island, Labrador, and fishing vessels on the Grand Banks. From 1776 to 1778, Governor and Royal Navy Vice Admiral John Montagu improved the fortifications at Placentia and St John's, although with the assistance of St John's merchants. The success of American privateers against British ships on the Grand Banks, and the entry of the French on the side of the Americans meant that the British government augmented the small, poorly equipped naval forces based in St John's. Local artisans and labourers formed a local militia in 1778, which St John's merchants agreed to support as the Newfoundland Volunteers in 1779 (renamed as the Newfoundland Regiment in 1780). Merchants had come to believe that the naval administration of Newfoundland had failed to protect their interests adequately and that they should be entitled to better protection of their property rights in St John's as they took greater steps to defend themselves.[5]

The British naval squadron unintentionally preserved the Labrador coast under the effective control of St John's. Quebec merchants had continued to demand recognition of their right to the seal hunt along the Labrador coast, and the British government had warmed to the overtures of Quebec governor Sir Guy Carleton in 1774. Influential supporters of the navy in the British House of Commons, many of whom were friends of Palliser, unsuccessfully opposed the navy's, and thus the Newfoundland governor's, loss of control over the territory. Under the Quebec Act of 1775, Labrador had again become part of the colony of Quebec, although the rights of British migratory ships to the cod fishery continued. Newfoundland naval governors continued to protect the migratory fishers on the coast, while the governors at Quebec found that they had little means to exercise jurisdiction. During the American Revolution control over Labrador fell to the naval authorities of St John's, who also commanded all of the British naval forces throughout the Gulf of St Lawrence and as far south as the Hudson River. As thinly stretched as it was, the naval squadron, under the direction of Governor Edwards, was the only protection that the Labrador coast had. Through 1779 and 1780, the authorities in St John's made the coast more secure against American privateers. At the end of the war, the Labrador fisheries from the Strait of Belle Isle eastward and northward had come under the effective government of St John's.[6]

The end of war in 1783 saw the readmission of international competitors into the fisheries of Newfoundland and Labrador. The Americans and their French allies won the war; their fishing industries suffered as British naval operations had kept both from fishing on the banks. Under the subsequent Treaty of Paris with its former American colonies in 1783, Britain allowed New England fishers to return to the banks off Newfoundland and Labrador and in the Gulf of St Lawrence. The Americans also gained the right to fish in inshore waters along the British coast of Newfoundland and Labrador, the Magdalen Islands, and Nova Scotia. By the Treaty of Versailles, signed in the same year, Britain returned to the French their fishing rights in Newfoundland, but the boundaries of the French Shore shifted from between Cape Bonavista and Cape St John to between Point Riche and Cape Ray. While British negotiators did not want it stated forthrightly in the treaty language, they conceded to the French an exclusive right to the fisheries of the French Shore, and the French continued their possession of St Pierre and Miquelon.[7]

By 1788 the British migratory fishery, buoyed by high fish prices, had revived, producing almost 52 per cent of the total British catch. But the resident fishery was a close competitor, and Palliser's Act encouraged it by declaring as fishing ships' rooms all unoccupied land along the shores at Newfoundland, regardless of ancient usage. This declaration reserved such land for the migratory fishery. Further, any land not used for the fishery for one full year would revert to ships' rooms. Migratory fishermen were the ones least likely to maintain year-to-year usage of shore facilities, while residents, by their very presence, were more likely to do so. Under the act, the processing of salt fish was the only legitimate use of ships' rooms. Warehouses, shops, and docks for the local carrying trade dominated the St John's waterfront, but these were not used for making fish. Although British houses still dominated the trade, local agents of these firms, like residents, knew that they held such property only at the pleasure of a governor's willingness to believe they used it for the fishery. In 1784, Governor Campbell was increasingly concerned about the congested St John's waterfront and faced a good deal of animosity from St John's residents when he tried to survey the ships' rooms. Over the next fifty years, discontent with the naval governors' attempts to regulate the alienation of ships' rooms to raise revenue for the expense of local government undermined St John's merchants' confidence in naval government.[8]

As the American Revolution destabilized West Country participation in the trade, more Irish and Scottish firms entered the fishery. From Waterford and Ross came the Irish firms of Ryan, Keough, Eustace, Meagher, Sweetman, and Morris. An occasional Scottish sack ship had carried provisions to trade at Newfoundland for fish to sell in Iberian markets as early as 1726. However, Scottish merchants became seriously interested in the Newfoundland trade from the 1760s with the growth of the Clyde and Ayrshire deep sea trades. Merchants from Greenock and Glasgow began to carry manufactures from Scotland to sell in Newfoundland. The Scottish merchants concentrated in St John's and northeast-coast centres such as Harbour Grace and Bonavista, while the Irish firms developed trade from St John's to Placentia Bay.[9]

The Irish and Scottish firms drew on residents' experience in the fish business rather than relying on partnerships with West Country firms. Scottish merchants supplied the provisions and access to markets that were already part of their colonial trades; they were more likely to provide credit to new residents as they tended to be less committed to long-term relationships with existing suppliers of salt cod. People in the trade referred to the new merchants as 'dealers' to distinguish them from the old West Country 'merchants.' The Scottish merchants found St John's a convenient place from which to deal, and they reached out even into the territory of the West Country firms. Irish merchants in St John's invested in huckster shops to supply the consumer needs of the Irish servants who came to the area. They also invested in public houses, which comforted servants with a warm meal, a drink, and a smoke away from the eyes of their masters. Most provided services to the people of St John's in return for the bills of exchange servants earned in the fishery, or by taking fish in payment directly. By the turn of the century, these Irish and Scottish firms competed with the West Country firms of St John's to such an extent that the latter survived by retreating into their outport operations. Firms such as Robert Newman and Company closed their St John's premises to specialize in the supply trade among the growing number of resident fishers on the south coast of Newfoundland.[10]

Merchants' origins could set them apart from each other. Roman Catholic merchants from Ireland, for example, were mortified that the authorities might consider them the same as Roman Catholic Irish fishing servants. Truck credit practices, the dangers of working on the sea, and poor opportunities for local farming were more important than ethnicity and religion in determining the harshness of such servants' lives. They turned not to the official structure of the church, but rather to itinerant priests for leadership, whether in faction fights to control access to employment in a particular fishing community, or in making public their grievances with merchants. The activities of the itinerant Irish priests had so embarrassed Catholic merchants that they had petitioned the church in Waterford and London to send a bishop to bring the priests under control. In 1783, Catholic merchants in St John's sent a deputation to Waterford to look for a suitable church leader. They wanted one from the conservative clergy of the Irish church who had resisted middle-class radicals in exchange for British state support of the church. The answer to merchants' prayers came when James Louis O'Donel, who had been born into a prosperous Tipperary farming family in 1737, became Prefect Apostolic in 1784. His family had provided the classical education that allowed him to enter the priesthood and to fit in with the English establishment. Although O'Donel's function was to make the church an instrument of class rule, he continued to face opposition from 'strolling' priests of the people, such as the Dominican Patrick Lonergan, who sided with fishing servants in their disputes with merchants.[11]

O'Donel had arrived just as the growth of residence made many merchants more aware of just how important local government was to their interests. Through the late 1780s, merchants pressured the government to provide St John's with more constables and better regulation of its many public houses. Governors, in turn, wanted the merchants to help out with government finances, because their legislative grants from Britain fell short of the expenses of regulating a resident population. The issue came to the fore in 1789, when a transport ship destined for the mainland colonies dumped a large number of Irish convicts in Newfoundland. Governor Milbanke, without funds to feed and house the convicts until they could be transported out of Newfoundland, asked the St John's merchants to help. They agreed to provide food but stopped short of paying half of the cost of transporting the convicts out of the island. Without real property to tax, the merchants agreed only to a voluntary tax on fishing vessels. Local magistrates handled the convicts on behalf of the governor and inhabitants, and collected taxes in the form of fees and duties for the construction of basic public works such as jails. Irish authorities claimed that the governor of Newfoundland had no right to transport the convicts back to Ireland because, in their opinion, they had been sentenced to transportation to a British colony. British authorities defended Milbanke by reiterating Newfoundland's lack of colonial status, although a local government had coped with a difficult problem.[12]

O'Donel and his priests worked to ensure that local officials would not be troubled by Irish residents as they had been by the convicts. They were joined by Thomas Yore, or Ewer, in 1788, who took up the pastoral duties of the Ferryland district. Yore became the merchants' champion in a fight against another radical priest, the Franciscan Patrick Power, who came to St John's well recommended from the church in Ireland in 1787. Power supported fishing families from the south shore of the Avalon Peninsula who complained about mistreatment by merchants. Power's influence extended to the Ferryland district and drew the ire of Yore. Local fishing servants tended to be from Leinster or Munster and frequently found it difficult to find employment in the fishery. Yore, also from Leinster, encouraged faction fighting between his countrymen and those from Munster to divide the supporters of his fellow Franciscan, Power. Even as he encouraged faction fighting, Yore vocally supported local merchants, with the full blessing of O'Donel. O'Donel's actions drew the ire of two bishops in Ireland, James Lanigan of Ossory and William Egan of Waterford, who both felt that the clergy should be fighting for the betterment of all of the people in their pastoral care. O'Donel was steadfastly with the merchants. By 1791, their united opposition drove Power from Newfoundland. The Irish Catholic merchants of St John's were suitably grateful; they had been paying O'Donel's salary of £1,500 per year and invited him to dine with them and the governor to celebrate his victory over Power and the fishing people of the area.[13]

The days when Newfoundland's civil needs could be met by paying a bishop's salary, or voluntary subscriptions and supplements from the governors' resources, were coming to an end. The resumption of trade with the United States fuelled more growth in St John's, where merchant firms competed with English houses for the trade of outport planters. The St John's economy grew even more as residents opened more public houses and taverns to profit from satisfying thirsty and hungry soldiers and fishing servants. The construction, maintenance, and operation of new warehouses, wharves, stores, and other mercantile premises as well as military fortifications brought more tradespeople, labourers, and smaller retailers and merchants to the port. By the turn of the century, the wars with Napoleonic France disrupted the migratory fishery even more, further encouraging the metropolitan development of St John's. By 1795, artisans such as carpenters, coopers, tailors, hairdressers, and shoemakers accounted for between 100 and 150 of the household heads of St John's, far more than the less than 25 planters and boatkeepers (property-owning fish producers) or the approximately 50 merchants and their agents. Such artisans faced insecure tenure in their waterfront property under Palliser's Act, although some, such as prominent watchmaker Benjamin Bowring, cooper John Job, and tailor Thomas Meagher, could take up property on the waterfront because they moved into the merchant business.

Other artisans, and many merchants, wanted legal reform that would grant them more security of property, in keeping with the greater complexity of St John's and of the island generally. Newfoundland's lack of a population of independent farmers and gentry meant that imperial authorities would not grant it the forms of colonial self-government that had developed in other British colonies. Under Palliser's Act, the naval governor, his surrogates, and the Courts of Session and of Vice Admiralty administered the law in the fishery. The courts of civil jurisdiction which had emerged after 1728 continued to exercise summary justice, but popular satisfaction with them declined as the migratory fishery expired. The increasing residence of West Country merchants, or their agents, and the more complex nature of their trade and credit relationships with fishermen, meant that people began to challenge the courts' jurisdiction.[14]

The complex commercial transactions in the resident fishery and the St John's trade required more than the attention of a naval government during the summer, supplemented by a year-round magistracy and surrogate naval judges. Various merchants' challenges of local judicial authority led the British government to appoint John Reeves to make recommendations for judicial reform. A fellow of Queen's College and legal adviser to the Privy Council on trade, Reeves became chief justice of Newfoundland's new Supreme Court in 1792. At heart a conservative defender of the moral principles of eighteenth-century gentry society, Reeves believed that merchants wanted to let nothing interfere with their power over fishing people.[15] On Reeve's advice, the British parliament, between 1791 and 1808, established a new court of civil judicature for Newfoundland. Originally enacted by 31 Geo III c. 29 in 1791, this new Supreme Court at St John's, presided over by a chief justice, had full authority in matters of debt, personal property contracts, other property disputes, and wage disputes. The British government intended the Supreme Court to enforce the general policies of King William's and Palliser's Acts, but the court established some civilian control over naval government, especially as it had become the appellant authority of the surrogates and other lower courts, which began to draw more on civilian personnel. The 1791 act also provided the first clear means of settling debts, recognizing the primacy of the wage lien and current supplier provisions embedded in Palliser's Act. The Supreme and Surrogate Courts exercised all authority in civil matters; the Admiralty Court, while retaining its rule over maritime affairs, no longer had the right to hear disputes involving seamen's wages. The Courts of Session continued but were restricted by the new legislation to hearing wage contests and disputes over small debts. While the naval governors continued to appoint surrogate judges, the office of chief justice had significant executive power. By 1802, the chief justice became the ranking British civil official at Newfoundland and therefore the head of local government during the winter when the governor was absent.[16]

Reeves's study of Newfoundland property law set in motion events that challenged the authority of naval government by threatening the informal property rights enjoyed by St John's developing mercantile bourgeoisie. The principle of continual occupancy articulated in Palliser's Act undermined land titles established by possession before 1685 under King William's Act. Reeves asserted that no secure real property rights existed in St John's, only more informal ones based on occupancy or the governor's pleasure. The decline of the ship fishery at St John's, and growing mercantile pressure on the waterfront, meant that merchants routinely encroached on both fishing ships' rooms and other unused space for their stores, warehouses, and other facilities while governors looked the other way. Governors had to accept that public opinion favoured this informal engrossment of waterfront property, and Reeves felt titles in grant or occupation must force government to recognize St John's residents' right to sell, lease, or mortgage property. Such recognition would allow the government to tax property to pay for a better civil establishment. Reeves called for a Newfoundland council made up of five justices of the peace, five merchants, five fishermen, and five others with the chief justice and two assessors to advise the governor.[17]

British officials did not believe that Newfoundland needed such a council or a law of real property to provide the revenue of an expanded civil administration. They still hoped that the migratory fishery would revive and believed that the dependency of resident and migratory fishing interests on the empire to encourage and protect their transatlantic trade meant that Britain did not have to fear their disaffection. Nonetheless, the French Revolutionary (1792–9) and Napoleonic (1800–1, 1803–15) wars strengthened the St John's bourgeoisie. The wars prevented the French, and later Americans, from fishing in Newfoundland waters, disrupted the Newfoundland residents' competitors in the trade, and led to an increased demand for cod. All of these benefited the resident fishery, while naval hostilities disrupted the migratory fishery.[18]

Word of the revolution in France led local merchants to support a new militia, the Royal Newfoundland Volunteers. While the French continued to be a threat, as when they pillaged and burned Bay Bulls in 1797, merchants had more to fear from a mutiny aboard one of the British naval vessels, the HMS *Latona*, sent out to protect the Newfoundland fishery. The *Latona* mutiny was part of the larger 1797 naval mutinies at Spithead and the Nore, as sailors rose in a Jacobin and United Irish–influenced protest against low wages, brutal working conditions, and military discipline. Governor Waldegrave and local merchants feared the mutiny would spread to the Newfoundland Regiment, a locally recruited regular army unit of fencible infantry. Officials held unfounded views that the Irish Roman Catholics in Newfoundland, who provided most of the enlistments for the Regiment, were always on the verge of treason in collusion with the French, but there is little evidence to suggest that the mutineers were overtly political. Instead, the mutineers rebelled against their poor working conditions and poverty, clad in the rhetoric of wider protests popular throughout the empire. Members of St John's Protestant merchant families constituted most of the Regiment's junior officers, and the Regiment joined the Volunteers in suppressing the mutiny, but not before many wondered which side the Irish soldiers would support.[19]

The *Latona* mutiny again raised the issue of the need for a greater civil establishment and local real property rights. Waldegrave recognized that St John's merchants and other members of its bourgeoisie expected secure rights to the property they defended. However, Waldegrave felt that the naval government needed only to extend more civil authority for poor relief rather than support real property rights or colonial status. Such relief would defuse Irish discontent and forestall any attack on the social order of St John's. The governor had no interest in acknowledging that St John's inhabitants treated their property as if they had real rights but wanted to find ways to tax them for poor relief and other local expenditures. Conscious of their lack of property rights, St John's merchants began to confront Waldegrave and his successors over efforts to regulate access to property and attempts at taxation in the absence of formal real property rights.[20]

Popular anger at the gross inequalities between classes in St John's prevented merchants from openly condemning the naval government. Poorly treated Irish servants in the Royal Newfoundland Regiment eventually rose up against their exploitation by local merchants and their poor treatment in the regiment. On 24 April 1800, nineteen soldiers tried to revolt, using the United Irish cry of 'Death or Liberty.' Authorities quickly rounded up the mutineers, summarily tried and executed some, and sent others to Halifax for court martial. Rumours circulated around St John's that as many as four hundred residents supported the United Irishmen, planning to plunder and burn the premises of the respectable citizens. The St John's merchants formed night patrols to watch the town's Irish Roman Catholics and rallied behind British authority, welcoming martial law and the sixty-sixth regiment from Halifax.[21]

The rising of 'common' servants, soldiers, and sailors demonstrated that Irish labourers had become a political force that neither the naval authorities nor merchants alone could ignore. They turned to Roman Catholic Bishop O'Donel's influence to discourage rebellion, seeing any support for the United Irishmen as sympathy for the French and treason against the laws of England. In doing so, O'Donel secured his position as a member of the Newfoundland elite and protected the Roman Catholic Church from having the governor enforce the more draconian elements of the English penal laws. Indeed, when a mild stroke forced O'Donel's retirement in 1804, local merchants support-ed the British government's granting him an annual pension. In 1807, O'Donel left Newfoundland, having secured a promise from his suc-cessor Patrick Lambert that the new bishop would continue to contain the discontent of Irish fishing people. As a final gesture of apprecia-tion, the merchants of St John's gave O'Donel a valuable silver urn.²²

St John's merchants were locked in a more uneasy relationship with the naval governors. On the one hand, they depended on the gover-nors as well as bishops to protect their material interests. On the other hand, they resented the governors' efforts to tax their businesses. Gov-ernors Gambier and Gower were determined to charge quit rents on leased property to pay for a greater Anglican Church establishment and charitable schools for children of the poor. The governors hoped that the schools would protect St John's social hierarchy by instilling British loyalty and order among St John's rougher classes. Although the governors accepted that the merchants should have real property rights, the property owners resented being asked to pay for an ad-ministration. After 1800, the debate between the St John's bourgeoisie and the governors was not about individual rights to engross private property, but about the type of administration that should tax or rent such property, and what policies it should pursue. Merchants' civic-mindedness left much to be desired; they crowded the waterfront with poorly constructed buildings without regard for fire safety and sanitation. Some earned such high rents from artisan and petty-trade tenants that the governors felt they should be taxed for civic purposes. However, merchants felt that they had demonstrated responsibility in supporting the militia and that they should have some say over the government that would use their money. Governor Gower was sym-pathetic and thought that the merchant-dominated St John's grand jury should have some control over spending on poor relief, roads, jails, and other municipal needs. But he stopped short of suggesting a colonial legislature should gain control over the funds he proposed to raise from leases.²³

Wartime economic conditions lessened merchants' concerns about more control over government. For most of the 1790s, war-related economic disruption had caused low fish prices but inflated the price of just about everything else. War with France in 1793 decisively dis-rupted British migratory production. The resident fishery again flour-ished, eventually spurred on by the 1807–8 American Embargo Act, and the War of 1812, which limited the otherwise formidable competition of the new American cod fishery. The British invasion of Spain opened peninsular markets to Newfoundland fish and encouraged rising prices. While wartime inflation afflicted residents, the ready supply of Irish labour helped to offset planters' wage costs that had been rising due to war-related shortages of West Country labour. Even during the hard times of the wars, resident planters had found that they could further diversify their economic activities by engaging in the seal hunt, trapping furs, logging, and building more boats for the resident fishery. As the fishery improved, but with the migratory trade all but finished, merchants advanced more credit to some of these planters. With this credit, some planters began to invest in schooners, vessels much larger than the boats they had previously used in the inshore fishery. Planters could use these schooners to sail for the rich fishing grounds of the north shore, or those parts of the Newfoundland coast usually held by the French under treaty right. Hostilities excluded the French from such shores, and the planters filled the beaches.[24]

These planters hired a lot of labour, but this did not change the nature of the resident fishery. Most planters continued to be year-round settlers who relied on the labour of their families and perhaps a servant or two hired for a share of the catch. Notwithstanding improved conditions in the fishery, planters who built schooners and hired servants found credit to be expensive, and wage rates were high, but they could sustain this only as long as the good fish prices of wartime continued. As some planters borrowed more money, a greater division of labour developed among them. Some took their schooners to the north shore but concentrated only on catching fish. Such planters did not dry their fish but shipped it back to their home ports, where other planters specialized in hiring labour to dry it for export. More perceptive planters, especially from Conception Bay, saw that merchants were doing well and tried their hand at the trade themselves. Such planters did not have the resources to engage in the import and export trades, but they could become the agents and dealers for those who could. These agents or dealers used their schooners to carry other fishers to the north shore, where they fished with their families for the summer just as they had on their own shores in Conception Bay. The planter-agents or dealers provided these fishers with passage and supplies on credit and carried them and their fish and oil back at the end of the fishing season, again on credit advanced against the sale of their catch.[25]

St John's merchants still hoped for a settlement of their rights to property in ships' rooms on the waterfront. The most recent governor, Admiral Holloway, had decided to enforce the law restricting merchants' access to these rooms. The friendship he struck up with James Macbraire, a northern Irish merchant who had become a prominent member of the St John's mercantile community, meant that Holloway accepted the merchants' use of ships' rooms. In return, Macbraire, and the other merchants involved in the Society of Merchants, formed in 1807, sided with the governor in his disputes with Chief Justice Thomas Tremlett. The problem of relying on the personal whim of a governor came to the fore when Holloway's successor, Admiral John Duckworth, used ships' rooms leases to pay for schools, police, fire-fighting, and other civic purposes. In 1811, the British government, acting upon Duckworth's recommendation, passed the Ships Room Act, which allowed the governor to lease unused ships' rooms but without requiring him to recognize merchants' previous encroachments on them as real property.[26]

Although discontent with naval government persisted in St John's, it continued to provide rudimentary administration to the other communities spread out over a long coastline. The career of Lieutenant David Buchan shows the range of duties within the domain of naval government. Buchan attempted to establish relations between the Newfoundland administration and the Beothuks camped at Red Indian Lake. As fur trappers continued to move into areas of Notre Dame Bay used by the Beothuks as winter refuge, conflict between the two peoples worsened. Throughout the last decade of the eighteenth century there had been attempts by local settlers to capture Beothuks who might be trained in the English language and to act as intermediaries between the two peoples. These attempts at abduction, as well as fishermen's brutal retaliatory raids on Beothuk encampments, could only make the Beothuks less receptive to overtures from the government.

Governors' previous attempts to use furriers such as William Cull to establish contact with the Beothuks failed miserably. Governor Duckworth, on his arrival in Newfoundland in 1810, and with the support of the local Methodist Missionary Society, attempted to do better. Duckworth selected Lieutenant Buchan, who commanded HMS *Adonis*, to seek out the Beothuks. Buchan arrived in Notre Dame Bay in January 1811, equipped an expedition from his crew with trade goods, and set out with Cull and two other local men as guides. On 23 January, the expedition encountered a band of Beothuks on the shores of the frozen Red Indian Lake. Although Buchan tried to convince the Beothuks of his good intentions, the long history of poor relationships with the British, together with the presence of Cull, meant that he was unsuccessful. The expedition ended in disaster, as some of the Beothuks killed two marines in Buchan's party, decapitating them, likely as a ritualistic symbol of victory. Although the deaths of two marines had marred the expedition, Duckworth accepted Buchan's proposal to try to make contact with the Beothuks again in 1812 as they hunted among the islands of Notre Dame Bay. Although years of armed reprisals and kidnapping attempts had made friendly contact between the English and the Beothuks unlikely, Buchan was determined to capture a Beothuk to train as an emissary. Buchan's subsequent expedition was cut short by the outbreak of war between Britain and the United States in 1812. Sadly this was not the last ill-conceived attempt to establish a dialogue with the Beothuks.[27]

While the naval government's attempt to establish relationships with the Beothuks failed, Duckworth's policies for St John's were not doing much better. His position on leasing ships' rooms continued to frustrate St John's merchants, even after he left the island at the end of the 1811 fishing season. Merchants, along with a growing number of professionals, wanted a local Board of Police to ensure that the substantial revenues from ships' rooms leases would be spent on local roads, a police force, the lighting and widening of existing streets, a marketplace, schools, and poor relief. One of these professionals, the surgeon William Carson, aggrieved because Duckworth forbade his attempt to establish a farm, condemned the arbitrary authority of naval government. He demanded self-government through a popularly elected legislature, as existed in the neighbouring colony of Nova Scotia. Local merchants such as Macbraire felt that Carson went too far in his strident attacks on Duckworth. They especially disliked the manner in which Carson depicted himself as the champion of popular rights and were happy enough to stop short of the potentially expensive burden of colonial self-government. Macbraire felt that judicial reform would be sufficient to meet merchants' particular concerns.[28]

Outside of St John's the limited ability of naval government to provide good civilian administration was becoming more apparent. St John's merchants could easily appeal decisions by lower courts to the Supreme Court. In the outports, authority over civil matters lay with the surrogates, accompanied by two justices of the peace, but the Supreme Court, and no longer the governor, was now their appellant judicial authority and administered criminal law. The Courts of Session could still hear wage and debt disputes, but only the surrogates could issue writs in cases of insolvency or rule on the customs and laws governing wages and credit in the fishery. Magistrates often served as government administrators, collecting duties and linking the outports with the governor at St John's as a sort of rudimentary local government. Some magistrates, such as Lewis Anspach in Conception Bay and John Bland of Bonavista, had reputations for being beyond mercantile influence and for serving as reliable sources of information for the government in St John's. However, the authorities doubted the independence of most magistrates from local merchants. Although the governors technically exercised a great deal of influence over the administration of justice, they preferred to devolve responsibility for the supervision of the surrogate judges onto a 'Supreme Surrogate,' a justice of the peace with an official salary and the power to hear cases all over Newfoundland. Although senior naval officials tried to distinguish their civil and military responsibilities in Newfoundland, government continued to appear very much as a naval institution.[29]

The limits of naval government became apparent in 1815 with the end of the wars with Napoleon. Postwar depression struck the island as war-related high prices in the fishery collapsed. As early as the spring, merchants and planters began to reduce the scale of their operations dramatically. Irish servants continued to pour into St John's, hoping to find work, but there was little work available, and that only at low wages. The Irish organized into rival Leinster and Munster gangs. The gangs attempted to control the local labour market through pacts, refusing work unless paid a minimum wage. Fights broke out as the Leinster and Munster gangs disagreed about who had a right to work, and at what price. Another strolling Franciscan, John Power from Munster, had come to Newfoundland in 1808. Power antagonized Bishop Lambert, but endeared himself to the Irish servants generally by forming a liaison with a woman and travelling about the northern outports conducting himself as a common man. The current governor, Keats, wanted the church to get rid of Power, whom Lambert had already suspended. Lambert and his loyal priests were Leinstermen; the dispute with Power inflamed the faction-fighting. The divisions among the Irish frustrated their attempt to regulate the labour market. By the summer of 1815 the gangs had collapsed, and those who could find work received only half the wages paid by planters in 1814.[30]

The economic problems underlying the gang rivalry worsened during the winter of 1816–17. The year started badly when a disastrous fire swept through more than 130 St John's homes and mer-

chant premises in February 1816. The continued absence of imports of
cheap provisions from the United States aggravated unemployment
and poor wages in the fishery. Merchants further restricted credit to
planters, causing distress in fishing households. The Court of Sessions
in Harbour Grace ordered unemployed servants to report to St John's
for shipment out of the island or be flogged and jailed. Unemployed
servants, mostly Irish, in St John's, Carbonear, and Harbour Grace
formed bands that rioted for relief and broke open merchant stores to
seize food. Authorities preferred to think of the rioters as a disorganized rabble, and called them 'Rals,' an Irish term for rascals. Despite
the best efforts of Lambert's successor as Roman Catholic bishop,
Thomas Scallan, to keep the servants quiet, the rioters displayed discipline and organization, taking only the food they needed to survive. Scallan continued to press for more political rights for Roman
Catholics, suggesting that this would calm discontent, but such rights
would not feed empty stomachs or put money in the pockets of distressed servants.[31]

The governor, Francis Pickmore, had left Newfoundland for the
season, and the responsibility for dealing with this 'Winter of the Rals'
fell to Captain David Buchan as the senior naval officer and surrogate.
Pickmore had hoped that Buchan could use public works to employ
some servants and deport the rest. Buchan did not have the revenue
to spend on public works, realized he did not have the legal right to
deport people simply for being unemployed, and issued naval stores
to relieve distress. Many servants continued to flock to St John's because it offered some hope of work in areas outside the fishery. Such
hopes were unfounded. Increased military spending and the growth
of the resident fishery had encouraged the town's economic development during the wars. The town had acquired other trappings of
an administrative centre: the government had established an official
newspaper, the *Royal Gazette*, along with a printing office in 1807 and
a post office in 1809. Like the outports, however, St John's prosperity
depended on the fish trade, and it too suffered in the wake of war's
end. Another disastrous fire in November 1817 made life even more
difficult for people in the port, and the return of the French and Americans to the fishery meant that fish prices were unlikely to improve.[32]

The effect of international relations in the fisheries on British subjects residing in Newfoundland encouraged local officials such as
Buchan to think about how the resident fishery might be reorganized to survive postwar depression. Although the treaties of Paris in
1814 and 1815 between Britain and France returned to the latter its

fishing rights in Newfoundland as they had existed in 1792, it had become clear that Newfoundland residents expected a concurrent right to fish off the French Shore. France nonetheless insisted on its exclusive right and returned in full force as a major competitor in the cod fishery. American competition also returned, although the Anglo-American Convention of 1818 deprived the Americans of their rights to fish within three marine miles of the Newfoundland and Labrador coastline, thereby excluding them from a shore-based fishery. New England fishers increased their fishing effort on the banks adjacent to Newfoundland and Labrador, driven by the opportunities of the expanding domestic American market and the need to provide more employment to local farming and fishing households. While the Americans could not use the shores of Newfoundland and Labrador for fisheries, the same was not true for residents' fellow colonists from Nova Scotia. Fishing fleets from Lunenburg increasingly resorted to the Labrador coast in search of new fish stocks to exploit, using local shores to dry their fish as did Newfoundlanders, but also expanding their schooner fisheries on the banks off Newfoundland. Everywhere they turned, resident Newfoundland and Labrador fishers faced more competition even as international fish prices declined.[33]

Competition in the Labrador fishery was a problem for British fishers at Newfoundland and Labrador. Many planters survived the depression by retreating into household production, but some of the better off survived as dealers for merchants, carrying fishing families to the coast of Labrador. The growing importance of the Labrador fishery had led British authorities to return jurisdiction over Labrador to Newfoundland in 1809. There Newfoundland planters could fish as they had on the north shore, which had been returned to the French under treaty rights, but the fishing season was shorter, the voyage longer, and the conditions for drying fish poorer. To keep their schooners occupied at Labrador while waiting to carry back passengers and catches, planters had their schooner crews fish as well, paying them in a share of the catch. The business that kept these planter-dealers and agents afloat, however, was their supply of credit (as intermediaries of larger merchants) to those who relied on household production in the inshore fishery. Even more important, the planters who owned schooners found that they could make money by using their schooners in an expanded spring seal hunt. The profits of the seal hunt offset the persistence of low prices in the cod fishery, so much so that it is doubtful that residents would have survived without them. While the

seal hunt allowed residents to persist, it did not allow many to pros-
per as depressed conditions in the cod trade prevailed.[34]

The British government hoped that the patriarchal authority of the
household organization in the fishery, prosecuted largely by family labour, would offset social problems caused by such depressed
conditions and foster greater social order. David Buchan had left
Newfoundland for two years after the winter of 1816–17, staying
in England when not on expeditions to the North Pole. England at
that time was experiencing similar social upheaval in the wake of the
postwar depression, even as official opinion suggested that the family
should become the foundation of a renewed social harmony and the
patriarchal duty of the male household head was to ensure the public
peace of his household. Such thought was unrealistic, and the consequent frustration of officials such as Buchan, who returned in 1819,
provoked a political furor that brought naval government to an end.

In 1819, Buchan, along with another surrogate judge, Anglican minister John Leigh, ordered that two Conception Bay planters, Philip
Butler and James Lundrigan, each receive thirty-six lashes of the cat-
o'-nine-tails for their contempt of court. Butler's and Lundrigan's debt
problems were part of a larger wave of post-1815 insolvencies that
peaked in 1820 but lasted until 1825. The matter had arisen from suits
for debt by their supplying merchants. Merchants pursued delinquent
debtors by asking the court to seize fishing people's produce and/or
equipment. The surrogate courts did not order corporal punishment
for other fishermen who treated these writs with contempt (indeed,
the surrogate courts had used corporal punishments such as whipping
only on a couple of occasions for thefts in the 1780s). The surrogate
judges usually jailed a defendant, if he was acting alone, or ordered
that person to behave until his debt was paid, and would intercede on
the behalf of fishers if they thought merchants were jeopardizing their
families' ability to avoid starvation. The sentence of whipping was
out of character for Buchan and Leigh, who had earlier dealt leniently
with fishermen charged with contempt in debt cases.

The only difference between Butler and Lundrigan and the other
offenders was that their cases involved wives openly defying peaceable patriarchal social order. Butler's and Lundrigan's crime was not
contempt of court but their failure to be proper patriarchs, something which must have troubled Buchan greatly given his experience
of the Winter of the Rals. The surrogate judges had expected Butler
and Lundrigan, and all other men for that matter, to maintain order

within their households. Such order would be in keeping with the patriarchy of English common law, particularly in inheritance law, which recognized few property or civil rights for women within the family and still allowed men to use corporal punishment to discipline the public lives of women. Official patriarchy existed in naval government. There was no place for women in the administrative structures of government at Newfoundland; no one, for example, could hope to have their case tried in court before women as judges or juries.

Despite such formal patriarchy, their importance to the fishery meant that women assumed important public economic and social roles in their communities. By the second decade of the nineteenth century, women took care of most of the shore work of curing fish and oversaw most of their households' supplementary farming. Families which had an excess of female labour often hired out daughters to do shore work for those fishing families who lacked a sufficient number of women and girls. In Conception Bay, the courts tended to recognize husbands' assumption of the property rights of their wives upon marriage. Nonetheless, the courts recognized the rights of women to inherit property upon the death of male relatives and continued to recognize women who acted as the de facto heads of some fishing enterprises and traded with merchants on their own account, whether they acted through male relatives or on their own in court. Likewise, the Placentia courts heard women's complaints but also recognized their right to inherit property on a 'share and share alike' basis with male relatives. Their pivotal role in the production and reproduction of outport society and economy gave women a public life and a prominence which defied the official, patriarchal proscriptions for behaviour of the period.[35]

Women managed the day-to-day activities of their homes and surrounding gardens. This made them most likely the first to meet a constable on his way to serve a writ of attachment on the fishing families' belongings as a result of a merchant's suit. As they might deal with each other in cases of slander, or even disputes over scarce, precious topsoil and manure, women could greet such officers of the court with violence, public ridicule, or gossip – yet other challenges to official gender proscriptions. In Butler's case, his wife refused to turn over her household's property to answer a writ to satisfy a claim for £236 by their merchants, Trimingham and Co. Lundrigan's debt of £13 was much less than Butler's, but his wife, Sarah Morgan, threatened to blow out the brains of the constable who tried to serve a writ. While Buchan and Leigh claimed that they ordered Lundrigan whipped because he would not appear in court, their remittance of twenty-two of Lundrigan's lashes only after he promised to make sure his family left their fishing room suggests that Morgan's forcible possession of the fishing room had most bothered Buchan and Leigh. Compared with their wives, James Lundrigan and Philip Butler played a small but unforgivable part in the actual contempt of court. They had stood aside and let their wives openly defy the courts in defence of their households. The surrogates' singling out the males for punishment reflected the English judicial system's preference for believing that women's femininity rendered them incapable of responsibility for serious breaches of public order and the local courts' refusal to allow married women to take part in legal actions independent of their husbands. Whatever the reason, the surrogate courts were not prepared to recognize women's unfeminine and public defiance of their authority by prosecuting them alongside their husbands.[36]

Reformers such as William Carson portrayed the incidents more as examples of the supposedly brutal and arbitrary authority exercised over civilians by naval authorities. They appropriated the whippings as a convenient outrage, which only constitutional change might remedy. Reformers helped the two planters to bring countersuits against Buchan and Leigh for damages in the Supreme Court in November 1820. While Chief Justice Forbes ruled that the surrogates did have the right to punish Butler and Lundrigan, he expressed disapproval of the harsh sentences meted out by the surrogates in these instances. The suits became political show trials, embarrassing the surrogates for their use of excessive authority. Reverend Leigh even apologized and promised restitution in the Lundrigan case. Neither surrogate ever added to the controversy by openly discussing their reasons for the whippings. Debates took place in the British House of Commons which confirmed the Newfoundland Supreme Court's ruling that whipping was by then considered an excessive punishment for contempt.[37] The Butler and Lundrigan affair had effectively undermined the legitimacy of naval government in Newfoundland.

Improving relations between settlers and the Beothuks was another area that proved beyond the competency of the naval government. In 1819, the furriers John Peyton, Jr and Sr, decided to kidnap and train a Beothuk as an interpreter for the governor. They retraced Buchan's ill-fated expedition, captured a woman, Demasduit, but killed her husband, Nonosabasut, in the process. After being kept captive in Twillingate for a while, Mary March, as her captors named her, was brought to St John's. Her brief time in the capital was pivotal in changing Newfoundlanders' views of the Beothuks, for while they had once feared dangerous wild people, the woman before them was obviously not. Demasduit sat for her portrait to be painted by Henrietta Hamilton, the governor's wife. Many members of the small elite in St John's now suspected that the fishermen were more savage than the Natives. The governor sent Buchan to return her to her people, but she died of tuberculosis before making it home. Given the history of misunderstanding and distrust between the two peoples it was not surprising that no good came of this incident.

By 1823 there were too few Beothuks left to sustain their communities, encouraging three hungry and sick Beothuk women to surrender to some fishermen rather than face starvation. John Peyton cared for the three at Twillingate before sending them to St John's, where, like Demasduit before, they made a sensation. Buchan, chastened by his earlier experiences, had them returned to a tilt in the woods near Twillingate, where Peyton could keep an eye upon them. Two soon died of tuberculosis, leaving only the young Shanawdithit, as far as she knew the last of her people. For the next five years Peyton employed her in his home as an unpaid maid and sent Governor Hamilton a bill for her upkeep. While she helped raise Peyton's children, a committee of citizens, led by the Newfoundland-born and Edinburgh-educated William Cormack, formed the Boeothick Institute. In addition to the genuine horror the members felt at reports of atrocities, the Institute exemplified the nineteenth-century bourgeoisie's interest in using natural history and science as ways of taming the wilderness and bringing it within the knowledge and control of civilization. The Boeothick Institute was dedicated to rescuing any remaining Beothuks and learning what could be recovered about their history. Cormack undertook a couple of unsuccessful expeditions in search of Beothuks, including an epic walk across the breadth of the island with his Innu guide James John of Gander Bay and subsequent expeditions accompanied by Mi'kmaq guides. The Institute concluded that Shanawdithit was likely the only living Beothuk, prompting Cormack to arrange for her to be taken from Peyton's house and brought to St John's. Under Carson's medical care and Cormack's guardianship she was interviewed for information about her people. On 6 June 1829 Shanawdithit died of tuberculosis. Her passing prompted much remorse among subsequent generations for the role that Newfoundlanders had in contributing to the extinction of the Beothuks. Not surprisingly given the imperialistic science of the day, Shanawdithit's skull was removed and sent for study to the Edinburgh museum at which Cormack's mentor worked.[38]

The public controversy surrounding the naval government's failure to protect the Beothuks, along with the Butler and Lundrigan affair, discredited naval government. The Butler and Lundrigan episodes undermined the legitimacy of the naval government's administration of justice, especially considering that Buchan was the island's chief surrogate. While Governor Hamilton thought that the summary justice of the surrogate courts should be strengthened, he faced stiff opposition from Chief Justice Francis Forbes. Forbes appreciated the cheap and relatively summary justice of Newfoundland but insisted that Newfoundland law must live up to English legal tradition. He argued that Newfoundlanders were British colonists who had rights to the rule of English law, which were daily being trampled by surrogates who, as career naval officers, surgeons, ministers, or merchants' clerks, had no legal training. Forbes further argued that the courts must be more sympathetic to masters than servants in the fishery and wanted servants hired on shares to be recognized as co-adventurers who would have no privileged lien for wages under the wage and lien system. More paternalistic surrogates ignored Forbes's rulings on this matter, and the chief justice was determined to end their influence.[39]

Colonial Office officials were increasingly sympathetic to Forbes as they realized that the civil requirements of Newfoundland were likely to become much more expensive and beyond the ability of the naval state to provide. The political furor that developed around the Butler and Lundrigan atrocities encouraged this view. The Irish-born merchant Patrick Morris had joined Carson and other Reformers in an 1820 committee of St John's inhabitants. The committee petitioned Governor Hamilton, complaining of arbitrary judicial authority, the injustice of taxation without representation, and the lack of a local legislature. Debate about the petition in parliament led to more Reform pressure throughout 1822 and 1823. The Reformers hoped that popular outrage at the Lundrigan and Butler affairs, as well as official displeasure with the legal inadequacies of the untrained surrogates, would encourage the home government to grant Newfoundland self-government by legislature. The British decided to grant minimal colonial government, but with judicial authorities still possessing a great deal of executive power. The British government merged executive and judicial authority by the 1824 reform of the Supreme Court and the appointment of a council along the lines of a system developed for New South Wales to advise the governor in ruling the colony. The Reform efforts resulted in a new Judicature Act in 1824 (5 Geo.V, c. 47), which replaced that originating in 1791. The British government recognized that Newfoundland was in fact a settled colony, replaced the surrogates with circuit courts presided over by magistrates under the authority of civilian judges of the Supreme Court, and appointed a civilian governor with the power to alienate crown land for agricultural purposes.

The new Judicature Act ended the authority of the surrogates in judicial matters and established a permanent Supreme Court with full civil and criminal jurisdiction over the colony and fishery. This new Supreme Court was to have a chief justice presiding over a Central District from its seat in St John's, while assistant judges would preside in circuit courts over southern and northern districts. The appellant Supreme Court for these district courts sat at St John's and served also as the Court of Oyer and Terminer as well as of General Gaol Delivery, and as a Court of Record. Besides having a civil jurisdiction, the Supreme Court gained authority over all crimes on the seas and islands of the Newfoundland fishery, as well as over suits on trade and commerce, leaving the Vice Admiralty Court with power over only naval matters. English legal practice would govern all civil and criminal cases, the latter being heard either before a jury at St John's or by circuit judges in the outports with either juries or, if they could not be raised, three assessors. If juries could not be raised for civil cases, the judge could act alone. The chief justice and his assistants now had to be barristers of three years' standing either in Great Britain or the colonies.[40]

The merchants of St John's supported the limited reforms of 1824. The depression in the fishery that had begun in 1816 had undermined many of the business partnerships between Scottish and West Country firms and interests in St John's. Many of the former junior partners and agents of these British firms set up business in St John's on their own and began to pursue the fish trade, sealing, and local trading. As St John's began to transform into the metropole of the British Newfoundland fishery, its merchants became more interested in the issue of colonial government, but within strict limits. Merchants like Meagher and Macbraire, as absentee landlords, delayed considerably the evolution of municipal institutions which might interfere with their property rights. St John's merchants' jealous guardianship of their town's revenue for St John's, not Newfoundland, improvement, eventually persuaded local merchants that gaining control over the island through a colonial legislature represented the best political means of satisfying their metropolitan impulse in the Newfoundland trade. For such merchants, more representative colonial institutions were to advance their own interests, not those of the colony as a whole, although of course they saw no distinction. In their hands, a colonial government would really be a St John's government.[41]

Newfoundland had once been perceived as a great ship moored near the fishing banks for the convenience of English fishers. First the American Revolution, then the wars with France and the United States, made the Newfoundland fishery a resident one, complete with a nascent local bourgeoisie. After the Napoleonic wars the needs of this growing settled society could not be met by naval authorities. The colony gained a civilian administration, but that fell far short of satisfying the aspirations of some among the bourgeoisie of St John's. They soon began a fight for more representative colonial institutions, but in a manner that would lead the colonial government to turn its back on the sea.

5

A Colonial State, 1824–1855

The imperial government sent Sir Thomas Cochrane as governor to oversee the first official colonial government. Arriving in 1825, Cochrane, a naval officer, controlled much of the executive and regulatory authority of what was a civilian administration. He felt that Newfoundland's narrow economic base and small, dispersed coastal population required institutions of government that would be different from the British North American colonies with a more agrarian base. The new governor set the tone for succeeding administrations, which had to govern a complex and difficult society. Various political movements for reform persisted in opposing the new colonial regime, demanding instead representative, then responsible, government. Eventually, a consensus about what the nature of colonial self-government should be emerged in St John's, but it had significant class and sectarian dimensions. More important, the reform consensus overlooked the integral role of marine resources, which defined the colony's economy and society, in favour of expectations about colonial development that were ill-fitted to local circumstances.

The most developed part of the colonial government was the judiciary. The chief justice and assistant justices of the Supreme Court brought greater civil authority to the outports through the new circuit courts established in 1826. The Supreme Court judges also sat on the governor's Executive Council with the St John's garrison commander. By serving as president of the Council, the chief justice was the chief executive authority of the island during the governor's absence. As a result of the 1824 Judicature Act, the circuit courts and justices of the peace performed many civic as well as judicial duties, and their court-houses served as local government buildings. Most communities only had one justice of the peace, which led circuit judges to administer district affairs personally, approving (for example) the appropriation of district funds from licensing and fees for courthouse and jail repair, hiring constables, and relieving the needy. Where they were more numerous, justices of the peace served in courts of sessions as a form of government through virtual representation that was common in the British colonies of settlement.[1]

The Judicature Act gave the governor the right to institute a Court of Civil Jurisdiction for the coast of Labrador. Prior to 1824, the only effective colonial administration had been that of the Moravian missionaries at their stations along the northern coast. To the south, a variety of small traders had been moving northward to Hamilton Inlet and Davis Inlet, although many of these were bought out by the Hudson's Bay Company (HBC), which established posts at Rigolet and North West River in 1836. Traders and missionaries acted as 'substitute governors,' regulating the people who depended on their posts and representing local interests to colonial and imperial officials as they saw fit. However, the civil court for Labrador, presided over by naval captain William Paterson from 1825, heard cases and gathered information for authorities in St John's about Innu and Inuit, the Moravians, visiting Americans and Europeans, the fishery, and the fur trade. The court visited communities along the southern Labrador coast by hired vessel. By 1827, the Labrador court had taken on more administrative duties, acquired jurisdiction over minor criminal matters, and functioned much like the circuit courts in Newfoundland. While the court was an effective extension of colonial jurisdiction over coastal Labrador, the government in St John's discontinued it in 1834 because of its high costs, dodging its administrative duty to Labrador, and abandoning it to a variety of informal administrations. Governments in St John's continued to collect customs duties and other revenues from the area, collecting more from the territory than it spent there on services.[2]

The intensification of the Labrador fishery meant that more people of European descent settled on the Labrador coast. Some were New-foundland-born, but many continued to be British servants brought out by the British mercantile firms that operated on the coast. Others were deserters from British naval vessels that patrolled the coast. Over the next few decades personnel from the HBC travelled throughout the interior from its local headquarters at North West River promoting the fur trade among the Innu of the interior. From the Orkney Islands or Quebec, these early employees often settled on the coast themselves so that they could trap and trade on their own account just as the original servants of fish merchants had done on the coasts of Labrador to the south and east.

As fur traders elsewhere in the continental north found, the knowledge of the Innu and Inuit was critical to the success of such settlers' trade and survival. HBC servants who wanted to settle did so by marrying Inuit or Innu women. Northward along the coast, the Moravians continued to expand their missions, making the territory of the Inuit more familiar to Europeans. However, smallpox outbreaks caused the Moravians to withdraw with the Inuit to Hopedale and Nain, making the HBC more dependent on the Innu. The Innu preferred to follow the caribou and were reluctant to concentrate on the fur trade. While the HBC worked at luring the Innu into dependence by supplying them with guns and ammunition for the hunt, the company had to rely more on settlers, or those of their employees who married First Nations women.[3]

In Newfoundland, more isolated outports, such as those on the south coast, could not resort to the virtual representation of the Court of Sessions because they did not have enough justices of the peace to sit together. Cochrane found it difficult to imagine how the colony could develop further without the basis for commercial agriculture and an independent gentry. Wartime prosperity had encouraged rapid population development, but immigration collapsed in the post-1815 economic depression. The torrent of post-1815 immigration to the rest of North America bypassed a colony with meagre agricultural potential where the resources of the sea supported almost everyone. Yet fish prices remained so low that merchants were tight-fisted with credit, and government faced persistent demands for relief. Although he had little faith in its success, Cochrane encouraged agricultural development, seeking to lessen residents' dependence on the fishery. While fishing families had always raised root crops and livestock for their own use, Cochrane hoped that commercial agriculture might diversify the economy, balance class divisions through the development of an independent farming population, and provide a landed gentry whose existence might deserve a legislature. The governor planned to use able-bodied relief through road building to open up agricultural land to settlement but found that Newfoundland's ecology supported little besides root crops, especially potatoes, and the keeping of a small number of livestock for household use. The government continued to give out relief for road building, but no matter how many roads were cleared, or how much seed was distributed, farming did not thrive beyond the gardens that fishing families were able to tend with their own labour, particularly the labour of women.[4]

The particular legal complexities that affected the relationships between merchants and fishers in the context of poor postwar prices for fish ensured that the courts had plenty of business in the outports. In 1826, the government appointed a small number of clergy and merchants' agents as conservators of the peace, who could take complaints or depositions under oath and handle the paperwork of the judicial system but were unable to try cases. The legal complexities of the wage and lien system continued to preoccupy the outport judiciary. A planter in the Labrador trade or the seal hunt had to agree to pay his servants wages fixed by written contract long before knowing how the season might fare; masters were prohibited from reducing wages to avoid insolvency. Even if planters had successful voyages, the law of current supply limited their freedom to market fish. If planters tried to sell fish to anyone else, their current suppliers of credit might become nervous about losing their preferential liens and go to court to attach the planters' voyages, possibly forcing the latter into insolvency. To avoid this fate, planters had to continue to deal with current suppliers regardless of the prices such merchants charged for supplies or gave for fish. Current suppliers guarded their status as preferred creditors because they envied servants' even stronger claim. Finally, merchants had little reason to offer better prices for fish to planters who were not their regular clients because they were unsecured creditors if a planter's current supplier forced insolvency. In a bad season, the law allowed servants and current suppliers to protect their own investments while squeezing planters, who found that there was little room for their own successful capital accumulation by the employment of wage labour.[5]

The wage and lien system aggravated the greater problems of the long post-1815 depression in the fish trade. Everywhere, fishers retreated into household production as much as local settlement allowed. Conception Bay and the southern shore of the Avalon Peninsula were the demographically most mature areas with well-established families to supply sufficient labour for household fish production. Trinity, Bonavista, Placentia, and St Mary's bays, areas that had been disturbed by conflicting Anglo-French exploitation, would not reach the demographic point at which families could supply their fishing households with enough labour until the 1850s, and the remainder of the island (held by the French) would not do so until the 1870s. In such places, merchants continued to employ labour directly to produce salt fish and other marine products. Merchants, who operated in the Strait of Belle Isle, found that many of their servants preferred establishing their independence by settling locally, establishing families often by marrying women from Newfoundland who came to work as cooks and shore crews, and trading fish, seals, and furs to the Birds and other West Country and Jersey firms on their own accounts. Subject to truck, such ex-servants nevertheless preferred the relative autonomy of task-oriented work within the household to time-regimented work for a firm. Merchant firms continued to bring out servants and specialized tradespeople but tried to lower their overhead costs by restricting their operations to trade alone while continuing to rely on servants for supplies of fish. Merchants in St John's specialized in trade with small outport traders and withdrew completely from the direct production of salt fish.[6]

It was the seal hunt rather than agriculture that made settlement possible. In the first half of the nineteenth century, the hunt on the northeast coast shifted from a shore-based to an offshore operation. Building and supplying schooners for the offshore hunt required capital resources beyond the ability of planters and smaller outport merchants to supply; they turned to the larger merchant firms of Harbour Grace, Carbonear, and St John's for credit. St John's firms had the most resources, and they slowly consolidated their control over the industry by processing the seals brought by vessels from the many smaller outports of the northeast coast that did not deal with Harbour Grace and Carbonear firms.[7] The seal hunt continued to be vital to the economic survival of the outports, but the gulf between fishers, masters, and merchants, and the gap between the outports and St John's, became even wider as the benefits of the hunt concentrated in the hands of the colony's largest merchant firms.

The economy of St John's was more diverse. While the post-1815 depression had hurt British merchants' trade in the town, many of the clerks and agents they had sent out found their own local business opportunities. One such clerk was Charles Fox Bennett, who had come to St John's in 1808. Bennett established his own trading firm in partnership with his brother Thomas in the 1820s. While the Bennetts traded fish for European imports, they did not invest in the seal hunt or in ships. Instead, the Bennetts opted for brewing, distilling, and saw milling, industries that took advantage of the port's growing local consumer demand. The growth of the judiciary and executive, as well as the continued presence of the military, meant that there were many government employees and functionaries ready to spend their cash salaries on the goods and services their comfortable lifestyles demanded. Military officers and Supreme Court judges alike had to have suitable homes and domestic servants. They required locally prepared foodstuffs and the services of artisans to fix their silver watches and mend their fine boots. The port's elite required teachers for their children, surgeons to nurse them, lawyers to write their wills and fight their legal battles, and ministers and priests to assuage their guilt and assure them of their righteousness. Although tailors, bakers, carpenters, butchers, and shoemakers had also suffered insolvency and bankruptcy in the wake of 1815, their trades survived, as did the urban professions of a growing middle class.[8]

People who worked in the fishery continued to be the largest proportion of the St John's population. A few immigrants continued to arrive throughout the 1820s. These tended to be the poorest of the Irish who could only afford passage on the ships that supplied the fish trade, not passage to more attractive destinations in the Canadas or the United States. Many of these probably hoped to continue on their way to other parts of North America but often abandoned their passage when their vessel called at St John's. Such was the case of the thirty-two passengers of the brig *James* in 1827. Typhus aboard ship forced them off in St John's, where they sought the help of the Irish-born Roman Catholic Bishop Michael Fleming as they tried to find work. More ill passengers left the overcrowded *Freedom*, having travelled from Waterford without sufficient supplies, sleeping on top of its cargo of salt for the fishery during the voyage. Many of the passengers had dysentery, but this did not stop the labouring people of the port from taking them into their homes. The illnesses quickly spread throughout the town and into nearby Quidi Vidi and Logy Bay. District surgeons investigated the problem and assured authorities that 'respectable' people need not fear; cases of illness 'were generally confined to the hovels of the poor,' and typhus usually afflicted only those who had poor diets, poor access to clean water, and were usually fatigued, that is, the St John's 'lower classes.' William Carson rightly complained later in the summer that it was shocking that the authorities had taken little action to help the poor.[9]

Although they lived in appalling conditions, fishing people and immigrants in St John's and its vicinity could find work as unskilled labourers or tradespeople in the construction of the many government buildings and churches that proceeded through the 1820s. Building contractors and real estate developers took advantage of the general desperation for employment to pay low wages, prompting the development of unions among construction workers as early as the last years of the eighteenth century. In 1799 and 1800, journeymen carpenters employed in building an Anglican church and in constructing a house for Dr John Macurdy, a St John's landlord, had united to strike for better wages. At that time English law did not allow workers to form combinations to improve their working conditions; the Supreme Court ordered the arrest of these carpenters and declared their unions illegal. When out of work, many carpenters and labourers worked in the fishery, leading colonial officials to have a low opinion of their skills, while skilled artisans left the colony to search for better prospects elsewhere.[10]

Many tradespeople plied their skills in areas linked to the fishing industry and shipping. Sailmakers, ships' carpenters, and especially coopers were important to the local economy. Most goods carried aboard ships in the nineteenth century were packed in barrels, including cod and seal oils, two of the colony's most important exports. It is not surprising, then, that a cooper, Laurence Barron, led skilled artisans from many trades into an alternate form of organization that would not run afoul of the law. Barron formed a Mechanics' Society in 1827. In addition to Barron, the society's executive included a shoemaker, two tailors, a baker, and a bookkeeper. Unable to improve their lot legally by bargaining for better wages, the mechanics used their members' dues to assist each other in times of sickness and death. The Mechanics' Society emphasized the virtue of self-improvement; by 1846 it had established a reading room where its members could find books, newspapers, and other journals, as well as meet to discuss and debate the issues of the day.[11]

Although commercial agriculture was very limited, the demand created by St John's farming meant that money might be made even in selling small quantities of high-priced fresh produce, dairy products, eggs, and meat. Irish immigrants to the city, many of whom had trades or had experience as farm labour were not content to live simply as labourers or fishers; the Irish constituted a disproportionate number of those who tried to take up farming in the outlying parts of the town. In the area near St John's, some successful commercial farms supplied some fresh meat, milk, poultry, eggs, and vegetables to the town. Farming remained limited even close to the market of the capital. Many of the most successful farms were owned by government officials, military officers, and merchants who had the money to improve the small amounts of good land that could be found at the edges of St John's. Their farms never came close to being able to supply the demand for food in the town let alone the colony. From the first decade of the nineteenth century, much of the livestock raised by local farmers had actually been imported from Prince Edward Island or the neighbouring British North American colonies by butchers and merchants to be fattened, milked, and finally slaughtered. The residents of St John's consumed pork products, butter, oats, and even potatoes imported from the same neighbours, even drawing on the supplies of Cape Breton and eastern Nova Scotia, which, although not well endowed agriculturally, had much better resources than most of Newfoundland.[12]

Without a vibrant local agricultural economy, few fishing people could find local substitutes for merchant imports and continued to remain dependent on merchant credit. Ambitious local political reformers used the potential discontent of a people suffering through tight credit for their own ends. Rather than build a political movement based on confronting the fundamental problem of the competing needs of producers and merchants in fisheries that had proved to be Newfoundland's only good resource base, reformers misdirected popular frustration against merchants' supposed opposition to economic diversification through agricultural development and merchants' alleged wish to undermine fishers' rights in the wage and lien system. Reformers claimed merchants could do this because of their inordinate influence over a colonial government that did not represent the people of the colony.[13]

Governor Cochrane found that it was expensive to support agricultural development, build roads, relieve the poor, and fund the judiciary. As early as 1825 the governor had been exploring some form of municipal government for St John's and in 1828 proposed an *ad valorem* duty to raise the revenue required by the expense of government. St John's merchants objected to the new tax on imports, which would have to be passed on to fishing families. Such families would likely demand a higher price for their fish or they would starve. Merchants feared that such higher prices would make them less competitive in European markets. The local press also complained about the appearance of taxation without representation. The governor's proposal, and subsequent debate in the press, fuelled the reform movement. The Reformers, led by William Carson and Patrick Morris, revived the anti-naval rhetoric of their indignation over the whippings of Butler and Lundrigan. A number of St John's merchants, including the leaders of its Chamber of Commerce, began to support the Reformers' demands for representative institutions.[14] Merchants such as Thomas Brooking, William Thomas, and Newman Hoyles supported the demand because they objected to having their property taxed without representative institutions. Reformers such as Carson and Morris worried as much about gaining control over access to government patronage. Carson, the surgeon and aspiring gentryman, and Morris, the petty trader, were part of a new St John's bourgeoisie of small merchants, doctors, lawyers, and other urban professionals who had done well by the wars but had never acquired the status in colonial administrators' eyes of the agents and merchants of the British firms and those with military connections. In the absence of local political government over which they could exercise some control, the Reformers found that they had no way to force government to reward them with the perks of political office to which they felt entitled.

Most of the residents of Newfoundland and Labrador cared little about the desires of an elite few in St John's and larger towns such as Harbour Grace and Carbonear. The political patronage of Reformers would not improve fish prices, make credit more readily available, or feed their families. There were plenty of local grievances the Reformers could use to build popular support. The Butler and Lundrigan affair was one; another was the need to secure local control over the funds generated by the leasing of property in St John's. The Reformers needed something more, however, if they were to really fire public support and gain the cooperation of the British Colonial Office and the imperial government, which alone could grant representative government.[15]

The Reformers found a perfect cause in the ongoing problem of public relief. Carson argued that there would be no relief problem in Newfoundland if the government only managed its economic policy better. He repeated constantly that agriculture was undeveloped because of mercantile influence on an oligarchic colonial administration, not because of the ecological conditions of the colony. Only a government elected in the colony, Carson argued, would govern in the local interest by developing systematic agricultural colonization of the interior, partially by a road-building scheme. Carson and Morris's rhetoric began to appeal to the Colonial Office. The British government paid for public relief, argued the Reformers, but a colonial legislature might bear this burden. A representative government would finally develop properly the colony's resources, and poverty would disappear. In making this argument, the Reformers were taking advantage of the growing popularity of imperial reformers who wanted to lessen the imperial government's financial commitments by granting self-government to the colonies, including the responsibility for local taxation and expenditure. The Newfoundland Reformers were also echoing the opinions of reformers in the neighbouring British North American colonies that colonial governments were better able to manage local development than officials appointed by the imperial government.[16]

Governor Cochrane supported imperial reform and had hoped that his agricultural development policies would prepare the way for representative government. In 1831, Cochrane's government allowed leases at the low rate of nine pence per acre on land in the vicinity of St John's. By doing so, Cochrane was asking the Reformers to put their money where their mouths were. If a trader such as Morris was really serious about Newfoundland's agricultural potential, let him lease an estate, hire labourers and rent to tenants, farm the land profitably, and contribute to the maintenance of the colony through the small amount of rent the government asked for. The Reformers would not take Cochrane's challenge; instead they complained that they could not earn enough from their farms to pay even the pittance of nine pence per acre. Cochrane took the Reformers' whining as evidence that Newfoundland would never have a landed gentry, and in his view without a gentry, there was little social basis for the establishment of a legislature. The governor felt that he must encourage agriculture but that there was no reason to establish representative government any time soon. Carson and Morris felt that Cochrane's opposition to representative government was narrow-minded; the governor could not contemplate allowing Newfoundland colonists, such as themselves, to take their proper place in the empire. No matter how difficult the problems to be overcome, it was the right of every British subject, at least if they were white, to make the attempt themselves.[17]

Some Reformers had tried to formulate a colonial development strategy with fisheries as its centrepiece. An 1824 investigation by the Colonial Office into the economic state of Newfoundland heard local complaints about the manner in which the Americans and French used subsidies, called bounties, to encourage the recovery and growth of the fisheries on the Grand Banks. Patrick Morris suggested that similar imperial assistance to the Newfoundland fishing industry would help relieve economic distress. Anxious to minimize colonial expenditures and conscious of the declining importance of the fishery in an empire now dominated by Britain as the 'workshop of the world,'

British officials would not agree to bounties for the fishery. Reformers found even more frustrating the British government's refusal to give Newfoundland fishing vessels concurrent fishing rights to those of the French on the French Shore. The imperial government would not offend such an important trading partner as France for the sake of one small colony. The imperial government's position made Morris even more determined to support representative government and entrenched his support for local agricultural development. An elected colonial government, he thought, would be more amenable to the need to assist local industries. Without British subsidies fishers would have to accept lower fish prices to compete with the French and American products, and the only way that Newfoundlanders could make up the lost income would be by expanding supplementary farming.[18]

The misery of the fishery had begun to tell on the side of the Reformers. The winter of 1831–2 had been unusually severe and long, forcing the government again to issue seed potatoes to avert famine. In Conception Bay, crowds looted merchant stores for bread and other foodstuffs. Local men hoped that the spring seal hunt would provide some money, but local merchants hoped to make up for the recent string of poor fisheries from the hunt as well. These merchants gave credit to the planters who captained the sealing schooners. These planters, in turn, advanced sealers berths on their ships and credit against their future wages, determined by a share of the total catch, at the end of the hunt. Sealers were not paid for their work in cash but kept accounts with their planters' merchants for needed equipment, which they acquired on credit. Such accounts were open to truck practices by merchants and planters. Truck had been a mutual, though unequal, paternalistic accommodation between sealers, merchants, and planter-dealers. Fishers constantly required credit to purchase equipment, provisions, and other supplies, and to hire occasional labour for their household enterprises, but faced frequent, cyclical depressions in the industry due to wars and variations in market demand and supply. Merchants extended credit to allow fishing people to survive the disruptions of the market and continue to supply fish for their international trade. In return, merchants manipulated prices of goods they sold residents to offset losses in the fish trade. Simply put, fish producers and merchants needed each other. Fishing people might use truck to preserve their households' independence from direct service to another master, especially as merchants provided winter supplies, but it was hard to escape debt.[19]

Persistent poor conditions in the fishery meant that merchants in the Newfoundland trade constantly risked overextending credit to fishing families for which they could only take fish in payment even if the market for fish proved poor. This was particularly a problem for West Country and Jersey houses that might be investing in other areas of the transatlantic trade, that were far removed from the day-to-day administration of the fishery in Newfoundland, and that did not have alternate local sources of revenue, such as renting premises, that kept the more modest merchant houses of St John's afloat during bad years. Such was the case for the Bristol and Harbour Grace firm of H.W. Danson, which ended in bankruptcy in 1831. Danson's business failed in May before he had settled accounts with the sealers who had worked for him or his dealers that spring. The sealers had to forcibly seize casks of seal oil to compel the trustees of Danson's estate to pay their wages but learned in the process that truck could not guarantee that merchants would survive economic vicissitudes and hence that credit with an insolvent merchant did not count for much.

The next year, the sealers determined to get rid of truck. They met at Saddle Hill, which they renamed 'Liberty Hill,' in January, and agreed only to go sealing for masters who paid in cash. While Carbonear merchants quickly came to terms with the sealers, the Harbour Grace firm of Thomas Ridley did not. As a result, some of the sealers attacked a ship belonging to the firm. The authorities tried to intervene, but the sealers, led by people from Carbonear, continued to use violence to intimidate planters and merchants who would not meet their demands. Merchants yielded in March, and the seal hunt began.[20]

The sealers had been well organized and united, demonstrating to the colonial administration that fishing people, when organized collectively, constituted a powerful political force. Reformers began to pitch for representative government as a pro-fisherman program, promising it would break the merchants' hold on government. A colonial legislature would manage the full development of colonial resources to guarantee prosperity. Thomas Ridley, joined by Carbonear merchant Robert Pack, doubtless trying to improve his image among the angry sealers, jumped on the reform bandwagon. Under increased pressure from the Reformers, and with the dominant British liberal sentiment in the House of Commons favouring colonial representative institutions, the Colonial Office instructed Cochrane in 1832 to create a legislature. This legislature was bicameral, consisting of an elected lower house and an appointed council of seven with legislative and executive powers. The governor retained the right to adjourn, prorogue, and dissolve the legislature and did not have to be guided by the wishes of the House of Assembly.[21]

Newfoundland had the broadest franchise of the empire, universal manhood suffrage, but the governor was not responsible to an elected assembly. The House of Assembly largely controlled the manner in which government could raise revenue, but it did not control spending, especially the hiring or the payment of salaries, particularly those of the executive councillors. Gradually becoming known as Liberals, the Reformers continued to fight for Assembly control over spending.

Many of the smaller merchants and professionals of the old reform movement such as Morris were Irish Roman Catholics. They also wanted constitutional change to ensure that members of their denomination received a fair share of government patronage. Opposition coalesced around mercantile and Protestant hostility in a loose political group known as the Conservatives. Cochrane preferred to appoint Anglicans from the mercantile elite of St John's to most important government positions, believing they were the most respectable people available. The Conservatives defended their hold on government patronage, but they also fought against Liberal attempts to secure additional revenue for colonial development through taxation of the fishery.[22]

The governor knew that British financial support for the government of Newfoundland was about to end. The Assembly would have to find a way to pay for the expansion of government services in areas such as administration of justice, fisheries regulations, and public relief, but the governor wished to retain his authority over appointing most government officials. The colonial government, through the legislature, was now responsible for paying for the Supreme Court, a costly burden that included paying for a clerk and sheriff for each of the circuit courts. The cost of the judiciary was high, but even then the imperial government retained most of the authority and means of enforcement for fisheries law, which mattered most to the colonial economy. In 1834, the legislature had failed to convince the British government to enforce treaty restrictions on French and American vessels involved in smuggling. The colonial government enacted fisheries regulations in 1836 that penalized the Americans and French for fishing for bait or cutting timber for the fishery outside treaty areas and punished any Newfoundlander for trading bait or timber with them. The British government disallowed the law, arguing that only it had the right to make laws within the empire that might affect treaties with foreign powers.[23]

Patrick Morris led the Assembly in this unsuccessful engagement with British authorities. He fought on, but amid less important, if more venal and sensational, patronage issues. Other Irish Roman Catholic Reformers, particularly Morris's nephew John Kent, played the sectarian card in the attempt to secure the benefits of office. A member of St John's aspiring shopkeeper bourgeoisie, Kent had become a successful auctioneer and commission agent in the early 1830s. Ambitious, Kent courted Johanna Fleming, the sister of the Roman Catholic Bishop Michael Fleming, and embarked on a political career during the election of the first House of Assembly in 1832. Kent's attack on the Executive Council's control of patronage while seeking a nomination for a seat in St John's earned the enmity of Henry Winton, the Conservative editor of the *Public Ledger*, a St John's newspaper. Kent responded by suggesting that Winton's politics were nothing more than bigoted opposition to Roman Catholics' sharing political power. Winton, in turn, demanded that the bishop declare his political neutrality.

Bishop Fleming would not stand for Winton's suggestion that he had no right to a public political opinion and openly voiced his support for Kent, William Carson, and the Protestant merchant William Thomas, who appeared to sympathize with the Reformers. The bishop openly led a campaign for the Reformers. As a result, Kent and Thomas won their seats, but Carson's own squabbles with Edward Wix, the Anglican archdeacon, cost him victory. The long-term political significance of the election was that 'the cross of Christ was dragged into St John's politics.'[24] Important matters were to come before the electorate of Newfoundland and Labrador, but within the blood sport of narrow sectarianism.

Reformers such as Carson found that the support of the Roman Catholic bishop was indispensable to their election and fight for control over patronage. Carson won a by-election to the Assembly in 1833 with Fleming's support and sectarian rioting on his behalf. Bishop Fleming used Reform support to help bully opposition within his church, such as that from the liberal Irish Roman Catholic merchant Timothy Hogan, or the carpenter Patrick Kough, who opposed the autocratic Fleming. Hogan and Kough were from Wexford, tried to get along with the government, and supported the non-sectarian Benevolent Irish Society (formed in 1806) and its non-denominational Orphan Asylum School (formed in 1827). Hogan opposed Fleming's efforts to exert episcopal control over church finances, establish denominational education within the Asylum School, and enmesh the St John's church in supporting the liberal nationalism of the followers of the Irish Reformer Daniel O'Connell, who began to advocate for the repeal of the union between Ireland and Britain. While Fleming justified his policies as an effort to unite the local church under papal control, the bishop campaigned for control over government patronage by a newer Waterford bourgeoisie, composed of people such as Morris, John Kent, and Laurence O'Brien. By promoting Munster interests along with his lieutenant Father Edward Troy, Fleming promoted sectarian strife with the older Leinster interests and further associated moderate local reform without representative government with subservience to British colonialism.

Governor Cochrane thought Fleming was an opportunistic demagogue who would commit almost any outrage to mobilize 'the lower orders' to fight for his political candidates. Fleming, deeply conservative, may ironically have seen himself as an Irish Reformer in the tradition of O'Connell, fighting to liberate Roman Catholic settlers from a colonial state that denied their clerics the right to perform marriages, had insisted on public oaths for office that Catholics could not take, refused public support for their schools, and discriminated against Roman Catholics in appointments to leading political offices such as the Executive Council.[25]

The Irish were not homogeneous; a huge gulf separated the Irish members of the St John's bourgeoisie and the vast majority of the Irish who worked in the town and in the fishery generally. Fleming may have been an O'Connellite, but the movement had a specific class agenda. In Ireland, O'Connellite priests had fought for the rights of the local Catholic bourgeoisie against the Protestant Ascendancy by deflecting the discontent of their fellow Roman Catholic labourers and tenants against Protestantism. In Newfoundland, Irish Catholic employers treated their employees no better than did Protestant ones, but priests channelled the discontent of the poor away from the economic circumstances that produced their poverty and toward official Protestantism and British rule. Fleming and his supporters used sectarianism to convince the 'lower orders,' as someone like Kent might have termed fishers and workers, that their interests were the same. Significantly, the Liberal–priest alliance did not rely on grounds other than that they were all Irish Roman Catholics together. They relied on the old Reform attacks on the supposed neglect of local colonial development by governors who promoted only the narrow interests of fish merchants. The dominance of Anglicans on the Executive Council, in turn, reinforced the association of mercantile privileges with those of the established church. The Liberal alliance with Fleming could be portrayed at once as a just, if sectarian, battle against the monopoly of privilege and as a fight for fishermen's rights.[26]

Simmering discontent about the wage and lien system provided the Liberals with strong ammunition. A new Fisheries Act, which had accompanied the Judicature Act of 1824, recognized and expanded upon fishing servants' wage liens and continued to recognize the liens of current suppliers. The Colonial Office wanted the new colonial government to amend the law as seemed appropriate. In 1829, Cochrane had asked magistrates throughout the colony to convene public meetings of planters and merchants to review the wage and lien system. Few people suggested at these meetings that the system was as much a problem as was the overall depressed condition of the fish trade. Planters and merchants did complain that the law gave servants too many privileges and felt that employers in the trade should be able to renegotiate wages if fish prices proved lower than expected, or if catches were bad due to bad weather or environmental perturbations that may have disrupted fish populations in local areas. Merchants further felt that their liens for current supply should be given priority over those of servants for wages. The Supreme Court under Chief Justice R.A. Tucker, supported by Attorney General James Simms, agreed, but recommended that the entire wage and lien system be abolished, including current supply. The Liberals had fought with Tucker (who resigned in the course of the dispute), in his role as president of the Executive Council, over money bills in 1833. In his place, the Colonial Office appointed the Upper Canadian Henry John Boulton, fresh from disgrace and accusations of corruption as attorney general of Upper Canada. A Conservative, Boulton detested the Upper Canadian reformer William Lyon Mackenzie.

As president of the Executive Council, Boulton had no intention of making any concessions to the Liberals in the House of Assembly. At the same time, as chief justice of the Supreme Court, Boulton was determined to follow Tucker in seeing the wage and lien system ended. The chief justice felt that the wage and lien system contradicted English civil law. Usually, he argued, the first creditor, not the last (as in the case of current suppliers in the fishery), had the most secure lien against an insolvent's estate. In a series of court cases in 1835, Boulton ruled that merchants were not liable to pay all of an insolvent planter's servants' wages if the planter had not caught enough fish to pay them, and they had no liability for contracts between masters and servants if they were not parties in the agreement. As president of the Executive Council, Boulton declared that it would never assent to another law re-establishing the system. At a time when colonial politicians had begun seriously debating the proper management of the colony's critical marine resources, public debate degenerated into much sound and fury about laws that had, at best, merely aggravated the dominant trend in the fishery for planters to retreat from the hiring of servants in the first place.[27]

Boulton's further reforms in jury selection, the incorporation of a law society, and the regulation of barristers and attorneys all provided further ammunition for Liberal attacks on the supposed arbitrariness of his role as both chief justice and Council president. There were fears among many in St John's that Boulton's changes in the selection process for juries would make it easier for lawyers to challenge the appointment of Irish jurors. The issue was important because most of the people imprisoned by trial were Irish. Bishop Fleming had taken action in a number of cases where miscarriages of justice either were in process or had already taken place. In one case, Fleming prevented the execution of a wrongfully convicted Roman Catholic from the Labrador coast named Hackett. In another case, the bishop catalogued a long series of incorrect procedures in court that led to the execution of a Harbour Grace labourer, Peter Downey. Finally, Fleming's assistant Father Troy, convinced of her innocence, had tried unsuccessfully to save Catherine Snow from hanging for the murder of her husband, Conception Bay planter John Snow. Fleming, Troy, and the Liberal press labelled Boulton 'a bigot and partisan,' and popular outrage greeted the fate of Downey and Snow. In both cases the public injury of apparent miscarriages of justice was exacerbated by the insult and indignity of the public display of the executed bodies. At Harbour Grace, anonymous threats against a local magistrate led to the quick burial of Downey. In Port de Grave, the local priest led a crowd to seize the body from the district surgeon for a public burial.[28]

The Liberals capitalized on the outrage when Patrick Morris sponsored a bill in the Assembly that would have supposedly aided Roman Catholic–dominated fishing servants to secure payment of their wages. Boulton used his position as Council president to throw out the bill, claiming he was simply continuing legal changes instigated by his predecessors in the general application of English law to Newfoundland. Fleming accused Boulton of undercutting the rights of poor fishing servants in the interest of the colony's fish merchants. Carson, Morris, Kent, and John Valentine Nugent led a mass, open-air meeting of protest against the chief justice early in the summer of 1835. This meeting produced a petition to the British government accusing Boulton of a 'rancorous hostility to the interests of the poor.' Throughout 1835, Robert Parsons, editor of the *Patriot*, a Liberal newspaper, repeated one message on Boulton's decisions about the wage and lien system: '*Boulton's law* [has] made us a pauper population ... and put the just dues of the Fisherman and the Shoreman into the pockets of the Merchant!'[29]

Boulton, whose wife Eliza was a Roman Catholic and who got on well with the Scottish clerics who dominated the church in Upper Canada, was unprepared for Fleming's hostility. When Boulton charged Parsons with contempt, the new governor, Prescott, had the garrison prepare to take to the streets to keep the peace. Fleming ruthlessly attacked any who sided with Boulton. The editorials of the bishop's nemesis, Henry Winton, earned him such popular enmity that a crowd accosted him, mutilating his ears, on a trip between Carbonear and Harbour Grace. Most were certain that Winton suffered at the hands of the Roman Catholic fishing people he had first criticized during the sealers' protests of 1830–2 and continued to offend by his criticism of Fleming and defence of Boulton. Robert Parsons's editorial pen always insinuated that Boulton was the puppet of the colony's fish merchants, and Reformers suggested that the only remedy would be a government more responsible to the people of the colony. Boulton responded that the Liberals cared nothing for fishing servants' wage liens but knew a good political rallying cry when they heard it. By 1837, Boulton claimed that he was a bulwark against an unholy political alliance between the Liberals and an insubordinate Roman Catholic Church, which willingly used violence to attain their goals. Boulton successfully defended his decision on the wage and lien system before the Privy Council at London in 1838. However, the Colonial Office demanded his resignation because of Boulton's reputation as a bigot and decided that future chief justices would no longer preside over the Executive Council.[30]

The political excesses of sectarianism proved too much for Parsons, who had little interest in seeing a political oligarchy rule Newfoundland from the bishop's palace any more than from the governor's office. Parsons broke with Fleming's faction in 1849, when the bishop opposed the candidacy of James Douglas, a Liberal Presbyterian merchant, in a St John's by-election. Parsons supported Douglas and newer Irish Roman Catholic politicians like Ambrose Shea, who saw themselves as true Newfoundland natives, not Irish-born foreigners. The Newfoundland Natives' Society had recently emerged to champion the careers of the native-born over the Irish and English born.

Shea, from a merchant family that had come to Newfoundland in the early 1780s, did not have the same sense of grievance against the British as did the newer bourgeois families of St John's such as the Kents and the Morrises. He welcomed the formation of the Newfoundland Natives' Society, supported it as editor of a local newspaper, the *Newfoundlander*, and became its president in 1846. The Irish Catholic faction of the Liberals, which dominated the Assembly, cut off Parsons's patronage as the Assembly printer for supporting the natives and led him back to the Liberal fold. Nonetheless, afraid of lower-class radicalism, Parsons would not support Liberals like Morris, who continued to court the political support of fishers by unsuccessful efforts to restore the wage and lien system in law.[31]

By 1841 sectarian violence forced the British parliament to appoint a Select Committee to review affairs in Newfoundland. The committee interviewed Cochrane, delegates from the Assembly, and various opponents of Fleming, and heard a number of merchants' concerns that Conception Bay sealers continued to press for better pay through collective action. The franchise, these merchants argued, did not belong in the hands of such people. All of the evidence left the British government with no doubt that the social and political fractures of the colony ran deep. Uninterested in resuming responsibility for Newfoundland, the Colonial Office recommended that electoral influence with the colonial government be lessened by amalgamating the House of Assembly with the appointed Legislative Council. Further, the Colonial Office recommended a more conciliatory governor for Newfoundland. This governor could use his powers of appointment to ensure that the more cooperative elements within the Liberal movement could be promoted within the amalgamated legislature.[32]

The British government appointed a new governor, Sir John Harvey, the first to have previous experience in colonial administration, who arrived in the fall of 1841. Harvey wanted to mollify the Liberals by friendly overtures to Fleming, appeasing Carson and Morris with a Newfoundland Agricultural Society and patronizing them with appointments to the Executive Council. The prickly Carson passed away in 1843, but Morris became a government supporter. The governor further assuaged Fleming by using the 1843 Education Act to provide public support for Roman Catholic schools, such as those being established by the Sisters of Mercy, an Irish teaching order. Providing public support for denominational education was Harvey's attempt to subordinate the class divisions between fishers and merchants and dampen the sectarian flames that had been fanned by Irish Roman

Catholic members of the St John's bourgeoisie. Harvey hoped to in-
still a unifying sense of British nativism in Newfoundlanders by rallying people from all classes and creeds behind the British flag in a
culture of improvement. Government would inspire this culture of
improvement by adopting much of the development platform of the
old Reformers.[33]

The need for economic development drove Harvey's support for
the culture of improvement. Representative government had done
nothing to relieve persistent low prices in the fishery and merchants'
restriction of credit, all aggravated by unusually long, severe winters
and poor potato crops. Regular outbursts of store breaking and other
forms of collective protest by hungry and starving fishing people in
the 1830s drove prominent Liberal supporters such as Robert Pack to
demand able-bodied relief through road construction beyond the vicinity of St John's. Harvey hoped that the Newfoundland Agricultural
Society would foster improved living standards through agricultural
diversification. Although he had made agricultural improvement a
plank in his old Reform platform, Morris, as an executive councillor
in the amalgamated assembly, and enjoying Harvey's support, fought
unsuccessfully for greater imperial assistance in regulating the fisheries and subsidizing the development of a bank fishery to compete
with the Americans and French.[34]

Morris encouraged the colony to develop the fishing industry
without the assistance of the empire. In 1845 the Newfoundland government had established a token bounty of 30 shillings per ton for
three years to encourage colonial participation in the bank fishery.
At the same time, the colonial government passed a law prohibiting
the sail of bait to foreigners by Newfoundlanders, despite grumbling
in London. Repeatedly, through the early 1850s, Morris led colonial
demands for British assistance in the development of the fishing industry, including the protection of fish resources from exploitation by
other nations, but to little avail. Without British support, especially
for the enforcement of regulations at sea, the colonial government had
little real effect. The government felt that it had no option but to promote interior economic development through agriculture. The prospects were daunting. Beginning in 1845, disastrous blights plagued
the Newfoundland potato crop. Around the island, people could not
grow enough potatoes to feed themselves throughout the winter and
often resorted to eating their small stocks of seed potatoes. To make
matters worse, fire swept though St John's during the winter of 1846–
7, followed by disastrous gales around the island.[35]

Rather than assist the colony, the Colonial Office in 1847 revived the bicameral legislature, and Governor Harvey requested a transfer to Nova Scotia. The new governor, Sir Gaspard LeMarchant, was inexperienced as a colonial administrator. Suspicious of Roman Catholicism and a supporter of the establishment of the Church of England as a bulwark of political order and social stability, LeMarchant aggravated sectarianism by supporting the recently appointed Anglican Bishop Edward Feild's Tractarian and High Church ideals. Feild had fought against the evangelical piety popular among Anglican fishing people in places such as Harbour Buffett in Placentia Bay. These people cooperated with their Methodist neighbours through the Newfoundland School Society and objected to Feild's desire to centralize control over the Anglican Church and to harness their funds to pay for it.

Throughout the nineteenth century, Wesleyan Methodism became more popular because of the accessibility of its itinerant preachers, its enthusiastic revivalism, and its continued emphasis on the common experience of faith. The Church of England opposed Methodism, in the long run failing by 1833 in its bid to have Methodist clergy excluded from the right to solemnize marriages in Newfoundland. From a modest presence in St John's, Conception Bay, and Trinity Bay, the Methodist Church had spread to Bonavista Bay, the Burin Peninsula, and Notre Dame Bay. A district of the British Wesleyan Conference in 1815, the Newfoundland church became part of the Wesleyan Methodist Conference of eastern Canada in 1855 and had been attempting expansion into Labrador. An opponent of public support for Roman Catholic schools, Feild attacked Wesleyan Methodism, despising its 'low' revivalism, and attacked Methodists' rights to denominational education and the solemnization of marriages and baptisms. In doing so, Feild alienated Presbyterians and Congregationalists, whom he perceived as threats to the loyalty of his church's membership.[36]

By supporting Feild, LeMarchant had made his government a target for discontent from dissenting Protestants as well as Roman Catholics. Furthermore, the governor, like the Colonial Office, felt that merchants should relieve the poor with more credit and did little to provide public relief. LeMarchant felt that interior agricultural improvement would succeed if poor Newfoundlanders would desist in their moral failings and laziness, and he actually cut relief in 1848. By 1849 two things were evident: the governor's agricultural policies had failed, and there was a lot of public resentment about his administration's crude misunderstandings about the nature of the relief problem.[37]

While much popular anger was aimed at LeMarchant, the social relationships of fishing communities meant that it would not be directed purposefully against the existing social order. Although the government had passed the Chattels Real Act in 1834, following earlier Supreme Court decisions in recognizing the right of women to inherit the property of fishing households, this did not diminish the overall nature of patriarchy in Newfoundland. The Butler and Lundrigan affair forcefully reminded people in the outports that the legal responsibilities of citizenship were supposed to be a male affair, no matter how much that might be challenged by the importance of women in fishing society. Planters could use a variety of patriarchal, non-economic disciplinary measures, often harsh and extralegal, to regulate the labour of women and children in their families for household production. The burden of making salt fish fell on women's and children's shoulders. If planters had to hire labour to make salt fish, they usually paid women lower wages than men, even if both did the same work. The almost life-and-death struggle for many families to earn their livelihoods might pit fishers against each other. Instances were reported of women fighting each other over topsoil, and members of neighbouring families sometimes came close to killing each other when their livestock got into each other's vegetable and potato gardens.[38]

Patriarchy was a potent form of social relationship that cut across class divisions by defining paternalistic ideology within the colony. Paternalism was particularly important in defining the credit relationships between fish merchants and their clients. Many would doubtless have agreed with a Harbour Grace newspaper correspondent in 1847 who described fishermen as being worse off than the 'slaves and serfs of Russia' because of merchants' truck practices. Yet others suggested that truck insulated fishing people from the ups and downs of international fish markets. A merchant who provided credit in good years and bad thus acted as 'a father towards his planters.'

Because they did not enjoy the same power as merchants, fishers negotiated their relationships with their creditors from below. Merchants controlled prices to increase the likelihood of their profit but could not do so with impunity. Fishing people used many practices to negotiate the terms upon which they received credit: some went to court and won decisions against merchants whom they felt had unfairly manipulated accounts; others used extralegal threats and violence by assaulting merchants, taking fish to competitors, or throwing agents or bailiffs into the harbour over disputes about court proceedings instigated by merchants.[39] At heart, most fishers believed that they had a right to be treated fairly by merchants in order to earn enough to keep their households and families competent. They could be very loyal to a merchant who lived up to their expectations and might defend one threatened by forces from outside their community. Such was the case in 1848, when fishers in Brigus, under the cover of darkness, stole the goods seized by the firm of Bowrings in St John's from their local, bankrupt merchant, Richard Leamon. The colonial government, apprehending further trouble, sent troops to the area. Authorities feared that local fishing people would become even angrier as the result of the seizure of their local merchant's assets by a St John's merchant. Leamon might have been a usurious merchant, but he was their supplier.[40]

Regional differentiation within the colony also tied fishing people to their merchants. A merchant from Brigus, Charles Cozens, continued to enjoy popular support among his neighbours despite suffering bankruptcy in 1834, nearly losing his seat in the House of Assembly, and deciding not to run in the next general election. Cozens started over again as a merchant, became a local magistrate and chairperson of the local relief commissioners for Brigus, and demanded better assistance by the government for the poor of his district. In time he became a local political broker whom the government in St John's continued to patronize with political offices.[41]

As control over the fishery continued to consolidate in St John's, the cleavage between town and outport grew. Outport resentment against St John's was becoming a staple of colonial politics, but the city had its own troubles, particularly for residents who were poor. The tiny 'hovels' of the labouring classes, as the local magistrates liked to refer to them, were inadequate shelters against the cold. Poorly constructed, and warmed and lit by open flames, these homes were constantly at risk of fire, and many were destroyed by the fire of 1846–7, to be replaced by relief sheds, which continued to house the impoverished for the next fourteen years. The poor clustered in neighbourhoods close to the harbour but could use dogs and sleds to travel outside the town to cut wood for their own use as fuel and to sell to the better-off residents of St John's.

Like most of the pre-industrial cities of North America, St John's had a lot of livestock. In addition to horses used in work and transportation, even the wealthiest homes might have one or two animals to provide meat, eggs, or fresh milk. Suburban farmers and the local authorities complained regularly about the dogs of the poor, suspecting that they harassed or killed livestock, but poor people needed the dogs to help in cutting and selling wood – their only way of supporting themselves in winter, since able-bodied poor relief in road building and other public works stopped with the onset of cold weather. Private charities, usually affiliated with a church, and often organized and led by bourgeois women, sought to forestall the social discontent and instability that might arise from poverty. One notable effort at poor relief was the St John's factory, begun in 1832 through the fundraising efforts of women and designed to teach women and children how to make cloth and nets. In addition to securing a small grant from the government, and raising money through donations, these women organized balls and theatrical performances whose proceeds went to the factory.[42]

By the 1830s notices routinely appeared in colonial newspapers about failed inshore fisheries in the longest-settled areas of Conception, Trinity, and Bonavista bays. Dramatic cyclical declines in Newfoundland salt cod exports, together with steady population increases throughout the nineteenth century, suggest that a basic ecological problem resulting from overexploitation of cod stocks underlay the poor catches. The fisheries supplied most of the work for Newfoundlanders, and the absolute number of people employed in the fisheries rose with overall population. Effort, in other words, rose constantly, but catch rates did not. Evidence continues to mount suggesting that nineteenth-century fishing people were periodically depleting discrete bay stocks or substocks of cod in inshore waters. Fishers in Trinity Bay, for example, witnessed signs of local cod stock depletion by the 1830s.

Declining fish catches led some firms, such as that of Slade and Kelson, at Trinity, to contemplate cutting winter credit to clients who failed to catch enough fish to trade against their accounts. Such restriction prompted the firm's manager, William Kelson, to fear violent reaction from fishers who might starve without their winter supplies. Kelson sympathized with popular protests among fishers against the many new types of fishing gear being deployed in waters around the island, particularly cod jiggers (fish-shaped lures attached to hand lines) and trawl lines (lengths of line, often called bultows, with hundreds of baited fish hooks that were anchored and buoyed in the water), and the more intensive use of cod seines (nets used by crews working in two boats to encircle and capture fish). He led protests which argued that these new gears would allow only the better-off few who could afford them to catch more of the increasingly sparse resource, leaving the mass of fishing society to poverty and possible starvation. Kelson's movement failed in 1849 when the Newfoundland government denied the need for conservation, accepted new gears as the prerogative of private capital, and blamed inshore fish scarcities on French and American over-fishing offshore.[43]

The cyclical recoveries in Newfoundland's total fish exports likely resulted from several factors that may have prevented awareness of ecological stress. While increased effort in the Labrador fishery probably masked the inshore failures, fishing people also began to build larger boats that could travel to newer, outer headland fishing grounds. Then, as exports recovered in the 1840s, the use of cod seines, trawl lines, and gill nets became more widespread than the older hook-and-line method of fishing.

The careers of Kelson and Cozens suggest that fishers sympathized with paternalistic merchants as much as they might despise the sectarian-tinged castigations of merchants by the older St John's Liberals. A new generation of Liberals appeared under the leadership of Phillip Francis Little, a Roman Catholic lawyer from Prince Edward Island. Little fought for responsible government but defined it as party government: the governor should be obliged to select the Executive Council, or cabinet, from whichever political party had the support of the most members of the elected House of Assembly. It was time, in Little's mind, for government policy to be inured against the vagaries of governors' comings and goings, and for patronage and policy to be controlled by those who had the support of the electorate. Although older Liberals had continued to use the issue of the wage lien to cultivate popular support, their efforts failed. Appeals to fishing servants further carried the sectarian taint of the Fleming era, and the Liberals under Little wanted to find a broader, more respectable basis of support.[44]

The question of public funding for schools provided an opportunity. The Education Act of 1845 was to expire in 1850. The act provided funding for separate Anglican and Roman Catholic schools, but not for Methodists and other smaller denominations. The Anglican bishop, Edward Feild, vehemently opposed the extension of funding to Methodists and wanted a new act to provide most of the funding for Protestant schools to a separate Church of England board. Feild had the support of Charles Fox Bennett, who had been a Conservative member of the Legislative and Executive Councils and was a determined opponent of responsible government.[45]

Little prevailed in building Methodist support for his party and for responsible government despite sympathy for Feild among some prominent Roman Catholic Liberals such as Ambrose Shea. The Roman Catholic bishop, John Thomas Mullock, openly supported Little's campaign for responsible government. While Mullock supported Irish nationalism and opposed Feild's efforts to entrench the authority of the Anglican Church, he was much more moderate than Fleming, whom Mullock had succeeded in 1850. Mullock also had a reputation as a stronger advocate of Newfoundland's economic development and as a Newfoundland nativist rather than a local Irish nationalist. Together, Little and Mullock portrayed the Liberal fight as a progressive, pro-development, and non-sectarian movement against the reactionary stance of Field, Bennett, and other opponents of responsible government such as the St John's Commercial Society, the organization that represented St John's merchants.[46]

Under Little, the Liberals won a majority in the House of Assembly in the general election of 1852. Throughout the campaign the Liberals cultivated an image of themselves as the friends of Wesleyan Methodism. Although many Methodists remained unconvinced that they would be best represented by a party that had such strong Roman Catholic support, enough supported the Liberals to help that party win. When the new House met, the Liberals made clear that they would be satisfied with nothing less than responsible government. While Newfoundland's new governor, Hamilton, sided with the anti–responsible government forces throughout 1853 and 1854, the tide had turned. Faced with constant pressure from the House of Assembly for assistance in the development of a bank fishery and in limiting the fisheries of Newfoundland's rivals, the British government was determined to extract itself even more from the politics of the colony. Since 1849 there had been rare unanimity between the House of Assembly and the Legislative Council in the belief that the British government must act to help Newfoundland face French and American competition in the fishery. The refusal by the British introduced a split between Liberals and Conservatives on this issue, as Charles Fox Bennett led a group that decided that Newfoundland should turn to economic diversification. Opposing Liberals, led by Ambrose Shea, hoped that the British might negotiate reductions in American bounties for fish during the talks that established reciprocity between the United States and British North America in 1854. While such reductions did not develop, Shea's group accepted the 1854 treaty in the hope that freer access to the American market would lead to better prices for Newfoundland fish.[47]

The British government wanted to be rid of the political demands coming from Newfoundland. With a general election looming, Governor Hamilton did his best to block responsible government by postponing the election. Bishop Mullock denounced the action, and Little travelled to London to condemn the governor's behaviour and to petition for his removal. In Newfoundland, some of the older Liberals tried to revive the old Irish Roman Catholic tactics of Fleming's time, but they were brought to heel by Mullock. The Conservatives tried to fight the Liberals by splitting off their Methodist supporters through fear of the old Irish Roman Catholic sectarianism. Core Methodist support held for the Liberals, and they again won a general election. In the new legislature, Little claimed that only the Liberals had the confidence of the people; the new administration must be constructed from its members. The Colonial Office instructed the new governor, Darling, to ask Little to form a government.

Throughout the election, the Liberals had resurrected the hoary wage lien issue to appeal to fishermen. The new Liberal government, in the fall of 1855, passed an act establishing fishing servants' preferential lien for their wages on fish received from planters by merchants. The lien did little for fishing people; just as had the previous 1824 Fisheries Act, the new law defined the wage lien in terms of planter insolvency.[48] By doing so, the law implicitly recognized that the real problem facing fishing people had little do with whether or not someone guaranteed to pay wages. The cost of hiring labour could not be justified within a fishing industry dominated by the trade of a low-value commodity in international markets and persistent problems with localized depletion of natural resources.

The Liberals had won the battle for responsible government in 1855 but, with their Conservative opponents, had unleashed potent sectarian and class forces. Despite their many appeals, the Liberals hammered home one consistent message to British officials: Newfoundland had great economic potential in its landward resources. These resources required only the guiding hand of a colonial government responsible to the people and not to selfish merchants. Once developed properly, Newfoundland would no longer depend on troubled fisheries alone, and there would be little need for public relief of the poor. The Liberals had promised much and now would have to try to deliver. Whatever was to come of such promises, the Liberals had shifted colonial state policy and much of the colony's political culture decisively from an awareness of the extent to which most people depended on the resources of the sea.

6

Responsible Government and Landward Industrialization, 1855–1895

Philip Francis Little, Newfoundland's first premier under responsible government, had to live up to twenty years of Reformers' and Liberals' promises. They had argued that a colonial government that was responsible directly to the people of the colony, not to the Colonial Office or the arbitrary whims of an individual officeholder, could diversify the economy and ease the old rancour of political life. Sadly, 'responsible' government would become the quixotic ideal of generations of politicians who were never able to come to grips with the material reality of people who lived by the sea. Beginning with the misguided attempt of early governments to foster an industrial economy such as that which was developing in Canada, Newfoundland administrations rarely addressed the fact that most people depended on marine resources.

Once Newfoundland politicians took control over the executive, their attention turned away from the fishery. Despite the fact that Newfoundland's life was international trade, Britain continued to control foreign relations, and so the colony was unable to negotiate directly with foreign countries. Worse, both the French and Americans had rights to parts of Newfoundland's coast and waters, secured by British treaties. These treaties prevented the Newfoundland legislature from developing the resources of the island's west coast and from regulating the fishery. The Liberals had hoped that free trade with the United States would increase American demand for fish, revive prices, and perhaps stimulate new fisheries, but the Reciprocity Treaty had not limited American fishing in Newfoundland waters, while the French retained an exclusive right to fish on the 'French Shore,' limiting its development by Newfoundlanders.

Angered by the growth of French fishing on the Shore and on the Grand Banks, Newfoundland officials expected the British government to insist on concurrent Newfoundland rights to the French Shore and to support its efforts to regulate the bait trade with French fishers. Motivated by a desire to avoid conflict with France, however, in 1857 the British government sided with the French, allowing Newfoundlanders only limited rights to fish on parts of the west coast and confirming much of France's claim to exclusive fishing rights. France could even expand its rights to fish in Labrador waters and on the south coast of Newfoundland.

A colonial delegation to London persuaded the British to back away from the 1857 convention, and British Colonial Secretary Henry Labouchere agreed that London would not thereafter enter into any international agreement which diminished Newfoundland's rights without the consent of its domestic legislature. But his 'Labouchere Dispatch,' hailed as the colony's Magna Carta, did little to assist Newfoundland with the practical problem of managing the fishery. Although the colonial government claimed the right to regulate all fisheries in local waters for conservation purposes, British authorities intimated that if such regulations bothered the French, Britain would become less vigilant in policing French treaty rights.[1]

Denominational politics further hampered the Liberal government. While Methodist support had been essential to their election, the Liberals' strength lay with their Roman Catholic constituents, and Bishop Mullock expected to be rewarded for supporting responsible government. Methodist alienation from the government grew when, in 1858, Little resigned to accept an appointment to the Supreme Court, and John Kent, the old sectarian warrior of the Fleming years, succeeded Little as premier. Kent represented a conservative, pro-clerical, and St John's Irish wing of the Liberals that was increasingly at odds with a more outport-oriented, pro-native, and occasionally anti-clerical progressive faction, and his leadership made it difficult for the Liberals to present themselves as a party of progress and development. Through 1858 the Conservative opposition demanded an end to French claims to an exclusive fishery on the French Shore, and James Tobin, a member of the Legislative Council and the colony's financial secretary, supported the opposition by insisting on a stringent enforcement of concurrent rights on the French Shore. The Liberals wanted the governor to suspend Tobin, and certainly he made the government look hesitant in its fisheries policy and the opposition vigorous by comparison.

In 1859, the British government announced that it would appoint a joint commission with the French to investigate possible solutions on the French Shore, but it failed to resolve the issue. Frustrated by British influence over its fisheries, and faced with poverty at home, the colonial government fell back on the old habit of trying to encourage more agricultural development, while the opposition demanded unsuccessfully that the government establish a fisheries board to manage fisheries in such a way as to supplement economic diversification.[2]

Under Kent, patronage rather than principle dominated policy. He courted the St John's electorate by able-bodied relief spending on local road construction, a policy that appealed to the large working-class population of Irish Catholic origin in the town. This antagonized Bishop Mullock, who had never been warm toward the old Liberal's style of Irish sectarianism and who had expected the government to encourage a broader program of agricultural improvement through road construction and railway development. Ambrose Shea, now speaker of the House of Assembly, favoured similar development policies. Continuing to lead the nativist wing of the Liberals, Shea appears to have led those Liberals who were tired of Kent's sectarian patronage. Early in 1859, Shea threatened to resign as speaker: he had expected to be consulted before Kent took up a position with the Anglo-French Commission investigating the fishery and may have hoped to take the position himself. Kent passed a resolution in the House begging Shea to stay on, but the Liberals were now divided. While spending money on relief in the St John's area might temporarily alleviate poverty, Mullock could not see how it would lead to lasting development and disapproved of the government's inattention to the outports. In 1860, Kent refused to honour a deal Mullock and Little had earlier negotiated with a New York firm to acquire a steamer to improve communications with the outports. The refusal was a personal affront to Mullock, who now believed the outports could expect nothing good from the Kent government, and in June, he publicly denounced the Liberal government, setting the stage for its collapse.[3]

The Conservatives wanted to build a new political alliance between Protestants and Roman Catholic advocates of development and favoured integrating fisheries management into a broader program of development. The Liberals, by contrast, appeared reluctant to fight the imperial government's disallowance of new colonial bait legislation to regulate the French fishery in 1860. Conservative leader Hugh

W. Hoyles, sensing Kent's weakness on the French Shore issue, pressured the government to establish conservation measures that would limit the French fishery. Conservative newspapers noted the oddity of the colonial government establishing a board to oversee agricultural development but not one for fisheries. Even Governor Sir Alexander Bannerman (who had come to Newfoundland in 1857) pointed out that the Newfoundland government needed to establish fisheries policy, and there were growing demands from fishers around the island for conservation regulations that would restrict the plethora of new fishing gears being deployed around the coast. However, although the Liberal government investigated the seal hunt, it did little else.[4]

While the Conservatives championed sounder colonial development policy, the Liberal government was mired in relief controversies. More of Kent's supporters revolted against his arbitrary administration of relief. In January 1861, members of the House of Assembly claimed that they should sit on relief boards, while Bishop Mullock wanted relief to be administered by clergy. Bannerman, who disliked his limited authority under responsible government, let Kent know that he would dismiss the administration if it lost his confidence. In February, Kent proposed to pay government salaries, including the governor's, in local colonial currency rather than the more valuable British pound sterling. The justices of the Supreme Court as well as the governor protested, and Kent responded by accusing the governor of being politically allied with the Conservative opposition. While such an accusation may have had merit since Bannerman seemed sympathetic to Hoyles's party, premiers normally did not question the integrity of the office of the governor; Bannerman used the episode as an excuse to dismiss Kent's government and request that Hoyles form an administration.

Bannerman's actions were constitutionally questionable, offended the spirit of responsible government, and dismayed Bishop Mullock since Hoyles recruited Laurence O'Brien, a Roman Catholic merchant, to augment what was primarily a Protestant administration. Mullock had wanted the Liberals to bend to his will and had not anticipated losing influence over government to a largely Protestant Conservative party that had never supported the broad economic diversification platform of the Liberals. Initially, he portrayed the Conservatives as greedy merchants seeking to squeeze dry the Catholic fishers of Newfoundland just as Irish landlords were squeezing their tenants, but the Anglican bishop, Edward Feild, declared his support for Hoyles, his old political ally. However, popular opposition to the Conservatives forming a government without an election forced Bannerman to dissolve the Assembly.

Victory in the ensuing election hinged upon two districts in Conception Bay. Both sides used violence and intimidation, which quickly assumed class and sectarian overtones. Fishers and sealers rallied to the Liberal candidate in Harbour Grace, James Prendergast, but local magistrates refused to open the polls. Tensions ran high throughout Carbonear and St John's, as Liberal supporters threatened or attacked the property of Conservative merchant candidates. Violence tainted the elections in the district of Harbour Main, where no Conservatives ran, and where rival groups of Roman Catholics fought each other. Two candidates, Hogsett and Charles Furey, had the local bishop's support, and another two, Thomas Byrne and Patrick Nowlan, preferred to have less clerical influence. The governor intervened, declaring the Harbour Main returns invalid. The Liberals believed they would have won the seats and, therefore, a majority in the House of Assembly. As it stood, the election result was fourteen Tory seats and twelve for the Liberals. When the legislature was called into session, Bishop Mullock and the Liberals encouraged public protest, which led to violence outside the Colonial Building. Troops dispersed the crowd by opening fire, killing three people and wounding twenty, including a Roman Catholic priest. Sporadic violence continued in Harbour Main, but the new Conservative majority agreed to allow the Liberal candidates to take their seats in the Assembly. Later winning two more seats in a Harbour Grace by-election, Hoyles ended Liberal domination in the Assembly.[5]

Once election fever had cooled, fisheries policy emerged as a pressing concern in districts around the island. The Hoyles government capitalized on popular indignation about French fishing rights to regulate the herring fishery in 1862. New legislation prohibited seining during the spawning season, established a minimum mesh size of 2.5 inches, and forbade the barring of herring in coves and using seines within a mile of settlements on the south coast, thus limiting French access to herring bait. Then, later in 1862, the Hoyles government bowed to popular pressure for fisheries conservation by appointing Conception Bay MHA John Rorke to a select committee to inquire into the fishery.

The legislature received many petitions from around Newfoundland demanding restrictions on new fishing gear, such as bultows and cod seines. In Placentia Bay, popular violence against people who deployed these gears forced a Supreme Court investigation. Rorke's committee received evidence from 104 merchants, fishers, planters, magistrates, and government officials throughout the winter of 1862–3. Fishers and merchants, including a few from Labrador, testified about a variety of wasteful practices such as the catching and dumping of juvenile fish, and many warned that the day might come when cod would be exhausted. Most favoured a variety of conservation measures and gear restrictions, but a small number argued that the state had no business restraining the right of individuals to use whatever fishing gear they chose. Rorke proposed an omnibus fisheries bill that would have introduced sweeping measures to ban some gears, such as bultows, and regulate the use of others, such as cod jiggers, seines, and gill nets. In the end, anyone could find something to oppose in the bill, despite agreeing with many of its provisions. Liberal opposition to the bill, along with Hoyles's recognition that the imperial government would not support its regulations if they affected the French or the Americans, led to its failure to become law.[6]

The Conservatives also turned to interior development by able-bodied relief programs in road construction. The government's boards, designed to oversee the administration of road programs, quickly became mired in sectarian patronage struggles over who would run them. An invitation in 1864 by the Canadian proponents of British North American union to send delegates to a conference at Quebec seemed opportune to consider solutions to the colony's difficulties. Premier Hoyles thought a united British North America could afford better fisheries management and would also have the resources to invest in economic diversification. The colony remained plagued by economic depression in the fishery, and, with most of the capital generated in Newfoundland tied up in the fish trade, there seemed little way to break out of the constant relief problems that strained government coffers and fuelled sectarian strife. Hoyles hoped that an infusion of Canadian capital might trigger change and sought to build a bipartisan consensus for union by appointing Frederick Carter (a Conservative MHA) and Ambrose Shea (as a voice for the Roman Catholics) to represent Newfoundland at the negotiations between delegates of the British North American colonies. Since his experience with trade negotiations with the United States in the 1850s, Shea argued that the Newfoundland economy would grow and diversify through closer ties with continental economies. He had become an enthusiast for railways as engines of economic development and saw Canadian capital and interest in railway development as useful for Newfoundland. Along with John Kent, Shea urged the government to abandon fisheries reform and devote its efforts to a renewed economic diversification strategy. In short, while Carter emphasized the potential for confederation to improve the regulation of the fishery, Shea hoped political union would encourage industrial diversification.[7]

This mutually favourable view of confederation led Shea into the Conservative fold. Hoyles retired from electoral politics in 1865, and his successor to the leadership of the Conservatives, Carter, convinced John Kent and Shea, along with Ambrose's brother E.D. Shea, to join him.[8] The Conservatives did not make confederation part of their platform and held on to power in the fall election of that year. Carter had inherited a predominantly Protestant Conservative party but welcomed Roman Catholic and Methodist Liberals into his coalition, thus blunting criticism that his party represented only one section of the population. Those Liberals who had not been incorporated into Carter's coalition unsuccessfully ran as an opposition party.

Carter's new government began to share seats in the Assembly, Executive Council positions, government offices, judicial appointments, and public monies among the major denominations – Roman Catholic, Anglican, and Methodist – on a proportional basis. All political parties adopted this 'denominational compromise,' which became a fundamental, if unwritten, rule of Newfoundland politics. Bishop Feild had never accepted anything less than full state support for a separate Anglican school system, even as the Methodists continued to gather in strength, forming a separate Newfoundland Conference in 1874. Carter cultivated Methodist and Anglican support in 1875 by guaranteeing both public funding for separate school systems. The government took other steps to lessen the likelihood of violence and intimidation during elections. Elections were held over one day throughout a district rather than over a period of days, which made it more difficult for roving bands to move from one community to another as the polls opened in each town. Carter also increased the numbers of police, instituted the secret ballot, and continued the Hoyles administration's ban on mummering, a Christmas custom in which people disguised their identity and visited each other, occasionally using their disguise as a cover to harass political enemies.[9]

Shea and Kent advocated union with Canada as a means to secure economic diversification. Shea and Carter suggested that Canada might assist Newfoundland with problems such as the French insistence on exclusive fishing rights, but much of the confederation debate focused upon union as a source of funds for diversification. In the 1860s, the influence of Irish nationalism in the Newfoundland

Roman Catholic church led Bishop Mullock to oppose confederation. This opposition fuelled the old pattern of sectarian politics, depicting confederation as a British invention that would interfere with the development of a unique local culture, including Irish influence and the special status of denominational education. The Province of Canada, formed from the union of Canada East and Canada West in 1841, moreover, was notorious for provincial squabbling over Roman Catholic and French-Canadian minority rights.

In the past, Mullock had restrained the Irish nationalist elements within the church in debates over Newfoundland's development, but he did not believe that Canada could help with the colony's economic problems. Most of the merchants agreed, arguing that the colony's fishery could not benefit by the transcontinental railway, despite the fact that the Maritime provinces had turned from maritime industries to embrace the continental reorientation of much of the British North American economy that went with confederation. Opponents of confederation argued that paying higher taxes, through import duties, to support such a railway would raise the cost of living and catching fish, while Newfoundland would not benefit from access to Canadian markets since the colony sold all of its fish in southern Europe, the West Indies, and Brazil. Newfoundland confederates promised federal backing for landward diversification as well as for better fisheries management, but their opponents responded that if the colony had interior resources to be developed then they should not be subject to Canadian influence.[10]

The Carter government campaigned for confederation in the general election of 1869, but it faced an opponent who had powerful nationalistic appeal. Charles Fox Bennett was a St John's merchant, but no one could accuse him of being uninterested in the economic diversification of Newfoundland: he had supported the Newfoundland Agricultural Society from its beginning and had long been a leading industrialist in St John's; his company had quarried slate in Conception Bay and invested in mines. By 1869 he had become a vocal proponent of interior development. Confederates continued to promote union with Canada as a solution to problems in the fisheries but emphasized that Canada, as a pioneer in colonial landward diversification, could help Newfoundland escape greedy monopolists such as Bennett. The Confederates spoke time and again of the vast natural resources of Newfoundland, which only awaited Canadian capital to be developed, but their opponents portrayed Carter and Shea as 'political Iscariots' willing to betray such resources into the hands of Canadians. Preference for a local national policy of development prevailed.[11]

The 1869 election ended in defeat for the Conservatives and for Canadian confederation, but the Canadian model based on railways and interior development took hold. The Bennett government relaxed controls on crown land legislation to open timberlands for investment and began to spend more on road development, while Bennett personally benefited from his government's removal of royalties on mining income. Although Bennett encouraged mining, he did not support extensive government involvement in building a railway because he felt it imprudent for government to get involved in projects that would necessitate heavy expenditures and borrowing. Then, in the early 1870s, stagnation in the economy led to an increase in emigration, and the press demanded that government invest in railway building. The world was gripped in railway fever, and people everywhere believed in the gospels of railway, progress, and development. At the same time, Bennett found himself uneasy as the leader of what was nominally a Liberal party with roots in the fight for responsible government and Catholic rights, both of which he had always opposed. In the 1873 election, he barely retained the premiership, and then only by dragging out the confederation issue again. The Conservatives abandoned their support for confederation, however, and portrayed Bennett as a leader who had betrayed his own principles for the Catholic vote. In 1874, Bennett resigned as premier. His party lost a general election later that year in part because it had not moved vigorously on the railway.[12]

Although Carter's Conservatives regained power in 1874, their economic diversification policies married older Liberal traditions to a new-found enthusiasm for railways, fuelled by the colony's difficult relationship with imperial authorities over French rights and a simmering dispute with the United States over its rights in Newfoundland waters. Throughout the 1860s, Newfoundland administrations pressed the imperial government for the right to grant land on the French Shore and to appoint magistrates; London finally agreed in 1869 that the Newfoundland government had very limited rights to resources on land that was located up to one-half mile from the high-water mark. The geological survey of Newfoundland by Alexander Murray suggested that the west coast had plenty of mineral resources as well as timber and land suitable for agriculture. Indeed, Nova Scotia investors had taken advantage of the jurisdictional wrangling between Britain and France to set up completely unregulated sawmilling operations in the Bay of Islands, paying no royalties or taxes, using wasteful cutting practices, and polluting streams and coves with their refuse, thereby harming local fisheries. The Newfoundland government wanted to establish clear jurisdiction over the natural resources of the French Shore for its potential revenue and economic development, but it also claimed an interest in conservation.[13]

Colonial government officials worried about the settlers from many different origins who lived on the French Shore. In the late eighteenth century, English- and French-speaking settlers from the island of Jersey had come to the Strait of Belle Isle, St George's Bay, and Bonne Bay. Originally these servants of such firms as Nicolle began wintering to trap furs and engage in a commercial salmon fishery; later they began fishing and trapping on their own accounts as settlers. Mostly Protestant, the settlers were joined later by other people of English origin from the south coast of Newfoundland. Initially, the French opposed such settlers as an infringement of their rights, but after 1815, French enterprises came to depend on settled salmon fishers to provide the staple of their trade. The local salmon fishery became so intensive that the rivers showed signs of depletion by the 1840s.

Unlike settlers elsewhere, many of those on the west coast had a Canadian connection. After 1820, Roman Catholic Acadian migration from the west coast of Cape Breton became much more important to the social development of the area from St George's Bay to Bonne Bay. By the mid-nineteenth century, the largest group of people living on the west coast was French-speaking. Settlers from St Pierre and deserting sailors and fishers from the French navy and migratory fishery on the French Shore joined the Acadian families and quickly began to populate areas such as the Port au Port Peninsula. Mi'kmaq had been migrating to the west coast from Cape Breton as early as 1763, but more began to arrive, having fled Cape Breton, where they suffered from the effects of overhunting, to settle across from Sandy Point. The Mi'kmaq relied on fur trapping, caribou and seal hunting, the eel fishery, and crafts such as basket weaving and moccasin making. The Roman Catholic community of the west coast became more complex after 1860 as kin groups of Highland Scottish settlers from Prince Edward Island and Inverness County, Cape Breton, came to the Codroy Valley, Highlands, and Campbell's Creek to search for better land. Newfoundlanders also moved to the west coast to escape the troubled fisheries of their homes after 1870. Many of these English-speaking settlers were from Conception Bay and migrated to the region by way of the Labrador fishery. They moved south from Labrador, searching for new opportunities in the herring fisheries and timber industries of Bonne Bay and Humber Sound. Other settlers from the south coast of Newfoundland and from the Maritimes came to exploit the previously untouched forests of the coast. Especially important was the establishment of a large sawmill by Halifax investors at Corner Brook, worth more than $40,000 in 1865. The attraction of the growing sawmilling industry, as well as the better agricultural resources of places such as the Codroy Valley, meant that west coast settlement also spread into the interior shores of the coast's great bays, St George's, Bonne Bay, and the Bay of Islands. The availability of timber also led to local shipbuilding, mostly of schooners.[14]

While the fisheries of Labrador continued to attract the interest of Newfoundlanders, the government continued to pay it little attention. Governed informally by the HBC factor at Rigolet and North West River, the latter community continued to grow in importance as the trading centre for the fur trade and salmon fisheries. Donald Smith, who managed the HBC's local activities from North West River, encouraged the development of roads and farming, solemnized marriages and baptisms, acted as the local judiciary, and provided basic medical services to the people who depended on the HBC. Throughout the late nineteenth century, settlers took over and operated the HBC's salmon fishing posts and trap lines, many of which became the nuclei for settler communities. Across Hamilton Inlet from North West River, Sheshatshiu was a seasonal gathering place of the Innu. Roman Catholic missionaries from Quebec, Jesuit and Oblate, active among the Innu of the Lake Melville area since the late eighteenth century, began to send priests to HBC posts beginning in 1867. Attracted to North West River by Oblate missionaries and the opportunity to trade for hunting rifles and ammunition, some Innu had begun to frequent North West River but were not welcomed by settlers there. To avoid conflict, the Innu kept to Sheshatshiu.

Along the coasts of Labrador, fishers from Newfoundland continued to move northward, commonly frequenting areas above Hamilton Inlet by the 1860s and 1870s, and the Moravians began to minister to the fishers from Newfoundland, partially to control their relationships with the Inuit. Along the southeast coast, many fishers decided to take up permanent residence. They saw lucrative opportunities for trade with visiting American schooners. The residents joined the families of former servants of West Country merchant firms who had decided to settle locally and fish on their own account. As in the trading territory of the HBC, southeast-coast settlement occurred by intermarriage with small enclaves of Inuit that persisted in the south until epidemics and assimilation took their toll by the end of the nineteenth century. As elsewhere in Newfoundland in the early days, fishing families lived in 'outside' stations on the coast during the spring and summer, engaged in salmon and cod fisheries, and then, in the fall and winter, moved into bays and inlets, setting nets for seals, hunting game, and cutting wood. The Newfoundland government provided small funds for schools, medical services, poor relief, and public works, but, overall, its attention to community needs in Labrador continued to be minimal.[15]

The Newfoundland government was more interested in the French Shore, where lucrative herring and lobster fisheries, the latter a recent development in response to a growing American market for the canned product in the 1870s, attracted the interest of St John's merchants. But it was the landward potential of the French Shore that fed many politicians' desire that its inland resources come under Newfoundland jurisdiction. A new generation of colonial politicians believed that landward industrialization would make Newfoundland a neighbour of consequence to Canada and the United States, and one that Britain would have to treat better. While still in opposition, Carter's leadership of the Conservatives had nearly been usurped by younger politicians such as William Vallance Whiteway, who were committed to this more nationalistic approach. Whiteway pushed forward plans for a railway across the island and terminating in St George's Bay on the French Shore. Carter was aghast at the prospect of antagonizing the French yet was able to negotiate for the right to appoint magistrates for the French Shore in 1877 by arguing that Nova Scotia timber cutters were taking wood there without paying taxes or observing Newfoundland law. While the new magistrates collected taxes and enforced the law, the British would not purchase territorial rights from the French, and London insisted it had the right to appoint magistrates, thus avoiding the question of colonial sovereignty.[16]

Carter wanted Newfoundland to gain control over the French Shore but feared the expense of a railway and the ire of the imperial government if the colony acted hastily. While he may have sympathized with the nationalism of the younger members of his party, the colony still depended on British negotiation and enforcement of international fisheries agreements. The abrogation of the Reciprocity Treaty with the United States in 1865, for example, had displeased Americans who wished to fish locally and Newfoundland merchants who desired freer access to American markets for their fish, especially herring from the French Shore and salmon. Britain and the United States negotiated the Treaty of Washington in 1871, which recognized past American treaty rights to fish in Newfoundland waters, most notably as stipulated in the Convention of 1818. This time, the British government accepted that the Newfoundland legislature would have to ratify the treaty. Many Newfoundland politicians did not like the access to bait fish gained by the Americans and wanted recognition of the colony's right to regulate American fishing for herring and salmon. The Americans, however, purchased herring as bait from Newfoundlanders living on the south coast, for whom the trade was an important part of their livelihoods. The colonial legislature accepted the deal, and the treaty came into effect in 1874. The United States agreed to compensate Newfoundland financially for the fishing rights it gained through an Anglo-American tribunal that was to make an award by 1877.[17]

A desire to assert Newfoundland autonomy more than to regulate the fishery motivated colonial politicians' stance on the Treaty of Washington. Landward economic diversification meant that the government supported open access in the fisheries and ignored fishers' demands for conservation regulations. As more intensive fishing technologies appeared, many officials took greater catches as evidence that fish stocks were inexhaustible, and, following brief periods of intense opposition, fishers accepted new gear introduced by better-off planters because merchants gave credit only to those willing to use the equipment or those who worked for such users. In a coastal ecology that provided few alternatives, people had to keep fishing regardless of poor catches or market conditions because they needed to maintain access to the merchant credit to purchase the necessities of life. Government inaction soon wore down fishers' concerns about the possibility of depleted fish stocks.[18]

Marine-resource depletion was especially evident in the seal hunt. The expansion of the schooner hunt locked sealers into a pattern of 'rapid expansion, intense competition and ruthless exploitation' that ended 'in declining resources and failure.'[19] The growth of the seal fishery had allowed population growth to occur during the nineteenth century despite the limits upon the expansion of the cod fishery posed by declining stocks. As the need for seal exports rose and the available seals declined, merchants invested in new technologies there too. By the 1860s, the old schooner hunt of the outports had given way to larger iron-hulled, steam-driven vessels which could penetrate deep into the ice packs in pursuit of remaining herds. Such steamers required capital beyond the means of most outport employers, and the ownership of the industry transferred from outports to St John's.

Throughout the period, newspaper correspondents wrote of the need for conservation. The Bennett government in the early 1870s had acknowledged popular fears that seal herds were being annihilated but did little about it. Beginning with Whiteway's government in 1878, half-hearted attempts were made to pass seal conservation legislation, but there was constant pressure to relax such laws. Men fought for employment in the seal hunt both because it provided some much-needed cash each spring as their families' winter credit had been exhausted and because the work had become a male right of passage in outports of the northeast coast. Merchants also needed to employ the steamers in which they had invested so much. The colonial government passed few and ineffective regulations to protect seal populations.[20]

American fishing rights in Newfoundland waters raised concerns about depletion of fish stocks in the context of the colonial bank fishery. The colony had long complained about the unfair competition from the subsidized French bank fishery, which used bultows; after 1874 more American vessels deployed them as well. The use of bultows meant that American schooners in the bank fishery required more bait, of which they wanted cheaper supplies to offset the higher cost of the bultows. Greater numbers of American vessels appeared in Newfoundland inshore waters in search of bait. Many of those Newfoundland merchants and fishers who wanted to enter the bank fishery feared that this increased American presence would jeopardize cod stocks and deplete bait fish such as herring. Moreover, the Americans caught enough fish to satisfy their domestic market so did not need to buy from Newfoundlanders. Newfoundlanders faced additional competition from banking schooners that sailed from Nova Scotia ports such as Lunenburg. From 1870 to 1900, Nova Scotians expanded their effort on the fishing banks off Newfoundland, fishing there from June through September. In 1876 the Newfoundland government established bounties to subsidize its own bank fishery. The development of the more easily stored dory also dramatically lowered costs in the banking industry, allowing Newfoundlanders to adopt the bultow. Together, these initiatives allowed the development of a small but vital bank fishery based upon the Avalon and Burin peninsulas. Like the Americans and Nova Scotians, Newfoundlanders prosecuted the bank fishery during the summer months but increasingly pushed their season into the fall and winter to take advantage of the ice-free waters of the south coast.[21]

The Treaty of Washington now seemed to be an impediment to the development of the colony, and it was difficult for Newfoundlanders to see how to proceed on the issues of bait and American fishing rights. Many south-coast fishers sold bait to Americans, and they feared that limiting their rights to purchase bait would lead the Americans to catch bait themselves. In the short term, most people hoped that the settlement of the Anglo-American tribunal would provide compensation for the rights the Americans gained, but the 1877 award was a disappointment. Compared with the $4.5 million awarded to Canada, Newfoundland received only $1 million. The American government, in turn, was indignant that it had to pay compensation and that the Anglo-American commissioners had agreed that American fishers must recognize Newfoundland's right to regulate the fishery in its territorial waters.

Matters came to a head in 1878, when the government decided to restrict the harvest of herring by banning fishing on Sundays. In January, a fleet of American bankers arrived in Fortune Bay to engage in a winter herring fishery. Rather than purchase bait by treaty right, the Americans decided to catch herring themselves. Local fishers were dismayed at the prospect of losing valuable winter income and feared that the Americans might sell bait to the French as well. About two dozen American vessels, equipped with huge herring seines of unusually small mesh size, began to sweep the bay at Long Harbour. On Sunday, 6 January, angry crowds began to gather on local beaches when it became apparent that the Americans would not obey Newfoundland law. Members of the crowd attacked some of the Americans, seized and destroyed their seines, dumped about two thousand barrels of herring, and drove the Americans away. The imperial government later conceded that the Americans were indeed in violation of the Newfoundland law that prohibited fishing on Sunday, seining in a closed season, and barring herring within a cove or other confined space. This was small comfort to Newfoundland, however, because imperial authorities maintained that colonial laws passed after the signing of a treaty between Britain and a foreign power, or which departed from the terms of a treaty, could not be imposed on foreigners.

The Fortune Bay dispute, as it became known, demonstrated that fishing people could affect the highest levels of international relations. Already aggrieved at the Halifax award, the American government complained loudly about alleged mistreatment of its fishers in the hope that it might get out of the obligations of the award, reduce the payment, or get additional fishing rights in compensation. The Newfoundland government worried when the Americans suggested that the incident might irreparably damage Anglo-American relations. At that point, the British Foreign and Colonial Offices stepped in, threatening the small steps Newfoundland had taken toward greater colonial sovereignty. Ambrose Shea came to the forefront of the fight to maintain Newfoundland's rights. He argued that the British must support Newfoundland's right to regulate the bait trade; it was a matter of the colony having the right to decide how its resources should be best developed. To Shea, Newfoundland's right to regulate the bait trade was simply another implication of responsible government. In the end, the British government agreed that the Americans would have to obey Newfoundland law.[22]

Fisheries issues did not disappear from the agenda, but Whiteway, who succeeded Carter as premier, had other priorities. On many occasions Whiteway stated that he did not think that government could do much to regulate fisheries, and he did not want to do anything to jeopardize Newfoundland's portion of the Halifax award, most of which he already had earmarked to support railway development. He advised the British to allow the Americans to resume their fishing rights quietly under the Convention of 1818, since British warships on patrol in Fortune Bay were not about to provoke the Americans by trying to enforce Newfoundland laws. Indeed, a new British government in 1880 paid $750,000 in damages to the Americans and, while Whiteway got his $1 million, it was a low price for selling the opportunity to regulate its fisheries. He did not completely abandon the fishery, however, but conservation took a back seat to the government's priority – industrial diversification. In 1879 the government dedicated $4,000 from the Halifax award for a commission of inquiry on the fisheries and $102,300 to build telegraph lines. While Whiteway considered appointing a superintendent for a permanent bureau of fisheries, the government established no actual commission until 1888.[23]

The disputes with France and the United States reinforced Whiteway's commitment to colonial development through railway construction. He hoped such development would open up the agricultural, timber, and mineral resources of the island, tie the French Shore more closely to the capital, and serve as a symbol of progress for a dynamic new nation. The premier suggested that financial assistance for railway development by the British empire would compensate New-foundland for the lack of support on issues such as the French Shore, but in 1880, Whiteway had to announce government support for a more modest project when it became clear that no British help was forthcoming. He proposed a rail line from St John's to Hall's Bay, No-tre Dame Bay, with a branch to Harbour Grace. Notre Dame Bay (especially its mining areas) and the Avalon Peninsula were two of the most densely populated areas of the colony. The lumber industry of the Gambo and Gander rivers was developing quickly, and the lands at the bottom of Trinity and Bonavista bays were more suitable for farming than any that could be found around the fishing communities of the outer headlands. The government awarded a contract to a New York syndicate to build the railway in return for annual subsidies of $180,000, loans, tax exemptions, and a land grant of 5,000 acres per mile.

The resulting Newfoundland Railway Company (NRC) began construction in 1881, although the government had not investigated its financial resources carefully enough.[24] Whiteway's mercantile opponents worried about the expense of even this modest project, not because they opposed the railway in principle, but because they did not think it was worth potential bankruptcy for the colony; they feared that their trade would be taxed through tariffs to raise revenue for its construction. Whiteway's party had begun as a Conservative one backed by Liberals such as Shea, but he now found himself the leader of the Liberal party, as the Conservative merchants of St John's had abandoned the premier.

Outport people also feared the railway. The rail bed and surrounding right of way would intrude on the gardens, pastures, local woodlands, and other areas used in common by people. Earlier developments, such as the Electric Telegraph Company in 1857, had led residents of Twillingate, Fogo, and Green Bay to protest, occasionally by cutting telegraph poles, the enclosure of woods they had always used for materials for the fishery. Rather than seeing the woods as the common property of fishing people, however, the government viewed them as 'waste' land that could be granted to the telegraph company to encourage development projects.[25]

The proposed railway would be a greater problem on the south side of Conception Bay, a densely settled area with a plethora of private and common property rights held by fishers and farmers. The Conservative opponents of the railway, seeing popular anxiety as an opportunity, encouraged rumours that the railway company would annex farm land, establish booths to charge tolls for anyone who wished to cross the rail track, and charge people if their animals crossed the line. They also suggested that the railway was a plot to manoeuvre Newfoundland into confederation with Canada. When a group of engineers tried to survey a right-of-way through the south side of Conception Bay from Topsail to Indian Pond in 1881, people followed the engineers as they worked. Rumours spread that the stick used by the surveyors, tipped with a piece of red flannel, stood for the Canadian flag and that wherever the surveyors measured, people would lose their land. At Foxtrap, the crowd began to throw stones at the engineers, driving them away and seizing their tools, and the arrival of a small force of police led to open rioting. Additional protests occurred episodically through 1882. While men and women of all ages, as well as children, participated in the rioting, women were prominent in what became known as the Battle of Foxtrap, using their aprons to carry caches of stones, which they used to great effect in driving away employees of the railway and police.[26]

Whiteway responded as a Liberal by painting the Conservatives as pawns of the fish merchants. He emphasized the importance of the railway in stimulating economic diversification and jobs that would finally break the grip of fish merchants and truck on Newfoundland. To counter worries about the expense of the project, his government approved a narrow-gauge railway rather than the more expensive broad-gauge lines being constructed in Canada and the United States. The governor of Newfoundland, John H. Glover, opposed the contract because he worried about the growing importance of American capital in the colony and thought (with much mercantile support) that the syndicate did not have the needed financial resources. By 1882, the NRC, borrowing heavily against the government contract, was sinking into financial trouble and becoming a potential political liability.

Whiteway's Liberals faced a strong coalition of St John's fish merchants, who backed the 'New Party' led by prominent merchant Walter Baine Grieve and James J. Rogerson in the general election of 1882. The New Party's platform was opposition to the railway contract, but it did not prevail in the face of the Liberals' ability to make an asset from an apparent liability. Whiteway presented the railway as the sword that would slay the merchant dragon of Water Street. The Roman Catholic Church hierarchy supported Whiteway, as did merchants in Conception Bay and Notre Dame Bay, who stood to gain by the railway as it passed through their areas. The government also used employment on the railway as a patronage measure. The strategy paid off. Whiteway gained a majority of 27 out of the 33 seats in the House. The NRC was bankrupt by 1884, leaving the colony with debt and eighty-four miles of poor narrow-gauge rail line on the Avalon Peninsula. Nevertheless, Whiteway had built a broad interdenominational coalition to support his economic progress platform. As long as it seemed that their hopes might be realized, the coalition remained solid.

The coalition weakened as it became apparent that the merchants of Water Street might be right. There had been no take-off in economic diversification as a result of the railway, and the colony had become mired in a financial mess while the fishery languished under heavy taxes. A.J.W. MacNeilly emerged as leader of the New Party and immediately took advantage of Whiteway's close association with the failed railway. Under MacNeilly, the New Party also played the sectarian hand by allying with the Orange Order against Roman Catholic support for Whiteway. On Boxing Day, 1883, members of the Order marched through a Roman Catholic neighbourhood in Harbour Grace. Conflict followed, deteriorating into open fighting that left three Orangemen and one Roman Catholic man dead. The community was so divided that a subsequent trial found it impossible to find witnesses who could prove the guilt of the Roman Catholics accused of the Orangemen's deaths. The trial was a huge political show, with Whiteway and the Grand Master of the Orange Order serving as the prosecution, and Catholic politicians acting for the defence. A British naval ship, the HMS *Tenedos*, stood by at St John's in case of additional violence. A supporter of Whiteway, MHA Alfred Penney of Carbonear, introduced a motion in the Assembly in February 1885 declaring the acquittals a miscarriage of justice and risked alienating Roman Catholic support for the government. Whiteway proposed a weak amendment, but he had lost the support of important Catholic members of his government such as Robert Kent, W.S. Donnelly, and Ambrose Shea. He resigned as premier, and many of his Protestant supporters coalesced with the New Party to form the Reform Party. Under Sir Robert Thorburn, the Reform Party won the ensuing general election of October 1885.[27]

The sectarian political role played by the Loyal Orange Association (LOA) in the 1880s reflected the persistent paternalism of popular politics. The absence of public means for the relief of working-class and fishing people distressed by the economic downturns of the 1860s produced much discontent. Roman Catholic members of the St John's establishment recognized that they could allay disgruntlement and mobilize the political support of working people through charity and patronage dispensed through the Benevolent Irish Society (BIS), which had developed a largely Roman Catholic constituency. Not to be outdone, Protestants turned to the LOA in 1863, which spread quickly throughout Protestant outports, especially along the northeast coast, helped by the patronage of politicians such as MacNeilly. Members of the BIS and the LOA were not simply dupes of colonial politicians. For the many fishers who joined the LOA, for example, holding office and playing public roles in its marches, funeral processions, and mutual-aid activities gave them publicly recognized and respected leadership roles in their communities. In the 1870s, the Roman Catholic Church formed the Star of the Sea Association and the Anglican Church organized the Society of United Fishermen, which had a mutual assistance mandate for their members similar to the LOA's.[28]

Working-class paternalism did not mean that workers were quiescent. Rather, they asserted themselves within their community but without engaging in class conflict. By their presence in church-affiliated organizations, for example, workers were able to demand that the St John's mercantile and professional bourgeoisie take notice of their needs. Again, and more directly, as in the west end of the city, where most of their number lived, skilled workers and artisans dominated the lay administration of the Anglican parish of St Mary's and fostered a more democratic and communal approach to decision making than existed in the upper-class-led St Thomas's in the east end. The St Mary's congregation visibly insisted upon its respectability by requiring High Church ritualism and organizing its poor relief as communal fundraising and social occasions rather than as bourgeois acts of dispensation.[29]

Throughout St John's, the growth of manufacturing meant that tailors, typographers, joiners, retail clerks, seal skinners, shipwrights, wheelwrights, sailmakers, tanners, and a variety of other skilled workers formed craft unions. Like the sectarian fraternities, these unions concentrated on providing benefits to their members and occasionally striking to protect their interests. They could be very effective in dealing with employers: in the 1870s, for example, organized coopers had been so successful in establishing and enforcing employers' observance of a fee schedule for daily wage rates that some St John's merchants recruited German coopers who were anxious to escape the proletarianization of their trade at home. However, the craft unions did not involve themselves in party politics.[30]

The most dynamic organization to catch the attention of working people was religious in nature. In 1886, representatives of the Salvation Army first came to St John's. The Army's parades and open meetings soon attracted young people, especially the many single working women, often domestic servants from the outports, who were otherwise alone and without much support in the city. These women found that they could engage in the same work and attain the same rank as men in the Army's service. In one year, the Salvation Army expanded rapidly to Brigus, Carbonear, Greenspond, Bonavista, Catalina, and Twillingate. By the end of 1887, it had established additional barracks in Burin, Grand Bank, and Bay Roberts. In St John's, young working men and visiting fishing crews learned that they could attend the Army's worship and social activities without worrying about the state of their clothing and without feeling uneasy in barracks that emphasized humility and practicality rather than ostentation and idolatry in their decoration. Working people from the outports who joined the Army became its missionaries, holding meetings on the flakes and stages, stores, lofts, and shops of coastal communities throughout the colony. The uniforms and the regalia of the Salvation Army were novel and entertaining but, more importantly, represented the outward manifestations of a commitment to the equality of the saved before God and the ability of the members from any social background to become officers.[31]

The Thorburn government believed that the best way it could help the people of the colony was to turn its attention back to the fishery. Whiteway had encouraged diversification within the fishery as part of his larger industrial diversification strategy but had paid little attention to the management problems of marine resources. Government had promoted the bank fishery, and the exploitation of new fishing grounds off the northern coast of Labrador as older ones showed signs of exhaustion, and had used the telegraph to allow fishers to shift effort rapidly to those areas reporting good catches. It also encouraged the construction of larger inshore fishing craft that could sail farther out into headland areas looking for newer fishing grounds. There was also diversification into the herring and lobster fisheries, and the 1888 Fisheries Commission, under the supervision of Adolph Neilsen, considered, then established, a cod hatchery.[32] While this demonstrates an awareness that cod stocks were not bearing up well under all this new harvesting pressure, such efforts also point to government reluctance to conserve marine resources by limiting the harvest. A cod hatchery could not address the complex problems of declining fish resources in the wake of the strategic failure to reduce Newfoundlanders' dependence on the fisheries.

Neilsen did not advocate conservation as much as the belief that science could enhance the natural resources available for exploitation or undo the environmental damage fishing had inflicted. As superintendent of the Newfoundland Department of Fisheries, created in 1893, the Norwegian-born scientist was instrumental in establishing an industrial whale hunt conducted from Newfoundland and Labrador shores. There had been earlier Newfoundland and Scottish experiments with commercial whaling, but these had been small in scale. In 1896, a joint Newfoundland-Norwegian Company, the Cabot Steam Whaling Co. Ltd., established whale-processing factories at Snooks's Arm, Notre Dame Bay, and Balaena, Hermitage Bay. The company used the latest in steam-vessel, cannon, and exploding-harpoon technologies to slaughter a variety of whale species. Soon, Newfoundland companies established more than twenty-one whaling stations around the colony, producing whale oil and bone. Unused whale offal initially posed a significant pollution problem wherever the factories appeared, but the consequent appearance of large flocks of gulls around whale factories led to the development of an operation to convert the offal into fertilizer.

Whalers hunted every species, including the planet's largest animal, the blue whale. The jeopardy to whale populations was clear, particularly since the Norwegians had come to Newfoundland, with the willing assistance of local capitalists, because Norway's own whale stocks had been exhausted in a westward pattern extending from Finnmark through Iceland and the Faeroe Islands. Newfoundland did not escape this pattern of depletion, although the government attempted to save the industry by legislation (which served as the model for later Canadian regulations) in 1902. By 1906 the whale populations were in trouble, and many Newfoundlanders who had become skilled in the work and management of the industry moved on to the emerging whaling industry in British Columbia.[33]

Fisheries industrialization was most pronounced in the lobster fishery. American, Nova Scotian, and Newfoundland investors built canneries, employing about one thousand people, on the French Shore in the 1870s and 1880s. The French government protested that the processing facilities were within the high-water mark that delimited its rights and interfered with French fisheries. St Pierre–based merchants built factories on the west coast and recruited labour from the

A group of men in a boat emptying a cod bag, 1905. While whales, seals, salmon, and other marine animals had brought Europeans to Newfoundland and Labrador for centuries, none of these had the enduring economic, social, and cultural significance of cod for settlers and their descendants. Courtesy of the Maritime History Archive, Memorial University, Location no.: PF 315.057.

Ruben Lewis, the Chief of Newfoundland Mi'kmaq, with his family outside a *mamateek* (wigwam), c. 1900. Long before Europeans arrived, a number of First Nations had either inhabited or resorted to Newfoundland and Labrador. While the Beothuk became extinct in Newfoundland, the Mi'kmaq continue to be one of the province's many peoples. Courtesy of The Rooms Provincial Archives, Newfoundland and Labrador, A 2-1.

Newfoundland Ranger W. Green (Service no. 153) with Innu at North West River, c. 1940. Although the Innu's home lands included much of the Labrador interior, their interests have rarely been important in the priorities of other peoples in Newfoundland and Labrador, and they had little direct contact with government officials until the arrival of the Rangers under the Commission of Government. Courtesy of The Rooms Provincial Archives, Newfoundland and Labrador, VA 127-44.2.

Three Inuit women at Hopedale, Labrador, 1886: Martha, Tarna, and Sarah. Inuit had lived at what is now called Hopedale by the early seventeenth century. Under the Moravians, the community integrated the Inuit into European trade and became a vehicle of attempted cultural assimilation. Courtesy of The Rooms Provincial Archives, Newfoundland and Labrador, A 7-90.

Women and children from Petty Harbour, 14 September 1886. Throughout the outports of Newfoundland and Labrador, such women and children dominated the drying of salt cod, the staple export of the region until well into the 1950s. Courtesy of The Rooms Provincial Archives, Newfoundland and Labrador, A 7-80.

Five privileged young women sitting on a bench near a garden fence, c. 1900. The greater social and economic diversity of St John's supported a well-developed bourgeoisie, which enjoyed much better living standards than most of the peoples of Newfoundland and Labrador. Courtesy of The Rooms Provincial Archives, Newfoundland and Labrador, A 7-102.

French sailor, c. 1890. Until 1904, France retained treaty rights to the fisheries of Newfoundland. French fishers and sailors constantly visited Newfoundland and occasionally added to the much larger group of Acadians who formed most of the francophone population of the west coast. Courtesy of The Rooms Provincial Archives, Newfoundland and Labrador, A 5-6 / Robert Edwards Holloway.

Isidor Wilansky's group, men of the St John's Jewish community, 1926. Largely through the efforts of his wife and business partner, Esther Wilansky, Isidor Wilansky opened a retail shop in St John's in 1919. The Wilanskys became leading members of the small but vital St John's Jewish community. Courtesy of The Rooms Provincial Archives, Newfoundland and Labrador, A 19-17 / S.H. Parsons and Sons.

Members of the Chinese community welcome the Chinese General Consul to St John's, 1938. From the mid-nineteenth century, Chinese immigrants had been part of the social fabric of Newfoundland but came under discriminatory Chinese Immigration and Aliens Acts by 1906. Courtesy of the Archives and Manuscripts Division, Memorial University Libraries.

Workmen repairing railroad, c. 1900. The railway was the centrepiece of colonial economic diversification in the last quarter of the nineteenth century. The railway produced significant new employment for workers, many of whom became leaders of the labour movement. It also produced massive public debt without much economic diversification, facilitated patronage politics, and contributed to the collapse of responsible government in the 1930s. Courtesy of The Rooms Provincial Archives, Newfoundland and Labrador, A 12-45 / R.E. Holloway.

A cooper standing with Job Brothers and Co. herring barrels, 1903. Despite colonial efforts to foster economic diversification and manufacturing in St John's, maritime work continued to dominate the social life of the city. Coopers, along with longshoremen, were especially prominent in labour organization. Courtesy of the Maritime History Archive, Memorial University, Location no.: PF 315.156.

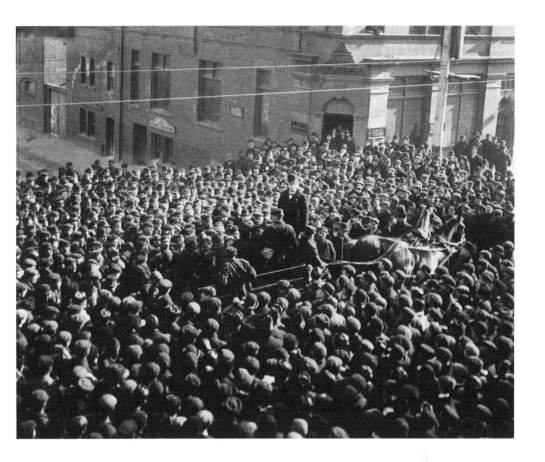

A.B. Morine addressing the sealers' strike, 1902. Collective organizations had little influence among fishing people until the formation of the Fishermen's Protective Union in 1908. However, the mass employment and harsh working conditions of the seal hunt meant that sealers sporadically acted together, such as when they refused to work in 1902 in response to reductions in their share payments. The sealers secured representation by Morine, a prominent local journalist and politician who originally hailed from Nova Scotia. Courtesy of the Maritime History Archive, Memorial University, Location no.: PF 315.250.

Temporary morgue at King George V Institute prepared for fatalities of
SS Newfoundland sealing disaster, April 1914. The deaths of 78 sealers
stunned people throughout Newfoundland and Labrador, reminding them
of the cheapness of life for many working people, and provoking outrage
against the mercantile organization of the sealing industry. Courtesy of
The Rooms Provincial Archives, Newfoundland and Labrador, A 18-34.

Dedication ceremony, prior to the unveiling of the National War Memorial, St John's, 1 July 1924. The beginning of war in 1914 diverted popular attention from the social divisions brought to the fore by the SS *Newfoundland* disaster. The losses of the Newfoundland Regiment, most notably at Beaumont Hamel in 1916, and later public commemorations, contributed to the founding mythology of a supposed Newfoundland national identity. Courtesy of The Rooms Provincial Archives, Newfoundland and Labrador, A 11-171.

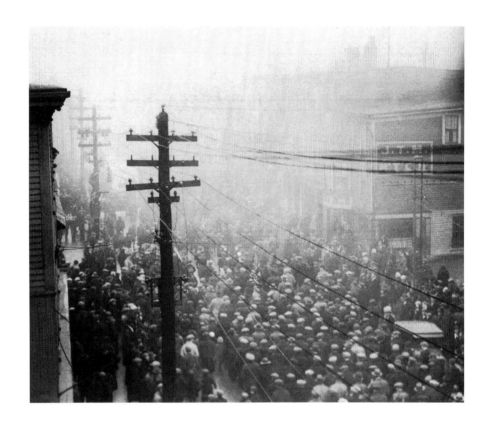

Unemployed people marching west on New Gower Street after leaving the Colonial Building, 5 April 1932. Their attack on the Colonial Building, the home of the Newfoundland legislature, was one of a series of protests by the poor against the miserable relief provided by governments burdened with war debt and years of ruinous spending on landward diversification. Courtesy of The Rooms Provincial Archives, Newfoundland and Labrador, A 2-166.

Three men working inside Bowater pulp and paper mill, c. 1940. The pulp and paper industry was a notable success in an otherwise dismal record of landward diversification. Unions among its skilled workers became leaders in dominion-wide labour organization, and fared better than most other workers during the depression of the 1920s and 1930s. Loggers, however, remained some of the worst-treated of workers. Courtesy of The Rooms Provincial Archives, Newfoundland and Labrador, A 38-108.

A heavy-bomber hangar under construction: men pour footings on the column line, Goose Bay, 24 July 1953. The economic boom triggered by military-base construction during the Second World War led to wider social and economic change, including support for confederation with Canada, with some of the most profound effects taking place in Labrador. Courtesy of The Rooms Provincial Archives, Newfoundland and Labrador, B 13-100 / U.S. Army.

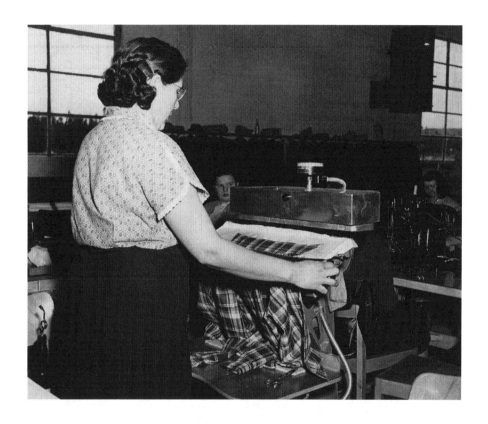

Woman operating a pressing machine in a clothing factory (between 1952 and 1961). Limited import-substitution manufacturing had been fostered by tariff protection since the late nineteenth century. Integration into the Canadian economy after 1949 forced much of this manufacturing to close, despite early attempts at further encouragement by the Smallwood government. Courtesy of The Rooms Provincial Archives, Newfoundland and Labrador, B 13-146 / Newfoundland Dept. of Mines and Resources.

Drill platform of Ocean Ranger, lost 15 February 1982 with 84 lives. Despite
increased provincial support for industrial-staple development, the local
economy remained dependent on a poorly managed and over-capitalized
fishing industry throughout the 1970s. The rush to encourage offshore
oil exploration contributed to an environment in which safety was not a
priority. Courtesy of The Rooms Provincial Archives, Newfoundland and
Labrador, A 41-36 / Mobil Oil Canada, Ltd., and G & C Associates.

French colony as well as from the French Shore, but appear to have depended on non-French factories to supply the French market. Luckily for Newfoundland, global strategic and trade issues meant that the French and British were ready to settle the long-standing problem of the French Shore. Whiteway's government had been well disposed to a settlement proposed by imperial negotiators that had arisen from an 1881 complaint by the French government, although imperial wrangling delayed its implementation. Thorburn's party, more oriented to fish merchants than railway promotion, preferred a fisheries development policy based on undercutting French competition through more bait legislation. Through 1888 the Thorburn government passed bait regulations that limited the French cod fishery, which made France less conciliatory on the irritants arising out of French treaty rights. Finally, French attempts to interfere with the construction of lobster factories led to heated protests by Newfoundlanders. In 1889, the British and French agreed to a *modus vivendi*, recognizing a French right to fish for lobsters and providing for the continuation of Newfoundland canneries only with the consent of British and French officials who policed the French Shore.[34]

Although some local protests began against the *modus vivendi*, they wilted in the shadow of a looming economic crisis. The Thorburn government replaced the Whiteway railway policy with a modest program to promote Newfoundland fishing rights at the expense of the French, to build roads, and to encourage more agriculture. His government found, as had many before it, that Newfoundland's ecology and limited markets would not support much agricultural development. With the exception of the Codroy Valley, some land around Corner Brook, and the farms in the vicinity of St John's, Newfoundland remained a maritime economy in which people fished and hunted seals, although work in shipping, usually on schooners, whether in taking fish to markets abroad or in coasting for cargoes along the eastern seaboard of North America, became the most important supplementary activity of outport men by the end of the nineteenth century.[35]

Thorburn completed the railway to Hall's Bay, but Whiteway campaigned as the Liberal party's friend of the working man, promising to revive the economy by a reinvigorated program of railway development, although he had no idea about how to pay for it. One possibility lay in the proposal of the Nova Scotia–born A.B. Morine, who had come to St John's in 1883 to take up the editorship of the *Evening Mercury*. Morine saw his political fortune in persuading the Newfoundland government to enter into confederation with Canada. In frequent contact with the Canadian government, Morine promised that New-foundland, as a province, would no longer be a competing interest at the negotiating table with the Americans or British imperial officials on matters related to fishing rights. Whiteway found attractive the notion that Canada would provide the financial resources and capital to back economic diversification in Newfoundland. Confederation, however, was inconsistent with the economic nationalism of many of Whiteway's supporters, such as his lieutenant Robert Bond, who did not like Morine's growing influence over Whiteway and suspected that confederation would again prove too unpopular to be carried successfully. The Liberals turned away from confederation and won the general election of 1889 on their old development platform.[36]

While nationalism remained important in Newfoundland's political culture, significant economic problems threatened to undermine it as the nineteenth century came to an end. One reason Thorburn's government had supported agricultural resettlement was the persistent poor fish catches in long-settled parts of Newfoundland and Labrador. While the Whiteway government supported the fisheries commission, its economic development policies overshadowed the body. Probably the most significant problem was the persistence of poorly understood ecological problems in the fishery, particularly on the northeast coast. By the 1890s colonial newspapers identified two related trends. First, shortfalls in catches encouraged the introduction of new fishing gears. Second, these new gears contributed to a decline in the quality of the fish. Fishers had been setting gill nets since the 1860s and cod traps, a box-shaped net fixed in the water with buoys and anchors, by the 1890s, which allowed fish to be caught without the presence of fishermen. These gears were, of course, less discriminatory than trawl lines and trapped both large fish and small. So, while catching capacity doubled by 1884, catches fell and had to be boosted by expansion into new areas off the south and west coasts of the island and on the Grand Banks, where fishers could work ice-free waters during the winter. Since the 1860s, fishers had moved steadily northward along the Labrador coast. This 'floater fishery' was different from the previous one, which had largely been conducted from shore stations by residents ('stationers') carried by merchants in the Strait of Belle Isle. The floaters remained aboard their vessels, roaming the northern Labrador fishing grounds. The farther north they moved, the shorter the fishing season, but cod traps were an intensive fishing gear. The smaller average size of Labrador fish, longer period of handling, and poorer weather conditions for drying contributed significantly to the poorer reputation of Newfoundland salt fish in international markets.[37]

Merchants responded by purchasing Labrador fish *tal qual* ('as it comes,' or bought for one price regardless of quality). The practice of *tal qual* gave fishers even less incentive to put time and effort into producing a good-quality cure, since a larger quantity of poorer fish would pay them more. Poor quality led to poor marketing practices, which in turn exacerbated the problem of quality. Merchants tried to make money from a poor-quality product by shipping as much fish as fast as possible to market in the hope of beating competitors. Fish buyers would not initially be sure how much fish would be available that season, and paid premium prices. Once other shipments arrived and started to undersell each other, fish began to flood the market and prices dropped. Every merchant knew that the best prices tended to be those paid first, so they preferred to ship quantity over quality if it would make the difference in getting a full cargo before competitors. Merchants knew that the overall effect of their marketing strategies was to glut the market and lower prices for everyone, but in the competitive culture of Water Street they could not combine to set a floor price.

Other factors were beyond merchants' control. They faced high import tariffs in Spain, Portugal, and Italy, the strongest markets for high-quality salt cod – the merchantable and Madeira grades. The best markets for poor-grade fish were in Brazil and the West Indies, which did not use high tariffs to tax fish imports for revenue. The Foreign Office in London was often sympathetic to Newfoundland's desire for lower duties upon fish, but Newfoundland was too small a part of the British empire to be worth antagonizing European trading partners by pressuring them to lower tariffs on fish. Taken together, these market conditions make it hardly surprising that merchants saw little reason to cooperate with each other in trying to produce a good product for high-end markets.[38]

The many new fishing gears and larger vessels required to bolster catch rates meant that the overhead costs of the fishery continued to rise even as the price for Newfoundland fish fell. To make matters worse, the number of people who relied on the fishery for a living grew at a rate that outstripped catch rates. In effect, the human population continued to grow while the resource population shrank, and merchants now sought to decrease their labour supply.[39] Although many young people left the outports, the demand for credit, for both provisions and new gear, grew even as merchants found investment in the industry less attractive. St John's merchant firms had come to dominate the colonial industry throughout the nineteenth century because, unlike the old transatlantic firms, they concentrated on the managerial requirements of the trade and other activities through rough periods while pushing the risk of advancing winter supply to outport merchants. By the end of the nineteenth century the largest firms specialized in the wholesale and retail functions related to the import and export business. Such specialization, in combination with the worsening market conditions for salt fish, meant that the large fish merchant firms became less interested in the business of producing fish as a commodity for sale in international markets. Now they were only taking fish as a medium of payment from the outport consumers, who had no cash to pay for the goods they bought. Even as the demand for credit among households increased, St John's firms withdrew capital from production in the industry by concentrating on investment in their importing, exporting, and wholesale operations. They invested, for example, in expensive steamers to facilitate even more rapid marketing, and in the other economic projects sponsored by the government.

Much of the day-to-day supply of the fishing families was left to smaller merchants and dealers in the outports. Outport merchants reacted to the erosion of their profit margin by restricting credit to only those fishers who used more capital-intensive gears and boats. Cod traps served as useful collateral for merchants' credit, but they could not stem the ecological and economic problems associated with declining catch rates, quality, and fish prices.[40]

The looming crisis of the fishing industry precipitated the bank crash of 1894. The combination of faltering catches in long-settled areas, poor prices for fish, and the concentration of St John's firms on investment in the import and export business meant that they relied increasingly on the colony's commercial banks, the Union Bank, founded in 1854, and the Commercial Bank, founded in 1858. St John's firms and the banks had many of the same people on their boards of directors, so the banks were quick to lend money to the merchants without worrying too much about the security of their loans. The banks had neither diversified portfolios nor significant cash reserves. In the 1880s, a number of senior merchants retired to Britain and took a great deal of the funds of their firms with them, further impoverishing the liquidity of both the exporting firms and the local banks which facilitated the trade. As it became clear that the mercantile operations were immersed in a long-term problem of debt and shortage of cash, the banks turned to the Newfoundland government's Savings Bank, the Reid family, British banks, customers' agents in England, and to funds raised through the sale of Newfoundland bonds to keep the financial system afloat. The Great Fire of St John's in 1892 destroyed a large part of the city and much capital, but created short-term liquidity as insurance payments and assistance flooded the city. But between 1890 and 1894, a decline of fish exports by more than 24 per cent, and a 6 per cent drop in fish prices precipitated the final crisis. When a senior partner of the English firm of Prowse, Hall and Morris died on 6 December 1894, that firm decided to call for payment on bills drawn on it by the Commercial Bank. Lacking sufficient cash, the bank closed its doors. The Savings Bank, fearing a run, called in its loans to the Union Bank, forcing the latter to close. A number of prominent merchant firms, including E.J. Duder, Thorburn and Tessier, and John Munn and Company, did not survive the crisis. In the short term, the bank crash led to severe unemployment and retail profiteering.

Unable to address the difficult problems of the fishery, the Liberal government added to the looming financial crisis by its railway policies. The Whiteway government had awarded a contract to a Canadian syndicate dominated by the family of Robert G. Reid to finish the Hall's Bay line for $15,600 per mile. Faced by another election in 1893, the Liberals had asked the Reids to construct the line from Hall's Bay to Port aux Basques. It raised a tariff on imports to provide revenue for the project and, hoping that railway-promoted economic growth would be worth it, borrowed the bulk of the money. In the short term, the tariff raised the cost of living for fishing families and deepened their dependence on credit or public relief for winter supplies. The depression in the fish trade triggered by the bank crash aggravated the situation, forcing the government to borrow just when few had confidence in lending money to Newfoundland borrowers. A.F. Goodridge, the premier of Newfoundland, unsuccessfully requested the financial assistance of Britain. The British government could not see how a short-term loan could solve such a systemic economic crisis. Imperial authorities may have been interested in seeing the colony fall into bankruptcy. Such an end would likely mean that the empire would serve as trustee and take control over a colony that had been since the 1830s a thorn in the imperial side on issues of treaty rights to the fishery, tariffs in foreign markets, and requests for subsidies for the industry.

The British refusal, and a related request for a royal commission investigation of the colony's affairs, led to the resignation of Goodridge and the formation of a new government under D.J. Greene. Greene's government managed to borrow enough funds to reopen the Union Bank and guaranteed a return of 80 per cent on its notes. The government further guaranteed 20 per cent on notes issued by the Commercial Bank. In January 1895, reeling under the ongoing problems caused by the Great Fire, the poor in St John's demonstrated in anger at the government's inadequate action. Charities organized by the governor and his wife defused some discontent, but the government found itself again unsuccessfully asking for British assistance. Greene resigned, and Whiteway returned to power as premier.

Whiteway thought that union between Newfoundland and Canada might provide a solution to the financial crisis. As one of the Newfoundland delegates, along with Robert Bond and A.W. Harvey, to the Halifax Conference in 1892, Whiteway had decided not to pursue suggestions of union at the time. Beggared by its economic development policies, the Newfoundland government now agreed to a conference with Canadian officials, held on 4 April 1895 in Ottawa. The Newfoundland delegates, including Robert Bond and E.P. Morris, felt that the Canadian government was unwilling to provide sufficient financial assistance, and the imperial government refused to provide additional financial support. Acting on behalf of the government, Robert Bond raised enough money in Montreal and London to keep the colony going, in part through personally guaranteeing the loan with his own money. The government reduced expenditures, and Canadian banks stepped into the void left by the Newfoundland institutions.[41] This gave stability but in the long run hurt the colony since the Canadian banks were less flexible when crafting credit arrangements to facilitate exports. Newfoundland now used the Canadian dollar as its currency yet had no influence over exchange rates, which affected exports. Nonetheless, the failed negotiations with Canada left many in Newfoundland feeling bitter and pessimistic about what they could expect from closer relations with their Canadian neighbour.

The social and ideological crisis of the bank crash may have been as important as the economic and political crisis. Truck credit practices had caused fishing people to mistrust merchants, and this was worsened by the practice of *tal qual*. An inquiry into the crash in 1895 led to prominent merchants who sat on the banks' boards of directors, including Robert Thorburn, A.W. Harvey, Walter Baine Grieve, and William J.S. Donnolly, being charged in the Supreme Court with issuing false financial statements. While the case dragged on through 1897, the prosecution's inability to determine whether or not overdrafts in one instance might serve as assets in another allowed the merchants to avoid punishment. For the firms that survived the crisis, business carried on as usual, although merchants tried to avoid extending credit to fishing people whenever possible. By the turn of the century, outport merchants wanted to get out of the fish business by becoming more conventional retailers.[42]

Forty years of responsible government had brought Newfoundland to a crisis. Frustrated by its lack of resources, and certain that little help could be expected from the empire, colonial authorities allowed the fishing industry to develop to the point of over-capacity, despite periodic demands from fishers that something be done to curb the problem of resource depletion. Merchants funded these problems by over-extending credit and engaging in ruinous competition with each other. Newfoundland governments dabbled with regulations and stock enhancement, but the multitudinous problems of the fisheries led most of them to embrace landward diversification, especially costly railway development. The railway was, ironically, part of a first nationalist fervour, as enthusiasts dreamed of a new industrial economy that, no matter how unrealistic the hope, would allow the colony to turn its back on the sea. Such commitment to landward diversification blinded many to the financial storm clouds that threatened to deluge the colony in ruin.

7

Twilight of the National Policy, 1897–1908

Close to a half-century of responsible government had brought Newfoundland to a crisis, but the colony was about to enter what many would later see as its golden age. Although the Reformers and Liberals who had fought hard for responsible government had promised economic wonders for the colony, it still depended for its life on the earnings derived from the sea. The fight over confederation with Canada had reinforced nationalistic expectations about the potential of the colony's landward resources for economic development. The ignominy of the bank crash, in which Newfoundland had been bailed out by Canadian banks, had not dampened nationalist fervour as the colony approached the four hundredth anniversary of Cabot's 'discovery' of Newfoundland. Nationalist intellectuals remained convinced that a great destiny awaited Newfoundlanders. Having weathered the adversities of the past, such nationalists hoped they might look forward to the potential prosperity of the future, and many still placed their faith in a national policy of landward economic expansion. The limited achievements of the national policy, however, forced people to pay more attention to fisheries matters.

To many Newfoundlanders, the four hundredth anniversary of John Cabot's voyage was an opportunity to put difficulties behind them and embrace what they hoped would be a more prosperous century. 'Cabot fever' swept St John's and merchants raised money to build a commemorative tower, the Cabot Tower, which altered the horizon of the capital city and remains a famous landmark to this day. More modest events accompanied the tower plans. St John's residents held public debates, billiards tournaments, and public celebrations to honour Cabot and to celebrate Newfoundland. The Newfoundland government issued a postage stamp that proclaimed Cape Bonavista as 'the landfall of Cabot.'

For many, such as Roman Catholic Archbishop Michael Howley, Cabot's landfall was more significant than just being an important milestone in British imperial development. Howley, the first leader of the colony's Roman Catholics to be Newfoundland-born rather than Irish, was a member of St John's non-sectarian nationalist intelligentsia. He believed Cabot was the perfect mythical founder of a Newfoundland nation and could represent a Newfoundland that was greater than the sectarian political mess that at times it had seemed to be. A Catholic Italian who sailed in the service of an English monarch before the great breach with Rome, Cabot, as symbol, could draw together Irish Catholics and British Protestants in Newfoundland political culture. For the Liberal historian and Newfoundland booster D.W. Prowse, the celebration of Cabot's supposed discovery of Newfoundland made it no mere colony; it placed Newfoundland at the forefront of British imperial development and was an augury of great things to come in the island's development.[1]

Although Cabot euphoria swept St John's, there continued to be good reasons to fear for Newfoundland's future. Robert Bond, Whiteway's colonial secretary, had little success in negotiating a new trade arrangement with the United States. Following the Fortune Bay dispute (see chapter 6), the American government had abrogated its trade arrangements with Newfoundland under the 1871 Treaty of Washington. In 1885, the colonial government had begun to negotiate a new arrangement with the United States but deferred to negotiations between imperial and American officials in 1887. The ultimate failure of those negotiations led the British, in 1889, to allow the Newfoundland government to negotiate with the Americans. Bond negotiated directly with James G. Blaine, the American secretary of state. The two agreed that American vessels would be able to purchase bait and procure supplies and crews in Newfoundland, while Newfoundland fish, fish oil, and marine-mammal oils could enter the American market without paying duty.

The agreement, known as the Bond-Blaine Convention, drew criticism from the Canadian government, which expected Newfoundland interests to play second fiddle to its own desire to use the British North American fisheries as a bait to lure the United States into a limited reciprocity agreement. The Canadian prime minister, Sir John

A. Macdonald, also suspected that Blaine was anxious to promote American interests by dividing the British North Americans as much as possible. The British government vetoed the deal in 1891, much to the ire of many Newfoundlanders, and then tried to placate the Newfoundland government by lending it money for the railway, but Newfoundland retaliated against Canadian fishing vessels by enforcing its bait act against them. The Nova Scotia bank fishery began to suffer and Canada retaliated by imposing punitive tariffs on Newfoundland fish, while Newfoundland responded in kind by taxing imports of Canadian manufactures and foodstuffs. Premier Whiteway had been more inclined to compromise with Canadian and imperial officials, but Bond, who had the majority support of the cabinet, forced the government to stand firm. The status quo returned in 1892, when the British made clear that they would disallow discriminatory tariffs and that Newfoundland could not refuse Canadians access to bait.[2]

Meanwhile, the Newfoundland government continued to ransom colonial resources in the pursuit of landward development. The bank crash led to the defeat of the Whiteway government in the election of 1897, despite their attempt to buy votes through awarding contracts for branch-line construction to the Reid syndicate. The opposition, now popularly referred to as the Tories, formed a government under the leadership of J.S. Winter and the minister of finance A.B. Morine. Faced with massive financial obligations yet determined to proceed with railway development, Morine negotiated a deal that would hand over to the Reids much of the colony's new economic infrastructure outside of the fishery in exchange for completion of the railway. This deal, known as the Reid Railway Contract of 1898, provided the Reid Company with additional land grants of 5,000 acres per mile of railway operated. Robert Gillespie Reid would operate the railway for fifty years, after which it would become the property of his heirs in exchange for a payment of $1 million to the government and the return of 2,500 acres per mile of the original grant. Reid also purchased and agreed to operate the government dry dock in St John's and to build and operate a coastal steamer service on behalf of the government for a subsidy of just more than $91,000 a year. Reid assumed control of the ferry service linking Port aux Basques to North Sydney, the island's telegraph system, hydroelectrical rights for the supply of St John's, and colonial assistance to build a new railway station and surrounding street improvements in the west end of St John's.[3]

The Tories believed that they had arranged for the Reids to carry the burden of railway development. Furthermore, the government felt that the Reids would fund much of the future industrial diversification of the colony as they developed their land grants. The Liberals, now led by Robert Bond, who had become increasingly critical of Whiteway's policies in the dying days of the last administration, saw the contract as an unjustifiable transfer of control over Newfoundland's economic destiny to a private monopoly. To make matters worse, that transfer had been negotiated by expatriate Canadians, especially Morine, who had been on the Reid payroll as the company's solicitor even while negotiating on behalf of the government.

Robert Bond successfully fought the 1900 election on the issue of the Reid contract, which he immediately set out to break, despite his colleague Edward Morris's support for the deal. Bond's fight with the Reids was an early example of the electoral success a party leader might expect if he could portray himself as the defender of ordinary Newfoundlanders against big outside interests, whether industrial or government, or whether they were Canadian, British, or American. Reid's family transferred its investments to the newly formed Reid Newfoundland Company and returned to the government the right to assume ownership of the railway (for $1 million plus interest) after fifty years of operation. As well, the Reids surrendered the lands given to them under the 1898 deal in exchange for $850,000, and Newfoundland acquired the right to resume control of the telegraph system. Otherwise, the provisions of the 1898 contract remained. The Reids retained control over much of the economy outside of the fishery, while the government assumed extra financial liabilities and the responsibility that went along with national control over future economic development. Bond wanted to limit the Reids, but they continued to have the quiet support of Morris, who represented the strong Roman Catholic constituency of St John's. Morris's working-class constituents in the west end of the city stood to benefit by the Reids' proposal to move the railway's machine shops from Whitbourne to the city, and Bond could not afford to alienate this constituency.[4]

There were other events that indicated that Newfoundland was achieving a more independent national status. One development was of symbolic and lasting significance. In 1902, Governor Cavendish Boyle composed a four-verse poem, which was set to the music of Hubert Parry in 1904 and chosen by the Newfoundland government as the colony's official anthem: the 'Ode to Newfoundland' (which continues to this day as the provincial anthem of Newfoundland and Labrador). More administrative in character was the Supreme Court's acquisition of jurisdiction over the vice admiralty court in 1890 and exclusive right to regulate inferior courts in 1904. Other developments were more international in scope. Until 1904, colonial governments had failed in their attempts to undercut the French fishery on the French Shore through bait legislation and pressure on an unsympathetic Colonial Office (see chapter 6). Now, led by Prime Minster Whiteway's opponents from the old Reform Party (which had become the Patriotic Association), the anti-French public sentiment forced the government into a more public stance against the French fishery. Initially, the British government was so upset with the Newfoundland government's stand that it considered withholding financial assistance for rebuilding St John's after the Great Fire to coerce the colony into accepting treaties legislation that might mollify the French. In the end, the British provided £15,000 to assist people made homeless by the fire without such strings attached. But the rise of Germany as a military power had caused Britain and France to settle various irritants between the two countries, including the French Shore, for the sake of their alliance. In 1904, the French agreed to give up their treaty rights to the French Shore in return for access to fisheries, bait, and ports in Newfoundland during the summer, but subject to Newfoundland law, and without the right to use the shore in their fisheries. The French retained a legal claim to rights on the French Shore until 1972, but the limits imposed by the 1904 agreement effectively ended its fisheries there.[5]

Within St John's and the surrounding communities of the northeast Avalon Peninsula, the ignominy of the Bond-Blaine Convention, the Cabot celebrations, the public fight against the Reids and their 'Canadian' henchmen, and the successful struggle against the French may have reinforced local economic nationalism. The city had undergone considerable economic change in the last quarter of the nineteenth century despite the shock of the bank crash. As Water Street merchants decided to invest outside of the fisheries to avoid such economic catastrophes in the future, they moved into manufacturing consumer goods. The notorious unpredictability of the fishing industry meant that credit-rating agencies (such as R.G. Dun and Company of New York) frowned on the efforts of local merchants to diversify. While such agencies were willing to forgive a merchant's occasional financial embarrassment due to a downturn in the fishery, seeing it as preferable to personal problems ranging from dishonesty to mental illness, they were reluctant to recommend that anyone invest in a new enterprise in the colony.

Local businessmen (women rarely participated in the businesses of the elite except occasionally as the widows of businessmen) relied on family connections for capital; indeed, under merchant capital, an important way for a single businessman to raise funds was to marry well and gain the backing of a wealthy father-in-law.[6] There were opportunities for investment in activities related to the fishery. Prominent merchants Moses Monroe and Charles Bowring, along with Robert Thorburn, were major investors in the Colonial Cordage Company, which manufactured ropes, lines, and twines. Some fish merchant firms, such as those of the Bowrings, Jobs, and Tessiers, also operated large cooperages that manufactured barrels for the fishing industry. Other merchants had invested in the dry dock.

Given the risks of the local environment, merchants who wished to diversify their investments turned to manufacturing. There had always been small-scale manufacturing of food such as baked goods, clothing, footwear, furniture, and other goods to satisfy the consumer needs of St John's. Merchant firms had a long relationship with the craftspeople who made these goods, largely in providing their wholesale requirements and retailing some of their wares throughout the colony. Throughout the 1870s and 1880s there had been a rapid shift in mercantile investment from producer goods required by the chronically troubled fishery to consumer goods. Merchants soon found, however, that the stable demand for such goods in the colony was also inelastic and small, limited by the employment of the vast majority of the population in the fishery compared with the very small population of St John's who received their incomes in wages or salaries and lived by purchasing goods. Most consumer manufacturing found little demand in the fishing outports, where cash for purchasing was at a premium, thus providing a poor market for the production of capital goods. The clothing and baking industries, for example, were so small that it never made sense to produce sewing machines or ovens in the city instead of importing them. By the late 1890s, investment in manufacturing began to slow, although it continued through 1914. The development of the railway, as well as diversification in forestry and mining, provided some additional consumer demand.[7]

The development of St John's manufacturing in the late nineteenth century led to the growth of an urban working class. Workers in the marine capital goods, consumer goods, and services industries organized unions and began to strike for higher wages, shorter hours, union recognition, and safer working conditions. These unions also opposed wage reductions and the use of non-union labour. In 1893, the St John's unions attempted to form a Workingmen's Union of Newfoundland

(WUN). This was to be a council of all trade unions which would act as a lobby group to remove legal impediments to unionization, fight for higher wages, provide mutual benefits, and promote government policies to encourage St John's manufacturing development. The WUN did not last long, probably because of the economic instability associated with the 1894 bank crash. In 1897 the Mechanics' Society united all trade unions into one central body to pressure government for tariffs which would encourage manufacturing in the city. Collective bargaining was not on the Mechanics' Society agenda, and many of its members drifted away as the economy improved by 1900.[8]

A much more successful working-class organization was the Longshoremen's Protective Union (LSPU), which organized workers in the port trades. Dockworkers, although indispensable to the economic life of the city, received poor pay for very irregular hours. Most worked by the day or hour, depending on the needs of shipping. To make matters more difficult for those who tried to make a living on the docks, their ranks swelled constantly with the arrival of fishers and other rural labourers during the off-season, or whenever a fishing vessel was laying over in port. The increasing metropolitan importance of St John's, enhanced by local manufacturing, railway, and dockyard development, provided a better base for the longshoremen's union. The shipment of perishable goods meant that shippers could not withstand long work stoppages, which the LSPU used to good effect. The variety of stevedores, fish packers, barrowmen, cullers, stowers, and helpers who worked on the docks meant that workers needed a union that was not limited by a narrow craft or occupational base. In 1902 and 1903, work stoppages for higher wages resulted in the workers' foundation of the Steamboat Labourers' Union, which by 1904 had become the LSPU and represented all dock labour. The concentration of labour on the docks and employers' reluctance to face strikes meant that the LSPU could build a strong, well-financed, and disciplined organization. Throughout the twentieth century the LSPU flourished and was well known for the support it gave other workers who were trying to establish their own unions.[9]

The growing dependence of manufacturing on differential protective tariffs on imports harnessed the St John's working class to the interests of local capitalists. A tariff of 5 per cent was placed on the imports of raw materials that manufacturers might require to produce goods. Finished goods such as boots and clothes were subject to a tariff of 10 per cent to protect local manufacturers from the competing imports of foreign industries. Such tariff protection also helped governments to raise revenue for railway development, and the Bond government further encouraged secondary manufacturing through subsidies, premiums, drawbacks, and tax exemptions. They reasoned that if Newfoundlanders spent most of their money on imported goods, capital would continue to drain away from the colony, while the purchase of local goods would not only retain capital but would also generate much-needed employment outside of the fishery. The whole strategy was premised on the success of what had become Newfoundland's national policy: the railway would open up interior resources, such resources would prompt industrial development and the growth of a consumer market, and eventually domestic manufacturing would not require protection.[10]

Much depended on the colonial government's ability to foster significant employment in industries other than the fishery. The industry which had given the colonial government the earliest hope had been mining. The Hall's Bay rail line had linked St John's with the mining district of Notre Dame Bay. C.F. Bennett had begun to operate a copper mine at nearby Tilt Cove in partnership with the prospector Smith McKay in 1864. The discovery of copper touched off a prospecting boom and a rush to file mining claims between the 1880s and 1914. Prominent Liberals, such as Whiteway, invested in mines such as that at Little Bay. Robert Bond invested in a speculative asbestos enterprise on the Port au Port Peninsula. The close ties between the mine investors and the Liberals meant that they gave the industry a free hand. This reached its zenith in the Newfoundland Consolidated Copper Mining Company (NCCM), whose directors included William Whiteway. The company used its Liberal connections to dominate the copper industry of Notre Dame Bay. Largely unregulated by government, the NCCM skimmed the high-grade accessible copper ore, left other ore inaccessible in the tailings, and gave no thought to the longevity of the mines. The NCCM used truck to supply its employees, charging them high prices for food and maximizing profits. When combined with speculative staking and sales of mineral rights, the high potential profit led to a boom in mining exploration.

In addition to serving as an important stimulus for railway expansion, the possibility of mineral discoveries on their land grants served as an important inducement for Reid investment in Newfoundland. The Reids operated iron, copper, and coal mines as well as granite quarries. They found most of the mines unprofitable, which reflected the Newfoundland Geological Survey's overestimate of the colony's mineral resources. Despite the Reids' problems, there was still reason to believe mining had a bright future. While the copper industry in Notre Dame Bay, as well as the pyrite mine at Pilley's Island, had begun to wind down in the 1890s and the last of the local mines at Tilt Cove closed in 1917, there was new interest in the iron ore of Bell Island, Conception Bay, close to St John's. The farming and fishing family of John and Jabez Butler, on whose land the ore lay, sold their rights to the land to the Nova Scotia Steel Company, which started a mine in 1894. In 1899, the mine became part of the holdings of the Whitney Company, which became known as the Dominion Iron and Steel Company.[11]

The Newfoundland government expected more from forestry because of its efforts to foster agricultural settlement. The coastal forests backing outports had always provided fuel and material for the buildings, boats, and fish flakes that people required. Crown Lands' Acts between 1844 and 1875 provided for the transfer of crown land to private property primarily for agricultural development, as well as for the development of sawmilling and railway expansion. In the last quarter of the nineteenth century, as the fishery stagnated, the colony had used bounties to encourage people to resettle to the bottoms of bays rather than emigrate from the colony. Some of the new communities developed substantial agrarian bases that allowed the withdrawal of effort from the fisheries. But most resettled people found logging to be more important than farming, largely because soils still had to be supplemented with fertilizers from the sea. Outport people opened up forest land primarily to find material for the larger vessel construction required by expanding outer headland and Labrador fisheries. The mines in Notre Dame Bay created demand for lumber for construction and mine props. The potential of the forestry industry had been an important factor in the government's decision to change the route of the Hall's Bay rail line so that it angled toward the west coast of Newfoundland.[12]

The Crown Lands and Timber Act of 1875 and the Crown Lands Act of 1884 had ended the indiscriminate and possibly illegal cutting on the French Shore. Otherwise, the Whiteway and Bond governments had let the lumber industry, which initially exploited almost exclusively white pine, develop almost unchecked. Although newspaper editors and correspondents occasionally expressed concern over resource depletion, the boosters of railways and forest industrialization kept up pressure to have all of the colony's resources surveyed and leased to developers. Within about thirty years, the commercial sawmilling industry had annihilated the pine stands of central Newfoundland, dried up the basis of the island's export trade in lumber, and disappeared. The government passed legislation in 1890 to foster a pulp and paper industry which would exploit the previously 'underutilized' soft woods. The Exploits, Gander, and Gambo rivers, along with the shores of Red Indian Lake, would likely be the site of the lumber and pulp industries. The government was excited about the prospect of growing Canadian timber shortages spurring on local industry by attracting more Canadian investors. It had hoped that development of the Reid railway would encourage even greater investment in forestry, and such hopes appeared to be fulfilled in 1899–1900.

The Newfoundland government had agreed upon an exchange of over 206 square miles of timber rights around Red Indian Lake between the Reids and Lewis H. Miller, from Crieff, Scotland. Miller built a large sawmill at the lake and constructed a branch rail line through to the coast. The new venture, Timber Estates Company, intended to mill white pine for export. Initially, the Reids hoped that Miller's would be the first of a number of forestry and other enterprises that would create traffic for their railway. Miller found that his timber rights did not include enough trees of lumber quality and that the land would not support the farms that promoters had hoped would be a by-product of cutting.[13]

The exhaustion of commercial-quality pine led the Reids to turn their leases over to Alfred and Harold Harmsworth (British newspaper barons and later Lords Northcliffe and Rothermere) for pulp development. Premier Bond saw the Harmsworths' proposal for a pulp and paper complex as a symbolic justification of his economic nationalism. More immediately important, the industry would create much-needed traffic for the railway, which had been operating at a deficit. Although the premier felt justified in limiting the Reid enterprise by the renegotiation of the 1898 contract, he believed that the railway was destined to be a powerful force for economic diversification and wanted to ensure that it was successful.

In 1903 Bond's government agreed to unprecedented concessions to the Harmsworths. In addition to the rights acquired from Miller, they received a ninety-nine-year lease for an undetermined section of land. The company chose land around Grand Lake, for which they had to pay only a reduced rent of two dollars per square mile. The Harmsworths had to pay the usual royalty of fifty cents per thousand board feet cut of lumber, but could cut pulp logs without any charge, and received all mineral and water as well as timber rights. The British capitalists had a choice of 10,000 acres outside their grants for mill and shipping facilities and could import any equipment and materials they needed duty-free. In return, the Harmsworths had to spend $20,000 in three years and pay the government $1 million within twenty years. By 1905, the Harmsworth operation had been incorporated as the Anglo-Newfoundland Development (AND) Company.

While Bond expected the public to be pleased, his political foes and St John's newspapers immediately attacked the deal. Those who were allied with the Reids argued that it was inconsistent for the premier to have attacked the railway contract of 1898 as an egregious form of monopoly and then help establish a near-monopoly in the forest industry. Others, led by A.B. Morine, attacked the deal as a gift of the colony's resources to the AND Company with little in return. The AND contract passed through the legislature, and the company had a mill in operation at Grand Falls by 1909, but Bond was more cautious in his subsequent negotiations for the establishment of the A.E. Reed pulp company at Bishop's Falls.[14]

The pulp and paper industry generated employment, but much of that was yet to come as St John's merchants invested in local manufacturing. While the forestry industry had shown some promise in diversifying the economy outside of St John's, the lumber industry had also demonstrated that the potential for resource exhaustion was great, and therefore the opportunities for significant long-term employment outside of the fishery were limited. Meanwhile, employment in mining was waning. Nonetheless, government support meant that merchants continued investing in local manufacturing, often with devastating effect on the smaller manufacturers who had long been a part of the St John's economy. Several small bakeries, for example, which had been producing ship's biscuit for the local fishing and shipping industries since the early years of the nineteenth century, could not withstand the competition of merchant-backed factories that imported machinery and raw materials for mass production. The new factories found the old markets for baked goods too limited, and diversified into making soft breads, pastries, cakes, and confections for the local market. Small tailoring and boot- and shoemaking establishments similarly fell to merchant-owned factory production. The Jobs with their Royal Stores, for example, integrated their manufacturing with retail establishments. These merchants secured markets and squeezed out smaller producers by using a few of their own products and larger volumes of imported goods to undercut local tailors, dressmakers, and milliners with a greater variety of cheaper goods. Ownership and control of local manufacturing concentrated as large firms restricted credit in the fishery even more.[15]

By 1910 there were signs the national policy of the Liberals was failing to live up to its promise. Railway development, mining, and forestry had failed to create the boom in population, employment, and wealth for which many had hoped. Despite the disappointing results, the government had promoted these industries by selling for a pittance much of the colony's resources into the hands of mostly foreign-owned and -controlled corporations. There had been few positive developments in the fishery; indeed the crisis of credit in the aftermath of the bank crash had continued to trouble that industry. Moreover, the differential tariff had made life more expensive for fishing people, who were already antagonized by what they perceived as the influence of Water Street merchants on government; but, rather than confront the problems of the fishery, the government invested most of its energy in economic diversification. The tariff structure cost fishers money and meant that the colonial economy had provided little opportunity for the profitable development of backward linkages from the fishing industry. Investment in producer goods for the fishery would perhaps have been productive, even this late in the day, but St John's manufacturers took advantage of the government's desire for diversification to gain protection from foreign competition through investment in the manufacture of consumer goods.[16]

The economic and social distinctions between St John's and the outports grew. While working-class organizations episodically tried to deal with poor working conditions and wages, St John's workers remained politically tied to their merchant-employers' campaigns for even greater assistance for manufacturing. In the outports, on the other hand, many fishing people saw their cost of living rise as the colonial government protected local markets for industry. To make matters worse, outport people paid higher prices on the necessities of life that were produced by capital generated partially by St John's firms' restriction of credit in the fishery.

Emigration persisted as an integral part of life in rural Newfoundland. If the national policy did not succeed in the short term in stemming emigration, then the government tended to feel that the colony was only losing its most unskilled and underemployed people. Bond hoped that the national policy would trigger a new immigration of skilled workers, agriculturalists, and entrepreneurs from Britain or northwestern Europe. The new immigrants would more than make up for those who left Newfoundland by developing the resources opened up in the interior by the railway. From the mid-nineteenth century, there had been a trickle of German, Norwegian, Dutch, and Danish immigrants, who came to work as merchants, ships' captains, medical professionals, engineers, and entrepreneurs, particularly in mining and forestry. The colony became a home to smaller numbers of Chinese immigrants and refugees from among the persecuted minorities of Eastern Europe, such as Polish Jews, or of the Ottoman Empire, such as Maronites, Druze, or Christian Syrians. These new immigrants became an important, if not particularly welcome, part of Newfoundland's society and economy. Jews from Russian territories, for example, usually young men, looked for business opportunities. Often finding a cold shoulder among the business owners of St John's, many took up peddling by foot or on coastal boats throughout rural Newfoundland and the coast of Labrador. Jewish pedlars found outport people more sympathetic but felt that the residents of St John's appreciated their success and patronized the businesses many eventually opened in the city. Once established, Jewish immigrants sent for family members to join them in Newfoundland. Nevertheless, increasing immigration amid a fairly open-door immigration policy meant that in 1906, fearing a flood of non-Anglo-Americans, the Newfoundland government passed the Chinese Immigration Act and the Aliens Act. The first was especially repugnant, imposing a $300 head tax on each Chinese male immigrant, attempting to limit the colony's Chinese community to a total of two hundred people, and barring the entry of Chinese women. The Aliens Act allowed the government to deport immigrants who it felt were not supporting themselves properly.[17]

While St John's had many of the trappings of a colonial capital, including the architectural symbols of the Colonial Building and Government House, the homes of the legislature and the governor respectively, in much of Newfoundland and Labrador the government was something with which people had infrequent contact. The government also provided few services to its citizens and relied upon merchants, clergy, and individual members of the Assembly to hand out public relief or employment in public works in rural districts. No area of the colony was as poorly served as Labrador. In the north, the Inuit were left to the Moravian missions to be regulated and administered. Rarely did the government have any contact directly with the Inuit but expected the Moravians to act as its agents. The Moravians continued to foster more fixed settlement by their Inuit followers around the missions at Hopedale, Nain, Okak, and later at Hebron,

Zoar, Ramah, and Makkovik, using a form of truck trade in the Inuit's cod fisheries and sealing to support the missions. The Moravians used debt to discourage Inuit business with traders to the south, thinking they were protecting the Inuit from a more corrosive trade, unfettered by Christian principles.

The missionaries further emphasized the importance of education, creating a written form of Inuktitut. Although this written language allowed the Inuit to study scripture and engage in more formal education, it was a form of orthographic imperialism. The Moravians imposed a Greenlandic and Germanic language on the Labrador Inuit, without regard for their spoken grammar and usage. Many Inuit preferred to avoid economic and cultural dependence on the Moravians by retreating to the northern tip of the Quebec-Labrador peninsula. These northern Inuit were content to trade with the Moravians and other traders, such as the Hudson's Bay Company (HBC), when it was convenient but were unwilling to become dependent on them by taking up cod fishing or commercial sealing.[18]

The Innu impinged upon the consciousness of St John's even less, despite the well-publicized exploits of the Hubbards. In 1903, Leonidas Hubbard, an editor with an American nature magazine, carried out an ill-fated expedition to what many American readers thought of as the exotic world of the Labrador interior. With his friend Dillon Wallace and guide George Elson, Leonidas Hubbard followed an inaccurate map, and they lost their way on the Susan River. Although Wallace and Elson survived, Hubbard perished. In 1905, Mina Hubbard, the wife of Leonidas, successfully completed the voyage he had planned. Her rivalry with Wallace, who had returned for a similar adventure, was well known, and Hubbard received much less public celebration in St John's than he did, likely because her successful leadership of an exploration party into the Labrador interior defied contemporary bourgeois expectations about women as the weaker sex.

Nonetheless, Hubbard's diary and published account of her expedition provided much evidence about the Innu. Hubbard recorded signs of Innu occupation everywhere in the interior. She also met with Innu under tense circumstances. The Innu had yet to have a good hunt that year and had been concerned about the manner in which settlers from North West River, people of mixed European and Inuit ancestry, had been intruding on their trapping grounds. One of Hubbard's party, Gilbert Blake, was a settler. The occasional Roman Catholic priest or HBC trader was the Innu's principal contact with other cultures. The HBC had been making the Innu more dependent on the fur trade with it by limiting ammunition for their caribou hunt, a policy that had sometimes brought the Innu to the brink of famine. The Innu had begun to assert their sovereignty over the Labrador interior by protesting settlers' trapping and the Newfoundland government's granting of timber rights to lumber companies.[19]

Perhaps no area of people's lives was more in need of aid than medical care. The dangerous occupations at sea and in the woods and chronic low incomes meant that malnutrition and the diseases that accompanied it were prevalent in areas such as the south coast of the island and coastal Labrador. As the Inuit settled in mission communities and became incorporated into the fishing economy, they no longer ate as much fresh meat and consumed much more flour and other European staples. The resulting poorer nutrition made them more susceptible to epidemics of such diseases as influenza and endemic diseases such as tuberculosis. The Moravians gave the Inuit what little help they could, but the settlers and other residents of the southern coast were on their own. Into this vacuum stepped Wilfred Grenfell. An experienced physician who was motivated by the Christian ideal of working among the poor, Grenfell first visited Labrador in 1892 and found a widely dispersed population of impoverished people in desperate need of medical attention. Over the next few years he combined visits to the coast by sailing vessel and steamer with public speaking and book writing in England and the United States to raise money to support his medical mission. The government of the colony was happy to have Grenfell treat the ill and raise money to build hospitals at St Anthony on the island and in several coastal communities such as at Battle Harbour, but were less happy with Grenfell's descriptions of northern poverty when they were trying to present the image of the colony as a prosperous and progressive place in which to invest. He recognized that medical care was a palliative that did not address the root causes of hardship and condemned the nature of merchant–client relations as being responsible for people's low incomes. On Grenfell's initiative several cooperatives were formed to give people an alternative to merchant credit, and a series of craft industries were begun to give people sources of income other than the fishery. Although often paternalistic in his messages, Grenfell and his Mission provided Labrador with a high-profile representation throughout North America that was difficult for the Newfoundland government to ignore.[20]

Small-scale handicraft production helped pay for the operation of the hospitals, but it could not compensate for the long-term decline in fish landings. The fishery had continued to languish as merchants withdrew capital from it, and colonial governments began to borrow heavily from foreign capital markets to fund economic diversification. The national policy itself burdened the fishery. Government tariffs raised the costs of the industry, while the appearance of new forms of employment on the railway and in forestry provided fishing people with alternate sources of income. Such income probably freed fishers from dependence on the credit of any particular merchant. In the context of the long-term restriction of credit in the trade, this meant that fishers were free to look for the best credit terms available. Merchants could not count on the dependence of their clients in a trade already risky due to such diverse problems as localized stock depletion, weather, international currency exchange, and market fluctuations. While smaller outport merchants had little choice but to continue extending credit in exchange for fish and other products such as cod oil, at least to the most dependable of their clients, the St John's firms had decided that investing in the fishery through extending additional credit was too unstable and risky. But as long as the vast majority of the population lived by fishing, merchants had no choice but to be involved in the complex credit and debt relations of the trade.

By the end of the nineteenth century, however, many firms could see the advantage of wholesaling and retailing in the cash markets of St John's and had high hopes for the development of similar markets in the industrial enclaves of forestry and mining. In the short term, merchants saw little point in investing a lot of money or time to reform the fishery. The fish trade was a highly competitive business to be squeezed ruthlessly to obtain profit that might then be invested in other sectors of the economy, or consumed as the personal wealth of the grand families of Water Street.[21] Under such circumstances, investing in a new industrial sector such as mining seemed more secure. Not only did investment in such an area seem to promise a way out of the troubled fishery, but there were also numerous American companies willing to provide capital to fund prospecting. Before 1908 no more than a few thousand people were ever employed in mining, but there were enough families enjoying the benefits of steadier employment and higher incomes than could be found in the fishery to pressure government for more. American capital also entered the forestry sector.

Until the 1880s, St John's merchants had provided most of the capital and ownership of the colony's shipping fleet. While merchants favoured the small schooners in the fishery and coastal shipping trade, by the 1860s they had also invested in the larger sailing vessels of the ocean-going trades. Declining earnings in the fishery meant that most merchants withdrew capital from the shipping industry through the 1880s. A small number of St John's and Conception Bay merchants increased their investment in shipping, particularly steam-driven vessels that were built outside the colony, and extended control over a greater portion of the colony's shipping fleet. Steamers had proven much more productive in the seal hunt, but the higher overhead costs of steamers meant that very few firms could afford them. The seal hunt was subject to many of the same uncertainties as the cod fishery, and owners would be hard pressed to find profitable uses for the steamers once the sealing season ended.

The pattern of investment in the seal hunt suggests an underlying weakness in this economic development. Firms tended to invest more in steamers after a particularly good hunt. The intensifying depletion of seals meant, however, that the best seasons increasingly went to those who employed steamers because these vessels were far more mobile in the pack ice and could better hunt for increasingly hard-to-find herds. By the early years of the twentieth century it became apparent that seal herds were in such bad shape that even the investment in steamers could no longer be justified. Over the long term, the cycle of investment and resource depletion encouraged merchants to withdraw capital from the fishery and landward investments.[22]

The merchants who invested in the seal hunt tried to offset declining rates of return by squeezing more out of their labour by using the share system of payments, a divisive system that pitted sealers against each other, and a variety of means such as 'berth' fees and charging sealers for their equipment. Nonetheless, time spent working together and living under harsh and dangerous conditions encouraged sealers to see that they had much in common, leading to collective action, such as a brief sealers strike in 1902. In that year, 211 sealers of the SS *Ranger*, a wooden-hulled steamer, left their vessel in St John's to protest their wages and sparked a wider strike by sealers from other vessels. Paid only by shares, the sealers had witnessed the steady deterioration in their earnings throughout the last quarter of the nineteenth century. Vessel owners made extra money, besides the sale of seal oil and hides, by charging the sealers for coal to fuel the vessels and for cleaning the vessels after the hunt. The sealers continued to purchase all the equipment they required for the hunt in truck from the vessel's owners. On 8 March 1902, the international price for seal oil had dropped so low that the sealers could not see how going to the ice would be worth all these charges. Merchants were offering only $2.40 for every 112 pounds of seal fat while the strikers wanted $4.00 to $5.00. Governor Sir Cavendish Boyle met the strikers and suggested they consider a compromise price of $3.25. The men of each ship agreed and chose a delegate from each vessel to meet with the owners, enlisting the representation of A.B. Morine. But the merchant firms – Baine, Johnston, Job's, and Bowring's – would only commit to looking into the matter. By 10 March it was clear the owners would make no concessions. Sympathetic residents of St John's took the strikers, most of whom had made their own way into the capital from communities on the northeast coast, into their homes. When some of the sealers broke ranks to return to their ships, the strikers formed a vigilance committee to prevent them from doing so. The owners requested the governor provide armed protection for sealers who wished to return to work, while the sealers, with Morine, asked for Premier Bond's assistance. The strikers stood firm in a demand of $4.00 per 112 pounds. An offer of $3.50 tempted many of the strikers to return to their ships. A crowd of angry sealers rushed to the wharves to prevent this return and were joined by local supporters among the townspeople. An appeal from Morine, and an assurance that Bond would back the settlement, led the strikers to return to their ships.[23]

Although an important part of the rural economy of the northeast coast, the seal hunt did not completely transform rural independent fishermen into part of a working class even though it was a harsh experience with the exploitation of capitalism. Sealing remained something resorted to for a few weeks out of the year by young men who were part of families working in fishing households for the rest of the year. The share system in the industry tended to lead to extreme competitiveness between the crews of different vessels, and even among the crews of individual vessels. While shares continued to dominate the payment of wages, employment levels dropped. Working conditions became more proletarian, but the work became a much more urban, St John's, phenomenon throughout the early twentieth century.[24]

The resource depletion and class conflict within the sealing industry in the early years of the twentieth century reveal the limited nature of the investment opportunities for merchant capital in the marine-resource sector of Newfoundland and Labrador. Merchants tried to utilize the unused capacity by employing their steamers to carry fishers to the Labrador coast in the summer and carrying salt cod to markets at the end of the fishing season. Unfortunately the large freight capacity and speed of the steamers encouraged greater competition between merchant firms and led to even more glutted markets and low fish prices. The resulting persistent drop in fish prices in turn undermined the bank fishery, the other major area of merchant investment, despite the subsidies provided by the Newfoundland government. By the early twentieth century, the bank fishery was a small part of the overall industry, although it was very important to the communities of the south coast of Newfoundland.[25]

Aware of the various problems that characterized the Newfoundland cod fishery, a number of fish merchants looked to the Americans for possible alternatives for the industry. In particular, the merchants of Gloucester, Massachusetts, had been turning more to the sale of cod in the domestic market to escape the same limits of low international prices. The fishing industry of Gloucester successfully defended protection of the American market for fish from competing imports and could rely on the railway transportation network radiating out from Boston to permit efficient marketing. The domestic market allowed the Gloucester industry to invest in new processing and packaging techniques to provide a high-quality, value-added product. Gloucester investors could afford to equip their banking schooners with auxiliary engines. All of these innovations were well known in Newfoundland, since Gloucester schooners came every year to acquire bait and ice from Newfoundland suppliers.

Merchants from St John's with ties to those in such south-coast centres as Burin, Fortune, Grand Bank, and St Lawrence, as well as local firms from those communities, considered the feasibility of adopting similar innovations as the Americans'. Unlike the Americans, these Newfoundland firms could not rely on a large, protected domestic market for fish to make the investment worthwhile. The St John's firm Bowring Brothers Ltd. had experimented with the introduction of a steam trawler in 1901–2 but found that it was too costly to operate in the absence of a nearby market for fresh fish. Although the Bond government had hoped that the combination of the railway, a good ferry service to the mainland, and cold-storage technology would allow Newfoundland-caught fish to be shipped to mainland markets, the cold-storage methods of the day were not adequate to facilitate the shipment of fresh fish over such long distances. The introduction of auxiliary engines gave American schooners an advantage in pursuing pelagic species such as herring and mackerel. Unable to justify the expense of such engines due to the poor returns of the international cod fishery, Newfoundland bank fishers could not break into these subsidiary fisheries, which, like the American cod fishery, enjoyed protected markets. Throughout the first decade of the twentieth century a number of merchant firms attempted to produce new fish products, from scotch-cured herring to a form of canned cod with the ill-advised name of 'fish cheese.' None of these operations were able to break into the American market.[26]

Without more lucrative markets for fish products, few merchants were willing to combine to take control over marketing in the colony's established salt-fish markets. Occasionally merchants would form an association, such as the Fish Exporters' Association of 1900, but Water Street's culture of competition meant that one or more firms usually broke ranks to try to get a better price. In this case, Bowring's broke away from an agreement to fix prices in the Brazilian market. Premier Bond attempted to improve the position of Newfoundland fish in the American market. The premier had come under increasing political pressure from the colonial press to do something to stem the tide of emigration to the United States. In 1902 Bond began this process anew through the negotiation of the Bond-Hay Treaty. This treaty would have allowed American fishers the right to purchase bait in Newfoundland on the same terms as Newfoundlanders, as well as the right to trade in colonial ports. The duties on many American imports would be removed or reduced, while Newfoundland would gain free access to the American market for metal ores and all fish products except fresh or unsalted cod. The last provision left many Newfoundlanders wondering if the treaty was worth much, but salt-fish exporters thought that the American markets for salt fish were good enough to justify it. Unfortunately for Bond, Gloucester fishing interests managed to stall American approval of the Bond-Hay Treaty. The American Senate's delay of the treaty led the Bond government to take retaliatory measures against the American fishery at Newfoundland, but to little effect. American vessels could no longer be licensed to purchase bait and supplies in Newfoundland, and the Americans were excluded from the winter herring fishery of the Bay of Islands based on a particular construction of the Convention of 1818 that argued that Americans did not have a right to fish off coasts inside the headlands of Newfoundland's major bays. The government's actions angered the American and British governments as well as the many Newfoundland fishers who depended on employment on American ships or on sales of bait to the Americans. The British and Americans eventually worked out a compromise that restored most of the Americans' fishing rights. Bond's government was embarrassed, and his party split on the issue.

Bond had other difficulties. The ambitious E.P. Morris left the government on a pretext and founded the People's Party. The People's Party supported amicable relations with the United States and hoped for an infusion of American capital to reinvigorate the national policy. Morris spoke much about Bond's futile efforts to develop markets while jeopardizing possible sources of investment in new manufacturing enterprises that would allow more Newfoundlanders to stay at home. Morris, a man who was comfortable rubbing shoulders with his working-class constituents, made much about being a man of the people, while portraying Bond as aloof and arrogant, a patrician who had little sympathy with the sealers during their strike. While Morris claimed to be interested in fisheries development, it was clear that his real interest lay in promoting the Reid enterprises and the national policy generally. The People's Party's development policies were not all that different from the Liberals', except in Morris's support for the Reids.

By 1908, it was apparent that the movement to secure better markets for fish products in the United States had failed. Without new market opportunities, merchants remained mired in their old marketing habits and continued their long-standing practice of withdrawing capital from the fishery.[27] It was also clear that marine-resource industries offered little room for additional investment in the manner to which merchants were accustomed. As the seal hunt had demonstrated, investment in more capital-intensive technologies quickly exacerbated the ongoing problems of resource depletion, which were already evident in the cod fisheries. Although the initial experience of railway development might have suggested to colonial governments that the alternative – landward diversification – was fraught with difficulties, they felt that there were few options. The twentieth century had begun with resurgent local nationalism, and the spectacular apparent success of establishing an interior pulp and paper industry, despite major concessions to foreign capitalists, offered hope for the future. In St John's, railway development and protective tariffs prompted local manufacturing, but at the expense of outport people's quality of living. The industrial constituencies of the city became a powerful political force, which an astute politician like Morris discovered might be mobilized by patronage, especially through further railway development. Few people thought much about taking new approaches to the better use of the mainstay of the colony, its marine resources. While many were inclined to view the Newfoundland national policy as progressive and forward looking, occasional voices would demand that the colony pay more attention to the better management of its fisheries. One such voice was that of William Coaker of the Fishermen's Protective Union.

8

The Politics of Hope and Demoralization, 1908–1934

Morris's People's Party, which came to power in 1909, continued the free fall into debt that began with the Liberals' landward economic diversification policies. Regardless of partisanship, the colony's political and economic elites developed no effective policies to address the problems of the fishery. New working-class movements periodically offered opportunities to redefine priorities for Newfoundland, but they fell apart because of the structural problems of mining and forestry or because of their dependence on the protectionism and investment of St John's merchants. The appearance of the Fishermen's Protective Union (FPU) initially seemed to promise reform but foundered on the political goals and personal inclinations of its leader, William Ford Coaker.

The FPU originated in the contraction of merchant credit that followed the bank crash of 1894. Fishers without credit had to work on shares for those who did, especially those who owned cod traps and the larger skiffs required to operate them. Successful trap owners, called trap skippers, could afford motors for their boats, allowing them to go further to set their traps. Most skippers and their employees were related; community and family considerations rather than the market governed skippers' relationships with servants, and all depended on merchants' credit. Merchants recognized that cod traps, and later motor boats used to tend them, served as adequate collateral that could be seized in case clients defaulted on their debts. Class differences emerged among fishers when some skippers began to act more as merchants themselves. Such skippers and planters in the Labrador fishery used truck practices to supply their servants with equipment and provisions. Community identification continued to tie trap skippers and their crews together, particularly as it became clear that it was the merchants of Water Street who cut credit. As such, trap skippers emerged as important, if paternalistic, leaders of their fishing communities.[1]

The fishery continued to be the economic mainstay of the island, making the restriction of credit all the more troubling. On the northeast coast, mining had declined, leaving people dependent on locally depleted cod stocks, reduced seal herds, and a steamer-based industry concentrated in St John's. The southern shore of Conception Bay, like most of the fishing communities of the northeastern Avalon Peninsula and its southern shore, benefited from the growth of St John's. People found work in the city's new industrial enterprises, and its growing population created a market for a variety of marginal agricultural surpluses and fresh fish. The opportunities for such employment were limited; despite all of the effort directed at economic diversification, six out of every ten people who worked in the colony were still fishers, and many others worked in the preparation and handling of fish products. The fishery dominated economic life from Ferryland south and west across St Mary's, Placentia, and Fortune bays. Merchants continued to invest in the bank fishery, which helped to maintain the total volume of fish exports of the colony. Working conditions were terrible in the bank fishery, but merchants used a combination of fixed wages and shares to encourage rivalry among the schooner crews and paternalistic ties with schooner masters.[2]

Discontent in these fisheries was never the same as on the northeast and west coasts, where credit restriction had eroded paternalistic truck practices. The slump during the 1907–8 exporting season was particularly severe partially because, although there had been a good fish catch, merchants' usual rush of salt fish to market produced a glut and a slump in prices. Merchants cut in half the price they had offered for fish the year before, threatening even trap owners. Trap skippers responded by taking a leading role in the formation of the FPU. By 1908, the FPU in turn mobilized the many more fishers who were brought together in the Labrador floater fishery and seal hunt, harsh work which fostered solidarity among the crews. The stationer fishery at Labrador, which had closely tied together families on the southern Labrador coast with those of the south shore of Conception Bay, had also been hit hard by the poor season of 1907–8. The floater fishery, however, drew fishers together in a more collective enterprise, unlike the household character of production among the stationers. The nature of work in the floater fishery and the seal hunt, combined with the leading role played by trap skippers in their home communities, provided a strong base for the FPU in communities such as Port de Grave, Bay de Verde, Trinity, Bonavista, Fogo, and Twillingate. Bank fishers provided little support for the FPU, favouring the denominational and fraternal organizations such as the Star of the Sea Association, the Society of United Fishermen, the Orange Lodge, and the Masonic Lodge.[3]

William Ford Coaker gave the FPU much of its specific character. Coaker was not from a fishing community; he had been born in St John's in 1871. As a boy, Coaker had quit school to work with other boys as fish handlers for Water Street merchants. Treated as cheap and casual labour, fish handlers worked hard for little pay. Coaker's response was to organize a successful strike in 1884 for better pay. Coaker may have absorbed some of the unionist views of other workers on the St John's waterfront; he later claimed to be familiar with elements of socialist thought. Coaker's values could be attributed to his Anglican upbringing to some degree; at heart he believed in the right of every individual to participate equally in the pursuit of wealth. Hard work, honesty, a commitment to fair play, and a sense of duty should be enough for personal success. Coaker went on to manage a fish cannery and eventually set up as an independent shopkeeper in Notre Dame Bay. After his small business failed during the bank crash, he began to farm near the small community of Herring Neck and fished on the side. A supporter of Bond, he received patronage appointments as a telegrapher and chair of the local road board in 1897 but lost both positions when the Tories came to power.

Coaker viewed merchants as ruthless exploiters. Sympathetic to the hardships of his neighbouring fishers and their families, he saw his own problems as part of theirs. Merchants, furthermore, were St John's people who used their influence over government to control Newfoundland and Labrador for their own interests, while venal city politicians courted self-interested city voters to the detriment of outport people. In 1903, Coaker organized a union of telegraphers and established a small newspaper that focused on the fisheries. His editorials addressed the plight faced by fishermen, whom he saw as a hard-working, God-fearing, and dutiful lot, the heart and soul of Newfoundland society. Given a fair chance, such fishers should have been able to earn good livings, but the power of merchants and their government lackeys meant fishermen never had a fair chance.

Between 1903 and 1908, Coaker conceived of an organization of fishermen that would counteract the influence of big merchants and indifferent governments in St John's: the FPU.

The FPU's basic philosophy bore the stamp of Coaker's individualism and incipient populism: fishermen should be independent, each having the right to accumulate the wealth from his labour. Embodied in the motto of the FPU, 'to each his own,' the ethic of Coaker's FPU was directed at merchants' use of credit to exploit the hard work of fishers. The FPU was primarily a cooperative of inshore fishing people that attempted to eliminate merchants as brokers in the marketing of fish. While a collective enterprise, the FPU's goals were nonetheless individualistic.

In 1909 the FPU held a founding convention that organized the union much like the Orange Lodge, the first democratic organization many fishers had experienced. The FPU's constitution allowed any male fisher, farmer, logger, or manual labourer to join a local in their community. Each local would then elect representatives to district councils that, in turn, would elect representatives to a supreme governing council. The annual conventions of the FPU elected its president, with Coaker being acclaimed in the position at the first convention. In the same year, Coaker established an FPU newspaper, the *Fishermen's Advocate*, to voice fishers' concerns, offer solutions, and politically educate their neighbours.[4]

While occasionally interested in the organization of fish production, the FPU spent much of its energy on giving fishers more control over the conditions under which they sold fish. The FPU wanted to see more government involvement in an impartial inspection and grading of fish quality, rather than leaving it in the hands of merchant-employed cullers. The union further criticized *tal qual* as a disincentive to the production of good-quality fish. Most importantly, the FPU wanted fishers to control the marketing of fish.

Initially, Coaker suggested that fishers should organize a loan fund through the FPU so that they could purchase supplies without having to rely on merchants' credit. Coaker put his ideas into operation by establishing the FPU's own mercantile enterprise in St John's: the Union Trading Company (UTC). By using bulk buying, the UTC would be able to supply goods at prices below those offered by merchants and therefore break their prices. The allegiance of the membership of the FPU to the UTC was impressive; by 1919 it was a successful mercantile venture whose earnings funded much of the work of the FPU. While the UTC successfully competed with merchants, it did not precipitate reform of the fishery. The FPU's other business enterprises, the Union Electric Company and a shipyard, show the extent to which the Union mobilized fishing people's dues to build a business empire. It was headquartered in its own town, Port Union, which boasted union-owned bungalows for workers, a department store with an elevator, and a movie theatre.[5]

Coaker felt that the FPU must organize politically to reform the fishery. Merchants had recently organized in a Board of Trade through the efforts of William G. Gosling to develop markets, regulate fish quality, support fisheries research, and lobby government on fisheries policy. Gosling's efforts had the sympathy of E.P. Morris; the People's Party platform called for market development, cold storage facilities, steam transportation of fish to markets, bait facilities, fisheries diversification, and a ban on steamers in the Labrador fishery. By supporting the Board of Trade, Morris looked dynamic in comparison with Bond, who was still flailing about on the issue of better access to the American market. While leading merchants supported the board, they only supported a voluntary inspection for salt fish and preferred to blame fishers' supposed illiteracy and conservatism for the persistence of poor quality. The FPU, by contrast, wanted government control of a mandatory inspection process that would be free of mercantile influence.[6]

Initially, Morris's rhetoric of being the working man's friend appealed to Coaker, as did the People's Party's pro-development policies. The split between Bond and Morris over the issue of access to American markets for Newfoundland products had been a further attraction. The People's Party's development platform, while mostly consisting of plans stolen from the Liberals, antagonized Water Street merchants, who favoured Bond's attempt to gain freer access to the American market and who rejected the Reid railway plan as too ambitious. Morris, on the other hand, continued to support the railway as essential for diversification and had the support of many of Newfoundland's smaller businesspeople, especially newer outport merchants, journalists, and professionals who felt that the expansion of outport branch lines would assist in the development of new industries throughout the entire colony.

In his struggle with Bond during the general election of 1908, Morris had angled for the support of fishing people and the FPU by promising better fisheries reform and an old-age pension scheme. However, Morris's failure to establish government-controlled, mandatory regulation of salt-fish marketing and his refusal to enforce regulations against commercial cutting on a three-mile-deep strip of coastal forests reserved for use in the fishery alienated Coaker and the FPU. Through 1911, Morris continued to fish for FPU support, using the bait of a limited number of pensions worth $50 per year available only to men over the age of 75. Morris eventually proposed to allow an additional four hundred pensions in 1912 in a further bid to live up to an FPU call for a more generous provision of $100 per year to men over the age of 70. While Bond criticized the expense of Morris's plan, no one, including the FPU, criticized the manner in which it excluded women, who did so much of the processing of catches into salt fish.[7]

Coaker concluded that none of the St John's–based parties were likely to represent the interests of fishing people adequately. The People's Party represented city capitalists, not fishing people, sealers, and loggers. The Liberals' old association with the encouragement of manufacturing through tariff protection meant that they were largely a party of the city, not of the outports. St John's newspapers and the city's workers benefited from manufacturing, which pitted them both against the anti-protectionist stance of the FPU. The FPU's loose ties to the Orange Order on the northeast coast and its progressivism drew the ire of Roman Catholic Archbishop Howley, who encouraged opposition to the union.

Without much support among the bank fishermen of the south coast, the FPU was a regional movement. The way to gain influence over colonial policy, Coaker thought, lay in the same balance-of-power strategy that Morris had previously used with Bond. The FPU should form a political wing that would form alliances with whichever party was willing to promote the rights of fishing people, as articulated in the political platform of the FPU. The Union Party had an excellent chance of controlling the fourteen seats in the House of Assembly for the northeast coast. In a House of thirty-six seats, such control was critical in the balance of power but insufficient to allow one party to form a government.

The full political program of the FPU shook the foundations of party politics in Newfoundland. It demanded that government provide free and compulsory education in non-denominational schools. In the outports, night schools should be made available to people who could not attend during the day because of their work. Local fishing people should elect people from their own communities to run school boards, but these boards should not be controlled by appointees of the church establishment in St John's. Sectarian politics should also be removed from the composition of the road boards that provided able-bodied relief. People in the outports should elect the boards rather than rely on the patronage of St John's politicians. Further, the FPU advocated conflict-of-interest legislation and the use of referenda, both to ensure that the government in St John's remained responsive to the people and to limit its corrupt practices. Finally, they required government to bring in universal old-age pensions and develop a program of rural hospital construction.

Such a platform clearly threatened the autonomy and power of merchants and industrialists in the economy. The union wanted import tariffs adjusted so that outport people could have access to cheaper imported goods, a direct threat to the factory owners and workers of St John's. They wanted the government to legislate better working conditions and wages in the seal hunt and logging, and, most threatening of all, they desired that the state take control of the marketing of salt fish to end the ruinous, competitive marketing habits of the colony's major exporting firms. The FPU demanded that the government guarantee the quality of its fish products to foreign consumers by abolishing *tal qual*, by legislating a standardized fish cull, and by appointing government cullers and inspectors. Newfoundland must further appoint overseas trade commissioners to take more direct responsibility for the promotion of Newfoundland products in foreign markets rather than rely on British officials or agents of private companies to do so. While concentrating on fish marketing, the FPU was also interested in the conservation of fish stocks and wanted the government to reorganize, and provide more financial support for, a professional fisheries department.

Having parted ways with Morris, Coaker approached Sir Robert Bond about the possibility of a Liberal-FPU political alliance. In 1911 Coaker proposed that any FPU MHAs elected in the next general election would support a government led by Bond, as long as it agreed to fisheries reform. Ever the patrician, and an ally of Bishop Howley, Bond refused, arguing that he could not allow a specific interest group to 'coerce' legislation from the Assembly, although governments had acted on behalf of railway owners, manufacturers, merchants, and bishops in the past. Coaker organized a mass demonstration by sealers in St John's in March 1912, but neither Bond nor Morris would bargain with the FPU. Morris, feeling cocky because of the better condition of the economy, openly attacked Coaker, as did Morris's allies in the Roman Catholic press. Coaker turned to organizing fishers in crucial Liberal districts such as Twillingate, which provided Bond's own seat, Bonavista, Trinity, and Fogo. Having lost a seat in a by-election the previous year, the Liberals' political fortunes looked bad indeed. Under pressure from his northeast-coast supporters in the House, Bond accepted an alliance with the FPU.

Although Bond had supported landward development, he feared the growing public debt and despised Morris's use of railway branch-line contracts to buy votes. He insisted that the Liberals could only enter the next election on a platform of government retrenchment. The Liberal-Union alliance, as it became known, survived only because of Bond's promise to attempt some of the reforms demanded by the FPU's own platform and because of the efforts of more cooperative leading Liberals such as James M. Kent and W.F. Lloyd. At first glance, the result of the alliance in the 1913 general election was unimpressive. The Liberal-Unionists managed to gain only fifteen of the House's thirty-six seats, and Morris's hold on power remained secure. The FPU's Union Party, however, had fielded nine candidates. Eight of these won their electoral battles, and the other, Nathan Barrett, lost by only nine votes to People's Party candidate John C. Crosbie in the district of Bay de Verde. The six Liberals elected in northeast-coast districts, including Bond, succeeded because the FPU had not run candidates against them. Thus, while the Liberals depended on the Union Party for electoral support, the Union Party depended on the Liberals for legislative experience and support in St John's.

Unable to accept his political dependence on a party of fishermen, Bond resigned his seat and retreated to his estate at Whitbourne to launch bitter attacks against the FPU. The leadership of the alliance was assumed by J.M. Kent, while Morris's political fortunes began to change for the worse. His St John's constituents consisted largely of the Reid enterprises and all those workers who depended on the railway and its related enterprises for their livelihoods. Morris's use of branch-line construction to establish a broad base of support outside the city had begun to alienate the merchants of Water Street, who feared mounting public debt and higher taxes. Soon after the election in 1913, with the support of Water Street slipping away, Morris again courted the FPU. His government passed toothless legislation to prevent price fixing in the fishery by merchant combines, to create and expand a Workmen's Compensation Act to cover sealers, and to establish better working conditions for sealers. Morris agreed to a joint Union Party–Board of Trade call for a royal commission to investigate conditions in the fishery but faced stiff opposition within the Legislative Council, where the influence of the St John's merchants remained strongest. Morris provided no effective enforcement for his fisheries initiatives and refused to implement the fisheries commission's call for government regulation of quality standards, culling, and inspection. In consequence, the premier had little chance for support from the Union Party.[8]

While the government's economic policies benefited the St John's area, the life of outport people continued to be difficult. Nowhere was this more apparent than in the spring seal hunt. For many, the hunt was the first opportunity to earn some cash as their credit and stores from the previous summer and fall fishing season, and other work had been all but exhausted through the winter. The crushing ice floes, icy waters, and unpredictable gales of freezing rain and snow that mark spring in the North Atlantic always claimed ships and men. The scale of the disasters changed as the size of sealing vessels increased with the transition to steam power, reaching its most tragic proportions in the spring of 1914.

The higher overhead costs of steamers, combined with the increasing difficulty of finding seals, led the captains and crews of sealing vessels to take greater risks in order to have successful voyages. Sealing skippers divided their larger crews into four watches that they would send onto the pack ice to kill patches of seals. It was rare to find enough seals in one patch to keep all of the watches busy, so captains often dropped a watch in one place and then steamed to another patch of seals to drop more men over the side. Sometimes the steamer would return for a watch, but often the captain expected his men to walk to the vessel, towing seals behind them. However, if bad weather or ice conditions changed for the worse, there was a danger that the sealers might become stranded. Such was the case in 1898, when Captain George Barbour of the SS *Greenland* lost forty-eight men from one watch in a blizzard. What became known as the '*Greenland* disaster' first provoked public outrage about the dangers and working conditions of the hunt. Particularly galling was the rumour that the crew of another steamer had stolen panned seals belonging to the *Greenland*, forcing it to stay out longer.

The government introduced some reforms, but they did little to prevent other disasters, culminating in the loss of the SS *Southern Cross* in late March 1914 while en route to St John's from the seal hunt in the Gulf of St Lawrence. Despite the persistence of such tragedies, sealing captains had no difficulty in finding sealers to work on their vessels. Crews tended to defer to their captains due to the deadly combination of masculinity and paternalism in the industry. Outport people commonly saw the hunt as a rite of passage; boys were not men until they had bloodied themselves at the hunt. Fathers often took their sons with them to the hunt, or young men went with their older brothers or uncles. The persistence of payment by shares and the importance of earnings from the hunt meant that sealers admired skippers' reputations as 'real seal killers' or as men who could find the 'main patch' of the seal herds, thereby assuring a successful hunt for all.

The most famous of all, Captain Abram Kean, had a reputation as a hard master and canny hunter. He was the master of the sealing crew that had allegedly stolen seals from the *Greenland*. Although he was embarrassed by the allegations, the sealing captain nonetheless prospered in his profession. Sealers vied with each other to get a berth on Kean's vessels because of his track record. Likewise, men hoped to join the vessels captained by Kean's son Westbury, or one of his nephews' vessels. The Keans often went to the ice together in a fleet of steamers.

In the same year as the *Southern Cross* tragedy, Abram and Westbury Kean played a key role in the most infamous of sealing catastrophes: the *Newfoundland* disaster of 1914. That spring, Abram took the largest of the steamers, the SS *Stephano* belonging to Bowring Brothers, to the ice, while Westbury took the *Newfoundland*, which belonged to a competing firm, Harveys. Despite the competition of the vessel owners, Abram helped his son find the main patch of seals, although the *Newfoundland*, an older wooden steamer, had difficulty in navigating through the pack ice. On 31 March Westbury decided to send his entire crew over the side under the command of his second hand, George Tuff, to walk to the *Stephano*. Abram Kean brought many of the crew to a patch of seals, although they had struggled over the ice for over four hours. The weather grew stormy, so Tuff decided to lead the men back to the *Newfoundland*. The crew became lost, but both Keans thought they were safe aboard each other's ships and had no way to contact each other because of the absence of a wireless on the *Newfoundland*.

The result was what the author Cassie Brown called 'death on the ice.' The crew of the *Newfoundland* wandered in a raging storm of snow and freezing rain for fifty-three hours. Most were improperly clothed and had little food. Fathers and sons, brothers and uncles, and best friends from childhood tried to keep each other going. As hypothermia and exhaustion worsened, men began to hallucinate about their loved ones at home; others sank to the ice in a stupor. Some simply walked off the edge of the ice into the sea. Friends and family tried to pick up the living, but often without success. They might return later to find only the dead and face the gruesome choice of having to scavenge for caps, mitts, or food to stay alive. Early on Thursday morning, part of the crew finally struggled to a nearby steamer, the SS *Bellaventure*, which began a rescue operation. Seventy-eight men died on the ice. Of the fifty-five survivors many were permanently crippled.

St John's came to a standstill when people heard of the tragedy. Crowds gathered to watch the maimed and the dead unloaded from the ship. At the ice, the crews of other vessels began to mutiny as they heard the news but learned that their captains would not stop the hunt. People clamoured for an investigation, but a magisterial inquiry found that no one was criminally responsible. Three thousand people demanded Abram Kean's arrest, and unprecedented public criticism of the seal hunt and its captains spread throughout the island. Coaker accused Kean, a supporter of the Morris government, of being responsible for the disaster. When their fight threatened the government, Morris forced Kean to withdraw libel charges against Coaker. Two members of a commission of inquiry in 1915 agreed that Abram should never have sent the *Newfoundland*'s men over the side in a gathering storm. One other blamed the weather. Ridiculously, the commission faulted George Tuff for not doing the unheard-of: refusing to take the old man's orders and keep the *Newfoundland* crew aboard the *Stephano*; but it also acknowledged real responsibility when it recommended that shipowners must be held accountable for injury and death among their crews and install safety equipment, weather forecasting equipment, and wireless telegraphs aboard all vessels.[9]

Many of these recommendations became law in 1916, although relief came to survivors and families primarily by public subscription to a disaster relief fund. By the summer of 1914, the *Newfoundland* disaster had appeared to tap a mainspring of anger among fishing people about social inequalities. Some sealers threatened to never hunt with Abram Kean again. Yet by 1915 he was back at the ice and went on to more fame and fortune, eventually receiving an appointment to the Legislative Council in 1927 and, in 1934, being awarded the Order of the British Empire when he caught his millionth seal. As in the case of Morris, who was floundering in 1914, war saved Kean's political neck. Morris had been unable to get more financial support from the Reids, and popular anger growing out of revelations of past timber-speculation scandals had risen to a fury over the fate of the sealers of the *Newfoundland*. Morris again turned to the idea of Confederation with Canada as a way to find more money for the railway and to rescue the government from financial embarrassment, but this further angered his opponents in St John's, whether mercantile, manufacturing, or Roman Catholic. The outbreak of war led Morris's critics to back off as a part of the general rallying around the flag that accompanied Newfoundland's entry into the First World War.

The organization of Newfoundland's participation in the war was largely an affair of the St John's elite. Morris, to the outrage of Coaker, agreed to surrender government control over Newfoundland's war effort to an organization of private St John's citizens chaired by the governor: the Newfoundland Patriotic Association (NPA). The NPA oversaw Newfoundland and Labrador's war effort until 1917, raising most of the funds for the war effort because the government was nearing financial ruin largely through railway spending. Mostly composed of local businesspeople, professionals, and journalists, the NPA viewed the city's interests as the same as those of Newfoundland. The NPA made the war effort a non-partisan affair by recruiting the support of members of the Liberal opposition. It raised funds and established the Newfoundland Regiment. The first five hundred soldiers shipped out to the ringing cheers of nearly the entire population of the capital. The ready availability of recruits from the more casual labour market of St John's, the assistance of denominationally based cadet corps for city youth, and the almost complete lack of a recruitment system in the outports at the height of the summer fishery meant that there were more city than rural men among the first to go overseas. Nevertheless, by the end of the war, 73.1 per cent, or 5,014, of the 6,754 men who joined the Regiment and the Newfoundland Forestry Corp were from rural Newfoundland and Labrador. Rural recruitment increased every year until 1918, when over 87 per cent of the 2,094 enlistments were from the outports.[10]

The Newfoundland Regiment acquitted itself well through many of the toughest battles of the war. It fought the Turks at Gallipoli and the Germans in the muddy trenches of France in the Battle of the Somme in the summer of 1916. Transfer to the Eighth Corps of the British Fourth Army led the regiment to tragedy. Allied command assigned the regiment a leading role by asking it to capture an area in the vicinity of Beaumont Hamel, behind the German front line. On 1 July 1916, about 810 officers and men of the Newfoundland Regiment went over the top against the Germans. British command overestimated the impact of artillery bombardments on German defences, and the Allies had failed to destroy a strategic machine-gun emplacement. When the order came, the Newfoundlanders climbed out of their trenches with rifles in hand and advanced toward the German machine guns.

Within minutes the regiment was nearly annihilated. Only two offic- ers and 95 of the men from the regiment answered roll call the next morning. Fifteen officers and 95 other men lay dead on the field, while 16 officers and 479 men were wounded. One officer and 114 soldiers were missing somewhere among the mud, blood, craters, spent shells, and barbed wire. The attack was a military disaster.[11]

Almost everyone in St John's lost a family member or friend at Beaumont Hamel. However, in the middle of war, authorities in New- foundland and the empire could not afford to have the loss viewed as a strategic blunder. Huge church services manifested public grief. Priests and ministers joined British war leaders in preaching duty to empire and glory, but the commemorations of the loss took on mes- sianic overtones of sacrifice, resurrection, and redemption. The people of St John's had now encountered death on a scale so massive it made even the sealing disasters pale by comparison. Newfoundlanders had developed a new sense of national identity as their country seemed to have been baptized in blood at Beaumont Hamel. The myth of Beau- mont Hamel quickly emerged, 'emphasizing bravery, determination, imperial loyalty, Christian devotion, and immortal achievement' on the part of the Newfoundland Regiment.[12]

The importance of the British connection remained strong, but in 1916 a new nationalism overshadowed it. Elements of this national- ism – especially the notion of Newfoundland as the long-suffering but stolid cornerstone of empire, popular among members of the New- foundland elite, such as the judge and historian D.W. Prowse, and Sir Robert Bond – had been around since the late nineteenth century. The public commemoration of Beaumont Hamel transformed this nation- alism into a mass phenomenon, at least in St John's.[13]

By 1917, many people were less enamoured of wartime myths as they began to contrast the sacrifice of Beaumont Hamel with the sus- picion that members of the NPA were part of a St John's profiteering ring. The NPA struggled to maintain sufficient recruitment to replace the daily casualties, and there was popular mistrust of the manner in which the organization managed money that it had raised to care for relatives left behind by soldiers going overseas. Rising prices angered people who felt that Water Street merchants controlled imports to in- flate coal prices beyond the conditions created by the war. Additional fears grew that fish merchants created artificial shortages of salt and fishing supplies to extort higher prices and that wholesale and retail traders inflated prices even more. Water Street merchants drew the ire of outport people by selling off most of their steel-hulled steamers now that the price of used ships was high. These steamers had become an important part of the seal hunt, the marketing of salt cod, the export trade generally, and communication around the coasts of Newfoundland and Labrador.[14]

The growing tension about the NPA prompted the Morris government to resume control over the war effort in 1917. Many people wanted the government to take control of the marketing of basic goods such as coal to end the profiteering that a government commission had confirmed. Married troops further wanted the government to instate separation allowances, and many people wanted the government to provide pensions to people widowed or made unable to work due to wartime service. Without political friends, Morris turned to Coaker and the Union Party, which had recently abandoned its balance-of-power strategy in favour of allowing its MHAs to serve in Cabinet, hoping that this strategy would allow Union Party platforms to become government policy.

Morris had again been considering the possibility of Confederation. While this had the support of the Reids, it antagonized the merchants of Water Street and opened up the possibility of a marriage of convenience between Morris and the Liberal-Union alliance. Coaker thought that, should the financial position of Newfoundland become much worse, it would be better to join with Canada than to allow Newfoundland to be governed by an unelected council that advised the governor and was influenced directly by Water Street.

Although there was supposed to be a general election in 1917, Morris decided to put it off until he could shore up support for his government. Such postponements were common throughout the empire during the war, and the House of Assembly passed the necessary legislation. With the support of the Imperial War Cabinet, Morris invited the Liberal-Union alliance to join the People's Party in a National Government for the sake of a united war effort. Coaker accepted, but he insisted that the National Government must better regulate the export of salt cod and provide minimum fish prices. This concession was easy for the premier to make: by 1917 the wartime demand for food and the disruption of Newfoundland's competitors' fisheries had considerably improved the prices merchants got for their exports.

Coaker, along with fellow FPU member W.W. Halfyard, joined the Cabinet, as did four Liberals, including Lloyd, who had become Liberal leader. By the beginning of 1918 Morris, who was in London, had resigned the premiership for a peerage and lucrative directorships in Britain which allowed him to escape the potential political disgrace he faced at home. He never returned to Newfoundland. As the senior politician, and free of the taint that now afflicted the People's Party, Lloyd became premier. Suddenly, the FPU members of the House of Assembly found themselves shouldering the burden of an increasingly unpopular war, even as the imperial war effort demanded more sacrifice. The Newfoundland Regiment continued to pay the price of battle on the fields of France, distinguishing itself at Gueudecourt, Sailly-Saillisel, Monchy-Le-Preux, the Scarpe, Ypres, Poelcappelle, and Cambrai. The regiment made terrible sacrifices in these battles, especially Ypres, where the Germans first used poison gas, and Cambrai. St John's physician Cluny Macpherson invented a gas mask which helped reduce allied losses. The regiment's service led the king to grant it the right to call itself the Royal Newfoundland Regiment, but this did not put more men in the ranks.[15]

The treatment of some of the veterans of these battles revealed that the new nationalism in St John's had ethnic and regional limits. In September 1914, the Newfoundland government had passed the War Measures Act, which gave it sweeping powers to arrest, detain, exclude, or deport anyone the government deemed an enemy alien. The government detained almost everyone from Germany or the Austro-Hungarian Empire as enemy aliens, including Moravian missionaries in Labrador, although most of the people who came to St John's were Jews leaving Eastern Europe. The war years proved to be an uneasy time for most immigrants, except for Syrian Christians, who openly supported the British war effort because of the persecution of their communities in the Ottoman Empire. Even among those native to Newfoundland and Labrador, there were limits to what might be recognized in the nationalist mythology of the First World War. About fifty recruits for the Newfoundland Regiment, for example, came from the Lake Melville area of Labrador. One of these, John Shiwak of Rigolet, gained fame as a sharpshooter, but died during the battle of Cambrai. Nevertheless, authorities cared little for Shiwak's fellow Labradorians and, at the end of the war, dropped them off at Battle Harbour, an island community and important centre of the fishery on the Labrador coast, but over three hundred miles from home. There the former members of the regiment waited for the freeze-up to walk home to places such as North West River.[16]

Still without official representation in St John's, such ill-treated Labradorians had to rely on the influence of the Grenfell Mission. Dr Harry Paddon, who had first joined the Mission in 1912, took up the cause of the stranded veterans and pressured the government successfully to pay their travel costs. With Mina Gilchrist, Paddon had established a Grenfell hospital at Mud Lake but moved it to North West River in 1915. The hospital contributed to North West River's status as the administrative centre for much of Labrador. The hospital's nursing and administrative staff formed a local elite in North West River, and their descendants continued to occupy the important jobs in the hospital and the wider community. With the Moravians, the Grenfell Mission proved helpless in the face of the Spanish influenza epidemic that swept the Labrador coast. At the Moravian missions of Hebron and Okak, 207 of 266 and 150 of 220 residents were dead within five weeks of the arrival of the flu. About one-third of the Inuit people of northern Labrador died, and Okak was abandoned. The flu plagued people throughout Newfoundland, but most of the deaths occurred in Labrador, where people had much less medical assistance. In southern Labrador, furious at the inadequate response from St John's, the Grenfell Mission tended the sick and dying as best it could. Paddon, with Henry Gordon, raised funding for dormitory schools to house and educate the many children orphaned by the flu.[17]

Class divisions emerged alongside the ethnic and regional splits in the experience of the Newfoundland and Labrador war effort. A working-class challenge to the status quo was building in St John's and spreading out from the city along the Reid rail line. Workers' concerns about merchant profiteering, inflation, and lack of proper government regulation of the economy resulted in unprecedented union action. The railway was one of the first concentrated industrial concerns to depend on skilled workers and large numbers of semi-skilled and unskilled workers who, although previously overlooked by craft unions, now worked for the same employers. The Reid Newfoundland Company was vigorously anti-union, but metal workers at the railway had belonged to the International Association of Machinists (IAM), a skilled-workers' trade union. To strengthen their position with the company, the metal workers determined to bring all Reid employees into one industry-wide union. In 1917 they organized the Newfoundland Industrial Workers' Association (NIWA), reinforced by concerns about how wages were not keeping pace with wartime inflation.

Initially, the NIWA had the support of FPU member and Unionist MHA George F. Grimes, who had earlier been involved in the Newfoundland Socialist Party. Beginning with only 35 members, by 1918 the NIWA had spread its organization along the railway lines to Reid workers elsewhere and built a membership of 3,500, 2,800 of whom worked in St John's. The union established a newspaper, *The Industrial Worker*, under the editorship of Warwick Smith. The NIWA also organized workers not employed by the Reids and advocated political reform to benefit all Newfoundland workers. In 1918, failed negotiations with the Reids resulted in a strike made successful by an unprecedented labour unity between the NIWA, the LSPU, and the Truckmen's Protective Union. The NIWA also fought a successful strike on behalf of Port aux Basques workers. A Ladies' Branch, organized by Julia Salter Earle, drew members from women in manufacturing throughout St John's and fought for shorter hours, higher wages, and better working conditions. The Reids decided that it was better to accommodate the NIWA through a joint management–union committee, and thereafter the NIWA became much more moderate.[18]

Despite its early success, the NIWA established little political contact with the FPU, which encountered greater political difficulties as the end of war approached. Under pressure from the Imperial War Cabinet to provide more troops, the Newfoundland government had considered conscription. As a member of the government, Coaker supported conscription even though there was widespread opposition to it among fishing people as yet another oppressive policy coming from St John's. Inflated by his office, Coaker had not consulted the councils of the FPU about his stand. In the meantime, organizations led by St John's businesspeople and professionals such as the Orange Order, the Society of United Fishermen, and the Methodist Church Conference that had formerly supported the NPA campaigned vigorously for conscription. While Coaker appeared a turncoat, he knew that every other party supported conscription and that the FPU would be unlikely to form an alliance with any of them if it broke ranks on conscription. Likely to be tarred as treasonous or cowardly, the Union Party would never be able to secure the better regulation of the fishery.

Coaker had sacrificed much in the short term, but the byzantine politics of the capital made that count for naught. Working among the ambitious younger members of the House of Assembly such as Richard Squires was much like swimming with sharks, while the relatively new Roman Catholic bishop, E.P. Roche, a conservative and strident man known as the 'Borgia of Branch' for his ruthless politicking against those who opposed him or his church (the distinctions were small in his mind), began to work against Coaker. Roche had asked Sir Michael Cashin, the senior Catholic member of the People's Party rump, to either convince Bond to come out of retirement or form a government himself, rather than see a coalition persist with the Union Party. Neither was possible in 1918, but the forces of resentment against the FPU continued to grow. Both Liberals such as Squires and Conservatives such as Cashin squirmed at the Union Party's discipline. Coaker had agreed to a quick spring election in 1919 in which the National government would campaign as a party. The Union Party faced opposition from Squires and Cashin, who tried to bully Premier Lloyd into abandoning the Union Party for a new coalition dominated by Cashin. When Cashin tried to bluff the premier into submission by moving non-confidence in the Assembly, the premier seconded the motion, thus forcing Cashin to form a government before he was adequately prepared.

Although a popular politician, Cashin was inept at government. He included in his government A.B. Morine, who continued to advocate the interests of the Reids, now widely suspected as profiteering speculators. To make matters worse, Morine was the minister of justice and had become identified with the heavy-handed use of a British cruiser to arrest moonshiners in Bonavista Bay during the fishing season, even as it became known that Cashin himself had broken wartime prohibition laws to have liquor at a private party. Furthermore, Cashin had left Richard Squires out of government, which was unwise given that Squires enjoyed both Protestant support and the friendship of Roche and hence became leader of the newly renamed Liberal-Reform Party.[19]

With few political allies, the Union Party and Squires's party courted each other. As the election of 1919 loomed Squires began to attack Cashin's party, now known as the Liberal-Progressives, as the tool of the Reid monopoly. Squires promised impartial government, lower taxes, and proper development of natural resources. Coaker agreed that the Union Party would join the Liberal-Reform alliance in exchange for Squires's promise that he would have a free hand in fisheries regulations. Squires was able to make great political capital out of the Reids' and Morine's continued support for Confederation and won the election of 1919 handily. The antipathy of the Liberal–Reform alliance for the Reid interests made them unlikely as an ally of the NIWA's attempt to field three independent working-class candidates as a Workingmen's Party in St John's. The three candidates failed to be elected, and the NIWA soon declined. The narrow base of the NIWA in the industrial enclave of the St John's railway yards and dockyards meant that it could not survive the layoffs and reorganization of the railway as the Reid Company approached financial collapse in the postwar recession.[20]

Coaker became minister of fisheries in the new Squires government, hoping to reorganize the fishery. The prices for salt fish had begun to collapse in the wake of postwar recession, encouraging Coaker to act quickly if he was going to have much hope of reforming the fishery. The FPU had now developed an institutional interest in the reform of marketing in particular, quite apart from the desire to see each fisherman get 'his own.' The UTC had successfully played the same game as the other fish exporting firms. The membership of the FPU had invested much in the UTC, which, in turn, had extended a lot of credit to fishers during the war. Now that prices were collapsing, the UTC risked failure. As minister of fisheries, Coaker took advantage of the War Measures Act (still in effect) to impose regulations over the entire fish trade and thus forestall glutting and further price drops.

In 1920, he tried to establish a more permanent regulation of the fishery through two measures. The first, the Codfish Standardization Act, established a commission to improve the quality of the Newfoundland product by regulating all aspects of the catching, processing, culling, warehousing, and shipping of salt fish. By establishing a national system for the grading of fish, Coaker hoped that foreign buyers would no longer be able to offer low prices on the basis of poor cure. The second, the Salt Codfish Exportation Act, attempted to end the ruinous competition between Newfoundland fish exporters. The act established a board of four licensed exporters, but chaired by the minister of fisheries. Only firms granted a licence by this board could export fish. The main condition for receiving such a licence was observance of minimum conditions fixed by the board for the maximum amount of fish that could be sold in any season and the minimum prices for which such fish could be sold. Coaker's goal was to prevent fish merchants from undercutting one another's prices and glutting the market. In the long term, he thought, Newfoundland's fish markets would become much more stable.

Initially there was widespread support for Coaker's Regulations, as they became known, because they seemed to promise a rescue from the deteriorating market conditions of the Newfoundland trade. Never before, however, had a Newfoundland government intervened so much to regulate the actual terms of trade of any industry, let alone the trade Water Street merchants jealously guarded as their private preserve. Coaker's mercantile opponents in the Liberal-Progressive Party, such as Sir John Crosbie, resented the FPU's interference. Local banks further disliked the government's attempt to regulate the market and restricted credit to firms that cooperated with the Exportation

Board. In effect, the banks encouraged clients who chose to sell fish at prices below those set by the board in the hope of increasing overall income by volume rather than value. A stunning loophole in Coaker's Regulations allowed companies to get away with this practice because, should one lose its licence by underselling, it could always acquire another issued in the name of the company's general manager. Merchants such as Crosbie and A.E. Hickman further cooperated with foreign buyers, particularly the Italians, to frustrate the Coaker Regulations by refusing to buy on the Exportation Board's terms. Individual firms had long been more concerned with competing with neighbouring firms on Water Street than with their international competitors. Now such firms' banks encouraged each to pursue its own interest and ability to repay its debts in the context of a deepening depression. Not surprisingly, the firms broke with the Board to sell fish below price. By 1921, at the instigation of the Board of Trade, the government repealed Coaker's Regulations.[21]

The failure of the regulations opened a floodgate of political disillusionment with the working of liberal democracy in Newfoundland and Labrador. Without market regulations, fish prices dropped, and the Squires government found that Newfoundland's public debt and obligations to the railway left it with very little room to manoeuvre. Newfoundland had a war debt of about $35 million and an annual railway debt of $1.3 million. The railway had not led to significant industrial diversification; most people depended on the fishery, and even markets for newsprint from Grand Falls were falling off. The Squires government had come to power partially by campaigning against the Reid interests but now had to provide more assistance to the railway or risk higher unemployment. Newfoundlanders were wary of the plutocratic Reids and suspected, rightly or wrongly, that the railway family had Squires in their back pocket. Bitter at the failure of his regulations, Coaker stood by as the government flailed; he saw both Squires and the opposition caught up in a corrupt contest of political bribery, each trying to shore up its support with unemployed and desperate voters by promising more spending on relief and public works, all of which the government could ill afford.

By 1922, Coaker was ready to quit politics but remained in government largely to support its efforts to secure another pulp and paper development on the Humber River. By turning to another large-scale forestry industry project for economic salvation, the Squires government returned to earlier Liberal national policies of incurring huge public debt to attract foreign capital, but Coaker saw little other hope to solve the colony's looming economic and social crisis. The FPU leader was lukewarm in his support for Squires, who was rarely in Newfoundland. Deputy Premier Alex Campbell was usually at the helm, doling out relief money in the districts of Liberal-Reform members of the Assembly to shore up support. When Squires was active, as in his negotiations to acquire timber rights to support the Humber project, the premier's actions seemed somehow foul. The Reids controlled most of the timber rights that might support the Humber project and would gain by any arrangement for another pulp and paper mill. As a general election drew near, Squires supported a proposal by the Reids in partnership with the engineering firm of Armstrong, Whitworth and Company for the development of a pulp mill at the mouth of the Humber River, as well as a hydroelectric plant upstream at what was to become Deer Lake. The government negotiated a financing arrangement with the British Treasury in 1922, but the Reids continued to demand more money for the railway's operation and actually closed it that year knowing full well that neither the British government nor the Armstrongs would be interested in an industrial development that depended on the railway and other Reid assets. The Squires government had to purchase these rights for the sum of $2 million.

It certainly looked as if Squires had hypocritically participated in another speculative act of profiteering by the Reids, although his government had bargained them down from their initial asking price of $2.4 million. Nonetheless, Coaker supported Squires largely on the strength of the premier's Humber development platform. Squires won the 1923 general election on a campaign to put the 'Hum on the Humber' through a settlement of the railway and new pulp mill deals. His new government passed legislation guaranteeing mortgages for the Armstrongs. As part of the deal, the Reids would get $1.5 million from the engineering company and royalties and dividends on developed water power and newsprint once it transferred its timber lands to the new company. The government got an export tax of $1 per ton on newsprint and a waterpower royalty. The Armstrongs' licence to operate otherwise was the same as that of the AND Company. To facilitate the deal, the government agreed to buy and operate the railway, coastal steam service, Gulf ferry, and dry dock.[22]

Although he had secured a major industrial development, the premier was in a precarious position. He had originally become premier in 1919 as the candidate who would save Newfoundland from the People's Party's close association with big corporations such as the

Reids and the AND Company. But Squires had found no way to cope with the public debt and poverty without also seeking the goodwill of these same corporations. Many voters concluded that Squires was no better than the People's Party remnant, then calling itself the Liberal-Labour-Progressive Party. The latter was much more disorganized and therefore lost the 1923 election, or so it seemed. Squires's lieutenant Alexander Campbell lost his seat in the election.

Unwilling to lose him in Cabinet, Squires appointed Campbell to the Legislative Council. This action rallied the opposition, who saw Campbell as the mastermind of patronage who had contributed so much to their defeat. Cashin accused Campbell of using public relief to buy votes during the election and, with the assistance of prominent St John's lawyer W.J. Higgins, provided evidence suggesting that Squires might have been directly involved in political bribery and the embezzlement of government funds. This evidence forced the attorney general William Warren to demand unsuccessfully that Squires fire Campbell. Incensed that Squires had likely accepted a $43,000 campaign donation from the operators of the iron ore mine on Bell Island, to modify in their favour a 1919 labour contract Coaker had negotiated, the FPU leader supported Warren when he and his fellow ministers resigned from Cabinet, forcing Squires to resign.

The governor asked Warren to form a new government. Although the new premier had hoped to build a non-partisan administration, he could not entice the opposition to join with Union Party members. This left Warren in the embarrassing position of having to appoint a commission of inquiry into alleged wrongdoings by members of a party government that was essentially the same as his own. In order to make sure that such a commission was without doubt removed from any possibility of government interference, the new premier turned to the British government to recommend a commissioner; they suggested British official Thomas Hollis Walker. Hollis Walker thoroughly investigated the liquor control board, not corruption generally, which would in all likelihood have tainted many politicians on both sides of the House. His report, submitted on 21 March 1924, revealed inappropriate payments from the Liquor Control Department, of which $20,000 could be directly traced to Squires. The Hollis Walker report found that Squires had taken the money in the Bell Island affair as alleged and that Campbell had used government contracts to buy votes.

A political circus followed. The FPU supporters of Warren's administration had never been involved in the Squires's government's misdeeds. They immediately demanded that the government press charges against Squires, Campbell, and John Meaney, Squires's appointee as head of the Liquor Control Department. Squires, who had been arrested but was out on bail, scurried to the opposition benches with some of his supporters. Warren's government fell, but he hoped to build a new coalition with the opposition to rid himself of dependence on the FPU. Warren cobbled together a ministry that lasted five days before it failed. A.E. Hickman formed another Liberal government after Coaker declined the opportunity to become premier. Hickman faced the Conservatives led by Walter Monroe in the general election of 1924.[23]

Monroe was the candidate of the St John's business community and working class, and had the support of Roche and the Roman Catholic Church. He was president of the Imperial Tobacco Company and a director of the Colonial Cordage Company, two St John's manufacturing establishments that had benefited substantially by tariff protection. He had little sympathy for the anti-protectionist and anti–St John's rhetoric of the FPU, neither sentiment of which would sit well with the city's working class. In the political tussle that had followed the Hollis Walker report, the FPU's political candidates found themselves isolated and guilty by association with the Squires government. In the general political disillusionment that followed, it was easy for many people to confuse their old anger with Coaker (about issues such as conscription) with their present frustrations about political corruption and economic depression. Monroe capitalized on all of this to marginalize the FPU. Although the FPU tried to portray itself as lily-white in the 1924 campaign, Monroe made it guilty by association with Squires and his cronies. Monroe campaigned on the promise that he would bring good, clean, and honest business principles to the administration of government. Reinforcing the notion that Newfoundland's economic problems resulted from petty corruption rather than fundamental errors in policy, Monroe's economic policies continued those begun by the Liberals under Whiteway. Monroe's party won the election, including among its MHAs W.L. Linegar, the Workingmen's Party candidate and president of the coopers' union in St John's.

Like the Squires government, the new Monroe administration had to borrow money for relief and public works to combat the problems of deepening depression. Monroe actually made the financial conditions worse when, loyal to his class, he cut income tax, which was paid only by a small portion of relatively prosperous individuals. The mass of people continued to carry the burden of paying for government through the customs duties on all of the imported goods they consumed. To protect St John's manufacturing and replace lost revenue, the premier raised the duties. Such a policy could not help fishers buy more domestically produced manufactures, and it also raised their cost of living.

Monroe's economic policies, while pleasing to the residents of St John's who worked in its factories, looked to many more as a direct boon to the premier's own manufacturing interests. Even the higher duties did not apply equally to all. In some cases, the premier appeared to benefit personally, as when the government allowed the Newfoundland Light and Power Company, of which Monroe was a director, to import materials duty-free for its city streetcar railway. In other areas, Monroe had little choice. The ailing fishery meant that Newfoundland was becoming more and more the hostage of the large corporations that exploited its natural resources. The government had to allow the AND Company to import equipment duty-free in order to get it to develop a mine at Buchans, and had to financially induce the International Power and Paper Company to take over the pulp and paper development on the west coast. Both companies further demanded, and duly received, tax concessions to continue with development.[24]

There were, however, positive achievements during the Monroe administration. The most socially important political development was the concession of the right to vote to women in 1925. Women throughout Newfoundland, both outport and city, had supported the Women's Patriotic Association (WPA), founded by Lady Davidson in 1914. The wives of outport clergy organized the WPA's 183 branches there, with a total membership of over 7,000 in the first year of the First World War. The WPA concentrated on providing supplies that would make life as comfortable as possible for troops overseas. Having roots in the local temperance activities of the Women's Christian Temperance Union in the early 1890s, the women's suffrage movement was strongest in St John's. There, the wives and daughters of the city's business and professional elites now further demanded political equality with their male relatives based on their importance on the home front in the WPA during the Great War.

In 1909, banned from local Protestant literary and discussion clubs due to their male membership's fear of the British female suffrage movement, city women had formed a Ladies' Reading Room and Current Events Club. In each other's congenial company, the privileged women of St John's debated the political and intellectual fashions of the day, ranging from socialism to exotic religions, and gained confidence in their political abilities and entitlements, building on the education, cultivation, and social connections that only wealth could provide. In 1920, the feminists of the Ladies' Reading Room began an explicit campaign for women's equal political rights through the formation of the Newfoundland Women's Franchise League. Unlike the earlier organizations of women, the League included Roman Catholics and Protestants, and professional women such as nurse Mary Southcott and educators Emilie Fraser and Violet Cherrington.

The importance of the WPA to the war effort, as well as the same women's leadership of organizations such as the Child Welfare Association and the Newfoundland Outport Nursing and Industrial Association (NONIA), made it very difficult for male politicians of the Assembly to oppose their demands, and the FPU began to support the cause of women's suffrage. NONIA – founded by Lady Constance Harris, wife of Governor Sir Charles A. Harris, in 1920, and consolidated by her successor, Lady Elsie Allardyce, in 1924 – provided outports with professional nurses and midwives paid for by the knitting and other crafts of outport women. As the mayor of St John's, W.G. Gosling had included women's suffrage in the city's municipal charter of 1921. Richard Squires had opposed the women's suffrage movement as an indulgence by the upper crust of St John's. Monroe took up the cause, which provided him with another political tie to the city's working class. The achievement of suffrage led the Franchise League to reconstitute itself as the League of Women Voters. One of the new League's main platforms was 'equal rights for rich and poor ... work and good wages for all.' Julia Salter Earle used her familiarity with government, gained through her job as engrossing clerk of the legislature, to help in the fight for working-class rights. In 1925, Earle, with May Kennedy and Fannie McNeil, decided to run for St John's council. While all were defeated, Earle received twice as many votes as her bourgeois running mates combined and came very close to being elected.

The defeat of Earle and the others indicates that, although the franchise was an important step in the struggle for women's rights, the foundations of social patriarchy were still quite strong. The first woman to be elected to the legislature, Lady Helena Squires, ran in a Liberal safe seat in 1930 as a supporter of her husband Sir Richard, not as an advocate of women's rights. The Monroe government itself further entrenched social patriarchy by extending old-age pensions to some women only if they were widows receiving income in right of their deceased husbands.[25]

The elderly of rural Newfoundland and Labrador were not the only women to experience the inequalities of patriarchal society. Younger outport women, like their counterparts from the St John's area, found limited opportunities for work and poor pay in the city. Throughout the 1920s and 1930s, increasing numbers of young women looked for work in the capital to supplement the meagre earnings of their working-class or fishing families. Few daughters of the city's mercantile and professional families had to work; most working women were the daughters of households headed by unemployed men, longshoremen, carpenters, or labourers. Mercantile and professional households demanded domestic servants, the new clothing factories preferred to hire women as garment workers, the retail trades wanted women as sales clerks, restaurants looked for waitresses, and the offices of Water Street looked for female typists. Employers tended to hire young, single women, justifying their low wages by arguing that these women did not have families to support. Such rationalizations misrepresented the importance of young women's work to the survival of their parents and siblings. Very few women earned enough to live alone, and society morally disapproved of working women who did. There were few boarding houses for women in St John's. The churches and the Grenfell Association operated some accommodations, which could be much regimented, and by 1926 the YWCA had appeared.

If they married, women found that their household duties and employers' expectations left little room for paid employment. St John's was still a city in which many working-class households did not have running water and depended on wood or coal-burning stoves. The labour of fetching wood and water and cleaning and cooking under such conditions fell to women. Childcare further meant that few married women could work outside the home for wages, although they might sew or clean for neighbours. Most women had no representation in unions; there had been few attempts by labour organizers to address the concerns of women since the NIWA had begun to organize retail workers in 1918. Sadly, the postwar recession and demise of the NIWA ended the initiative.[26]

The Monroe government ensured that the resources of Labrador would remain within the grasp of Newfoundland developers by winning a dispute over boundaries with Canada in 1927. Quebec governments had never accepted Newfoundland's control over Labrador. Quebec objections had led the British government to establish a boundary between Quebec and Labrador in 1825 to return people of French-Canadian descent to Lower-Canadian jurisdiction. The act of

1825 established the line of 52 degrees latitude as the southern boundary of Labrador. In 1898, the Canadian government had passed an act that attempted to extend the northern boundary of Quebec into territory held under Newfoundland jurisdiction. Quebec companies were interested in the forest, mineral, and water power resources of the region, especially of Hamilton Inlet and the Hamilton River.

By 1907, Newfoundland had agreed to arbitration of the border dispute by the Judicial Committee of the British Privy Council. While Sir Patrick McGrath prepared Newfoundland's case, the Monroe government almost undercut itself in 1924. Desperate to raise revenue, the government considered selling Labrador to Quebec for $30 million, preserving only fishing rights along the coast for Newfoundlanders. Even with the sale price cut in half, the Quebec government preferred to wait for the outcome of the arbitration. The arbitrators quickly settled the border south of the 52nd parallel due to the precedents of the Hudson's Bay Company's grant of Rupert's Land, the Treaty of Paris and Royal Proclamation of 1763, the Quebec Act of 1774, the 1809 transfer, and the 1825 Boundary Act. The Canadian government, however, claimed that the Newfoundland government was only entitled to a narrow coastal strip for the fishery above the 52nd parallel. The Newfoundland government pointed to the delimitation of Rupert's Land by watershed, the precedents of resource use by settlers of Newfoundland descent, and the precedent of Newfoundland judicial jurisdiction to counter successfully the Canadian claim. In 1927, the Privy Council accepted Newfoundland's claim to all territory from the height of land north of the 52nd parallel. The Monroe government's offer of sale revealed that it saw Labrador as an asset, nothing more, to be sold or leased as the government thought convenient.[27]

The benefit of the decision for Labradorians was far less certain. The decision ignored completely the Innu's use of territory on both sides of the new boundary. The Newfoundland government refused to even consider the Innu as native to the Newfoundland side of the boundary, preferring to see them as traders and hunters from Canada. The government had little interest in understanding the Innu's use of much of the interior for the caribou hunt, and the people otherwise did not come to the coast to exploit marine resources. A dramatic reduction in caribou populations had forced many Innu to relocate closer to the coast in 1916. There they traded more with the HBC store, but the Innu resorted to interior bays for trapping and did not fish for cod or char. On the rare occasions when they impinged on the consciousness of Newfoundland government officials, the Innu appeared as visitors rather than as inhabitants, or as people with no real property rights.[28]

Victory in the Labrador boundary dispute did not help much to improve the popular image of the government or to restore public faith in the political system. Desperate to create employment by courting international corporations, and also unwilling to address the problems of the fishery rather than hoping for some sort of landward diversification boom, Monroe's government looked as bad as its predecessors. Coaker, bitter and stung by the ruthless and unfair campaign of Monroe in 1924, recommended to the 1925 annual convention of the FPU that Newfoundland should take a ten-year rest from democracy by appointing a commission of government. This did not stop him from coming out of retirement to join Squires in a successful election campaign in 1928. Coaker returned to government, hoping he could develop regulations for the fishery. By the end of 1929, however, the Great Depression was in full swing; prices in the fishery dropped even further, and few firms were interested in cooperating with Coaker. By 1932, it was obvious that the government had no stomach for effective regulations, so Coaker left politics to manage the business enterprises of the union.[29]

The Squires government struggled to borrow money as the world depression and demands for public relief grew, but this was becoming almost impossible due to its existing debt. In November 1929, the government had found itself unable to cope with a major public disaster when a tsunami struck the Burin Peninsula, causing more than $1 million in property damage and the loss of at least twenty-seven lives, and leaving many families without homes or the means of subsistence as winter approached. The government sent a relief ship with some supplies but relied on private subscriptions from Newfoundlanders and Labradorians, as well as from Canada, the United States, and England to provide the assistance it could not afford.[30]

As the government struggled, Coaker criticized it for not embarking on a program of financial retrenchment. By now, any leftist leanings had disappeared from the FPU leader's views. He had no confidence in the political culture of Newfoundland and felt that the poor who demanded public relief during riots in St John's in 1932 were simple dupes of politicians and merchants such as H.A. Winter and Eric Bowering, who would make any patronage promise to secure political power. The FPU leader looked elsewhere for the antidote for Newfoundland's political ailments. He found it in the fascist government of Italy, particularly as its corporatist organization of national fish purchasing, known as the *Consorzio*, had proven so effective in stymying the original Coaker Regulations. Coaker claimed that Newfoundland needed its own Mussolini to overcome the influence of merchants and industrialists in party politics. By contrast with the social unrest in Newfoundland, Coaker marvelled at fascist order – 'countless well-dressed policemen, Blackshirts, and national soldiers, Boy Scouts in black shirt uniforms in every city and town' – and apparent economic progress.[31]

There was not much of a political left to counterbalance the turn to the right signalled by Coaker's fascination with Italian fascism. New-foundlanders were aware of the postwar growth of socialism, indus-trial unionism, and independent labour politics across the Cabot Strait. Many Newfoundlanders, such as Silby Barrett, worked in the Mariti-mes, especially in the coal and steel towns of Cape Breton. The anti-labour stance of Roy Wolvin, the director of the British Empire Steel Corporation (BESCO) in the early 1920s, had been followed closely in Newfoundland because of BESCO's ownership of the mines at Bell Island. Although socialists were active in Newfoundland, the NIWA and the LSPU had adopted a more moderate political stance, which persisted as concern grew in the St John's newspapers about the vari-ous syndicalist, industrial unionist, socialist, and communist dimen-sions in general and sympathetic strikes, not only in Canada, but in the United States, Britain, and continental Europe. The potential for working-class radicalism and labour unrest in the 1920s scared people in St John's. Anything that smacked of working-class independence in Newfoundland was likely to draw a charge of Bolshevism. In St John's, Julia Salter Earle wrote, as 'The Working-Man's Friend,' that there was little to worry about. She felt that local workers were inter-ested in a Christian progressivism; they only wished to be consulted more on public affairs.[32]

Nevertheless, the press continued to worry. Throughout the spring of 1926, the newspapers had been closely following the worsening situation in the British coal industry. As a general strike loomed, locally the *Daily News* feared that such an action would 'shake the very foundations of the industrial life of Britain, and under certain circumstances, render conditions almost indistinguishable from civil warfare.' It greeted the development of a general strike as 'a revolu-tionary movement, instigated and developed by alien communists.'[33] At home, while the major forestry companies required loggers, people from fishing communities were reluctant to assume the high costs of travelling to low-paid jobs in distant camps. Unrest always seemed to be a possibility among loggers. Similarly, the press worried about the potential for unrest among the miners of Bell Island, some of whom had formed the Wabana Mine Workers' Union (WMWU) in 1922, affiliated with the International Union of Mine, Mill and Smelter Workers. In 1925, BESCO forced striking WMWU workers to take a pay cut by threatening to close the mine, something it had already done in Cape Breton. The next year, the demoralized WMWU collapsed, but workers' unrest continued because BESCO was scaling back operations and laying off workers.[34]

The St John's labour movement and the city's business community were becoming disillusioned with the workings of democracy in Newfoundland. Labour reformism had led to disappointing alliances with protectionists such as Monroe. The absence of a strong local socialist intellectual tradition meant that local working-class organizations did not benefit from critical analyses of the structural economic problems of their country. Most labour leaders indulged in the accusations of corruption and short-sightedness that the established political parties hurled at each other. The St John's bourgeoisie could offer no solutions. Its business leaders, whether merchants or manufacturers, had helped to block fisheries reform, and they and their families now stood frightened by the rising tide of social discontent. Rather than blame the inadequacies of their own particular political programs, everyone found it easy to blame democracy generally and the Squires government in particular. Without the financial resources to help the unemployed, the Squires government could only engage in futile gestures, such as building on an already restrictive immigration act of 1926. In 1932, the government prohibited working-class immigration in addition to that of most Europeans and all Asians, Africans, and Latin Americans.[35]

The onset of the Great Depression revealed the limited and fragile nature of Newfoundland's industrial development. Diversification policies had proved costly to a government already burdened with old railway liabilities, and now the debt of the First World War. The downturn in the international economy struck hard at export-dependent industries such as the fishery, leading to demands for public relief that the government could barely meet. Ongoing credit restrictions by merchants worsened the relief problem. Emigration, railway development, service in the war, and newer industrial development all gave some people a chance to skip out on their debts. Seasonal employment in other industries gave some fishers the chance to market more freely through merchants other than their usual suppliers.

Some trap skippers had even become successful enough to trade on their own account and vied with more established firms in trying to garner fish supplies made scarcer by declining catches. Long-established merchant firms responded by restricting credit even further in the 1930s. People reacted against credit restriction throughout Newfoundland and Labrador with threats of violence and store-breaking against merchant firms. Communities closed ranks to protect the perpetrators of such actions. Under pressure from merchants, the government extended even more public relief through merchant accounts but could not long bear the expense.[36]

The condition of the poor was appalling. About one-third of the Newfoundland population depended on public relief. As distress grew, so did public anger. During the summer of 1931, Premier Squires feared 'Red tendencies' among the crowds of unemployed people who had demanded better relief in Conception Bay and St John's. Squires asked the British navy to station a cruiser nearby to keep order. The Newfoundland government continued to cut spending and hired R.J. Magor, a Montreal businessman, to organize a much-reduced relief system. Since the 1920s, unemployed workers in St John's had been organizing under the leadership of unionists such as Jim McGrath, the president of the LSPU from 1905 to 1920. In 1932, McGrath was often at the head of delegations from the Unemployed Committee and at its protests against Magor's relief reforms. In February, a crowd assaulted Squires at the St John's Court House. Unrest spread to the north side of Conception Bay, where many of the miners who worked at Bell Island lived when not employed in the mines.

Government tinkering with the relief system did not improve it. Further austerity measures led to a protest at the Colonial Building in March. At least 250 unemployed workers demanded that the government help them, and their demonstration developed into a riot. People smashed windows, and their actions forced Squires to flee. Although the crowd dispersed, there were more meetings and marches by the unemployed throughout April, prompting Squires to call for another naval cruiser to cow the crowd.[37]

The relief crisis was one manifestation of the manner in which the Squires government found it increasingly difficult to meet all of its financial obligations. It could not meet the day-to-day running expenses of government, including hiring and equipping more police to control protestors, or meet the huge interest payments on the public debt. The government considered defaulting on the public debt by suspending or rescheduling interest payments, but this was anathema to officials in the British government. After all, by the Statute of Westminster, Newfoundland had been named as a self-governing 'Dominion' of the British Empire. The British Treasury feared that even a partial default on its debt by Newfoundland would affect the credit of all the British dominions. The Squires government had turned to four Canadian banks, especially the Bank of Montreal, hoping without luck for a bailout similar to that of the bank crash in 1894. At Squires's behest, the Canadian government convinced the Canadian banks to lend Newfoundland more money. In exchange, the Newfoundland government accepted a representative of the Canadian banks to control the use of the funds.

The Canadian banks feared that Canada's credit would suffer if Newfoundland defaulted. Desperate, the elected government surrendered control over its spending. In a last, desperate effort to stave off financial collapse, Squires tried to sell Labrador to Quebec, with no luck. Rising anger at yet more revelations about Squires's political malfeasance, which had contributed to the spring riot in St John's, forced him from office. Frederick Alderdice, with the support of Water Street merchants and Coaker, neither of whom was willing to support democracy in Newfoundland, led a United Newfoundland Party that won a subsequent general election. Alderdice attempted to alleviate the country's financial situation by leasing Labrador to British interests for ninety-nine years, but again the attempt failed. Public anger at the inability of the government to assist the poor had continued to mount and exploded in a series of riots in St John's and across the island during the winter of 1932.[38]

Alderdice also considered defaulting on Newfoundland's public debt, but yielded as well to imperial fears that such an action would hurt Newfoundland's and Britain's reputations. The British and Canadian governments arranged more loans for Newfoundland, but on the condition that it accept a joint commission of inquiry into Newfoundland's financial affairs composed of British, Canadian, and Newfoundland representatives. The British appointed Lord Amulree, a Labour peer, to lead the commission. Before he left Britain the Treasury and Dominions Office made clear to Amulree that Newfoundland was not to default and that the British taxpayer would not be expected to underwrite the colonial treasury unless the government in London, not Newfoundland politicians, had control over the spending. The Canadian representative on the Amulree Commission, Charles A. Magrath, did not feel that Newfoundland's problems were too severe. Magrath thought that a partial rescheduling of payments on its public debt and further financial help from Canada and Britain would see Newfoundland through its crisis, although he felt that the best option was Confederation with Canada. However, the Canadian government was unprepared to help further, and Britain remained determined to take political control over Newfoundland if it was to be the source of financial help. Alderdice had picked Canadian banking adviser Sir William Stavert to represent Newfoundland on the commission. The Canadian banks favoured Britain's plans to take over the direction of Newfoundland's affairs; Stavert consequently was no advocate of Newfoundland's constitutional independence.

The unfortunate precedent of the Hollis Walker report meant that the Amulree Commission was predisposed to find a people living in a society and economy that by its very nature mired them in despondency and corruption rather than to investigate the long-term structural problems of the Newfoundland economy. Amulree justified the suspension of democratic government, and did so by mistaking the appalling conditions of the depression with the long-term pattern of life in the colony. His report admitted that the seasonal and occupational pluralism of the outports usually kept people healthy, and that their current misery was primarily the result of credit contraction due to the depression.[39]

Finding a sympathetic ear in the Alderdice government, the Amulree Commission recommended that Newfoundland's democratic self-government be replaced by a non-democratic commission appointed by Britain. Coaker approved of the plan, as did Wilfred Grenfell and many other influential Newfoundlanders. There were few voices of opposition. On 16 February 1934, Premier Alderdice signed the papers that surrendered Newfoundland's dominion status and its democracy. Although local nationalism had been fuelled by the sacrifice of war, such sacrifice meant little in the context of the inexorable, if more banal, tide of economic waste and debt associated with the colony's version of the national policy. Nationalism may have been fostered at Beaumont Hamel, but it failed to thrive on war and railway debt, combined with neglect of the fisheries and cynicism about government's courting of international capital. By the mid-1930s, it appeared that a new class-based opposition to the waste of the national policy had emerged. It fell to the Commission of Government to stifle such opposition.

9

Commission, Depression, and War, 1934–1945

The Commission of Government arrived in St John's with the diagnosis of Newfoundland and Labrador's problems contained in the Amulree Report in hand. The commission intended to set right government finances and the relationship between fishers and merchants, workers and employers. Six commissioners were to govern; three Newfoundlanders took charge of the departments of Justice, Health and Home Affairs, and Education, while three British civil servants took control of the departments that were responsible for the country's finances and economy: Finance, Public Utilities, and Natural Resources. The governor chaired the commission. Approaching its task as if the real problems of Newfoundland and Labrador required only better administration and moral reform of society and politics, the commission failed to achieve significant economic reform. It lapsed into many of the policies of previous governments and, although it took more interest in the needs of Labradorians, tended to take the part of capitalists over working people. It took the advent of war in 1939 to bring about improvements in the lives of working Newfoundlanders and Labradorians.

In the early years of the depression, Newfoundland's paper companies responded to decreasing demand for paper by cutting back production and paying lower prices for pulpwood that was cut by logging subcontractors. The companies also reduced the wages paid to loggers and provided them with miserable camps in the woods. Loggers often travelled long distances by train to work, but the price of their fares was not included in their wages. At the same time, both the AND Company mill at Grand Falls and the International Power and Paper (IPP) Company mill at Corner Brook denied responsibility for the working conditions in the woods, since they were the domain of the subcontractors.

One of the first acts of the commission had been to pass a Public Enquiries Act that enabled it to look into complaints, such as those in the forestry sector, about poor wages and working conditions. But their track record was disappointing. In 1933, for example, the IPP Company hired loggers directly at 22 cents per hour and later asked the government to waive the legal minimum wage of 35 cents per hour. A two-week strike against the IPP action resulted in the government suspending the minimum wage law, a move that discredited the government in the minds of these workers. Throughout 1934 strikes and civil tension increased. Finally, the commission responded by appointing F. Gordon Bradley, the last opposition leader in the defunct House of Assembly, to investigate loggers' complaints.

Bradley crossed Newfoundland, gathering evidence of poor wages, dangerous work, and relentless poverty for loggers and their families. The paper companies blamed the loggers' plight on the depression, but Bradley pointed out that those well-paid, skilled workers in the pulp and paper plants who had strong unions, and managers and owners, did not suffer in the same way. Aghast at such an openly critical assessment of one of the country's leading industries, and fearful that the former politician Bradley would try to use the inaction of the commission to build a political basis of support among those who worked in the woods, the commission did not publish his report but made Bradley a magistrate. In exchange for suppressing what became known as the Bradley Report and Bradley's recommendation of a minimum price per cord for wood, the paper companies agreed to pay a minimum net monthly wage of $25 to those loggers they directly employed.[1]

The situation in the woods clearly illustrated for the commission the deep-rooted social problems embedded in the structures of economic development in Newfoundland and Labrador. Throughout 1934, to take another example, the British Commissioner Sir John Hope Simpson, responsible for the Department of Natural Resources, often remarked on the scandalous poverty suffered by loggers and their families in his letters to relatives in Britain. Hope Simpson claimed that the commission was determined to prevent the paper companies from running roughshod over loggers and that it would not allow them to be treated like 'sweated labour' in the manner that the Belgians had exploited the people of the Congo. And yet his wife, Lady Hope Simpson, upon touring the outports with Sir John, argued that poverty and depravity ran together among the living conditions of coastal Newfoundlanders: 'Savages have better arrangements. And savages manage their social morality better.' Hope Simpson further tended to feel that many loggers could not earn enough because they were unskilled at their work and did not have the initiative and fortitude to make a go at logging. Although critical of the IPP as an American company, Hope Simpson allowed that the British AND treated its loggers better. He spoke about loggers with the managers of both corporations over dinner and a bridge party at St John's finest hotel. Later in the summer, Sir John and Lady Hope Simpson travelled to the IPP mill site at Humbermouth, where 'the International Paper people' organized a pleasure cruise and 'gave us a slap-up lunch at the Glynmill Inn.'[2] Desperate to attract investment to Newfoundland and Labrador, the commission kept up appearances by chastising the paper companies, but Hope Simpson hardly confronted them.

Instead, the commission concentrated on uplifting the 'savages.' The commission took its lead from the Amulree Report, seeing Newfoundland and Labrador's social and economic problems as stemming from deep-rooted social and political demoralization. The new administration planned to stimulate the integrity of the people by giving them more orderly administration, primarily by creating a Newfoundland Ranger Force. More than a police force, the Rangers became the unelected administrators of basic government services in rural areas, while the Newfoundland Constabulary continued policing urban areas. The Rangers were responsible to the Department of Natural Resources rather than Justice, and controlled by a Newfoundland Commissioner. The force was an expensive undertaking for an administration that was supposed to restore public solvency, but Hope Simpson justified the expense to the British Treasury by explaining that the Rangers would oversee economic development and social revitalization in model communities the commission would foster, such as one at Markland, which would develop beaver farms for a local fur industry.

Hope Simpson wanted to use magistrates and Rangers in an integrated system of administration similar to that used by the British colonial administration in India, where he had been posted prior to Newfoundland. Magistrates, like the Rangers, were to report to the government on their district's natural resources, public facilities, economic developments, likely additional infrastructure requirements in such areas as public sanitation, and the operation of existing government agencies such as the post office.[3] It became clear, however, between 1935 and 1937 that the magistrates were too busy with their judicial work to be the political and administrative representatives of the commission, so the Rangers took over most of the functions of district officers. As the administrators of public relief, they had very little time left for all of their other duties, which included enforcing the regulations associated with the day-to-day running of almost every government department throughout rural areas. Travelling over great distances, the Rangers acquired an excellent reputation as sympathetic administrators who often ignored the commission's parsimonious relief guidelines to help people in desperate circumstances, and emphasized crime prevention in their policing duties.

The administrative role of the Rangers was much more significant than their policing work, particularly in Labrador. The commission established six detachments there between 1935 and 1936. Newfoundland's residents had an array of government representatives and officials to communicate their interests to the government in St John's. Labradorians, who had no representation in the old House of Assembly, had relied mostly on voluntary and irregular representation by church officials and philanthropists such as Grenfell to advocate for their needs. Now, the Rangers submitted to the government monthly, quarterly, and semi-annual reports on local conditions there, just as they did for Newfoundland, while reflecting the will of the commission by being more sensitive to local concerns, especially in the enforcement of game laws. Regulations such as the opening and closing of hunting seasons were based on ecological conditions on the island. They needed a more flexible application to fit the needs of Labradorians.[4]

The Commission of Government hoped that it could revitalize rural Newfoundland and diversify its economy through the development of model communities based on full-time commercial farming, thinking that such farming in centralized communities would have lower administrative costs. Markland, the first to be established (in 1934), is the most famous of these settlements, but the commission also sponsored eight others. They began as attempts to reduce some of the poor's reliance on government assistance and were potentially imaginative attempts to introduce principles of cooperative living and production to rural Newfoundlanders. Two of the land settlements, Sandringham (Bonavista Peninsula) and Winterland (Burin Peninsula), benefited from better agricultural resources, and on the west coast Lourdes thrived because settlers supplemented agriculture with fishing and logging. Yet the policy cost the commission a great deal of money and the farms were not profitable because the commission used its agricultural policy as an experiment in social engineering to eliminate denominationalism and reform the character of settlers. Although the commission had tried to introduce a more secular administration of the denominational school system in Newfoundland, it did not have the financial resources to engage in significant reform or the political support to challenge directly the churches' role in education. Similarly limited in what it might invest in the development of farming, the commission supported the Newfoundland Adult Education Association (NAEA), an organization dominated by J.L. Paton, the president of Memorial College in St John's, and W.W. Blackall, a member of the college's board of trustees. Committed to the notion that poverty resulted from moral failure and ignorance, the NAEA offered a form of self-help public education for the people who went to the new settlements. This education was short on practical advice, but long on middle-class exhortations that good Christian citizens dutifully did what they could to stay off public relief and away from political radicalism. The overall result was the failure of land settlement, much discontent among the settlements' residents, and little economic opportunity that would draw people out of fishing communities.[5]

The commission's social and administrative experiments did not improve the colonial economy, and the government lapsed into courting foreign capital while overlooking the well-being of industrial workers and their families. The commission had no interest, for example, in addressing the concerns of miners from St Lawrence, on the south coast of Newfoundland. In 1933, the New York capitalist Walter Seibert had proposed the development of a fluorspar mine there. Desperate for work, and with the local fishery in ruins after the 1929 tsunami, local people welcomed the development. However, Seibert imported cheap dry drills (banned in most other jurisdictions because of the dust they produced) for the miners to use. Working in deeper, poorly ventilated shafts, the miners had no protection from the dust, and had only contaminated water to drink, little safety equipment, and poor wages. During the early years of the commission, miners complained about conditions in the mine and occasionally refused to work unless they were paid better wages. Seibert's St Lawrence Corporation refused workers' demands, and the commission ordered local relief officers to decline assistance to any miner who refused to work because of poor wages or conditions in the mines. The commission was so anxious to attract investors that it did not want to alienate them by concerns about industrial safety, refusing to enforce 1908 legislation that established minimum working conditions in the mining industry.[6]

The commission turned to land settlement and courted foreign capital because of social discontent about the inability of government to help those impoverished by the depression. In St John's, the Unemployed Committee demanded better government assistance for the poor and unemployed. Pierce Power, an unemployed marine fireman who was well liked and trusted by the working poor of the city, emerged as a leader of the group in 1934. Through powerful speeches and demonstrations, he rallied unemployed men and women, sometimes attracting as many as one thousand men, women, and children, which earned him surveillance as an agitator by the police. Throughout the city, petty theft, assaults, and property crime increased as the poor fought to put food in their mouths and roofs over their families' heads. The Unemployed Committee received little sympathy from the commission, but it continued to demand simple things such as more coal for the poor, cash instead of dole orders, clothing, and freedom from eviction. Power led marches on Government House, organized larger demonstrations, and, in 1935, threatened to hold a parade on 6 May, Jubilee Day, the king's birthday.

Although the commission agreed to provide some employment, it reneged on a promise to let the Unemployed Committee decide who needed it, arguing that the police should do so instead. This incensed the unemployed, who gathered in protest over the next few days, culminating in a riot on 10 May. Eventually, the police dispersed the crowds, dealing out severe beatings to Power and some of the other Committee leaders. The beatings and subsequent trials of Pierce and other leaders broke the Committee's momentum. Pierce went to jail for five years for slashing the policeman who came to arrest him. Tired of police harassment, he had told the crowd that gathered at one meeting in 1935 that they had a right to dignity, that no one should be treated like a serf, and that 'We don't intend to die peacefully in a land of plenty.' Throughout Newfoundland, the working poor, especially loggers, continued to voice their discontent, and crowds continued to gather in protest against poverty and inadequate relief through the late 1930s.[7]

Land settlement schemes and diversification in the form of mining failed to lessen rural Newfoundlanders' and Labradorians' dependence on the fishery and logging for work, and both remained troubled industries throughout the 1930s. The Rangers, otherwise busy with overseeing the administration of model communities, outports, and other towns, served as a blunt instrument of the law during a loggers' strike at Deer Lake and Corner Brook in 1937. Although the commission's rhetoric suggested that it favoured trade unions, it was no more interested in confronting powerful companies than were the previous elected governments. Loggers took matters into their own hands by organizing a union, although the high unemployment of the depression made that difficult. Not only did the companies take advantage of the shortage of work to dictate employment terms, but the logging camps were isolated from union organizers and the government officials who were supposed to enforce the labour code. The piecework system also tended to emphasize a competitive masculinity among loggers, which the companies encouraged by suggesting that a real man would have no trouble cutting enough wood to make a decent living. The seasonality of employment, and their tendency to log only during the winter because they fished much of the year, meant that loggers' identification with the forestry industry was limited and unionization was difficult.

Despite their divisions, loggers placed more faith in worker solidarity than in the commission's willingness to represent their interests. Many loggers bunked with relatives and familiar co-workers in the logging camps and developed a loyalty to each other. In 1935, loggers had rallied around a new union, the Newfoundland Lumberman's Association (NLA) and its leader Joe Thompson. Thompson was a former logger from Point Leamington who had sons in the industry and who had organizational experience through service with the local Orange Lodge. He organized the NLA along lines similar to the FPU, retaining tight control over it through a highly centralized leadership. By 1937, most loggers belonged to the NLA, which led successful strikes to improve wages and working conditions for log drivers working for the AND and IPP companies. The NLA was moderate. Thompson believed that loggers could rely only on themselves to be well represented in their struggles with employers but that those employers and employees should be able to accommodate each other reasonably. While committed to cooperation, the NLA found that the paper companies were not. Tensions within the loggers' movement led to a split in 1938 as loggers from the Corner Brook area formed the Newfoundland Labourers' Union, and those from the Deer Lake area formed the Workers' Central Protective Union. The NLA also faced hostility from the rump of the more conservative FPU, which saw itself as the only legitimate representative of outport people.[8]

Loggers found little support from the skilled workers of the paper mills. The mill workers often saw any concession the loggers won from the mills as a threat to their own livelihoods, which they had improved through their own union struggles. Local 63 of the International Brotherhood of Pulp, Sulphite and Paper Mill Workers, a union that represented the skilled workers at the AND mill in Grand Falls, went on strike against the company in 1921 when it laid off workers, reduced wages and hours of work, and stopped providing town families with free coal. The strike ended in a compromise, which reflected the paternalistic relationship between the union's members and the AND: the company restored hours and increased production but did not increase wages or restore the coal rights. By the 1930s, Grand Falls had established a stable labour force, kept relatively happy by company paternalism, which extended into the provision of good municipal and health services by colonial standards. As in Corner Brook, the paper companies encouraged the division between mill workers and woods workers by not allowing the unskilled workers to live in the companies' planned town sites, for example, and subsidizing social activities that created a sense of community among mill workers that was not shared with the more poorly paid outside workers.

The depression hurt the pulp and paper industry. At Corner Brook, for example, IPP's total value of exports to the United States fell from $9,100,000 in 1930 to $4,100,000 in 1935. The company responded by introducing wage and hours cuts that amounted to a 50 per cent reduction in mill workers' real earnings by 1933. Yet the IPP continued to provide its skilled workers with good housing, water and sewage, electricity, schools, and health facilities long before they were readily accessible in most logging towns or other rural communities. Nevertheless, loggers in nearby communities such as Lomond who were lucky enough to find work earned between $1.00 and $1.30 for every cord of wood they cut rather than the $2.50 per cord they had been getting.[9]

The skilled workers of Grand Falls feared that the loggers and the itinerant unemployed of the outports who might come looking for work in their town would erode their privileged living standards. Unemployed people from fishing outports usually coped with hard times by leaving Newfoundland to look for work elsewhere. With the depression, emigration from Newfoundland ceased, because there were no jobs to be had in the United States or Canada. By the 1930s, outport people turned more and more to places such as Grand Falls and Corner Brook for work. Men found work in logging and the pulp and paper plants, but for women, domestic service was the main form of wage work available, while the daughters of mill workers got the small number of clerical, retail, and teaching jobs.

Some women from the outports had always hired out to perform domestic service for crews in the Labrador fishery or had gone abroad to work as servants. The poor state of the fishery encouraged outport people to move to the industrial towns to find work and young women to take positions with the families of managers and skilled workers in Grand Falls and, later, Corner Brook. Other girls took service to supplement their families' earnings back home. Often recruited by kin and family friends who had managed to secure work in the mill towns, such domestic servants linked the household economies of the outports with the formal labour markets of the enclave towns and helped fishing families to survive by their remittances.[10]

Usually marginalized in communities with few basic amenities outside of the pulp and paper towns, poorly paid and underemployed loggers were often slighted by their more skilled counterparts in the mills. Feeling displaced, the unskilled labourers, loggers, and their families found comfort, dignity, and hope in the relatively new Pentecostal ministry of Newfoundland. Pentecostalism began locally with the efforts of Alice Garrigus, the New Englander who came to St John's in 1910 and founded the Bethesda Mission on New Gower Street, in the heart of the working-class part of the city. As in the earlier experience of the Salvation Army, the Pentecostal missionaries faced public ridicule and harassment in their public activities, especially the baptism of converts in Mundy Pond. For ten years, the Pentecostal movement built slowly but gathered force after 1919 as disenchanted Methodists such as Robert C. English and Eugene Vaters turned to the more evangelical faith.

The movement attracted people who felt that the structure and hierarchy of the more established churches had little to offer the marginalized. The Pentecostal movement promised that the 'second blessing' of a personal, charismatic conversion made all people, regardless of gender, class, or ethnic difference, equal in their salvation. The fellowship of the faith gave poor people, such as the washerwoman Jessie Snow of Carbonear, who converted in the early 1920s, the strength to speak publicly and fearlessly in confrontation with the clerical elite of the other churches. Missionaries from Bethesda successfully established two missions at Humbermouth and Corner Brook West, just outside the Townsite, in 1925.

In the next year, missions spread rapidly eastward to Deer Lake and

Humber Canal, then to Grand Falls Station (later named Windsor) outside of Grand Falls, Springdale, Port Anson, Twillingate, Triton, Bishop's Falls, and Botwood. All of these towns were either homes to loggers or the unskilled labourers who serviced the needs of the pulp and paper industry. From these towns, Pentecostalism spread to the many smaller towns involved in the forestry sector and to mining towns, where workers experienced similar social problems. By 1935, 3,757 people of the Pentecostal faith were living in Newfoundland, of whom 2,278, or 61 per cent, were from White Bay, Green Bay, Grand Falls, Twillingate, Humber, and Harbour Main – Bell Island districts dominated by forestry or mining. Many of the rest were from the working class in St John's and the larger centres of Conception Bay North. The early Pentecostal movement was an industrial, working-class phenomenon, which began to spread quickly from towns such as Carbonear and Bay Roberts to coastal Labrador along the routes of the migratory cod fishery.[11]

Skilled workers' unions hardly fared better than loggers in their relationships with the Commission of Government. A Local 63 dispute with the commission in 1935 had reinforced the local's organizer Alphonse Duggan's belief that individual unions required a Newfoundland federation to bolster their influence. With the support of Ron Fahey and F.A.F. Lush of the International Association of Machinists (IAM) in St John's, Duggan had organized the pulp and paper unions, the railway brotherhoods, and the Buchans miners' union into the Newfoundland Trades and Labour Council (NTLC) in 1937, renamed the Newfoundland Federation of Labour (NFL) by 1938. The NTLC wanted local unions to be more loyal to it than to the American Federation of Labor (AFL), the international union to which most of its members were affiliated. With Duggan as its first president, the NTLC opted for a Newfoundland-first form of union organization and a reformist approach to advocating workers' interests with employers and government. Besides promoting the organization of workers, the NTLC fought for a five-day, forty-hour work week, the abolition of child labour, an improved Workmen's Compensation Act, the creation of a pension plan for government employees, and improved inspection of mines.

To counter employers' accusations, the NTLC denied that any foreign influence, such as that of the AFL or the more radical Congress of Industrial Unions (CIO), lay behind its work or that it supported socialism. In the late 1930s NTLC leaders, including Walter Sparks, who had recently organized railway clerks, and Irving Fogwill, organized a range of St John's workers. Between 1937 and 1938 they organized or rejuvenated fifteen unions and added four thousand new members to the NTLC. Among these were retail and office clerks, carpenters, plumbers, pipefitters, metal workers, barbers, and workers in the clothing, food, beverage, tobacco, and cordage industries. The NTLC unionized city council workers, telephone operators and electricians with the Avalon Telephone Company, and city printers. They also unionized shop workers in Grand Falls, Corner Brook, Botwood, and Bishop's Falls. Three existing St John's unions also affiliated with the NTLC: the Coopers' Union, the Bakery Workers' Protective Union, and the International Boot and Shoe Workers' Union.[12]

The Commission of Government was unwilling to recognize workers' efforts to improve their lot by organizing, but it hardly proved effective in dealing with the social and economic problems that plagued Newfoundland and Labrador during the depression. The government's efforts in public health care were yet another case in point. It replaced the Newfoundland Outport Nursing and Industrial Organization with government-paid nurses and funded a travelling clinic. The commission established immunization and public education plans to fight tuberculosis, smallpox, diphtheria, and typhoid fever – all illnesses to which the malnourished were prone. The government nonetheless did little to address the poverty-induced malnutrition problem that underlay the worst of the public health problems facing Newfoundlanders and Labradorians.

The greatest public health innovation came from a private source: the work of Dr John Olds, an American trained at Johns Hopkins Medical School, recruited to work at Twillingate hospital in 1929. Recognizing that the hospital's greatest challenge was malnutrition, Olds set up a baby clinic that gave mothers food and clothing as well as prenatal care education. He experimented with formulas of cod oil, brewers' yeast, and milk powder because of the high infant mortality rate among families that depended on the inadequate poor relief. Prompted by the Grenfell Mission and Olds's colleague Dr Charles Parsons, the commission had been forcing those on public relief to eat whole-wheat brown flour rather than white. People preferred white flour, which was both more palatable, rose properly when baked into the bread that was the staple of so many people's diets, and did not have the social stigma of 'relief flour.' Dr Olds recognized that the pre-depression diet was not particularly deficient, and that the commission's program was an insult. Not until 1938 did the commission follow Olds's strategy in targeting children by supplying them with cocomalt, a vitamin-enriched chocolate drink powder. Olds found that the commission was otherwise of little help to the outports in his area. Remarkably, the commission cut the operating grant of the Twillingate hospital in 1935. Rather than close the hospital, Olds developed a rudimentary health insurance plan whereby families paid $10 a year to ensure access to the hospital.[13]

Although aware of the link between poverty and poor health, the commission was loath to assist the poor directly with public money, as with old-age pensions. The desire to lessen the financial burden of the pension plan actually predated the commission, for in 1930 the government had established a Royal Commission on Health and Public Charities that recommended means testing to ensure that those who could be supported by families did not receive a pension. The commission's Department of Public Health and Welfare insisted on a stricter and more bureaucratic enforcement of means tests, although this remained limited by the small staff. While commission officials harassed pensioners and applicants with their investigations, they saved little money, while continuing to discriminate against women, refusing pensions to unmarried elderly women or elderly widows whose husbands had not collected a pension before they died.[14]

Developments in Labrador and Europe provided the commission with other possibilities for social and economic development. From the administration's earliest days, Sir John Hope Simpson had taken a great interest in the economic potential of Labrador. He first visited North West River in 1934 and, by 1936, had energetically promoted forestry in the area around Alexis Bay, which became known as Port Hope Simpson. The commission also promoted mineral exploration, eventually giving the Weaver Coal Company mineral and water power rights for 50,000 square kilometres of the Labrador interior. Throughout the 1930s, the commission received proposals from agencies such as the Jewish Colonization Association and members of the local Jewish community for the large-scale settlement of Jewish refugees in Newfoundland or, more usually, in Labrador. The ascent of Nazism in Germany and its expansion throughout central Europe had forced international Jewish organizations to find places that would welcome the thousands of European Jews who fled. However, commission officials worried about the supposed impracticality of large-scale settlements during a time of economic depression, feared opening a floodgate of Jewish refugees, and preferred instead settlement by British or 'northern' Europeans.[15] The commission was reflecting the dominant view in the local press and the professional community.

By the late 1930s, the commission's social experimentation, moralizing, and parsimony had not revived Newfoundland and Labrador's economic fortunes. However, a practical and promising perspective came from J.H. Gorvin, who had been seconded from the British Ministry of Agriculture and Fisheries to work as an adviser on rural development for the commission in 1937. Gorvin recommended that the commission build on the existing strengths of coastal communities and believed that the government should encourage outport families to maximize their use of inshore fishing and farming resources. He argued that rural reform would have to take place through the use of producer cooperatives, which would maximize the return to households rather than to merchants in the fishing industry. In the absence of other labour-intensive industrial developments, or the possibility of out-migration, Gorvin wrote, government must do its best to encourage the informal economy of fishing communities, especially in supplementary farming, by which outport Newfoundlanders continued to find much of their own food stuffs. Gorvin became the commissioner of Natural Resources in 1939 and planned for the co-operative revitalization of the fishery and outport communities in his 1940 Act to Facilitate the Economic Development of Special Areas of Newfoundland. The act earned Gorvin the support of the NFL and colonial cooperative organizations, but also the enmity of many in the St John's business establishment, as well as the governor, Humphrey Thomas Walwyn. Walwyn had Gorvin recalled from Newfoundland in 1941, effectively ending the commission's plans for rural reconstruction.[16]

Gorvin's fate as a commissioner is a reminder that, over the course of its operations, the Commission of Government experienced internal dissension and changes in its policy objectives. While the British-appointed commissioners occupied the most influential portfolios, they could face opposition from their Newfoundland colleagues. Thomas Lodge, the British commissioner for Public Utilities in 1934, for example, had been, with Hope Simpson, the enthusiast behind land settlements. He quickly acquired a dictatorial reputation among his Newfoundland colleagues, and Frederick Alderdice, who served as the commissioner for Education, opposed Lodge's desire to end denominational education. Frustrated with the practical realities of building consent for commission policies in Newfoundland, Lodge left in 1937. Although Gorvin was an exception, British officials subsequently appointed commissioners who would carry out moderate economic reforms without ruffling the feathers of Newfoundland's elites.[17]

The Commission of Government was, however, willing to spend money on the moral reform of Newfoundlanders and Labradorians as long as such expenditures involved no fundamental restructuring of their economy. It put resources into the development of a state broadcasting system in 1939, when the commission bought and amalgamated three privately owned radio stations as the Broadcasting Corporation of Newfoundland (BCN). The government planned to use the BCN to promote its policies and enhance the moral enlightenment of Newfoundland and Labrador, directing its efforts at what it perceived as the failings of a backward society dominated by a primitive inshore fishery and self-interested fish merchants. Although the Amulree Commission had recommended sweeping reform of the fishing industry by the introduction of producer cooperatives, better-quality inspection, and the elimination of truck credit practices, the commission largely failed to follow through. Gorvin's dismissal revealed that, whatever its rhetoric, the commission was not going to stand up to powerful mercantile interests in St John's. The government did, however, give the Salt Codfish Board authority to set minimum prices for exported fish in 1934 and, in 1936, created the Newfoundland Fisheries Board. The board regulated all aspects of the production, processing, culling, inspection, and distribution of fish, thus slowly bringing some order to merchants' marketing of fish. Nonetheless, the commission did not want to intervene directly by rationalizing the many firms that competed with each other in the fishing industry.[18]

Unable to improve conditions in the salt fishery significantly in the middle of the depression, the commission viewed the industry as backward and espoused the notion that a fresh/frozen industry would be a progressive force, stimulating fisheries modernization and industrialization. Local mercantile firms, however, struggling with the depressed salt fish trade, initially demonstrated little interest in risking capital in the new fresh/frozen sector, despite commission-sponsored education and research programs designed to promote industrialization. Fish merchants had a major currency problem: they conducted their business in devalued British pounds and had to sell their fish in southern European, Caribbean, and Brazilian markets for currencies of unstable value. But increasingly they found that they had to purchase supplies for the fish trade in more valuable American dollars. It was this, more than anything else, that eventually turned their interest to the factory-like production of larger offshore vessels and concentrated processing promoted by the commission. By the late 1930s, a number of firms, such as John Penny and Sons, began to invest in the new fishery, inspired by the American Clarence Birdseye's innovations in the process of quick-freezing fish fillets and marketing of frozen foods in more lucrative North American consumer markets. Such tentative steps towards modernization, however, remained hampered by the commission's lack of financial resources to support extensive programs of assisted shipbuilding, or to provide funding for the fisheries science that would need to identify new fish stocks for industrial exploitation.[19]

Having done little to aid the fish trade, the Commission of Government also accomplished little in forest management. Throughout its tenure, it complained about the supposed wasteful cutting practices of rural people, especially on the three-mile limit. As in the case of previous administrations under responsible government, the commission opposed the export of relatively unprocessed timber such as pit props for mines, although it continued the practice of allowing pit prop exports as a relief measure until 1937. Other than that, it established a national park, created demonstration sawmilling and logging operations, and started a forestry nursery on the Back River on the Avalon Peninsula, all of this to improve small-scale logging and sawmilling by rural people.

The real focus of the commission throughout the 1930s and 1940s was the industrial expansion of pulp and paper operations. Early on, the commission had hoped for a third pulp and paper complex on the Gander River, but the depression and limited wood supplies on the island frustrated this plan. With its American markets contracting because of the depression, the IPP at Corner Brook was approached by Bowaters, the major British buyer of its products. Bowaters was interested in taking over the operation to secure its paper supply and, if it could, more timber rights. The government agreed, allowing Bowaters the Gander timber limits that people had hoped would have supported a third paper mill. Bowaters took over the Corner Brook operation in 1938 and gained control over three-mile reserves in southern White Bay and Canada Bay. Although the company's legal right to these reserves was questionable, local people supported the transfer of property rights to the private sector, hoping that Bowaters might provide employment to alleviate desperate local poverty.

With the help of generous government concessions, Bowaters made a lot of money in Newfoundland during the depression. It maintained paternalistic relationships with the skilled workers and businesspeople who lived and worked in Corner Brook, but had little sympathy for those beyond its boundaries. With the AND, Bowaters assumed great influence over forest policy. The pulp and paper companies had become so dominant in the area of forestry management that agencies of the Commission of Government turned to them rather than the Department of Natural Resources for policy advice, and usually gave a sympathetic ear to company complaints about the supposedly wasteful cutting by coastal people on crown land.[20]

The commission had demonstrated little real interest in confronting the fundamental social and economic problems that arose from the mercantile organization of the outport fishery during the first seven years of its existence. Its limited administrative reforms and its failure in almost every major social and economic initiative it undertook began to provoke public discontent. In July 1938, Governor Walwyn warned that the unemployed of St John's continued to become angrier and more inclined to a '"bolshie" spirit.' But everything changed with Britain's declaration of war on Germany on 3 September 1939, which automatically drew Newfoundland and Labrador into the conflict. Through the Act for the Defence of Newfoundland (1939) and the Emergency Powers (Defence) Act (1940), the Commission of Government gained extensive powers to regulate society and economy for the war effort. It quickly organized the Newfoundland Militia, which became the Newfoundland Regiment in 1943, as a defensive home guard, thus avoiding the expense of raising an overseas force. Instead, over 3,400 Newfoundlanders and Labradorians enlisted in the Royal Navy, while 3,600 more joined the Newfoundland Overseas Forestry Unit, from which many went on to branches of the British armed forces or the United Kingdom Home Guard. Others supported the war effort by serving as merchant mariners in the British and Allied shipping that proved vital to the war effort in Europe. While most Newfoundlanders and Labradorians saw military action on the North Atlantic or in the theatres of war in Europe, Africa, and Asia, hostilities occasionally struck close to home. German U-boats torpedoed ships at anchor at Bell Island in 1942, causing 69 casualties, while 137 passengers and crew died as a result of a torpedo attack on the *Caribou*, the ferry which linked North Sydney and Port aux Basques.[21]

The strategic geographical position of Newfoundland and Labrador meant that it played a central role in the Allied war effort in the North Atlantic. Before the war, Newfoundland had already become important in the development of transatlantic flight, especially at the Gander airport and the Botwood seaplane base. The Canadian government took over the defence of these facilities and later agreed to build additional airbases at Torbay and Goose Bay. The bases at Gander and Goose Bay became vital links in the ferrying of military aircraft to Britain, while Torbay was home to fighter squadrons that provided protection against U-boats for convoys of ships headed for Britain, although anti–U-boat patrols flew from the other airbases as well. A Canadian naval base at St John's was the home for escort ships that sailed with these convoys. The Canadian government used its military presence in Newfoundland to assert its strategic autonomy within the Commonwealth and Allied war effort and bring Newfoundland into its sphere of influence. Nevertheless, Canadian investment in its bases was often poorly planned and insufficient for the operational requirements of the war effort. While Canadian naval forces based in St John's were crucial to the Allied cause in the Battle of the Atlantic, it was Canada's leading role in military aviation based in Torbay, Gander, and Goose Bay that made Newfoundland and Labrador so important to its emerging strategic position in the North Atlantic.[22]

In 1940, Canada and the United States formed the Permanent Joint Board on Defence to protect the Western hemisphere. Although still officially neutral, the United States leased an army base in St John's, an air base at Stephenville, and a naval and army base at Argentia in return for providing Britain with destroyers and military equipment. The Americans decided to build a naval air station and army base on the sites of the communities of Argentia and Marquise in Placentia Bay. The residents negotiated with American authorities and the commission to be relocated for the most part together in the nearby town of Freshwater. The huge workforce that built the base, about 1,500 Americans and 4,000 Newfoundland civilians, was a boon to the local economy despite the difficulties relocation had caused the original settlers in the area. A nearby anchorage proved significant in August 1941 as the site at which U.S. President Franklin Roosevelt and Britain's Prime Minister Winston Churchill agreed on the main points of the Atlantic Charter. Throughout 1940–1 the Americans also began construction on an airbase at Stephenville, on the west coast of Newfoundland. Over the next two years, about 1,500 civilians worked with American personnel on the construction of the base, which generated many of the same benefits as at Argentia.[23]

The construction of the Goose Bay airbase had the most profound social effect of all the military installations in Newfoundland and Labrador. In 1939, the Canadian government had begun to look for a site in Labrador that would serve as a place from which new aircraft could be flown to England and from which anti-submarine patrols could be launched. By 1941, the United States took the lead in identifying and surveying the Goose Bay site. Under the auspices of the Permanent Joint Board on Defence, Canada leased the land and, with the Americans, built a huge base for the Canadian Army, Royal Canadian Air Force, and the U.S. Army Air Force. Between June and December 1941 the Allies had put temporary structures in place. By the end of the war, Goose Bay had a modern airport, port facilities, and all of the housing and other infrastructure necessary to support a population of about eight thousand people. Over time, the base brought together an unprecedented combination of Innu, Inuit, and settler peoples.[24]

Military authorities relied on Labradorians for much of the labour required to build the base, and the Allies had agreed to hire local labour whenever possible. Although prices for fish and furs had improved, work on the base was far more lucrative and, what is more, paid cash, thereby allowing many Labradorians to escape merchant credit and truck practices. Not allowed to live on the base, workers first went home, at the end of their shifts, to tent communities outside the restricted area, much like the shantytowns that developed on the edge of the Stephenville base. Workers and their families lived there, clustering together with others from their original communities, until the major Canadian contractor, McNamara Construction, built more permanent housing. Finally, worries about potential explosions at nearby fuel storage tanks for the base forced their relocation to Happy Valley in 1943.

Labradorians cleared the forest, operated sawmills, and then worked in the laundries to allow the base to operate. Whatever their ethnic background, people who had been used to seasonal and transhumant work in fishing and trapping found the industrial supervision of base work difficult. Those from fishing communities would often leave to take up fishing again in the summer, to the frustration of military authorities and commission officials, who felt they were better off with base employment. Nonetheless, the better wages and incomes of base work, which forced local employers such as the HBC to pay more as well, continued to attract people. Those who did not wish to live in Happy Valley often moved to nearby coastal communities such as Cartwright, where the Allies also constructed related military installations.[25]

The construction and maintenance of such military infrastructure changed the economy of Newfoundland and Labrador. Thousands of local people found work for good wages during the construction phase of the bases. Many men and women continued to find employment in the operation of the bases once construction had been finished. Wartime demand for foodstuffs led to improved marketing conditions in the fishing industry. That said, economic problems partially offset the prosperity brought about by the military presence and revived fishery. Inflation and housing shortages, for example, were constant problems, especially in major centres, throughout the war, and conditions became so bad in St John's that the Commission of Government established a Commission of Enquiry into Housing and Town Planning in 1942. Based on its recommendations, the government, in cooperation with the City of St John's, began a program of suburban housing development at Churchill Park for working people who could afford to buy a house; they were not, however, interested in providing public housing for the working poor.[26]

The arrival of military personnel, the overseas service of Newfoundland and Labrador men, the movement of local people to take work on the bases, and the marriages and other relationships that developed between local people and military personnel strained family relationships. While most Newfoundlanders and Labradorians might separate legally, there was no legal basis for divorce in the dominion, and few had the means to resort to other jurisdictions where divorce might be granted. Throughout the war years, the commission faced increasing popular demands for the legal right of divorce. While Justice Brian Dunfield ruled in 1948 that the Newfoundland courts had the power to administer judicial separation, Newfoundlanders and Labradorians did not gain the legal right of divorce until they became Canadians in 1949. The presence of large numbers of military personnel created other social problems. Whether in Gander, St John's, or Goose Bay, the military brought or encouraged the development of entertainment facilities for troops, which local people attended. American authorities particularly worried that relationships with local women would leave American soldiers with venereal diseases (VD) and other health problems, little considering that these soldiers might leave local women with the same problems. Military authorities pressed the Commission of Government to institute public health campaigns, to take aggressive measures against VD, and to prosecute more vigorously people suspected of prostitution.[27]

The presence of so many Canadians and Americans, along with their entertainment and consumer goods, gave many Newfoundlanders and Labradorians a taste for the more affluent consumerism that had been developing throughout North America. The wartime economy also provided the Commission of Government with the resources to spend more public money on health, education, and housing. The commission further invested in transportation and other public infrastructure. Nonetheless, it recognized that wartime prosperity was unlikely to last long once the war was over. With British support, the Commission of Government had pressured American authorities to keep wage rates down, suspecting that better wages would draw workers from the mining and forestry sectors. Many people participating in the commission's resettlement schemes had abandoned their new homes for work on the bases, leading the government to fear that the local postwar labour market would be unable to provide Newfoundlanders and Labradorians with the same type of well-paid jobs as had the bases. Not surprisingly, when Newfoundlanders learned they were being paid more poorly than foreign workers for the same jobs, word leaked out that the commission intentionally held the wages down. Further, since the bases were sovereign American territory, Newfoundlanders could be detained by the military police for attempting to unionize their countrymen, making collective bargaining impossible.[28]

Although the commission was unwilling to concede to labour leaders' demands that Newfoundland and Labrador labourers on the bases be better paid, the war effort gave workers more influence, and the organized labour movement achieved limited but important goals. At St Lawrence, for example, miners had continued to press for improved working conditions. In 1939, amid an outbreak of illness likely caused by workers drinking water contaminated by the mining process, miners formed the St Lawrence Labourers Protective Union (SLLPU). Although the SLLPU immediately demanded that the government address health and safety issues in the mines, the government did little, while the company offered a 10 per cent wage increase. Already important in steel manufacture, fluorspar was essential to the manufacture of aluminum. The Canadian manufacturer Alcan established another mine in St Lawrence in the same year, and its employees boosted the SLLPU membership. By 1940, SLLPU members walked off the job at the St Lawrence Corporation. Facing renewed union activity throughout the dominion, and fearing that labour unrest would disrupt the war effort, the commission gave itself the power to intervene in labour disputes. Rather than acting right away, the commission asked local magistrates to hold an inquiry into workers' complaints. The inquiry found that miners and their families continued to live in appalling poverty and unhealthy conditions without adequate medical services. It took greater militancy by the union, reorganized as the St Lawrence Workers Protective Union (SLWPU) in 1941, along with strikes elsewhere in Newfoundland, to force the government to act. In the fall, the commission established a Trade Disputes Board, which recommended the next year that the mining companies would have to recognize and bargain collectively with the SLWPU. Although workers brought their health and safety concerns to the board, it recommended nothing. The union, caught up in the early process of collective bargaining, did not pursue the issue. Their safety neglected by their employer, and their interests hardly regarded by their government, the miners of St Lawrence along with their wives and neighbours and people from the nearby community of Lawn, heroically answered the call of basic human decency on 18 February 1942, when they rescued crew members from the American warships USS *Truxton* and *Pollux*, which had run aground on the nearby coast in bad weather. While 93 members of the *Pollux*'s crew perished, local people rescued 140 others. Only 46 of the *Truxton*'s 146 lived to tell their tales, which included stories of the hard work and generosity exhibited by the people of St Lawrence and Lawn in caring for them.[29]

Throughout the war, the organized labour movement generally had avoided confrontation with either government or employers for the sake of the war effort. Pleased with the cooperation, the commission appointed representatives from the labour movement to advisory committees, including the New Industries Board, the War Loans Committee, the Unemployment Assistance Committee, and eventually the Advisory Committee to the Cabinet on Demobilization and Economic Readjustment. The Commission of Government had originally established the Trade Disputes Board with the Strikes and Lockouts Board and the Woods Labour Board to impose settlements and to ensure labour peace in the crucial pulp and paper and mining industries. The boards acted only when collective bargaining could not resolve disputes but gave members of labour unions an opportunity to acquire bargaining experience without worrying about strikes or lockouts. The touchstone for these developments had been a strike by miners at the Buchans Mining Company Limited for better wages. The miners walked off the job without the consent of their leaders in the Buchans Workers Protective Union, refused to be bullied by a police squad sent to Buchans, and demanded that the Trade Disputes Board investigate. The board recommended a wage increase and a contract provision for cost-of-living increases. The board further demanded that the employer recognize and bargain with the union. The commission used the Buchans decision as a template for further industrial disputes throughout the war.[30]

Wartime employment and the flood of cash into the local economy, combined with rising prices for fish as the war progressed, eroded most of the old credit practices associated with truck. The Rangers dealt less with public relief and more with social problems often related to the transience required by base construction. Outport communities changed as large numbers of strangers moved throughout the dominion, and older community leaders found their influence waning in the shadow of a new consumerism arising from integration into the cash economy. The Rangers found that their new duties of enforcing wartime price controls and rationing made them unpopular. People who had suffered through the depression wanted a little sugar or other luxury items now that they had some spare cash after years of privation. Rangers were not only responsible for the registration of all men fit for service, but had to enforce school attendance in line with the School Attendance Act of 1942, which required that all children up to the age of fourteen attend school. Many families disliked this regulation because their fisheries and farms depended on the help of all family members, whether one was younger than fourteen or not. By the end of the war, the Rangers found that their policing duties had increased.[31]

High fish prices revived the household fishery during the Second World War, but market and currency problems in the immediate postwar period led to a dramatic restructuring of the industry. Once the war ended, and prices began to collapse, the commission was content to allow a group of private interests to respond by forming the Newfoundland Associated Fish Exporters Limited (NAFEL) in 1945, which had the sole right to export fish from Newfoundland. NAFEL was itself a nonprofit organization that used 10 per cent of its sales to cover costs but otherwise returned the remainder of the proceeds to its members, who had to guarantee the delivery of a good-quality product. As a private marketing organization, however, NAFEL had no mandate to develop markets for new products, new markets for old ones, or to reform production. The commission had never hired any personnel with much direct experience in the marketing of fish, much less in processing, and NAFEL's practice of marketing fish by consignment now meant that those individual firms that had always produced for particular markets would not know whether their fish would go to these same markets. As a result, there was even less incentive to cure carefully, and, without the power to establish standardized production, NAFEL could do nothing to improve quality. As European competitors resumed fishing, Britain's postwar currency problems plagued Newfoundland firms, whose traditional markets in southern Europe had paid for fish in the British pounds sterling, which were then converted to dollars to pay for Newfoundland's imports from the United States and Canada. With the devaluation of the pound sterling at the end of the war, however, the British government prohibited its conversion to American dollars and Newfoundland found itself short of dollars to pay for imports while holding pounds in accounts in Britain that could not be transferred.[32]

The commission believed that persistent poverty in the fishery was the result of rural dependence for earnings on producing low-value, salted fish that could only be sold in poor southern European and South American markets. However, a long process of ruinous competition among the merchants who marketed fish had meant that Newfoundland salt fish had a poor reputation in the marketplace as a hurriedly processed and poorly shipped product. Lower prices, of course, followed declining reputation, and merchants responded by cutting the credit they gave to fishing households. Continuing merchant opposition to salt fish marketing reform left the commission encouraging a fresh/frozen fishery on the part of a few new companies: in effect, a complete modernization of the fishery.[33]

The plan followed one developed by Canadian fisheries official Stewart Bates in 1944 to cope with similar marketing problems in Nova Scotia. Bates suggested restructuring the fishing industry along more capital-intensive lines, replacing independent fish merchant firms that exported salt fish produced by family labour with large fishing corporations that could standardize processing and export to more lucrative fresh/frozen markets in the United States. The new industry would be based largely on wage labour employed on large deep-sea trawlers that supplied processing plants concentrated in a small number of communities. Large vessels could stay at sea for up to two weeks, catching fish by towing large nets from their sides or, later, from their sterns. Bates suggested that frozen fish processors should take control over the whole process of production, from catching fish to selling it in the market, thus allowing processors to freeze excess catches and store product to await higher demand. A more efficient process of moving fish from the water to the dinner plate, he thought, would stabilize the old problems of uncertainties in the availability of the resource and in markets.

Although the Bates plan had been developed for a Nova Scotia economy that was more diversified than Newfoundland's, and could therefore absorb some of the household labour made surplus by the intensive capitalization of the industry, the atypical success of the wartime era fooled the commission into thinking that Bates's plan would work for the island, and it embraced fisheries modernization as the cornerstone of a policy designed to bring to a close the outport life of Newfoundland.[34]

While many people criticized the commission for its failures to resolve the economic problems facing Newfoundland, some now became frustrated by the lack of democratic institutions within which to resolve problems. Nationalistic Newfoundlanders turned to other avenues, among them F.M. O'Leary, who sponsored the journalist, former labour organizer, self-professed Christian Socialist, and Squires Liberal supporter Joseph Smallwood's *Barrelman* radio program. Smallwood had tried to bolster Newfoundlanders' confidence in the face of the depression and became a popular radio personality. In 1943 he left the program, suggesting that Newfoundlanders now had their confidence back, and moved to the Royal Canadian Air Force base at Gander to operate a pig farm. Smallwood's interest in farming was long-standing, and he probably drew some inspiration for it from the efforts of his political heroes, the Reformers of the nineteenth century such as William Carson, to establish an alternative to living from the sea.[35]

Other discontent with the commission was also making itself felt. Although the relative absence of industrial strife during the war enhanced the reputation of the NFL and its affiliates, there was growing frustration within the labour movement about the manner in which war-induced inflation was eroding workers' wages. Workers in the building trades were particularly sensitive because of the manner in which the commission had discouraged the Americans and Canadians from paying wages equal to what they might pay their own nationals for work in base construction. Cash-strapped, the NFL had not been organizing such workers, some of whom formed their own union with Harold Horwood as leader. Horwood enlisted the aid of Greg Power to organize the General Workers' Union at the Argentia military base, where he led a successful fight for union recognition and pay increases by waging a public and embarrassing campaign against American authorities there.

With the end of the war, the NFL decided that it was time to renew its organizing efforts and to fight for better wages for working people who had been plagued by inflation. It hired Horwood as a part-time organizer but suspended him in 1947 because his leftist radicalism did not fit with the NFL's desire for public respectability. Nonetheless, the NFL initiated a successful union drive that, by 1947, meant New-foundland had, on a per capita basis, twice as many organized work-ers as had Canada. In 1948, the NFL, with the support of the LSPU, backed a successful strike by railway workers for a wage increase. As almost all consumer goods were shipped by rail or sea, the coopera-tion of longshoremen and railway workers meant that food shortages and economic disruption reigned outside of St John's, which was the main port of entry for most imports. Without violence and with the cooperation of the labour movement, the railway workers forced the Commission of Government to give in to their demands. The NFL had hoped that the commission would introduce a labour relations act but recognized that it would have to wait for a return of responsible gov-ernment. Leading members of the NFL, such as Irving Fogwill, had already turned to the only democratic politics left in Newfoundland, St John's municipal elections. They formed the St John's District La-bour Party in 1945 and ran unsuccessfully in the municipal election of that year.[36]

The demands for a return to responsible government were going to be difficult to resist, but Clement Atlee, the Dominions Secretary in 1942, believed that Newfoundland would be better off joining Canada. He sent a delegation of three MPs to Newfoundland in 1943, which found that few people wanted Confederation, but they also were un-happy at the prospect of returning to responsible government as it had existed in 1932. The United States emerged from the war as the world's pre-eminent power that was on the eve of a struggle with the Soviet Union. Newfoundland and Labrador continued to be vital strategically to American interests in the North Atlantic, since the na-ture of its military leases meant that the United States had a sufficient presence there to protect its interests. The Canadian government, on the other hand, decided that bringing Newfoundland and Labrador into Confederation would be the best way of securing its interests in civil aviation and defence. Canada now stood in the shadow of its American partner; with Britain, it recognized the potential of friendly counter-balancing American hegemony if Newfoundland and Lab-rador became a province. British officials proposed, but ultimately rejected as expensive, a postwar economic reconstruction plan for Newfoundland. Canadian officials opposed the plan because it would make Newfoundland more viable as an independent dominion and therefore unlikely to join Confederation. The British and Canadian governments decided to bring Newfoundland into Confederation.[37]

The Commission of Government realized that the experience of war would lead to demands for change once peace arrived. Before the war, the unemployed, loggers, miners, and unionists had begun to rally against the commission's ineffectual and stingy social and economic policies. During the war, Newfoundlanders and Labradorians felt that they had done their part to defend democracy from fascism. Yet, these same people continued to be administered by an often unpopular and unelected government. At the international level, the Second World War had cost Britain dearly; it would be unable to maintain its pre-war imperial commitments, including its support for the commission in Newfoundland. Although Newfoundland's books were balanced, fulfilling one of the conditions under which self-government might be resumed, the commissioners believed financial solvency was a result of abnormal wartime conditions. Newfoundland and British authorities realized that the commission's efforts to reform the moral character of Newfoundland had been futile, that it had been unable to bring about significant economic reorganization, and that war had been the real catalyst for change. With war at an end, working people expected meaningful social and economic change. J.R. Smallwood's campaign for Confederation appeared to be the best way they might realize their hopes.

10

The Land of Milk and Honey, 1946–1972

Herbert Pottle, one of the first of Smallwood's cabinet ministers to abandon him, wrote that Smallwood saw himself as the people's 'Abraham' leading them into the 'new Canaan' of Confederation, but with a common touch: he was the prophet 'of the average "Joe."'[1] Smallwood appealed to the fishing people and loggers who comprised the bulk of the outport population, leading them to believe that he would stand up against the merchants of Water Street. Smallwood promised them better lives, but under his government the newest province of Canada experienced increased dependency on federal transfer payments and the courtship of big business to aid in natural-resource development. Smallwood's goal was to transform the province into a modern urban and industrial society dominated by consumerism. Over the long term, the milk and honey of Confederation soured as workers' clashes with Smallwood and his obtuse economic vision for the province and the area's dependency on the fragile resources of the welfare state all took their toll. Newfoundland and Labrador's experience as a Canadian province would not live up to the inchoate but real hope on the part of many Newfoundlanders and Labradorians that constitutional change might fundamentally alter the economic exploitation that they had endured for so long and maintain the greater personal economic autonomy that had come with war-related employment.

The British government and the Commission of Government in St John's decided to use an elected National Convention on Newfoundland's constitutional future, established in 1946, to promote union with Canada. Although opponents of the commission and Confederation argued, with some justification, that the British government should have restored full responsible government instead, there was little popular hue and cry against the National Convention. Most of the Convention's delegates felt that self-government should resume, but they took up the task of investigating the general state of affairs. A recent convert to the cause of Confederation, Smallwood was unshakeable in his commitment to it. Influenced by his youthful flirtation with the political left and the crushing poverty of the depression, Smallwood believed that union with Canada would shift the balance in favour of working Newfoundlanders, especially those of the outports, against the dominion's mercantile elite, concentrated in St John's. In his earlier *Barrelman* broadcasts, Smallwood had suggested that ordinary people were hard-working members of a Newfoundland nation, with the same entitlements to modern living standards and consumerism as anyone, merchants included. If such ordinary people could not marshal the resources to obtain their rights in an independent Newfoundland, then it was better to join Canada.[2]

Although Smallwood had distanced himself from the left, it is impossible to escape the class dimensions implicit in his message of consumer entitlement and in the nature of the team he assembled to fight for Confederation. His most important ally was F. Gordon Bradley, who had retired from the bar and moved to Bonavista in the mid-1930s, partially out of disgust with the St John's elite, who had paved the way for the Amulree Commission's recommendations. Bradley had long believed in the necessity of Confederation and wrote periodically about political matters for the FPU newspaper, the *Fisherman's Advocate*. Smallwood recruited a young, dynamic group, the first of whom was the self-described 'left-wing socialist,' Harold Horwood. Horwood claimed that he and Smallwood counted 'card-carrying communists' among their friends and that Smallwood professed that he wanted to bring socialism to Newfoundland in the fight for union with Canada. Horwood's colleague in the labour movement and local literary circles, W. Irving Fogwill, along with his wife Janet Fogwill, joined him in supporting Confederation. Another self-proclaimed socialist, Phil Forsey, supported them, as did Greg Power. A talented writer as well, Power became a close friend of Smallwood and the most important writer for the *Confederate*, the newspaper of the Newfoundland Confederate Association.[3]

Some leaders from the labour movement worked against Confederation, most notably Frank Fogwill. He had been elected to the National Convention as a labour candidate for St John's East Extern and supported Peter Cashin's fight for a return to responsible government. Although a firebrand, Cashin was unable to put together a convincing platform for a return to responsible government or to rally a party to his cause. In 1947, St John's business interests and professionals came together in a Responsible Government League (RGL), led by F.M. O'Leary. The RGL relied heavily on the notion that Newfoundlanders would not want to sell their nation to Canada or live under the yoke of Canadian taxation. Although Smallwood had failed in 1946 in a motion to send a delegation of the Convention to Ottawa to investigate possible terms of union with Canada, he used public broadcast of the debate to extol the benefits of Confederation and to ask Newfoundlanders if they really wished to return to responsible government and the poverty of the 1930s. In 1947, the Convention agreed to send delegations to Ottawa and London.

Ottawa officials agreed that if Newfoundland became a province, Canada would assume 90 per cent of its public debt, allow it to retain its accumulated surplus of $28.8 million, provide it with statutory subsidies and transitional grants until the new province had phased in its own provincial taxes, establish a royal commission within eight years to review the province's financial position; they also made concessions to Newfoundland's right to manufacture margarine and have a public denominational education system. The management of land-based natural resources would fall under provincial jurisdiction as provided in the British North America Act. However, management of fisheries would fall under federal jurisdiction, although the Canadian government agreed that NAFEL would continue to have exclusive rights to market Newfoundland and Labrador fish, which lasted until 1959.[4] The London delegation, on the other hand, came away with little more than a promise that Britain would continue to support the Commission of Government financially if Newfoundlanders decided that it should continue.

In the Convention, the RGL had the support of enough delegates to ensure that only Commission of Government and 'Responsible Government as it existed in 1933' would be on the ballot for a national referendum on the constitutional future of Newfoundland. Smallwood quickly organized a petition demanding that Confederation be added to the ballot as well, something which the British were happy to grant. The RGL had focused its attention upon preventing the people of Newfoundland and Labrador from having such an option and was now ill prepared to meet Smallwood's head start in convincing people to vote. In desperation, younger anti-Confederates formed the Economic Union Association (EUA) and recruited businessman Chesley Crosbie as its leader. The commission would not allow the Convention to travel to Washington to inquire about closer economic ties to the United States, ruling that such discussions were a matter of foreign affairs and not a form of government. Poorly organized and funded, the RGL and the EUA divided the responsible government campaign and could not escape the tarnish that they represented Water Street, although most of the country's business elite were ambivalent about the referendum outcome.[5]

The first referendum in June 1948 resulted in no form of government getting a majority, although responsible government gained the most votes. The commission dropped the option of continuing under Commission of Government and campaigning resumed before a second ballot. The campaign assumed sectarian tones as Archbishop Edward Patrick Roche advised Roman Catholics to vote against Confederation. His arguments were essentially the same as those of the RGL, yet his greatest fear was that Confederation could undermine denominational education in Newfoundland. Although there is little evidence to suggest that most Roman Catholics took political direction from Roche, Smallwood mobilized the Orange Order to support the Confederation cause. Although mean-spirited, this sectarianism little affected the referendum. The majority of those who had favoured continued commission appear to have backed Confederation in July, resulting in a slim majority for union with Canada.

The results reflected a remarkable division within Newfoundland society. Most voters on the Avalon Peninsula favoured a return to responsible government while the remainder of the island and Labrador supported Confederation. Sectarianism may have contributed to the division, but other factors played a major role. Exposed daily to the anxieties expressed in the media of many in the business community about the possible economic problems of Confederation, people on the Avalon Peninsula, regardless of denomination, were disposed against Confederation. Smallwood had used an anti–Water Street sentiment to good effect, however, portraying Confederation as a way for the powerless in rural Newfoundland to get out from under a plutocratic merchant-dominated political and economic system that gave them only poverty and want. In the districts of Humber and Grand Falls, pulp and paper companies were opposed to Confederation because they did not want to come under a more exacting federal taxation regime; this opposition probably encouraged loggers to support Smallwood. In St George's–Port au Port, voters of the mostly

Roman Catholic district supported Confederation. Although some analyses suggest these Catholics (Acadians, Scottish Highlanders, or Mi'kmaq from Cape Breton in origin) did so because of their Canadian connections, W.J. Chafe, who had been working for the Newfoundland railway at St George's, remembered that 'the American base at Stephenville had given the people a taste for North American prosperity,' which they hoped to preserve through union with Canada.[6]

Smallwood and the Confederate Association had convinced rural Newfoundlanders and Labradorians that their best hope for a better life lay in Canadian-funded transfer payments through family allowances, pensions, unemployment insurance, and other programs. Despite efforts to block the union, it became effective one moment before midnight on 31 March 1949, to avoid the symbolism of joining as the tenth province on April Fool's Day. The Canadian government, however, had intended that the Terms of Union would bring Newfoundland up to the standards of the Maritime Provinces, which had found Confederation to be more than a little disappointing in terms of economic development. The new provincial government would be hard pressed to use the terms of its union with Canada to fundamentally restructure the social inequalities of Newfoundland and Labrador. Apparently generous financially at the time, the Terms of Union had not been designed to make Newfoundland and Labrador better off than its neighbouring provinces.[7]

Smallwood capitalized on the localism of class relationships in fishing communities by building the campaign for Confederation as a way for outport people to strike at St John's merchants. The paternalism of outport culture meant that fishing people often continued to identify with their local merchants against 'Water Street.' Local dealers and merchants had been hurt by St John's firms' restriction of credit during the 1930s. Outport firms had further borne much of the strain of supplying their clients with more expensive products from St John's under the shelter of protective tariffs. Wartime prosperity had meant that many small firms concentrated more on the business of satisfying the consumer demands of local people. Although military spending had been reduced, government spending and the appearance of the first fish plants on the south coast provided fishing people with cash and encouraged merchants and shopkeepers to compete for their business. Such businesses would deal with St John's wholesalers when they could obtain affordable supplies, but by the early 1950s they turned to Canadian suppliers to procure goods at the best prices possible for their rural customers. When a small outport merchant, therefore, wrote to the St John's firm of F.M. O'Leary just after Confederation to gloat as he closed out his account because he planned to buy in future from Canadian suppliers, we can too easily regard the complex class antagonisms expressed in his message as a regional divide.[8]

In the long run, Smallwood and his allies had no intention of alienating capitalists regardless of the size of their interests. Instead, they quickly adopted the Liberal mantle, partly because that party was in power in Ottawa and partly because the federal Liberals were ideologically compatible with Smallwood's modernization agenda. Smallwood's early socialism paled beside his political involvement in the Liberal Party of Richard Squires, and he supported the same type of industrialization as had Squires. This left the anti-Confederates to join the Progressive Conservative Party, contaminating it with their reputation as opponents of Confederation and its accompanying social programs. During succeeding elections the Progressive Conservatives were unable to elect members of the House of Assembly outside of the anti-Confederate pocket on the Avalon Peninsula.

Smallwood always had his eye upon the partisan implications of everything his government and the federal government did. He had promised better old-age pensions, for example, which the federal government could use to quickly demonstrate, with hard cash, the material benefits of being Canadian. Despite federal officials' hope that they might have some time to establish their normal procedures, including a process of verifying ages, provincial minister Herbert Pottle advised Newfoundlanders to start flooding federal officials with applications to get a head start on establishing their eligibility. Smallwood wanted happy voters with pension and family allowance cheques in hand to support his Liberal Party in the first provincial election. He was even more blatant upon other occasions, as when he threatened the voters of Ferryland District that if they did not elect Liberal Greg Power he would ensure they would get 'not one red cent' of federal money until the next election. Over the next few years Smallwood's close connection to federal Liberal insider Jack Pickersgill helped the premier claim credit for federal programs.[9]

Smallwood retained an antipathy toward Newfoundland's economic elite when they seemed to be an obstacle to modernization and often viewed them in terms of the old Reformers' notions of parasitic merchants from the 1820s and 1830s. He hoped to enlist the federal government and international capital to help him transform the province's society and economy. Canadian officials encouraged modernization of the fishery after 1949, and Smallwood embraced the idea that persistent poverty in the fishery was the result of rural dependence for earnings on producing low-value, salted fish that could only be sold in poor southern European and South American markets. He agreed that ruinous competition among fish merchants made matters worse. A complete reorganization of the fishery, removing the old household-based salt fishery, seemed best.

Smallwood's government supported the modernization of the fishery, believing it could use federal money to build a diversified economy. He assumed that outport fishing people wanted to get out of not only the poverty that dominated their lives but also the insecurity and risk associated with independent household production in the fishery, and he wanted Newfoundlanders to join the 'modern world' by leaving the outports for wage work in the designated growth centres. The federal and provincial governments expected that any remaining inshore fishing communities would disappear as they encouraged the fishery to become more capital-intensive, mechanized, and centralized in a few urban communities.[10]

Smallwood did not have a clear plan or vision for the new Newfoundland he wanted to build, just a vague sense that people wanted secure full-time jobs in a modern, urban, industrial society. His government embarked on a disastrous program of industrial diversification that failed to provide employment to those fishers who were displaced by fisheries modernization; his attempted industrial diversification of the provincial economy resulted in a lot of ill-advised manufacturing failures and political chicanery. Smallwood believed that 'Water Street' was too short-sighted to take on industrial projects and hoped to use the accumulated surplus of the commission years as seed money to entice outside capitalists to bring their expertise and new industries to Newfoundland and Labrador.

To spearhead this plan he recruited Alfred Valdmanis, the former Latvian finance minister and wartime resident of Germany, as Newfoundland's director of economic development. Smallwood was impressed with Valdmanis's drive and energy and hoped that the former collaborator's contacts with German industrialists might allow his government to entice entrepreneurs from war-ravaged Germany to set up shop in Newfoundland. Valdmanis helped establish the successful North Star Cement factory in Corner Brook, but subsequent efforts such as knitting mills, confectionary factories, and film production were ill-suited to an economy that had few alternatives to marine resources and a small local market for consumer products, for which local manufacturers had already lost their market protection when Newfoundland became a Canadian province.[11]

The Smallwood government had passed the province's first Revenue and Audit Act in 1952, which created a treasury board as a committee of cabinet and put in place a relatively independent auditor general. Nevertheless, the auditor general did not report to the legislature, and Smallwood was loath to allow the office to challenge his administration's often questionable expenditures. The government quickly dissipated its surplus in subsidies to businesses that never got off the ground. Under Valdmanis's direction, the Newfoundland government courted foreign investment by providing 50 per cent of the start-up capital for new industries through various forms of public financing. In return, private investors were obliged to provide the rest of the capital but could do so in-kind. Some German businessmen felt they had been lied to about Newfoundland's economic suitability for their businesses, while many Newfoundlanders believed that foreign con artists had taken money from the gullible Smallwood without ever intending to establish viable businesses, not least because Smallwood had inadvertently encouraged many Newfoundland politicians to be jealous of Valdmanis, on whom he depended. In 1954 Valdmanis entered a guilty plea to the charge of accepting bribes from German industrialists who were looking for government concessions.[12]

With the Valdmanis experience ending in disgrace, Smallwood continued to face a dilemma. His vision of a modern Newfoundland was twofold. First, he wanted to improve provincial living standards by increasing the population's ability to consume private goods and public services. Second, he wanted to build an industrial economy that would support such expanded consumption. In the short term, Smallwood made rapid strides in the first agenda through federal welfare-state and transfer programs. The provincial government quickly expanded Memorial University from a junior college to a degree-granting institution and embarked on an aggressive program to build roads, schools, and hospitals during the 1950s. The government had failed, however, to generate significant industrial employment, especially in rural areas. Unsuccessful industrial development schemes drained the surplus left over from the Commission of Government and left the province without a tax base to generate revenue for government services.

Rural people were beginning to suspect that Smallwood might have been a false prophet. Loggers from communities in White Bay had already discovered that the premier favoured the large pulp and paper companies over them in the allocation of forest resources. Through-out the early 1950s the provincial government refused to return control of a portion of the three-mile limit of coastal forest to White Bay communities, despite support from their Liberal MHA, Sam Drover, and Ted Russell, who had been the minister of Mines and Resources.[13] Finally, in 1954, persistent complaints about the forestry industry led the government to appoint a royal commission on forestry, which recommended the management of crown timber resources for the benefit of large-scale industrial development of the woods.

Feeling that the Liberal government no longer represented the best interests of his constituents, White Bay MHA Sam Drover crossed the floor, eventually sitting as the Assembly's first member of the Co-operative Commonwealth Federation (CCF). Ted Russell, who had supported Smallwood during the fight for Confederation, had already left cabinet in 1951 over the development policies recommended by Valdmanis; Horwood and Forsey abandoned Smallwood over his development policies. The Liberals successfully ran Fred Rowe, the minister of Mines and Resources, against Drover in the 1956 general election, but Rowe recalled that Drover kept the support of loggers in his district. By now, it was very clear that the Smallwood government would prefer corporate interests over those of the people if circumstances forced a choice.[14]

Loggers forced the government to choose. Since the 1950s, they had belonged to the Newfoundland Lumbermen's Association (NLA), under Joe Thompson. The NLA had secured better pay for loggers but otherwise had become entangled in an increasingly accommodating relationship with the paper companies. By 1956, tired of his long career, Thompson responded positively to overtures from the conservative United Brotherhood of Carpenters and Joiners (UBJC) for a merger with the NLA. The CIO-affiliated International Woodworkers of America (IWA) made a competing bid for the support of Newfoundland loggers. Although, like many industrial unions, the IWA had grown initially through the organizational skills and dedication of people with communist sympathies, by 1956 such influences had been contained by a more moderate leftist leadership that could still sympathize with the CCF. The IWA began an enormously successful membership drive, enjoyed huge popular support among loggers and their families, and organized a strike in 1959 for higher wages and better living conditions in the woods camps.

The federal Conservative government turned down Smallwood's request to use the RCMP as strike breakers, prompting the premier to send out to Badger (central Newfoundland) members of the New-foundland Constabulary, a police force which normally operated only in the area near St John's. A subsequent confrontation with loggers left one constable dead, and this tragedy gave Smallwood an oppor-tunity to deal harshly with the union. In a remarkable radio address Smallwood presented the strike as a war between two sides. On the side of the multinational corporations in the pulp and paper indus-try, he said, were Newfoundlanders and democracy itself. On the side of the IWA were non-Newfoundlanders, communists, gangsters, and pimps, he claimed, despite the fact that (although initially wary) the NFL fully supported the IWA against Smallwood once it clearly had the backing of the vast majority of loggers. Smallwood, however, decertified the IWA as the bargaining agent for the loggers and ap-pointed a Liberal Party loyalist as president of a new, more concilia-tory union.[15] The forest companies later quietly granted many of the concessions which had prompted the strike, but the IWA had been dealt a fatal blow and it would take a long time for organized labour to regain its confidence.

The leakage from Smallwood's government benches continued. Al-ready troubled by Smallwood's growing arrogance, Greg Power final-ly left the government. The International Labor Organization and the Canadian Labour Congress condemned the provincial government's actions, but Smallwood felt he had triumphed. Spiteful about the NFL's support of the IWA, Smallwood did his best to undermine that labour organization. The NFL responded by forming the Newfound-land Democratic Party, which incorporated the small CCF organiza-tion in the province. Steve Neary, the secretary-treasurer of the NFL, nonetheless decided that the federation must improve its relationship with the government and accepted publicly some minor legislative concessions by the Smallwood government. As acting president of the NFL, he declared a truce with the government, but the IWA support-ers within the NFL did not accept his actions and were not surprised when Neary ran as a Liberal candidate in the next provincial election. Led by Esau Thoms, the group successfully fought Neary for control of the NFL executive, but the IWA struggle had weakened the organi-zation considerably.[16]

In a masterly stroke of political strategy, Smallwood diverted the popular anger over the IWA strike into public indignation about term 29 of the Terms of Union between Newfoundland and Canada, which had committed the federal government to reviewing the financial state of the new province within eight years of its entry into Confederation. As early as 1953, Smallwood had begun to build a case for more generous financial terms from Ottawa and for himself as a regional champion against federal policies favouring central Canada. Smallwood was upset with the paltry $8 million per year in perpetuity in increased subsidies recommended by the McNair Commission, which conducted the review, and Prime Minister John Diefenbaker's initial refusal to pay even that. Smallwood, the champion of Confederation, threatened in 1962 to take Newfoundland out of Canada amid an outpouring of provincial popular support for his position.

As matters stood, of course, Newfoundland received other transfer payments from the federal government according to the formula that applied to all provinces. However, even with federal money the province's expenditures still outstripped its revenues. The federal government continued to be a visible presence in the modernization of Newfoundland, especially so in the creation of the province's first national park at Terra Nova between 1957 and 1961. The National Parks Branch (NPB) of the Canadian Department of Northern Affairs and Natural Resources did everything it could to accommodate the Smallwood government's economic development agenda. The NPB accepted the location of the national park on the northeast coast of Newfoundland that would maximize the federal government's financial responsibility for the construction of the Trans-Canada Highway across the island (the federal government took complete financial responsibility for the highway within national park boundaries rather than the usual 50-50 per cent sharing of the costs with the provinces). More important, the federal government agreed that commercial logging would be allowed in Terra Nova National Park to feed a third pulp and paper mill on the east coast of Newfoundland, should one ever be constructed. The construction and operation of the park also provided a limited number of jobs to people in local communities such as Port Blandford, Traytown, and Charlottetown, but the federal and provincial governments forced no one to move to accommodate the park and even recognized local people's fishing rights and timber harvesting rights within its boundaries.[17]

The provincial government could not conduct its business simply by blaming all of its woes on the federal government. Aware that his failed economic policies, political scandals, and treatment of loggers jeopardized his support among rural Newfoundlanders, Smallwood began to give the fishing industry more attention. In 1962, he held a Fisheries Convention of businesspeople, fishers, scientists, and government officials. The premier remained convinced that the development of a modern, technologically intensive, centralized fresh/frozen fishing industry was of paramount importance to the province, but he had come to realize that many inshore fishing people continued to depend on the salt fishery. So Smallwood developed a plan for its revitalization based on the hope that the federal government would invest in it through the federal Agricultural and Rural Development Act (ARDA). Hence, in the next provincial election, Smallwood promised more public support for boat building and harbour facilities, exploration for new fish resources, and the construction of community-owned fish plants and stages. In 1963, the Newfoundland government further proposed that the federal government develop a national, community-based fisheries development policy similar to that provided in ARDA for other rural communities.

The federal government refused to accept the proposal or to support financially Smallwood's earlier campaign promises but held to the modernization plan first outlined by Stewart Bates. It was reluctant to invest in an industry that produced such a low-value commodity and that was subject to growing international competition. During these years, the Canadian government had pursued talks with the United States and, through the Law of the Sea Conferences of the late 1950s and early 1960s, aimed at expanding its territorial control over marine resources from three to twelve miles at sea. The United States, however, was uninterested in having its maritime rights limited, and, in the context of the mounting Cold War, Canada had little means to prevail on its much more powerful ally. The federal government saw little option but to encourage modernization of the Newfoundland fishing industry so that it might better meet its foreign competitors in designated growth areas.[18]

In 1965, the federal and provincial governments negotiated the Household Resettlement Program, which continued the province's earlier centralization program, but aimed to move people out of the fishing industry by creating 'growth poles' of resettled people as a local unskilled labour pool that might attract industry. In 1954, the provincial government had turned to resettling the widely dispersed populations of coastal communities into centralized locations, thus reducing the cost of delivering health care, education, and public utilities such as electricity. Many rural people initially favoured resettlement, especially women, who had borne the high costs of trying to arrange the education of their children and maintaining their families' well-being in the absence of well-developed educational and medical facilities. Disillusionment quickly set in, however, as resettled people found little work, inadequate housing, poor land for supplementary farming, and insufficient financial assistance from government in their new communities.[19]

Resettlement nevertheless encouraged consumerism as rural people depended more than ever on cash coming into the community in the form of make-work programs, community council work, unemployment insurance, and other forms of social assistance. The provincial government remained committed to raising the standard of living for most people in the province by increasing their ability to consume, and in this it had, not surprisingly, the support of the St John's business community. Although that community later complained frequently about the public debt that accompanied the expansion of the welfare state, postwar St John's businesses concentrated on the provision of wholesale, retail, and other services to provincial consumer markets made possible by government spending.[20]

The new resettlement program had its most traumatic impact in Labrador in the immediate context of the industrial exploitation of its interior resources. Smallwood saw Labrador as a resource to be developed for the sake of Newfoundland; it was to be the keystone of a provincial economic empire. Anxious to establish a team of empire builders, Smallwood had gone to the United Kingdom in 1952 to offer much of the Labrador interior for private development to such luminaries as Sir Winston Churchill and Anthony de Rothschild. A consortium of corporations, including Bowaters, the AND, Rio Tinto Company Limited, and, eventually, the Bank of Montreal and the Royal Bank of Canada, took Smallwood up on his offer. Incorporated in 1953 as the British Newfoundland Corporation (Brinco), the consortium acquired lease rights to a huge tract of the Labrador interior.

Between 1952 and 1954, Smallwood had struck up a relationship with John C. Doyle much as he had earlier with Valdmanis. Doyle's Canadian Javelin acquired lease rights to develop an iron ore mine at Wabush, close to a prospective new development by the Iron Ore Company of Canada (IOC). Although the IOC had been developing iron ore mining at Knob Lake on the Quebec side of the border since the 1940s, it only acquired the technical capacity to develop ore in Labrador West in the 1950s and announced that it would develop a project at Carol Lake, which became known as Labrador City. The mammoth project generated much business for Quebec and Newfoundland companies, and a town grew up rapidly around the mining complex. Of the hundreds of workers and their families who poured into the town, most came from Newfoundland. Some Labrador settlers found work with the project but faced prejudice on the part of others, and there were almost no job opportunities for Innu workers, a situation aggravated by poor transportation links between Labrador West and the coast. Similar developments occurred in Wabush. The provincial government provided few services to Labrador City and Wabush, which were mostly provided by the iron-ore companies. Over time, as the companies withdrew services, the residents of Labrador West found that the provincial government did not step in readily to fill the gap, causing many residents to realize that their communities had been developed primarily to generate wealth for others, in particular applying that analysis to the island of Newfoundland rather than the corporations that made money from mining ore.[21]

In the wake of the development of the iron-ore mining industry in Labrador, the Newfoundland government emphasized the importance of Labrador's natural resources to the economic development of the province. The original discussions between Smallwood and representatives of the Canadian government about the terms of union had included the idea that the Aboriginal peoples of the new province would come under the federal jurisdiction of the Indian Act and would be entitled to reserves and direct funding. Canadian and Newfoundland officials decided against this, arguing that there was too much intermarriage between the Innu, Inuit, and people of European descent, and that the Innu and Inuit would lose their voting rights under the Indian Act. The federal government still contributed financially for the provision of services, but did so by transferring funds to the province for use in all northern communities in which there were Innu and Inuit, thereby leaving Ottawa to pay for most of the province's responsibilities in Labrador.[22]

Resettlement was a means by which the province attempted to dispossess the Innu of their rights to much of the territory in which natural resources might be found. As on the island, the Newfoundland government argued that the centralization of the Innu in a small number of settlements would allow a more efficient delivery of better health and educational services. However, with the establishment of the Division of Labrador Affairs within the provincial Department of Welfare, the Newfoundland government committed to the resettlement of the Innu as a way to break their supposedly 'uncivilized' reliance on transhumant hunting. The division's policy was to assimilate the Innu into a sedentary lifestyle based on wage labour in the mining, forestry, or fishing industries. Authorities singled out the education of children as the primary means of achieving such assimilation. The practice of Innu at Sheshatshiu to go into the bush to hunt and trap was incompatible with the southern-based schooling that the government wished to develop in the community; school officials, teachers, and clergy did their best to make Innu parents feel guilty about taking their children into the bush when they were supposed to be in school.[23] The province demonstrated less concern about the Innu's traditional rights to natural resources than it had, for example, for the people of the northern coast of Bonavista Bay who might have been displaced by the development of Terra Nova National Park.

To encourage permanent residence in the community, in 1957 the provincial government had begun to construct houses, ostensibly to curtail tuberculosis, which health officials maintained spread easily in the tents used by Innu families. However, rather than build the houses directly, the government supplied the Innu with some building materials, but did not provide the facilities for running water or the same quality of building as those used by government officials and teachers: a practice of substandard housing that also characterized a later government housing project in the community from 1965 to 1968.

Throughout the 1960s, the Newfoundland government continued to pursue the centralization of southern Innu in Sheshatshiu. At the same time, the growth of Happy Valley-Goose Bay as a centre of provincial administration for Labrador affected the relations between residents of North West River and Goose Bay. Although tensions between settlers and the Innu over rights to hunting and trapping territory had been long-standing, the influx of outsiders without Native ancestry to work first at the Grenfell hospital and then with the military base or government offices affected the local people who worked alongside them. Newcomers mocked the settlers' Native heritage, and some settlers consequently minimized the importance of that heritage, especially in trapping. Although settlers and Innu trapped differently, they had traded with each other and got along well when members of one group had occasion to visit the hunting camps or trap tilts of the other. As more settlers from North West River worked for wages, the opportunities for such interactions diminished, and relationships between the communities worsened. Nonetheless, some settlers learned to 'play the native game,' to advertise their Native heritage when it was to their advantage.[24]

Conditions were worse in the new community of Davis Inlet. Since Confederation, the Newfoundland government had failed to induce the northern Mushuau Innu to settle in a central location. However, in

1967, the Newfoundland government moved the Innu to Davis Inlet on Illuikoyak Island under the Fisheries Household Resettlement Program, although living on an island made it much more difficult for the Innu to engage in the caribou hunt of the mainland. But government promised to assist them in developing a viable saltwater fishery there, despite little evidence to suggest that local resources would be able to support such an industry. Again, as in Sheshatshiu, the Innu did not acquire the same quality housing and facilities as the people from the south who came to run the school and provide government services. Without a water and sewage system or secure potable water supply, location of the community on an island also made garbage removal difficult. The Innu incorporated their community, which they called Utshimasits, in 1969, and established the Mushuau Innu Band Council under the authority of the federal minister of Indian and Northern Affairs but chose not to register under the federal Indian Act, an action which the Mushuau Innu saw as an act of submission, even though it would have provided a range of funded programs, benefits, and services. The poor quality of housing and sanitation contributed to health problems, as did the constant pressure on the Innu to stand by and watch their children be assimilated through public education.[25]

Although the provincial government had initially wanted to centralize communities to lower the cost of providing medical, social, and educational services, the program, in the case of the Innu communities, was beginning to generate as many problems as it solved. Moreover, while the province continued to fund the general expansion of health care services, these were inadequate to meet the industrial demands of modernization throughout the province, particularly in mining. At St Lawrence, for example, miners had continued to fight without much success for improved working conditions and health care. Miners continued to report health problems and, by the 1950s, cancers associated with elevated levels of radiation from radon gases in the mines began to appear among older workers. Other miners suffered from dust-related respiratory problems, including silicosis. A number of federal and provincial investigations recommended that the Newfoundland government take action to deal with the dust and radiation problems in the mines. In 1960, the miners refused to work, and their union president, Aloysius Turpin, wrote to Smallwood that the mines would remain at a standstill until the companies improved conditions. Subsequent wildcat strike action forced the government to appoint a royal commission in 1967 to investigate the situation. Although ventilation systems had been installed at the mines, poor conditions persisted. The Newfoundland government continued to do little about the poor enforcement of existing safety regulations and the inadequate workers' compensation system for miners and their families who suffered the ravages of industrial diseases. The Smallwood government did not accept the commission's recommendations that the government establish better industrial inspections and workers' compensation, and tended to treat the commission as window dressing to make the mining industry look more respectable.[26]

Throughout the 1960s, it was increasingly apparent to many rural Newfoundlanders and Labradorians that their province was not becoming the land of milk and honey that Smallwood had promised. To be sure, the expansion of the welfare state improved the quality of life and provided jobs for some. However, many people did not find work in the new Newfoundland of resettlement and failed industrialization. Integration into Canada meant that it was easier for them to move away to find work in the industrial centres of the mainland. Many of them found the reality of adjusting to life in the industrial cities of Ontario much different from the idealization of Canada set forth by Smallwood and the Confederates. A nostalgic romanticization of home intensified, fuelled by television and popular radio stations. From Newfoundland clubs in places such as Toronto, expatriates such as Harry Hibbs sang sadly about the homes they had given up. Much of this nostalgic popular culture painted an overly rosy picture of outport life, but the resentment underlying such nostalgia was very real. A passion developed among many Newfoundlanders living 'away' to return during the summer to visit home and relatives, and the Smallwood government encouraged this even more to promote the tourist industry through a 'Come Home Year' in 1966. Droves of Newfoundlanders returned home, bringing their stories of the difficulty of adjusting to life away and perhaps looking for signs of hope for a return in the superficial elements of modernization, such as the new Trans-Canada Highway or the network of provincial parks opened to foster a modern tourism industry.[27]

The benefits of modernization were uncertain even for those who were able to stay and find work in the new fishing industry. This was especially the case for women as modernization strongly reinforced social patriarchy. While there was a clear sexual division of labour in the salt fishery, the commercial importance of women's labour as 'skippers of the shore crew' muted a clear division of power and authority by gender in rural Newfoundland before the intensified commitment to modernization in the 1950s. The decline of salt fish production led to the disappearance of women-led shore crews. Government training and unemployment programs for the fishery emphasized that only men should become full-time, professional fishers, while, if women worked in the fishing crews of their husbands, only their husbands received unemployment insurance benefits. The province also issued social benefits to men but not women during downturns in the fishery. Women continued to dominate the processing of fish, but now as wage workers in fresh/frozen processing plants. Federal fisheries policies assumed that such women worked merely to supplement the 'real' wage of male breadwinners. At the provincial level, Smallwood was adamant that the fishery of the future was to be the more technologically intensive, offshore trawler industry but that women were to have little place in it. When the new College of Fisheries, Navigation, Marine Engineering and Electronics opened in 1964, it trained only men for the new employment opportunities of the industry. The prescribed ideal was essentially one of separate spheres, of public, virile men and private, passive women, but few men rushed into the poorly paid trawler work of the 1970s, preferring to remain in the smaller-scale, inshore fishery. The reality was family dependence on women's low wages for arduous work, wage levels being justified by employers' and government officials' belief that women worked only for pin money.[28]

Disillusionment with Smallwood ran deeper than partisan politics in the province. From 1952, Harold Horwood's columns in the *Evening Telegram* had served as the main public vehicle for criticism of Smallwood's industrial programs and autocratic political style. Although Horwood left the *Telegram* in 1958, Greg Power began to criticize Smallwood in the press, suggesting that the government was using public contracts to divert money to the provincial Liberal Party's coffers. By the mid-1960s, Ray Guy had joined the *Telegram*. Guy's satire revealed a deep, but clear-eyed, affection for rural Newfoundland, anger at the havoc wreaked by resettlement and unsuccessful industrialization, and contempt for Smallwood's leadership, whom he referred to as the OLF (Only Living Father of Confederation). Although Smallwood was an enthusiastic supporter of Memorial University of Newfoundland, and always respected its need for autonomy, he was dismayed and angry to find that the university had become a centre of academic criticism of his modernization and resettlement programs.

Unease with Smallwood extended into cultural expression. Horwood's novel *Tomorrow Will Be Sunday*, published in 1966, revealed his disquiet with the rural communities that still gave Smallwood their support, but also his misgivings about the impact of modernization on the province. Throughout the mid-1960s, Horwood, with Farley Mowat, the Canadian naturalist and writer who settled in Newfoundland with his partner Claire in 1962, began to promote a countercultural revival, based on a romanticized outport idyll, against the impact of modernization on Newfoundland. The bleakest view of Newfoundland society was by the novelist Percy Janes, whose *House of Hate* (1970) suggested that the spiteful patriarchy of its chief character, Saul Stone, arose from the hardships of outport life as well as the demands of life in fictional Milltown, loosely based on industrial Corner Brook. In Janes's novel, the milk that flowed from Canaan had soured indeed.[29]

Although real progress in living standards had been made in the 1950s on the basis of expanded welfare-state programs, Smallwood realized the Newfoundland economy had not developed the capacity to sustain modernization. He therefore turned to a succession of even larger-scale industrialization projects ('megaprojects') to generate employment and economic growth. In 1958, the Newfoundland government had already decided to support the expansion of a provincial power grid to further rural electrification. In 1963, the Newfoundland Power Commission took advantage of federal funds to develop the Bay d'Espoir hydro project, completed in 1970. The project guaranteed cheap, reliable power for megaprojects. From 1966 through 1968, the Smallwood government had successfully courted Albright and Wilson Ltd to build a phosphorous manufacturing facility at Long Harbour, Placentia Bay, through its Canadian subsidiary, the Electric Reduction Company of Canada Industries Ltd (ERCO). The large facility generated a lot of permanent jobs, but shortly after it went into operation in late 1968, it caused serious environmental problems when its effluent killed large numbers of fish in the bay. Smallwood also returned to the old dream of a third paper mill, originally believing that Come By Chance in Placentia Bay would be an ideal site. American industrialist John Shaheen had first suggested the mill for the area because it was close to a cheap source of hydroelectricity and had an ice-free port and plenty of fresh water required for paper production. However, the government found that all the timber was controlled by the owners of the Corner Brook and Grand Falls mills.

Shaheen, who had already developed the Golden Eagle Oil refinery at Holyrood, then convinced the premier that he could build an oil refinery at Come By Chance. The provincial government provided much of the financing directly through bonds or indirectly through loan guarantees, helped negotiate federal assistance for docks and wharves, and designated the refinery as a crown corporation so that it would be exempt from federal taxes. Shaheen invested little in the project. Smallwood also ensured the financial backing that would allow John C. Doyle to form Labrador Linerboard Ltd, which built a third forestry mill, the kraft linerboard mill at Stephenville. Plagued by scandal in the past, Doyle eventually faced legal charges alleging that he was defrauding the project and took refuge in Panama. These megaprojects gave ammunition to the critics who pointed out resources were being given away and the province driven into debt to fund developments that created few jobs.[30]

Smallwood sowed the seeds of his own demise with his efforts to modernize Newfoundland. His autocratic style of leadership had made him many enemies who were waiting for an opportunity to unseat him. He rejuvenated the Liberal Party during the late 1960s with a new generation of talented people, including John Crosbie, Edward Roberts, and Clyde Wells. Crosbie and Wells soon chafed under Smallwood's domination and left cabinet in 1968 when Smallwood proposed that the government should advance $5 million to Shaheen to help the industrialist prospect for capital to build Come By Chance. When the premier announced his retirement, Crosbie became a candidate for the leadership of the party. Smallwood could not stand the thought of anyone else being premier, especially Crosbie, whom he disliked, and in a bitter leadership convention successfully retained the leadership of the party. Smallwood remained the premier, but the Progressive Conservative Party was the real winner as many of those who wanted greater measures of democracy, including Crosbie, defected to it or, like Wells, retired from politics.[31]

Through the 1950s and into the 1960s, the Smallwood government hoped to develop the significant hydroelectric power potential of the Grand Falls on the Hamilton River, newly renamed Churchill Falls in 1965 as part of the land and water rights acquired by Brinco. Unfortunately there was no demand for the power within Labrador and Quebec refused to allow transmission lines to be built across its province to deliver the power to the American market. Political considerations dictated that the federal government would never intervene to force Quebec to allow the lines, so only by selling the power to the provincially owned Hydro Quebec could the power reach markets. Hydro Quebec consequently drove a hard bargain with Brinco in 1969 in a contract that permitted construction to begin. The project flooded thousands of square kilometres of Innu land without their being consulted, let alone compensated. The Innu lost forever important cultural sites at places such as Kanekuanegau and Meshikamau, which disappeared under the Smallwood Reservoir. The Innu and trappers from settler communities such as North West River lost trap lines, equipment, and hunting territory through the flooding of a region that was more than one-half the size of Lake Ontario. By the early 1970s, when electricity prices rose dramatically, the public learned that the ninety-nine-year contract contained no provision to raise the price, so Hydro Quebec reaped a huge annual windfall and the province of Newfoundland and Labrador nothing.[32] Over subsequent decades 'Churchill Falls' became symbolic of Newfoundland's weak position within Confederation and Newfoundland politicians' propensity to sign bad deals with capitalist interests from outside the province.

Perhaps more alarming for Smallwood in the short term were signs that his popular support was crumbling. One of the most disturbing signs was the first strike by the province's teachers in 1971. A professional association of teachers, the Newfoundland Teachers' Association (NTA), had existed since 1890. Although it did not bargain collectively, the NTA always sought better salaries, pensions, and insurance for its members, as well as professional development. Suffering drastic salary cuts under the Commission of Government, the NTA fared better during Smallwood's early years. The association made notable achievements through the 1950s, including mandatory membership for all teachers and pay equity between men and women in the profession. Through the 1960s, the NTA fostered a commitment to full post-secondary degrees among its members, and teachers became crucial agents of Smallwood's social modernization. Nonetheless, the Smallwood government was put off by the growing importance of the NTA and the social and political influence of teachers, and dragged its heels in bargaining with them over wages. In the spring of 1971, teachers began rotating strikes, but the government forced the NTA to desist. Smallwood underestimated the degree to which teachers enjoyed popular support and attributed his defeat in the ensuing fall election partially to them.[33]

The groundswell of social reaction against the Smallwood regime that had been building since the 1960s broke over the government at Burgeo. In rural Newfoundland, fishers were rallying around Richard Cashin and Father Desmond McGrath. Cashin and McGrath had founded the Northern Fishermen's Union in 1970, which within five months broadened as the Newfoundland Fishermen, Food and Allied Workers' Union (NFFAWU). An intense strike at Canso, Nova Scotia, in 1970–1 led to legal recognition of fishers' rights to unionize, at least in the offshore fishing fleet. Unionization began first in the processing plants of the Newfoundland industry. In the summer of 1971, militant workers in Spencer Lake's Burgeo Fish Industries plant went on strike for better wages following a tough certification fight. Lake used court injunctions and strike breakers, and the strikers retaliated with store-breaking. Lake left town, and the government had to expropriate the plant. Across the province, the NFFAWU successfully struck for union recognition and better wages to help plant workers realize the promise of a better material life held out by modernization proponents. The Newfoundland government decided in 1971 to allow offshore and inshore fishers to join the NFFAWU. Petty producers in the inshore fishery and wage workers in the offshore sector joined the NFFAWU as the union spread out from the plants. Further strikes, by inshore fishers at Port au Choix in 1974, and strikes against the owners of much of the province's trawler fleet in 1974–5, confirmed that the union was a major social and political counterpoint to the fading influence of the premier in rural Newfoundland and Labrador.[34]

Another rejection of Smallwood's modernization plans for rural Newfoundland came in the form of the Fogo Island Co-op. The co-op's roots lay in a decision by the island's main fish buyer, Newfoundland-Labrador Export Company, to shut down in 1963. A local improvement committee, which had been focusing on road development, approached Memorial University's Extension Services, which sponsored a conference in Fogo in 1967. The conference raised the possibility of a cooperative amid an initiative by the National Film Board (NFB). Through what became known as the 'Fogo process,' the NFB cooperated with local people in producing films for local communities, which allowed residents to articulate their desires for the future and to reflect on collective measures that might realize them. In December, the communities of Fogo Island rejected the possibility of resettlement by forming the Fogo Island Shipbuilding and Producers Co-operative Society. The co-op established a shipyard and acquired fish plants to process and store fish caught by members; its goal was to use local labour and capital in small-scale enterprises to sustain Fogo Island's communities. Although it obtained some government assistance to build its shipyard, the co-op found that the Smallwood government was not interested in helping it build a frozen-fish plant. The government preferred investment in much larger, centralized plants in accordance with its modernization agenda. Although the government was willing to let people experiment with cooperatives, and at one time Smallwood felt that they were a good alternative to more radical socialist options for rural development, it preferred to regulate rather than promote the community-based organizations. Nonetheless, the co-op persevered, becoming the largest employer on Fogo Island.[35]

Working-class discontent continued to build in mining communities through 1971. In St Lawrence, miners' continued frustration with poor employer and government commitments to safety conditions served as the backdrop for the St Lawrence Workers Protective Union's (SLWPU's) demand for a wage increase of $1.25 per hour. Before the fluorspar miners could go on strike against their recalcitrant employer, thirty women from St Lawrence and the nearby community of Lawn picketed a loading dock to prevent an ore carrier from departing. Although they supported the miners' demand for more money, a deeper frustration with the industrial carnage wreaked by dust, radiation, and accidents on the men who went into the mines underlay the protesting women's concerns. In September, the St Lawrence Company agreed to pay $0.40 more per hour in wages, with a further $0.19 per hour to be paid in a year, and made concessions on seniority, sick benefits, and vacation time. The provincial government further agreed to set up a special fund to aid disabled miners and their dependents. In central Newfoundland, miners at Buchans, members of local 5457 of the United Steelworkers of America, went on strike against American Smelting and Refining Company (ASARCO). The miners won higher wages but were back on the picket line in 1973. Perhaps sensing that the end of mining was near, as available mineral reserves were forecast to be depleted by 1979, the miners tried to get as much as possible from a company that was enjoying excellent profits. ASARCO owned the town site and cut services to the miners' families. Violence broke out on the picket lines as non-union employees tried to cross, but miners' wives and children reinforced the lines. After months of disruption, the company gave in and gave the miners $0.87 more per hour.[36]

While Buchans's mining days were numbered, other union activities suggested that workers were becoming dissatisfied with their lot in the new Newfoundland. Throughout the province, strikes and industrial unrest marked trades and the civil service. Public sector workers were especially important because of the massive growth in the federal, provincial, and municipal governments brought about by Confederation. The Smallwood government had bullied hospital workers in Corner Brook in 1963 who had joined the National Union of Public Employees (NUPE) and struck for better wages. NUPE joined with another national union of public employees to form the Canadian Union of Public Employees (CUPE) in 1963, and it began to organize throughout Newfoundland. Smallwood threatened to ban public sector strikes, and in 1967 Clyde Wells, then minister of Labour, introduced legislation to outlaw strikes at hospitals when workers at the Central Newfoundland Hospital in Grand Falls went on strike. CUPE kept organizing. Although the Newfoundland Government Employees' Association (NGEA) began as a professional association in the 1930s, by 1968 it represented provincial employees as a union. The NGEA led mass protests against the Smallwood government in 1970 when the provincial budget provided no wage increases. The government agreed to collective bargaining two months later by passing the Public Service (Collective Bargaining) Act. In 1971, the NGEA became the Newfoundland Association of Public Employees (NAPE), one of the largest and most powerful unions in the province.[37]

Disappointing megaprojects, the failure to industrialize the growth centres, antagonistic relationships with workers, and Smallwood's autocratic leadership style all combined to undermine his dominance of the political system. In Labrador, growing resentment about the lack of local benefits arising from the development of its resources, compared with the benefits realized by the island portion of the province, fuelled support for independent MHA Tom Burgess's New Labrador party, founded in 1970. By 1970 many young Liberals had defected to the Progressive Conservative Party, which under the leadership of young businessman Frank Moores seemed to offer a more professional alternative. The 1971 provincial election was a hard-fought contest between Smallwood and those who wanted to remove him from power. The result was uncertain and contested; 21 Conservatives were elected versus 20 Liberals and one representative of the New Labrador party. Yet Smallwood refused to resign the premiership while judicial recounts and the prospect of members changing party allegiance held out the hope that he could hold on to power. The election of 1972 returned a majority for the Progressive Conservatives. Although he attempted a return to political life in 1975, Smallwood's personal hegemony had ended.[38]

By 1972, Newfoundland and Labrador had changed. Throughout the province, most residents, with the notable exception of aboriginal people, took for granted the conveniences of the modern age. Social and educational services were available at unprecedented levels. Improvements in living standards had come at a price. Smallwood had dealt dictatorially with the organized labour movement. Outports had been disturbed by resettlement in the interest of economic modernization, but little had come from this. Overcapacity dominated the fisheries, and growth centres had failed to attract significant new industries. There were new industrial ventures in hydroelectricity and oil processing, but at great cost to government. The government had treated Labrador as a convenience for the island, but Churchill Falls had only provoked popular ire. The province had become dependent on federal financial assistance and management of its key marine resources. Dissatisfaction was building as people became interested in new notions of nation.

11

The Limits of Neo-nationalism, 1972–2003

Disarray within the Liberal Party helped the Progressive Conservatives come to power under Frank Moores in 1972. Many Newfoundlanders and Labradorians were unhappy with how the Smallwood era's economic diversification policies had disrupted their lives. The Progressive Conservative governments of Moores and his successor, Brian Peckford, seeking distance from Smallwood and modernization, promised (but failed to deliver) a more supportive approach to rural economic development, continuing to rely heavily on industrial staples, whether old ones in fish, forests, and mines, or the potentially lucrative new development of offshore oil. The Peckford government, inspired by the neo-nationalism of a new generation of well-educated and relatively affluent professionals, fought for greater provincial control over natural resources and greater constitutional autonomy for provinces. Its rural development policy boiled down to dependence on make-work programs to manoeuvre seasonally employed and underemployed residents onto federally administered programs, especially Unemployment Insurance, and its successor, Employment Insurance. Worse, at least in the case of overcapacity in the fishing industry, the Newfoundland and Labrador government had to shoulder responsibility along with federal authorities. The Liberal government of Clyde Wells accepted the importance of the federal presence in Newfoundland and Labrador but continued to shift the burden of retrenchment onto working people, a process begun by the Peckford government during the recession of the 1980s. Major natural-resource developments under the Liberal regime of the 1990s and early 2000s resurrected national commitments but, as in the case of the aboriginal peoples of Labrador, in new ways that challenged the limits of older neo-nationalism.

Everywhere, signs of trouble appeared in Smallwood's 'new' Newfoundland and Labrador. Rural communities languished even as urban development accelerated, fuelled by the expansion of government at the provincial and federal levels in St John's. The expansion of educational opportunities for rural people throughout the province, however, meant that many young people coming to St John's to take up positions in government were only too familiar with the persistent problems of their home communities. They feared the long-term implications of their province being without the economic capacity to support the consumer expectations of its population and resented the manner in which Newfoundland continued to be a source of raw materials and labour for economic development in other parts of Canada and beyond.[1]

The first generation of well-educated, relatively affluent Newfoundlanders to come of age under Smallwood reacted against his regime in a variety of ways. In general, there was widespread aversion to the government's modernization policies and a rejection of Smallwood's personal, dictatorial style of patronage politics. Memorial University of Newfoundland became the centre of a new interest in rural Newfoundland and Labrador's cultural, social, and other strengths. In 1968, a highly respected folklorist, Herbert Halpert, became the first head of the new department of folklore and started to gather the oral history and culture of the outports. In addition to the Division of Extension Services, Memorial's Institute of Social and Economic Research generated a range of social, historical, and geographical studies of rural Newfoundland and Labrador and provided support to regional development associations, which had begun first on the Great Northern Peninsula, then on the Eastport Peninsula and Fogo Island. Through Extension Services and the Centre for Community Initiatives, the university provided training and other forms of support to the rural development movement. By the early 1970s, the advocates of small-scale, rural economic development, reinforced by the research findings that had accumulated a great deal of new knowledge about the province, found support in the form of the Moores's Progressive Conservatives' attacks on the Smallwood government.[2]

The diversity of the new political and cultural consciousness in Newfoundland and Labrador also became apparent in the arts community. Throughout the 1970s, poets such as Al Pittman and Tom

Dawe, writers such as Cassie Brown, and visual artists such as David Blackwood produced works that extolled the virtues of mythic, communal outports in reaction to the modernization of Smallwood. A key contribution of Memorial University was its theatrical community, especially Michael Cook's Open Group, but also Dudley Cox's Newfoundland Traveling Theatre Company and, appearing in 1972, Chris Brookes's Mummers Troupe. Brookes moved the reaction against Smallwood to the left, drawing on the old tradition of mummering as a form of mischievous, class-based protest against elitism and privilege. Committed to a consensus-based, democratic, and open organization, Brookes nonetheless brought an ideological dedication to using theatre in the pursuit of social justice. He used the apparent farce of clowns, puppets, and masks to expose the underlying social, economic, and political roots of exploitation that dominated the day-to-day lives of Newfoundlanders and Labradorians. The Mummers Troupe developed its message for rural and working-class people throughout the province, identifying the forces of capitalism that undermined the basis of their families and communities. The Troupe hoped that its socialist theatre would offer Newfoundlanders and Labradorians an alternative to the 'cloned plastic-wrapped homogeneity of North American consumer capitalism.' Although it produced plays about the class inequalities underlying the IWA strike, the Buchans strike, and recent developments in the fishing industry, the Mummers Troupe hoped to mobilize popular indignation along nationalist lines. Brookes later remembered the Troupe as 'wrapping ourselves in the rhetoric of righteous regionalism.' Eventually, 'doctrinaire xenophobia' split the group, leaving it with a 'legacy of simplistic political analysis.'[3]

There was a less political undercurrent running through CODCO, founded in 1973. Its first members – Tommy Sexton, Greg Malone, Cathy Jones, Mary Walsh, Andy Jones, D. Olsen, and Bob Joy – took it upon themselves to be the critics of 'hypocrisy and pretension everywhere.' Although sometimes partaking of the neo-nationalist sentiments growing in Newfoundland at the time, the members of CODCO held nothing dear, including the rural and working-class sympathies of their counterparts in the Mummers Troupe. CODCO members identified with the marginalized, especially as Newfoundlanders in Canada, but seemed almost consumed by their anger and resigned to what Mary Walsh later referred to as 'the intrinsic unfairness of life.' Part of the group's political cynicism arose from the roots of its success in what Brookes called 'Newfcult.' He recalled that

CODCO's 'comedic caricatures of rustic Newfoundlanders were the talk of the town' in cities such as Toronto and Ottawa but 'were practically booed off the stage when they toured rural Newfoundland.' In St John's, however, CODCO's emphasis on the supposedly separate and much put-upon identity of Newfoundlanders within Canada played well to cultural conservatives who liked the neo-nationalist implications of their work but did not have to feel threatened by the leftism embedded in the Mummers Troupe's work.[4]

Frank Moores had talked tough on the campaign trail about the need to end the Smallwood government's close relationship with industrial promoters such as John Shaheen or John C. Doyle. The Progressive Conservatives had promised a new approach to provincial development, based on rejuvenating fisheries, forestry, agriculture, and other rural activities. Nonetheless, the new government continued the focus on heavy industrialization that characterized the late Smallwood era. Much of the government's effort went into trying to renegotiate the sale of hydro power from the Churchill Falls development to Quebec. The effort failed, even though the Moores government spent $160 million to buy the company from Brinco. In 1975, the Moores government propped up the Come by Chance oil refinery with $60 million, only to see it shut down the next year. Its further investment of $25 million in the Stephenville linerboard mill in 1976 failed to prevent the mill's closure in 1977. Finally, Alcan closed its mining operations on the Burin Peninsula in 1978. While most of these failures were the legacies of the Smallwood years, Premier Moores was not above accepting flights on a jet owned by Doyle, and did not object when a new ship, the *Frank D. Moores*, joined the *Joseph R. Smallwood* in Shaheen's oil tanker fleet.[5]

The Moores government brought little new to fisheries policy. It continued to allow overcapacity to develop in fish processing as other rural industries lagged, lending weight to the accusation that the fishery was nothing more than an 'employer of last resort.' Although the provincial Progressive Conservatives brought neo-nationalist rhetoric to their views about the relationship between St John's and Ottawa in fisheries management, it left most of the major work to the federal government. Throughout the early 1970s, many people felt that the local fishing industry could expand despite declining domestic fish landings if only foreign fishing effort could be limited. Such effort by large factory freezer trawlers had expanded on the offshore banks. Part of a larger Atlantic Canadian trend, Newfoundland fish companies began to invest in a larger offshore fleet and, with provincial encouragement, built more processing plants in coastal communities throughout the island and Labrador. Although the Moores government encouraged the development of fish plants, the province, like its predecessor, continued to be unsupportive of co-ops, such as that on Fogo Island.[6]

The politics of the seal hunt reinforced the notion among many people in the province that foreigners were doing their best to hold back the development of a thriving Newfoundland. Matters came to a head in 1977 when anti-sealing protesters, including French actress Brigitte Bardot, converged on St Anthony. There had been episodic protests about the allegedly inhumane nature of the seal hunt since the late 1940s. In 1964, the federal government had enacted regulations to ensure the humane conduct of the hunt. The measures, and subsequent efforts, including quotas and later openings of the hunt, failed to mollify a growing international animal rights movement, which called for an abolition of the hunt by the early 1970s.

Led by the International Fund for Animal Welfare and, in 1976, by the Greenpeace Foundation, the anti-hunt protest focused on bringing celebrities and observers to the hunt to protest, record, and eventually campaign for funding internationally. Throughout rural Newfoundland and Labrador, many people still made their livings by slaughtering animals, either in fishing or farming, and many continued to hunt for sport and food. Far removed from the necessity and pleasures of the hunt, but still often benefiting from the products of butchering and processing domestic animals, the bourgeois militants of North America and Western Europe attacked the seal hunt to defend the 'wild' and to allay their fears about their own complicity in the excesses of contemporary global capitalism. Although Greenpeace initially supported the smaller-scale 'landsmen' hunt conducted by inshore fishers in vessels less than 65 feet long, protesting only against the large-scale factory ships that were going deep into the ice by the late 1970s, it declared against the entire hunt in 1976. Composed largely of affluent, urban North American professionals, groups such as Greenpeace had no sympathy for the struggle of ordinary working people to make a living in rural Newfoundland and Labrador. Local people perceived the protest as a condescending critique of an economic activity that had much deeper social and cultural significance in rural parts of the province. Many felt that the international protest movement cynically and selfishly manipulated the court of international opinion to raise funds with which they supported themselves. Increasingly angry confrontations between sealers and protesters resulted in federal efforts to control the presence of the latter at the ice. In St John's, the seal hunt became a neo-nationalist cause when, in 1979, local businessman Miller Ayre, with John McGrath, announced the formation of the Codpeace Foundation. A parody of Greenpeace, Codpeace engaged in a number of publicity stunts about the manner in which seals victimized cod, using satire and sarcasm to puncture the inflated self-importance of the anti-hunt protesters and to help manufacture a more positive sense of Newfoundland identity.[7]

The development of Gros Morne National Park on the west coast of Newfoundland illustrated the persistence of rural decline and resettlement for many small coastal communities despite the efforts of the Progressive Conservative government. By 1970, the Smallwood government had become far more interested in the economic potential of tourism in the establishment of national parks and agreed with the federal government in 1973 to establish Gros Morne. The provincial government planned to resettle the 175 families of twelve communities to larger towns in the area to make way for the park. It offered financial assistance to these families but chose to induce their relocation by restricting their right to develop their property and by limiting their right to sell it only to the province. A local trend of resettlement to nearby communities such as Rocky Harbour, Cow Head, Woody Point, and Norris Point to gain access to better services was already under way, encouraged by resettlement programs, but people persisted in the fishing and logging outports of Lobster Cove, Green Point, Belldown's Point, and Baker's Brook, the last holding out until 1981, when the lack of services and government restrictions on their rights to sell their land forced residents to move. Although thirty families from Sally's Cove moved to Rocky Harbour and Woody Point, the protests of the remaining twenty against relocation, partially galvanized by the Mummers Troupe's 1973 play *Gros Mourn*, forced the province and the federal government to develop the national park around their community. The actions of the people of Sally's Cove led the National Parks Board to adopt a new policy on the development of new parks in 1979 based on a commitment to earning more local public support and using no expropriation of local people's property. Gros Morne was a boon to the growth centres such as Rocky Harbour and Cow Head. These communities continued to serve as homes to people working in forestry and the fishery, who were able to maintain fishing rights within the park. However, the towns also developed hotels, restaurants, and related services to cater to the needs of the many tourists who came to admire the natural beauty and geological significance of the park (recognized as a UNESCO World Heritage Site in 1988) while eating their lunches on the picnic sites established on the remains of resettled outports within the park.[8]

Throughout the Moores years, there was much popular sympathy for the provincial government, which grew from frustration with the inability of federal regional development programs to stimulate significant economic development. When Moores resigned as premier in 1979, his successor, A. Brian Peckford, initially seemed to best articulate the frustration and ambition of a younger generation of Newfoundlanders and Labradorians, who felt disappointed by their experience as the newest Canadians. In particular, although there was much local optimism about the possibility of offshore oil development, the federal government held jurisdiction over the exploration process and had allowed a free-entry system through the 1970s. By the late 1970s, only about 10 per cent of Newfoundland and Labrador's continental shelf remained available for exploration. Younger members of the provincial Progressive Conservatives took up the cry against mismanagement by the federal government of Pierre Trudeau. One of Peckford's colleagues, Leo Barry, minister of the Department of Mines and Energy, led the way in the province's development of its own exploration regulations, but Barry lost his seat in the 1975 general election, opening the way for Peckford to become minister in 1976. Peckford fought vigorously to ensure that Newfoundland and Labrador benefited as much as possible from offshore oil development. He maintained that only the province had the moral authority and regulatory capacity to develop the industry in the best interests of Newfoundlanders and Labradorians. Peckford's anti-Ottawa stance overshadowed the provincial Liberals, stained as they were by their continued association with the federal Liberal government. The provincial New Democratic Party had been enjoying some success under the leadership of John Greene, but its political asceticism, especially its refusal to embrace the political theatre of demonstrations, rallies, and political bombast, meant that it was no match for the fiery oratory of Peckford, who enjoyed the political capital of his image as the 'scrappy fighter from the outports, pitted against the too-smooth Pierre Trudeau.'[9]

The new premier was the archetype of the 'new Newfoundlander,' made by, but rebelling against, the government policies of the Smallwood years. In his later manifesto, Peckford recalled his youth in Whitbourne, his unhappy time in Toronto as a young boy in 1959, and his intellectual coming of age as a student at Memorial University in the 1960s. On a personal level, he resented the manner in which the 'St

John's crowd' made 'baymen' such as Peckford feel unwelcome. More important, he disagreed with the underlying principle of the Smallwood-era development programs, 'getting away from the fishery.' To Peckford, it was bad enough that Smallwood had no interest in rural revitalization; even worse were the 'dictatorial styles and obvious ineptitude' of the Smallwood government and its 'lack of any sound management of our resources, the iron ore deal, the Upper Churchill deal, the Long Harbour phosphorous plant deal[;] all stood in testament of the failure of the "develop or perish" syndrome.'

The problem was more than just Smallwood according to Peckford; Newfoundlanders and Labradorians had not joined Canada in Confederation so much as they had surrendered to it. This surrender was a symptom of a national inferiority complex buried 'deep in our psyche' and flowing 'from our whole history of colonialism, subjugation and exploitation. Newfoundland was frequently a resource base to be exploited for the benefit of the mother country.'[10] Peckford's desire to revitalize Newfoundland and Labrador struck a positive chord with a nativist element running through Newfoundland's growing middle class. Anxious about the limited success of modernization, and desiring a provincial cultural identity that might simultaneously contain social discontent within and present a united front to forces without, many residents of the province embraced romantic, popular forms that mythologized the best qualities of outport life.[11]

Peckford immediately set about saving Newfoundlanders from their colonial subjugation. His government commissioned artist Christopher Pratt to design a new provincial flag to replace the old Union Jack, which the legislature adopted in 1980. Soon after his election in 1979, Peckford demanded that the federal government make provincial needs the central objective in managing the northern cod stocks fisheries. Reviewing the historical importance of these stocks to Newfoundland, and pointing out that Newfoundlanders and Labradorians were responsible for about 98 per cent of the Canadian fishing effort directed toward them, Peckford demanded that they be reserved for the province's inshore and middle-distance fleets. Larger, offshore vessels should only be allowed a share of federally set total allowable catches when it was clear that there was a surplus that could not be taken by the smaller-scale Newfoundland fisheries. Even then, the offshore vessels must not be allowed to land the fish for processing anywhere but in Newfoundland and Labrador. Peckford adamantly opposed the federal government's practices of allowing non-Newfoundland freezer trawlers to fish for northern cod either directly or as a by-catch of fisheries for species such as shrimp. He decried the federal government's ignorance of his views, arguing that its 'approach to Northern Cod is analogous to the Province of British Columbia having no say in forestry or the Province of Alberta having no say in energy.' Further arguing that 'the management of the Province's fishing resource by the Government of the Province represents a historic and moral right of Newfoundlanders to the economic benefits of those resources in the surrounding sea,' Peckford demanded a short-term federal–provincial mechanism for fisheries policy, while giving notice that the province would seek constitutional change to entrench its jurisdiction over northern cod. The Peckford government additionally approached the Quebec government to renegotiate the Upper Churchill Falls hydro contract to allow a greater share of the economic surplus for Newfoundland and Labrador. At the same time, the Newfoundland government also asked mining and forestry companies for better royalty agreements, increased employment, and improved conservation practices.[12]

Offshore oil became the watchword of Peckford's own version of the 'new' Newfoundland. Years of exploration had finally resulted in a major oil find in 1979 by Chevron Standard Limited at the Hibernia oil well, located 350 kilometres east of St John's on the Grand Banks. Peckford had hoped that the election of a minority Progressive Conservative government in Ottawa in the same year would result in federal recognition of the right of Newfoundland and Labrador to jurisdiction and greater control over offshore resources. The defeat of the Conservatives by the Liberals under Trudeau dashed such hopes. The Trudeau government wished to maintain federal control over offshore oil development in order to promote a number of objectives: a secure Canadian supply of oil in response to the energy crisis of the 1970s, revenue for the federal government, and employment and economic opportunities for all Canadians without necessary consideration of regional preferences. The Newfoundland government and Ottawa locked horns on the question of jurisdiction over offshore oil, leading Peckford to win a provincial general election in 1982 by campaigning against Ottawa's position.[13]

Although Newfoundland and Ottawa were antagonists in the battle over which order of government would have jurisdiction over offshore oil development, both rushed to foster exploration and exploitation in the context of the energy crisis and the federal National Energy Program of the 1970s. The desire on the part of the federal and provincial governments for rapid development benefited the major multinational corporations such as Mobil Oil that were involved in the search for oil off the east coast. The Newfoundland government's interest focused almost entirely on which jurisdiction would control the economic benefits of development, and, like the federal government, it paid little attention to the regulation of offshore workers' safety. The offshore oil industry, sadly, took on a more tragic significance for the people of Newfoundland and Labrador in 1982. On Valentine's Day, a winter storm damaged and led to the sinking of the Ocean Ranger. All hands aboard the oil drilling rig lost their lives; fifty-six of the eighty-four crew members were Newfoundlanders and Labradorians. The tragedy was part of a rapid increase in major mishaps involving oil rigs in the offshore oil sector globally as exploratory drilling boomed throughout the 1970s and 1980s. Subsequent investigations, including a royal commission, concluded that the Ocean Ranger had been generally well built, although it was designed for, and tested in, the waters of the Gulf of Mexico – a very different marine environment than the Grand Banks. Tellingly, a critical ballast control room had been located too close to the water in a support column, including a porthole with glass insufficiently thick to withstand severe pounding; the rig also had a ballast control system that was difficult to use in emergency conditions. Worst of all, the workers who operated the Ocean Ranger did not fully understand how to operate the ballast controls during an emergency such as the storm that developed that February night. Having to abandon the rig, workers were without survival suits and found its lifeboats almost impossible to launch in the prevailing sea conditions. Although the royal commission that investigated the tragedy was unwilling to say that the Newfoundland government's local hiring preference had led the rig's operators to hire untrained workers, it suggested that hiring 'guidelines requiring a very rapid phase in of local residents can affect the overall level of safety of the drilling operations' and recommended more careful hiring and training to ensure safety. Other studies found that the offshore oil industry had paid insufficient attention to workers' safety and had dealt inadequately with their complaints.[14]

The Peckford government's constitutional jockeying with Ottawa did not give the province any more ability to deal with the day-to-day problems of growing unemployment and social dislocation in rural areas. The provincial government continued to license more fish plants as had the Smallwood and Moores governments. Issuing licences encouraged the proponents of new fish plants to apply for federal financial assistance under the Regional Development Incentives Act (RDIA), administered by the federal Department of Regional Economic Expansion. In effect, the province could take the credit for a new source of employment at almost no cost to itself and without taking any responsibility for the impact of the plants on fisheries management, which remained a federal responsibility. The plants generated only seasonal employment, but federal unemployment insurance benefits made up the difference, again at no cost to the province. Provincial policy seemed clever at the time, a way in which the provincial David could force the federal Goliath to yield more, and no thought was given to the ecological impact of such a policy. To the contrary, throughout the early 1980s the Peckford government cooperated with Ottawa in a number of subsidy and loan programs to encourage fishers to build larger inshore vessels and 'midshore,' or 'nearshore,' draggers to expand the search for cod, crab, capelin, shrimp, and any other species to supply the plants. The provincial government accepted the expansion of corporate offshore trawlers so long as they were based in and controlled by Newfoundland interests.

The province had no greater vision for the fishery than did federal authorities and was loath to intervene in the manner in which private companies organized the industry. Overcapacity had burgeoned since 1977, when Canada extended its jurisdiction over Atlantic waters from 12 miles to 200 miles. The federal government originally planned for fisheries expansion simultaneously with restrictions on the number of people who fished within the 200-mile limit to bolster incomes in that industry, but this did not happen. The insatiable demand of the processing sector for cheap raw material meant that the industry depended partly on the development of the small-scale inshore sector, and so the older small-boat inshore fishery also grew. Inshore fishing households subsidized their own costs of production by supplementing work in the fishery with other employment, especially the often unpaid work of women. They furthermore could accommodate low prices for fish by supplementing their incomes through a variety of strategies: cutting their own wood for fuel, repairing their own boats and fishing equipment, and exchanging a variety of services for each other such as childcare and home maintenance. Some rural people supplemented their household incomes by seasonal out-migration, but a substantial portion of rural people's cash incomes came from make-work programs, community council work, unemployment insurance, welfare, and other forms of social assistance. The net effect of the 200-mile limit was that Canadian fishing effort, and much of that Newfoundland and Labrador's, displaced foreign effort within the limit, and overcapacity in the industry grew unchecked.[15]

Fishing policies and outport livelihood practices together ensured a cheap source of fish with which to offset the higher capital costs of the offshore fleet amid the problems of offshore fishing, the periodic unavailability of fish, and, more important, the volatile nature of fish prices in international markets. The NFFAWU responded to the growing overcapacity of the fisheries by arguing that employment should be restricted to a full-time, permanent wage-labour force by excluding 'part-time' fishers, seeing the 'professionalization' of the fishery as the only way to guarantee its members good living standards. As overproduction and market gluts in 1977 and 1978 lowered the prices fishers received for their catches, the union had negotiated direct sales of unprocessed fish for better prices to Eastern European buyers. The Moores and Peckford governments, however, were incensed that the federal government permitted the sales and condemned them using a rhetoric that was at once anti-union and neo-nationalist, arguing that a cabal of federal officials and union leaders was giving away processing jobs to foreigners. While the provincial governments made much of their desire to protect 'our Newfoundland way of life,' they did more to protect the low prices offered by Newfoundland processors, fended off competition from Maritimes and foreign buyers, and depressed the incomes of Newfoundland and Labrador fishers.[16]

By the mid-1980s, the Newfoundland fishing industry was in crisis, largely because of the problem of overcapacity. The 1982 federal Kirby Task Force on the Atlantic Fisheries had recommended reducing capacity and increasing the efficiency of the industry by merging companies and introducing new processing technologies. By 1984, years of overcapacity, competition, and market gluts had driven most of the province's largest companies into bankruptcy. In Nova Scotia, federal funds provided the basis for the reorganization of National Sea Products, which had interests in the Newfoundland fishery. The Newfoundland government, in cooperation with the federal government and the Bank of Nova Scotia, bailed out the industry by taking over the assets of the firms and consolidating them in Fishery Products International (FPI). Under the leadership of chief executive officer Vic Young, FPI enjoyed initial success, although the industrial restructuring did not overcome the problems of overcapacity and dwindling fish stocks that were becoming more evident with each passing year.[17]

In the same year, the provincial government's efforts to get a better deal from the Churchill Falls development project encountered a major setback when the Supreme Court of Canada, setting aside an earlier favourable ruling of the Newfoundland Court of Appeal, ruled that Newfoundland did not have the constitutional authority to enact its Water Reversion Act, legislation designed to recall water rights from the Churchill Falls Corporation. Such a recall might have forced Hydro Quebec to renegotiate the unfavourable hydro contract. If these developments were not bad enough, the next year the exhausted zinc and copper mines at Buchans closed, throwing miners out of work and placing the town in economic crisis.[18]

The offshore oil sector was the only area in which the provincial government appeared able to make any headway. In February 1985, the Newfoundland government signed an agreement with the federal government on how they would jointly manage the development of offshore hydrocarbon resources. The Progressive Conservative government of Brian Mulroney recognized the Government of Newfoundland and Labrador's equal say over the management of offshore oil and gas resources through a Canada–Newfoundland Offshore Petroleum Board and acknowledged the province's right to collect revenues from the exploitation of those resources as if it took place on land. Soon after this Atlantic Accord, Peckford, with federal minister John Crosbie, announced that Mobil Oil would establish oil production at the Hibernia site by using fixed concrete platforms. Furthermore, the federal government would contribute 75 per cent of a $300 million development fund to allow the province to prepare for industrial growth. The developments in the offshore oil sector contributed significantly to Peckford's victory in the general election in April. Nonetheless, the fisheries, forestry, and mining sectors were troubled by downturns in international markets, global restructuring, and resource depletion locally. Without the financial resources to do much more than attempt to regulate more local control over development, and with so much of the natural-resource sector controlled by external corporate interests such as Bowaters in forestry, the Iron Ore Company of Canada in mining, and the Bank of Nova Scotia in fisheries, or by federal authorities as in the case of fisheries, Peckford was becoming a neo-nationalist Don Quixote, railing against the big foreign interests that allegedly were holding the province back.[19]

Although the developments in the offshore oil sector promised future economic benefits, the provincial economy was in bad shape in the mid-1980s. The international recession, which had been accelerating since the late 1970s, struck hard at a province dependent on industrial staple production in forestry, mining, energy, and the troubled fisheries. With the labour-intensive construction stage of industrial megaprojects, such as in hydro development, over, and as mining, forestry, and fish companies dealt with the recession by increasing productivity through mechanization, with attendant job losses and pay cuts, the province's working class bore the brunt. The Progressive Conservatives proved that they were not much different from the Smallwood Liberals in the days of the IWA strike by siding with corporate interests against the union movement. In 1984, for example, the government passed Bill 37 to void a Labour Standards Board decision in favour of Wabush iron ore miners, members of the United Steelworkers of America. The board had found that Wabush Mines had failed to give proper notice to miners in 1981 during a lay-off and had ordered it to pay $750,000 in back wages. Similar cases were pending against Fisheries Products International and Advocate Mines at Baie Verte. The bill eliminated the need for more notice and appeased Kruger Corporation, which was considering purchasing the Bowaters mill at Corner Brook. Kruger agreed with the province to take over the mill late in 1984. Bill 52, the Kruger Act, provided the company with $64 million in provincial grants, loan guarantees, and sales tax relief, but Kruger would not have been interested if Bill 37 had not absolved it of $6.7 million in back wages that had been owed to improperly laid-off Bowaters' workers.

At the same time, the province was embroiled in a battle with the Newfoundland Association of Public Employees (NAPE) over Bill 59, an Act to Amend the Public Services (Collective Bargaining) Act, 1973. The bill, passed in 1983, made more provincial employees ineligible for union membership, changed the designation of essential employees, and limited the right to strike, especially by outlawing rotating strikes. Having failed in challenging Bill 59 in the Supreme Court of Newfoundland, 5,500 public sector workers went on strike on 3 March 1986. They returned to work after a month, but 5,000 went on strike again in September when the government did not back down from the intentions of Bill 59. The Canadian Labour Congress became involved, and Bill 59 eventually earned the criticism of the International Labor Organization of the United Nations.[20]

The Peckford government's anti-union stance was compatible with the neo-nationalism it often espoused. Its defence of a 'traditional' rural Newfoundland against the impact of modernity was partially an attack on the manner in which the development of the welfare state had supposedly eroded the self-reliant producer values of simple outport folk. In response to NAPE's failed legal challenge to Bill 59, Memorial University philosopher F.L. Jackson, muse and occasional apologist for the Peckford government, attacked the union's president, Fraser March, as a traitorous fifth columnist who was undermining the true Newfoundland. As unemployment increased, government cutbacks deepened, and the cost of living rose, the people who were the economic backbone of the towns and cities of the province, government employees and others whose paycheques and salaries came from a public source, found Peckford's anti-welfare message appealing. The state, the premier argued, had no business taxing such people to pay for welfare and make-work projects in rural Newfoundland and Labrador. Something had to be done to save the people of the province from the moral rot of welfare dependency.[21]

In the spring of 1985 Peckford appointed the Royal Commission on Employment and Unemployment (RCEU) and invited sociologist Doug House of Memorial University to chair it. Throughout rural Newfoundland and Labrador, the provincial and federal governments, often through the intermediaries of local rural development associations, relied on government-financed make-work programs to qualify people for unemployment insurance. As the recession worsened, the cycles of make-work programs and unemployment insurance barely allowed rural people to keep body and soul together, let alone produce any meaningful economic development. Keeping in mind that unemployment and government retrenchment were acute Canadian problems in the 1980s, the report argued that rural people would face uncertain futures if they continued to require government assistance and make-work projects to generate significant, if short-term, employment. The RCEU also realized that the offshore oil sector was unlikely to generate enough employment to address the needs of rural parts of the province, and fisheries, forestry, and mining as practised were not going to be of much greater help. Balanced development of urban centres and rural areas of Newfoundland and Labrador would be achieved, the RCEU suggested, if governments adopted an ambitious, twenty-point program that included consolidation and reform of existing natural-resource industries; greater investment in the inshore fishery; continued promotion of offshore oil and gas development; the advancement of agriculture and aquaculture; the expansion of the service sector and tourism; and the provision of better infrastructure and governance that were sensitive to the needs of Labrador and First Nations. The report further recommended an ambitious program of public investment in people through better education; labour-market and entrepreneurial development policies for women and youth; income-security policies; investment in public education at every level; and a more participatory Labour Relations Tribunal. Underpinning all of the RCEU's recommendations was its belief that every order of government must use all means possible to facilitate community and regionally based development.[22]

By 1987, the Peckford regime was experiencing its own problems. Misinterpreting the Royal Commission's recommendation to invest in long-lasting infrastructure, Peckford became involved with Alberta promoter Philip Sprung, who was promoting hydroponic technology. The government became enmeshed in an ill-thought-out plan to make Newfoundland and Labrador a major player in the tomato and cucumber markets of the province and Atlantic Canada, committing $14,325,000 and improper loan guarantees to the purchase and construction of one of Sprung's facilities. The provincial government carried out no proper market studies and did not properly supervise the project. A later provincial royal commission, chaired by Hon. Mr. Justice S. O'Regan, concluded that the Peckford government lacked the expertise to become involved in the venture, took no steps to seek such expertise, and was unjustified in taking almost complete financial responsibility for the foolhardy scheme.[23]

While provincial affairs were beginning to look bad for Peckord, he continued to fight for a better federal–provincial arrangement for the management of local resources, advancing this cause through provincial support for the constitutional change proposed at Meech Lake in 1987. The main factor contributing to the development of the Meech Lake proposal was the ongoing concern about Quebec remaining outside the process that had led to the repatriation of the Constitution in 1982. The Meech Lake Accord, the result of a meeting of premiers and the Canadian prime minister at the federal retreat of Meech Lake, proposed constitutional amendments that would (1) recognize Quebec as a distinct society in Canada, (2) assure the decentralization of federal spending power and authority in matters such as immigration, (3) give veto power to all provinces in future constitutional amendments, (4) provide greater provincial influence over the composition of the Supreme Court, and (5) establish mandatory regular first ministers' conferences to discuss economic and constitutional matters.

The Peckford government supported the accord because it hoped that the agreement to decentralize federal spending power and authority might provide Newfoundland and Labrador with greater power to place provincial priorities at the fore of future fisheries and offshore energy development, as well as in any other area that might otherwise be the preserve of the federal government. Peckford did not see Meech Lake as an ideal solution; in areas such as Senate reform that would give the provinces more say about federal policy, Meech Lake was, at best, vague, and moreover, it recognized social distinctiveness largely on a linguistic basis for Quebec, not on the basis of other historical processes. Nonetheless, the provincial government wanted to be able to opt out of federal programs but still have access to equivalent federal resources to develop policies that would suit the development needs of Newfoundland and Labrador.

This was a difficult position to take. The failure of most of the province's development strategies since 1949 made it dependent on federal welfare-state policies in health, social assistance, and education to maintain a quality of life in keeping with minimum Canadian standards. The provisions for decentralization of spending powers did not excuse provinces such as Newfoundland and Labrador from designing programs that would deliver services to residents that were as good as those available elsewhere in Canada; rather, the accord would give the province greater freedom to design programs of delivery that made sense in the local context rather than conforming to models derived elsewhere. As long as federal funds flowed freely through transfer payments from richer provinces to poorer ones, this issue of local control probably did not matter much. But the 1980s had been a time of federal and provincial retrenchment, in which the disproportionate social and economic vulnerability of provinces such as Newfoundland and Labrador had made clear that they could not continue to meet national objectives in areas such as health care without some greater provincial autonomy.

National constitutional debates were not enough to save Peckford. The signs of economic distress seemed to be everywhere in the late 1980s, perhaps the most visible of which was the federal government's decision in 1988, with the blessing of Peckford, to finally shut down that icon of earlier Newfoundland nationalism, the Newfoundland railway.[24] In 1989, in the wake of the failure of the Sprung project, with unemployment continuing to soar, and with the province's financial situation worsening steadily, Peckford resigned as premier. Briefly succeeded by Tom Rideout, the Progressive Conservatives fell to the Liberals led by Clyde Wells in the general election of April 1989.

Premier Wells took a much different stand on constitutional issues. A fiscal conservative but strong federalist, the new premier opposed the distinct society clause of the Meech Lake Accord because he felt it would allow Quebec governments to violate the Canadian Charter of Rights and Freedoms and would privilege the legislative status of Quebec within Confederation. The federal government must, Wells felt, preserve its ability to treat all provinces equally and fairly; provinces would be best advised to ensure that they were heard equally through reform of the Senate. Otherwise, the federal government had to preserve its ability to provide essential services to all Canadians, but by being as frugal as possible to assist economic development in the private sector. The popular support he garnered within his own province and across Canada came from those who saw him as another provincial little guy standing up to Prime Minister Mulroney's bullies in Ottawa, or from people who thought of Mulroney as a tool of Quebec. Here, in Wells's stand against Meech Lake, was a chance to get back at the province that had for so long been enjoying the benefits of Labrador's Churchill Falls power development. Finally, there were those who genuinely believed that Newfoundland and Labrador, like the other poor provinces, could not afford to lose the redistributive functions of the federal government over national wealth. All of this sustained Wells through intense political pressure in 1990 to give Newfoundland's support to the accord by a vote in the House of Assembly, but opposition to the accord in Manitoba made the question moot.[25]

In the same year, one of the last vestiges of the former close relationship between the church and state disappeared with the closure of the Mount Cashel Orphanage in St John's due to a public scandal about child abuse within its walls. From the beginning, Mount Cashel had been run by the Christian Brothers of Ireland, an influential Roman Catholic teaching order in St John's. For years, many residents of the city included the institution's annual Christmas fundraiser, the 'Mount Cashel Raffle,' as part of their seasonal festivities. However, by the mid-1970s the Order and authorities in the Department of Social Services suspected that at least some of the brothers had engaged in physical and/or sexual abuse of the boys in their charge; in 1974, officials within the Irish Christian Brothers and the provincial Department of Justice had come to an arrangement that shut down an investigation by the Royal Newfoundland Constabulary.

The scandal dogged the church, forcing Archbishop Alphonsus Penney to appoint the Honourable Gordon Winter, a former lieutenant governor, to head a commission of investigation which built on the Constabulary investigation and a provincially appointed commis-

sion in 1989. The provincial commission had substantiated the allegations of abuse and recommended that the Constabulary be freed from
political interference by the Department of Justice and that the Irish
Christian Brothers' victims be compensated in timely fashion by the
province. The Order apologized to the victims in 1992, but the province paid no compensation until 1996.[26]

The provincial economy continued to be troubled, even though
four oil companies agreed to develop the Hibernia oil field under
the Atlantic Accord. In 1991, the provincial government established
a program of retrenchment in public finances. Most labour leaders
had welcomed a change in government amid the disintegration of the
Progressive Conservative regime and its labour policies, but Wells
believed that governments had little positive role to play in economic development and that the private sector must be unchained from
burdensome taxes and cumbersome regulations to create wealth. In
his earlier vigorous attacks on federal programs such as unemployment insurance for creating a culture of welfare dependence among
Newfoundlanders and Labradorians, Peckford had paved the way for
such thinking. Now government programs and public spending were
to be reduced and the working people of the province supposedly
made more self-reliant.[27]

Wells's March budget contained massive cutbacks in government
spending, imposed wage freezes for public employees, cancelled pay
equity agreements to redress gender discrimination in the health sector, and, in many cases, reneged on existing union contracts. Led by
NAPE, the public sector unions dogged the premier with a 'Clyde
Lied' campaign and reminded the public about the pay supplement
of over $90,000 a year that Wells had insisted upon receiving when
he agreed to be leader of the Liberal Party while it was in opposition.
The unions felt that his government had been duplicitous in negotiating some thirty-five collective agreements providing for 22.9 per cent
wage increases over three years and then intending to undermine the
increases by introducing Bill 16, the Public Sector Restraint Act. A coalition of unions mounted a legal fight against the government, and
the government tried to appease the labour movement by introducing
legislation later in the year to prohibit 'double-breasting' (a practice
in the building and construction trades whereby unscrupulous contractors would shut down unionized companies and then reopen as
non-union organizations to avoid their obligations to collective agreements). The government defended its budget on the grounds that it
could not afford a $114 million deficit, of which it was saving about

$55 million by its actions. Although the union movement's solidarity in opposition to Wells was unprecedented, it did not translate into support for the NDP, and the government continued its austerity measures in subsequent budgets.[28]

Premier Wells's commitment to retrenchment and federalism shaped the nature of rural development in the province. In 1989, soon after his election, Wells created the Economic Recovery Commission (ERC), with Doug House as its chairperson. The ERC was to revitalize the Newfoundland and Labrador economy along the lines set out by the RCEU. Existing rural development initiatives relied heavily on funding from Ottawa, through federal–provincial cooperation agreements, but the federal government, like the province, wanted to reduce spending. In 1994, the two levels of government established the Task Force on Community Economic Development, which recommended a community-based approach to further economic development. In keeping with the fiscal conservatism of governments at the time, and based on the belief that make-work programs were actually stifling individual initiative from below, the ERC and its agencies, along with regional economic development boards (REDBs) established as recommended by the task force, focused on capacity building. The provincial government hampered the effort by not allowing the REDBs to provide investment capital to new, small business initiatives, and by refusing to allow the ERC to use credit unions to raise local capital. Wells made much of his commitment to using the ERC and the REDBs to engage citizens in economic development, but his commitment to shifting responsibility for economic and social development from the province to community and regional groups coincided with his efforts to reduce public spending and offload spending onto more local levels of government.[29]

Hampered by bureaucratic hostility or indifference at the provincial and federal levels, the ERC found it difficult to deliver short-term success stories in the economic context of the early 1990s, and its long-term plans for a fundamental alteration of community economic development threatened many people who depended on UI and the patronage of the make-work system. The ERC proposed in 1994 a guaranteed basic annual income of $3,000 to supplement earnings from any other source, formal (paid and taxed) or informal (non-monetary exchanges of goods and services), along with supplements for education and work. Critics argued that the plan would lower the unemployment insurance benefits large families with multiple wage-earners received and would subsidize low-paying forms of employment, but without creating an incentive for employers to pay better wages. They felt that it romanticized the occupational pluralism, informal economy, and merchant credit of pre-Confederation outports as a way to attack the social citizenship of the welfare state, which defined the unemployment insurance system. Engaging in their own romanticized views of the quality of life underwritten by UI, such critics argued that the development approach embodied by the ERC sidestepped hard-nosed analysis of the impact of capitalism on Newfoundland, especially the manner in which corporate interests in industrial staple production drained the province's natural resources even as they demanded that workers make more and more concessions.[30]

In 1992, crisis struck the east coast fisheries. The cod stocks collapsed, and the federal government put in place a series of moratoria on ground fisheries, which made the ERC's goal of revitalizing rural parts of the province a much harder task. The provincial government had continued to foster overcapacity in the fishing industry by licensing too many processing plants. The federal government relied on overly optimistic internal scientific advice or ignored warnings about the impact of over-fishing and paid little attention to warnings from a number of fishers' organizations. To be fair to federal Department of Fisheries and Oceans (DFO) officials, the long-term process of fisheries modernization had divided communities and created complicated and often contradictory political pressures. For example, small-scale inshore fishers who used cod traps, long lines, and/or handlines, resented the higher incomes of the newer dragger owners and their crews. When overall fish catches had begun to drop by the mid-1980s, such resentment focused on the likely ecological damage the more intensive otter trawls were inflicting on fish stocks and on dragger skippers' use of small-meshed liner nets, which increased cod catches by preventing the escape of small fish through the larger mesh of the trawl nets.[31]

The federal government's responses to the closure of the fishery in 1992 – first through the Northern Cod Adjustment and Recovery Program (NCARP) and the Atlantic Groundfish Adjustment Program (AGAP), and later through The Atlantic Groundfish Strategy (TAGS) – compensated many people for the roughly 40,000 jobs lost in the fishery by 1993. But fishers complained that compensation was insufficient, and training programs were inadequate to convince them to leave the fishery permanently. The few people lucky to remain employed in the corporate sector worked longer hours for less money. Many inshore fishers survived the moratoria by diversifying the species they caught and ranging further offshore in their small craft, although they were prohibited by DFO from building vessels longer than 65 feet.[32]

The social upheaval of the crisis in the fisheries further divided coastal communities. As relatively new entrants into fishing, for example, women faced federal regulations that limited the entry of new fishers or part-time fishers. Moratoria compensation programs, such as NCARP, discriminated against them by paying them lower average compensation than men and rejecting a higher percentage of their claims for assistance. The increasing cleavage of communities along gender lines led many outport women to question the patriarchal conventions of their communities and to participate in groups such as the Newfoundland and Labrador Women's FishNet Organization. These groups explored ways to maintain the social and economic viability of coastal communities, but faced a tough battle in getting governments, unions, and other institutions to take women's problems as seriously as those of men. Other divisions grew in coastal communities, particularly as people who were directly affected by the moratoria, such as truckers and workers in businesses that supplied the needs of the fishery, received no compensation and came to resent fishers and plant workers who did.[33]

The federal government's overall approach to fisheries management throughout the 1990s was to promote fishers' withdrawal from the industry and privatization of rights of access to fish stocks through various quota systems. While some fishers left the industry through retirement, and others left Newfoundland and Labrador to seek employment in other provinces, many remained to face an uncertain place in reduced fisheries. As in the case of women's organizations, rural people generally found the shock of the moratoria to be socially divisive in ways that impeded the collective defence of their communities. For many individuals and families, out-migration for employment and better educations seemed best. Although oil-related industrial development on the Isthmus of Avalon offset local out-migration, it was insufficient to stem the swelling tide of people leaving the province.[34]

The fisheries crisis, which became known throughout Newfoundland and Labrador as the 'cod moratorium,' or simply the 'moratorium,' focused the anger of fishers against the federal government. The producers of popular culture often shaped this anger by playing the neo-nationalist tune, perhaps the best example being the 'Fisherman's Lament' from the self-titled debut album released by the band Great

Big Sea in 1993. In this song, the band spoke of 'brave Newfound-landers,' hard-working and formerly proud men emasculated by the fisheries mismanagement of 'some government bastard' in Ottawa. Full of understandable, if highly gendered, indignation against the inadequacy of the federal government's compensation package, the song suggested no awareness of the provincial fisheries policies and the expansion of local fishing efforts as having played a role in the ec-ological catastrophe of the ground fisheries. Great Big Sea was much more overtly political than such artists as Mary Dalton, whose 1989 collection of poetry, *The Time of Icicles*, had been partially a pastoral reflection on the post-Confederation rural decline of the province, or the songwriter and performer Ron Hynes, whose beautiful 'Atlantic Blue,' written in 1988, had mourned the losses of the Ocean Ranger disaster. Ray Guy had continued to produce much popular and popu-list mistrust about the impact of modernization on Newfoundland. All of these artists expressed a profound sense of loss, but with little notion about the part the peoples of the province had played in the many misfortunes of Newfoundland and Labrador, whether in de-pleted fisheries, previous support for Smallwood's modernization, or being bamboozled by the neo-nationalism of Peckford.[35]

These misfortunes continued, and were perhaps most visible in events that unfolded in Labrador. Incidents involving children at Davis Inlet gained national and international media attention in 1992–3. Throughout the 1970s and 1980s, the Mushuau Innu of Utshima-sits had laboured under the constant intrusion of the Akaneshau, or English speakers, on their culture and society. Although experienced hunters could use snowmobiles to hunt during the winter, it was im-possible for the Mushuau Innu to travel as a community to partici-pate in the celebrations of the hunt such as the mokoshan, or ritual feasting, which missionaries had discouraged in any event. The Ro-man Catholic Church had forbidden the people to communicate with animal spirits through shamans and shaking tent ceremonies. In the latter ceremonies, the Innu had used alcohol with drumming, danc-ing, and singing; the diminishment of the ritual left only the alcohol. Many people, young and old, turned to substance abuse to cope with the frustration and alienation that characterized Davis Inlet.[36]

The national and international media seized on news stories about children dying in a house fire in 1992 and the sensational videotape and pictures of Innu children sniffing gasoline in 1993, portraying life among the Mushuau Innu as hopelessly demoralized. Nothing could have been further from the truth. Since the late 1970s, the Innu of all

Labrador had begun to react publicly against the proliferation of low-level military flying from the Goose Bay airbase over their territory. From 1985 to 1995, the Innu Nation waged a high-profile campaign against low-level flying, building a great deal of international public support. The campaign rallied the Innu of Sheshatshiu and embroiled them in considerable controversy with local residents of Happy Valley–Goose Bay and North West River, who depended on the employment and related economic spin-offs of the military presence. Others felt that the Innu could not legitimately claim traditional rights to their territory because they had been forced to accommodate aspects of Akaneshau life. The Innu of Utshimatsits were less impressed by the struggle, which failed to prevent low-level flying. However, the Mushuau Innu were convinced that the Innu Nation must fight harder for a territorial land claims agreement. They held their own public consultations, achieved federal recognition in principle of their rights to land and resources, and demanded that the provincial government agree to the relocation of their community to Natuashish, at Sango Pond on the Labrador mainland about 15 kilometres west of Utshimatsits.[37]

On the island, the closure of the American naval base at Argentia in 1994 only added to the problems of an area previously hit hard by the shut-down in 1989 of ERCO at nearby Long Harbour, which resulted in the loss of 290 jobs in the Isthmus of Avalon. The bleakness of the 1990s – the scandals generated by abusive Roman Catholic clergy, constitutional farce on a national scale, massive unemployment, constant labour unrest, and the crisis of the fisheries – helped make the remnant of CODCO a Newfoundland and Canadian phenomenon. As early as 1978, two of its members, Tommy Sexton and Greg Malone, had endeared themselves to Newfoundlanders and Labradorians with their show *The Wonderful Grand Band*. This show combined music and sketches in weekly parody of political figures and the everyday unemployed. In 1987, the CBC aired a weekly show called *CODCO*, featuring Sexton, Malone, Mary Walsh, and Andy Jones. In 1991, Jones wrote a sketch, 'Pleasant Irish Priests in Conversation,' which outlined much of the behaviour that later came to light in the Mount Cashel affair. The CBC refused to air the show, leading to Jones's departure. *CODCO* declined without Jones and ended in 1993. However, Walsh, with Cathy Jones, Greg Thomey, and Rick Mercer, founded the weekly satirical news show *This Hour Has 22 Minutes*.[38]

In 1994, public discontent with Wells's retrenchment policies mounted when the government announced plans to privatize Newfoundland and Labrador Hydro, which many saw as an important source of revenue for government as well as of cheap electricity for consumers. Wells stepped down as premier in 1996. His successor, Brian Tobin, had recently been in the public spotlight as the federal minister of Fisheries and Oceans when, in 1995, Canadian patrol ships seized the *Estai*, a Spanish fishing vessel that had been illegally catching undersized turbot just outside the 200-mile limit in international waters. Although the legality of the seizure was questionable, and the long-term impact on international fisheries conservation was negligible, the incident made Tobin extremely popular.

As the federal cabinet minister from Newfoundland and Labrador, Tobin had been supportive of the initiatives of the ERC and related agencies in rural and regional development. However, as the province's new premier, with a solid mandate in a quick general election, Tobin shut down the whole effort in favour of a reorganized, highly centralized Department of Development and Rural Renewal (DDRR). Unlike Wells, Tobin was much more committed to an older style of federal Liberal spending, pragmatic in using government spending to redistribute wealth to poorer areas, especially if it meant consolidating popular support for the government.

Desperate to find economic activity outside of the fishing industry, and hampered by the political climate of retrenchment, the ERC had focused on an integrated approach to fostering small-scale economic enterprises. While the ERC did not overlook the fishery, its approach and modest successes opened it to further charges of impracticality and abandonment of the fishing industry. Tobin's reforms brought regional development under direct ministerial control, which was more vulnerable to old forms of patronage politics. While the provincial government continued to make some effort at rural development, the new premier's policies were 'neo-Smallwoodian,' preoccupied with 'resource megaprojects – oil, nickel, and hydroelectricity – rather than with fish and small-scale rural development.'[39]

The most important initiatives of the Tobin government had been set in motion during Wells's premiership. Apparent economic salvation came in the form of the discovery of massive nickel deposits at Voisey's Bay in 1993. The area of the mineral discovery encompassed lands claimed by both the Labrador Inuit Association (LIA) and the Innu Nation. The LIA had been negotiating with the federal and provincial governments since 1975 for a land claims settlement, but without much success. The Inuit and the Innu had begun to assert their authority over the land they claimed by exerting control over archaeological research in their territories. In 1992, the Innu Nation had begun its own permit process for researchers who wished to dig in their land, much to the consternation but eventual resignation of the provincial government. Presented with the opportunity of Voisey's Bay, the LIA and the Innu Nation threatened to bring development to a halt through court challenges and protests, eventually leading to development agreements between the company and both peoples, and greater progress on land claims with the federal and provincial governments. People of Inuit and settler ancestry who lived outside the land claims area of the LIA had founded the Labrador Métis Association in 1986, later called the Métis Nation, but made less progress in securing government recognition of their claims. The Tobin government insisted on development of Voisey's Bay in ways that would maximize provincial benefits and employment, leading his successor Roger Grimes to negotiate with Inco an agreement that the corporation would develop an experimental hydrometallurgical smelter near Argentia, Placentia Bay.[40]

The Tobin government carried out educational reform that the Wells government had begun and that followed up on-recommendations dating back to 1964 that the province should abolish public denominational education. Tobin kept the debate focused on the question of how the province could deliver the best-quality education to its youth. His government determined to place the education system directly under provincial control and received the support of 73 per cent of voters in a subsequent referendum on the subject in 1997. This vote opened the way in 1998 for a constitutional amendment of term 17 of the province's Terms of Union with Canada, ending its provision for denominational education.[41] The Tobin government was responsible for additional constitutional change when, in 1999, it proposed officially changing the name of the Province of Newfoundland to the Province of Newfoundland and Labrador. The federal government passed the necessary legislation to effect the name change, which became official on 6 December 2001.

Grimes became premier in 2001, following Tobin's jump back into federal politics in 2000. A leadership race between Grimes and cabinet colleague John Efford had been bitter and close, leaving behind a divided party. As premier, Grimes was at the head of a Liberal regime that had been in power for thirteen years. With royalties from new developments in offshore oil, such as the White Rose project, and Voisey's Bay still in the future, the Grimes government had to contend with a huge public debt, making the prospect of a budget that would mobilize public support for his government unlikely. Grimes turned to the tried-and-true approach: he claimed that the federal government was unfairly treating the province, particularly in the manner it clawed back revenue from the royalties generated by the exploitation of non-renewable resources through reduced equalization payments. In March, the premier announced a Royal Commission on Renewing and Strengthening Our Place in Canada. The commission went over old ground in decrying the unfairness of the Churchill Falls contract and attributing most of the responsibility for the fisheries crisis to Ottawa. The commission emphasized the problems of rural decline, out-migration, and mounting public debt in the province and suggested that a new, more collaborative federal–provincial relationship might be founded on such policies as a reform of the Atlantic Accord to allow Newfoundland and Labrador to retain more of the revenue generated by offshore oil.[42]

Grimes failed to rally Newfoundland and Labrador voters to the Liberal banner on the basis of the commission's milquetoast report. Standing against him in the 2003 general election was the charismatic lawyer and cable television tycoon Danny Williams, the new leader of the Progressive Conservative Party. The Progressive Conservatives had co-opted many of the commission's recommendations about a more aggressive provincial stance on its place in Canada in areas such as the fisheries, future hydro development in Labrador, and the Atlantic Accord. Williams led his party to a majority government. It was too much to expect that voters would believe that the provincial Liberals, the federalist party of Wells and Tobin, were going to be able to get a better deal from Ottawa. Although voters had seen it all before in the Peckford regime, they were apparently ready to place their hopes in neo-nationalism again in his ideological heir, Danny Williams.

Conclusion

Not a Nation

The new Tory government of Danny Williams girded itself to do battle again with Ottawa in the name of a fairer, better deal for Newfoundland and Labrador in Canada. It wrung tremendous concessions from Ottawa on the Atlantic Accord in 2005 that, if honoured by the federal government, will provide the province with much more offshore oil revenue. Williams's success provoked the envy of Saskatchewan's premier and the anger of the premier of Ontario, who suggested that it was time that Ontario received a new deal in Confederation. At home, Williams enjoyed tremendous popular support: the province was the regional David standing against Goliath at the centre.

Although the rhetoric of the Williams government put Newfoundland neo-nationalism back in the public eye, it actually delivered little in terms of achieving a better arrangement in the case of offshore oil revenues. What really counted was a weak minority Liberal government in Ottawa that was unable to resist the provincial government's demands amid a federal election campaign.[1] Newfoundland and Labrador seems poised to become 'have' rather than 'have-not,' although it remains to be seen to what extent this will be the result of neo-nationalist rhetoric, a minority federal government that might make further concessions to the province, or the fortuitousness of high prices in the international markets for oil and gas. It further remains to be seen how the people of Newfoundland and Labrador will partake of the benefits of 'have' status for the province. The provincial government continues to project a net population loss for Newfoundland and Labrador, expecting the provincial population, which was

576,495 in 1986, to fall to 500,736 by the year 2022. The government expects the province to lose working-age people, while there will be an absolute increase in the number of people 65 years of age and older. The province's population loss will likely continue to be from rural areas as people flee the decline of the fishing industry, while the St John's population, largely fuelled by the revenues from the offshore oil industry, will continue to grow. The concentration of the benefits of 'have' status appears set to take place on the northeast Avalon Peninsula even as the forestry sector continues to be troubled; these conditions challenge the government to find means to distribute benefits to rural Newfoundland and to its working-age people in particular. Aside from offshore oil, the only other economic opportunities appear to be in the mining and hydro power opportunities of Labrador, which will increase that region's importance.[2]

It is doubtful that the people of such a divided Newfoundland and Labrador will find solutions to their problems in the currently fashionable political rhetoric of neo-nationalism. Recent analyses of this phenomenon have pointed out that the current fascination of eastern urban Newfoundlanders and Premier Williams with the old national pink, white, and green flag has its roots in the older neo-nationalism of D.W. Prowse and Robert Bond. Theirs was the optimism of the old national policy, which promised that Newfoundland would become a modern industrial nation. Contemporary nationalism, however, has a more negative tone, a fascination with conspiracy theories about how Newfoundlanders and Labradorians were tricked into joining Canada, how Canada has not done enough for the province, and how provincehood has undermined cultural identity, blighted the economy, and forced people to leave. It is too easy to succumb to new nationalist fallacies by accepting the notion that the pessimism of the last third of the twentieth century was a reaction against modernity as represented by the failures of the Smallwood regime. This superficial view overlooks the extent to which Smallwood's basic ideas were the logical successors to the nineteenth-century tradition of Prowse and Bond.[3]

Nineteenth-century nationalism was out of step with the long-term historical pattern that characterized the experiences of the people of Newfoundland and Labrador. Prehistoric peoples depended on their use of coastal marine and estuarine resources, including anadromous fish species such as salmon and coastal fauna such as seabirds. The early Norse explorers who prospected for farmlands to settle along the North Atlantic littoral found no basis for settlement in Newfoundland. Later European merchants, whale hunters, and fishers found rich marine resources to exploit by migratory fisheries in the waters off Newfoundland and Labrador, but there were few terrestrial resources to tempt them to found colonies. By the seventeenth century, French and English interests developed colonies, the most impressive being at Plaisance and Ferryland. While colonists bravely attempted to find landward resources to exploit, and all colonies depended on supplementary farming, these ventures were primarily of military and economic strategic importance. The colonies staked rival empires' claims to Newfoundland or provided a basis from which to protect labour and capital deployed in the fishing industry and related maritime activities. Merchants, gentry-planters, and fishing servants settled because they wanted better access to local fisheries, needed to protect their establishments from First Nations, or wanted to improve their mercantile position. Year-round settlers found limited opportunities as furriers and wood cutters, but the economic activity that made their lives successful was the spring seal hunt. The limits of lands dominated by cold-ocean coastal, northern boreal, or arctic barrens ecologies meant that there was little terrestrial basis for the type of agriculture that formed the base of successful colonial development elsewhere in North America.

Imperial conflict resulted in Newfoundland and Labrador becoming secure British possessions by 1763, fostered the growth of St John's as the centre of British naval administration of the fishery and local settlement, but left much of the administration of Labrador to missionaries and traders. Between 1775 and 1815, the military and administrative establishment of the town provided the economic basis for artisans, professionals, and a small shopkeeper bourgeoisie in addition to the extensive mercantile enterprises that dominated the resident fishery. Willing to tax residents to pay for the cost of their administration, but unwilling to grant the institutions of colonial self government, the British government wished to maintain much of the structure of naval government in the first official provisions for colonial status in 1824. Members of the St John's bourgeoisie, unwilling to accept their lack of control over taxation and patronage, fought for self-government but had to find a means of convincing British authorities that their demands were justified.

To answer imperial arguments that Newfoundland had no agrarian basis for colonial self-government, colonial reformers founded a nationalist myth: that the island had the resources for agricultural diversification and interior development but that these had been frustrated by a cabal of self-interested British merchants and naval governors. On its own, this myth had little appeal to the fishing people who made up the vast majority of Newfoundland's population. The reformers embellished their appeal by suggesting to servants of Irish Roman Catholic origin in the most densely populated areas of the Avalon Peninsula that supporting Reformers allowed them to strike a blow for settlers against a British and Protestant mercantocracy. Anxious to shed the expense of administering Newfoundland, the British conceded representative institutions in 1832, and responsible government in 1855.

Colonial reformers, known as Liberals by the mid-nineteenth century, had raised expectations at home and in London that a colonial government would oversee economic diversification and prosperity free of dependence on a fishery that had been chronically troubled after 1815. The Liberals' myth, popularized and embellished by the writing of Prowse, quickly burdened the colony's politics and policies with a denominational cast, most notably in public education. Over the long run, colonial governments' railway and interior diversification policies undermined the basis of colonial competency. Unable to count on imperial support for the regulation of the fishery, an inherently international economic activity in terms of trade and resources, Newfoundland governments paid scant attention to the management of marine resources. Instead, to varying degrees, they built expensive railway lines, always hoping that some new resource Eldorado might be found at the end of the next line. An extensive agricultural interior never materialized, but there were forestry and mineral resources to be developed if colonial governments were willing to make generous concessions to international corporations. Most governments made the concessions because they were desperate to generate employment. Otherwise, they used railway employment and public battles over American or French fishing rights to court the voters of the colony. Colonial governments also used tariffs to protect local manufacturing.

Newfoundland's nineteenth-century political elite embraced a national policy of landward economic diversification that was very similar to that pursued by Canada in the last quarter of the nineteenth century. The major difference was that the Canadian proponents of their National Policy had a well-established industrial heartland in southern Ontario and in parts of Quebec, based on the opportunities of colonial agriculture, and had a huge agricultural hinterland and resource frontier to the north and on the prairies to exploit. Although many in Newfoundland eventually came to see Labrador as such a hinterland, it could not justify the expansion of the railway on the island, the key to the nationalist dream.

Nineteenth-century nationalists, in other words, ignored the obvious dependence of the colony on marine resources. Such ignorance is not surprising; Newfoundland never had much effective control over fisheries policy. It depended on the British for the enforcement of regulations and influence over international competitors. Although conscientious enough in representing Newfoundland interests in discussions of international trade barriers such as tariffs, the British tended to trade off those interests to the French and the Americans in matters such as fishing regulations and territorial rights. Without sufficient fiscal resources to afford enforcement of the few regulations they did make, Newfoundland politicians gravitated to the national policy, but it failed. While the government had some success in forestry and mining, these sectors never generated the kind of employment and markets that would support a local manufacturing base or sufficient traffic to justify the expense of the railway.

It is all too easy to ignore the extent to which popular agency drove colonial nationalism by the turn of the century. Fishers supported the economic diversification platforms of early reformers because it was an apparent way to break merchants' control over their lives in the fishery. The expansion of manufacturing, the railway, and related trades in St John's created an important, if regionally concentrated, working class. Although members of that class, especially skilled workers, formed unions to negotiate better employment conditions, they knew that their economic interests lay with the national policy, and colonial politicians often saw political opportunity in using railway construction as a form of patronage to court workers' support.

All this does not mean that fishing people and the working class were simply dupes of the colonial elite. Their history is replete with examples of collective actions aimed at protesting exploitation or of building alternative ideological visions in popular piety and evangelical religious traditions. However, the strength of the national policy, by widening the gulf between town and country, by setting the interests of industrial workers against fishers, ensured that there would be little popular support in St John's for the single most important pre-Confederation effort to better manage the fishery, the regulations proposed by Coaker of the FPU in 1920–1.

Ironically, the national policy delivered Newfoundland, although perhaps not Labrador, into the hands of those who would later become the antagonists of the neo-nationalists. The policy created massive public railway debt. This debt, aggravated by the high cost Newfoundland paid to participate in the First World War, contributed to the financial crisis and surrender of self-government in 1934. The severity of the postwar recession in the fishery revealed just how shallow and fragile economic diversification was. Already antagonized by wartime inflation and suspicions of profiteering by merchants, workers and fishers felt betrayed by politicians, suspected them of corruption, and were disillusioned with the outcome of years of economic boosterism and patronage. Like many in the business community, workers and fishers were ready for a rest from democracy and accepted the Commission of Government.

For all of its ambitious, if misguided, plans for social, economic, and moral reform, the Commission of Government served primarily as midwife to Newfoundland and Labrador's union with Canada. This does not mean that the commission broke with the nationalist past. Notwithstanding its experiments with model settlements and administrative reform, the commission essentially followed the same desperate program of economic diversification, especially in forestry and mining, as had past governments. Like previous responsible governments, the commission showed little sympathy for the plight of the unemployed, workers, and their unions and committees, and did little to alleviate the depression of the 1930s. Likewise, its refusal to implement the Gorvin plans for cooperative reform of the rural economy revealed that the commission was uninterested in challenging mercantile power in the fishery.

The impact of the Second World War provided economic opportunities and improved living standards where responsible governments and the commission had failed. The economy and the financial condition of the Newfoundland government improved because of military spending and wartime demand for salt fish. The commission realized that the latter would not last and had already begun a program of fisheries modernization based on the Canadian model that would continue under Smallwood in Confederation.

Government spending, in the form of base construction and operations, had provided many Newfoundlanders and Labradorians with much better lives than had any of the old nationalist policies for economic development. The exigencies of war helped to revitalize the organized labour movement. Many of its leaders joined with rural people to support Smallwood in the fight for Confederation. They did so because they realized that the proponents of a return to responsible government had little to offer except for the empty promises and broken dreams of a faded and tattered nationalist past. Confederation, on the other hand, offered financial support for expanding government services and programs, which would fill the gap left by the loss of wartime spending in Newfoundland and Labrador. Smallwood otherwise took up the same basic program of industrial diversification, first by manufacturing schemes and then by industrial-staple development. The premier found, as had others before him, that it was extremely difficult to secure the development of natural resources without striking unbalanced agreements with foreign investors and other governments. Anxious to secure investment, Smallwood betrayed the working people who had supported him, most notably in his ruthless repression of the IWA in 1958–9. For Smallwood, like the Commission of Government before him, loggers and other working people were primarily labour resources to be used in courting corporate investment. Such workers were supposed to acquiesce to their compliant role in the building of a nation but found that their own interests meant they had to demand more.

Although he carried on in the tradition of the nineteenth-century nationalists, Smallwood's flawed economic programs, his political megalomania, his apparent resource giveaways, as in the case of the Churchill Falls contract, and increased dependency on federal transfers, made Confederation the target for a new generation of politicians. It was easy to blame Canada for failures in provincial policies that contributed to crisis, even in areas of inordinate federal authority such as fisheries management. The retrenchment policies of every order of government in the 1970s and 1980s led to public resentment about program and employment cutbacks in the province, which politicians could easily redirect at Ottawa. Politicians from both provincial parties have appreciated the local political capital that accumulates from public, often vicious battles with Ottawa. Peckford's battles with Trudeau over control of Newfoundland's offshore oil resources had their antecedent in Smallwood's battle over term 29. Clyde Wells was not straying far from the field in his fights against the Meech Lake and Charlottetown constitutional proposals, which distracted from his confrontation at home with public sector workers. While Wells became something of a Canadian hero for his staunch federalism, it is easy to overplay his distinction from Peckford. Peckford's anti-Trudeau appeal in many parts of Canada was considerable, as was Wells's popularity at home as an Ottawa-basher. In every instance, Newfoundland premiers redirected popular anger over their anti-labour and fiscally conservative policies at a federal bogeyman.

The rhetoric of neo-nationalism in Newfoundland ignores the manner in which neo-nationalist ideals discount the experiences of class,
gender, ethnic, and regional divisions. These divisions render mean-
ingless the concept of a Newfoundland nation. As one grieving mother
of a worker lost on the Ocean Ranger said of the provincial government, 'They want to get on with the job of making big bucks and we
are an irritant to them to be disposed of as quickly as possible. When
it comes to human life and dignity, it seems they don't care a great
deal.'⁴ Nor are members of the working class of Newfoundland and
Labrador the only ones who ill fit the idealization of the beleaguered
Newfoundland national cause. The First Nations of those lands now
within the province's geopolitical boundaries have never had a place
in this nationalism. There is perhaps no better illustration of this than
the continued use of the Churchill Falls hydro development as a rallying cry for nationalism. Time and again, Newfoundland political
leaders have played on an island-based sense of grievance over the
deal between Brinco and Hydro Quebec. Premier Brian Tobin, as
just one recent example, justified his government's tough stance on
the development of Voisey's Bay by stating that 'Churchill Falls is
a scar on the psyche of Newfoundland and Labrador, and until we
demonstrated that we could negotiate good deals we would never be
able to set aside the belief that we had been scuppered yet again.' In
contrast with Tobin's views, consider the observation of Marie Wadden in her study of the Innu fight against low-level flying: 'The Innu
not only lived, hunted and travelled over land now underwater [the
Smallwood Reservoir], they also buried their dead there, and carefully marked sites where children were born and where legendary
and heroic deeds had occurred. The flooding of graves is considered
a blasphemous act by many Innu.'⁵
    While the fortunes of such First Nations have varied, they have
all had to struggle against the subjugation embedded in the colonial
approach of the Newfoundland elite to their rights. The anguish of
the oppression of one people by another was abundantly clear in the
views of the Mushuau Innu: 'We have been discriminated against by
the government. They don't care about us. Our voices are not heard.
White people always have their way. We are far behind other communities. Some of us think the government doesn't see us as human
beings. They think we are animals and we don't know how to run our
lives. They want to control everything in our community. They think
we are too lazy. They are racist.'⁶ Nonetheless, national oppression

does not mean helplessness, and the Innu have successfully used their own national consciousness and organization to force concessions for themselves and Labrador, to the contrary of long-held expectations by many in Newfoundland that Labrador was little more than a treasure store of resources for the island's benefit.

The development of Voisey's Bay is an example of what may be achieved once people become conscious of their real interests and pursue them in a determined way. The benefits agreements negotiated by the LIA and the Innu Nation are the first time that the natural resources of Labrador have been developed in a way that satisfied local people. However, even in this case, national identity has its limits, and potential social divisions remain hidden by an uncritical acceptance of national analyses. In the case of the LIA, for example, Inuit women, represented by the Tongamuit Innut Annait, held workshops in 1998 about the manner in which they felt marginalized by the process of land claims negotiations. Women from Nain, Makkovik, Postville, Hopedale, and Rigolet spoke about how they felt that male negotiators from the LIA and the federal and provincial governments were more interested in the industrialization of natural resources than in the social and cultural impacts of such development. Arguing that they would bear the brunt of such impacts, women wanted negotiators to consider the impact of land claims and industrial development on their lives. For example, women argued that full-time work at Voisey's Bay might undermine families' spending time together on the land, deprive them of traditional foods, and foster divisions among families and communities.[7]

Recent neo-nationalism continues to distract the peoples of Newfoundland and Labrador from its real impact on their lives. Craig Dobbin, for example, one of Newfoundland's leading capitalists, was well-known for his 'remarkable' and 'passionate' articulation of provincial grievance in the case of the Newfoundland and Labrador government's battles with the federal government over the distribution of revenues from non-renewable natural-resource exploitation and federal equalization programs.[8] But consider Dobbin's actions as opposed to his rhetoric. In 2004, while maintaining his public position that Newfoundland was getting a raw deal from Confederation and would be better off controlling its own natural resources, Dobbin's company, Canadian Helicopters Corporation, moved its head office from St John's to Vancouver. Dobbin admitted that he was too embarrassed to speak to the press about his action, but defended the move as an act of international corporate concentration and rationalization. '"Why Vancouver and not St John's?" "Because I had 350 people in Vancouver already working out there and I had 35 in St John's."'⁹

In the same year, the Williams government used what the United Nations' International Labor Organization (ILO) termed 'harsh' legislation to order thousands of members of the Newfoundland and Labrador Association of Public Employees (NAPE) back to work following a bitter public sector strike. The legislation established a wage freeze and extracted contract concessions from the public sector workers. The premier's support for the back-to-work legislation, which NAPE president Carol Furlong called 'an autocratic approach to collective bargaining' and 'a flagrant disregard to the human rights of our members and the basic principles of freedom of association,' earned the government of Newfoundland and Labrador its third censure in 2005 by the United Nations body. Nonetheless, the premier's subsequent public battles with the federal government over offshore oil revenues and equalization programs have eclipsed Williams's treatment of NAPE in the public eye as his government continues to be popular.¹⁰

Nationalism is an ideological construct partially based on the fabrication that peoples of diverse interests are really one and should mobilize in support of a particular interest group or party. Newfoundland and Labrador is the home of a variety of people who, on a day-to-day basis within the context of their communities, are defined far more by their class, gender, and ethnicity than by the mythical nationalist identities invented by political elites. Since Confederation, politicians have used a particular form of neo-nationalist Ottawa-bashing to distract the people of Newfoundland and Labrador from the failures of provincial policies and to co-opt their support. Yet the supposed failings of Confederation for Newfoundland and Labrador – economic dependency and underdevelopment, the undermining of a 'traditional' outport culture, the depletion of natural resources, and out-migration – are all problems that predate Smallwood and union with Canada. The problems have their origins in the nationalist policies of the nineteenth century. The ecological constraints that were the material reality of life for most of the people of Newfoundland and Labrador provided scarce leeway for determining how the resources of a largely cold-ocean coastal environment might be used. The resources of the sea were paramount, but they have rarely been at the centre of Newfoundland development policies. Instead, governments ignored the slender margin by making generous concessions and regulating the labour market to court foreign capital investment in what were for the most part much less promising landward developments. To be sure, the forestry and mining industries generated limited employment, profits for investors, and revenue for governments, but that has yet to be balanced against the costs in the depletion of woodlands, environmental degradation, and the industrial carnage in communities such as St Lawrence. The offshore oil industry may be the economic saviour of Newfoundland and Labrador, but that depends on whether the province may use the wealth generated by the industry to invest in people and communities in ways that sustain both them and the ecologies in which their fortunes are inextricably bound.

Notes

Introduction

1 Hiller and Harrington, *National Convention Debates*, 95.
2 Rose, *Cod*, 19–25; quote from 25.
3 Geoffrey H. Farmer, 'The Cold Ocean Environment of Newfoundland,' in Macpherson and Macpherson, *Natural Environment*, 61–7; Rose, *Cod*, 26–43.
4 Farmer, 'Cold Ocean Environment,' 66–7; Rose, *Cod*, 43–55; 'Labrador Current,' *Encyclopedia of Newfoundland and Labrador* (hereafter *ENL*), 3: 223.
5 Robert J. Rogerson, 'The Tectonic Evolution and Surface Morphology of Newfoundland,' in Macpherson and Macpherson, *Natural Environment*, 24–7; 'Geology,' *ENL*, 3: 502–11.
6 'Labrador Current,' *ENL*, 3: 223–4; 'Climate,' *ENL*, 1: 452–3; Colin E. Banfield, 'The Climatic Environment of Newfoundland,' in Macpherson and Macpherson, *Natural Environment*, 67, 129.
7 'Agriculture,' *ENL*, 1: 11; 'Geography,' *ENL*, 2: 496–7; 'Agriculture,' in McManus and Wood, *Atlas*, quotes from figure 16.2, plate 16.
8 'Forestry: The Physical Characteristics,' in McManus and Wood, *Atlas*, plate 17; 'Pine Trees,' *ENL*, 4: 302–3; quote from 'Geography,' *ENL*, 2: 495; Joyce Brown Macpherson, 'The Development of the Vegetation of Newfoundland and Climatic Change during the Holocene,' in Macpherson and Macpherson, *Natural Environment*, 189–217.
9 'Flora,' *ENL*, 2: 221–7; Karyn Cooper, 'Alien Anthropophytic Vegetation of the Avalon Peninsula,' in Macpherson and Macpherson, *Natural Environment*, 251–65.
10 Pastore, 'Collapse of the Beothuk World,' 52;
11 Rose, *Cod*, 55–78; Busch, *The War against the Seals*, 42–3; Tuck, *Ancient People of Port au Choix*, 2–4.

12 'Fauna,' *ENL*, 2: 20–7; Roberts J. Mednis, 'Indigenous Plants and Animals of Newfoundland: Their Geographical Affinities and Distributions,' in Macpherson and Macpherson, *Natural Environment*, 218–32.
13 This brief introduction to the environment and ecology of Newfoundland and Labrador does not fully address the impact of human activity, which is clearly evident in the introduction of animals such as moose, the depletion of major fish species such as cod, the extinction of animals such as the great auk, the depletion of white pine, or the introduction of plants from Europe. The importance of such activity should not be underestimated but may only be understood once the systematic study of such phenomena, complete with an examination of their interrelationship with non-human environmental and ecological processes, has been undertaken.

1: The First Peoples by the Sea

1 Tuck, *Prehistory*, 11–16; Renouf, *Ancient Cultures, Bountiful Seas*, 7–20.
2 Busch, *The War against the Seals*, 42–3; Tuck, *Ancient People of Port au Choix*, 2–4.
3 Tuck, *Ancient People*, 80–6; *Prehistory*, 22.
4 Tuck, *Ancient People*, 17–18, 86–91, 201; Jelsma, 'A Bed of Ochre,' 140–62.
5 Tuck, *Ancient People*, 92–3.
6 Hood, 'Archaic Indians,' 163–85.
7 Tuck, *Prehistory*, 44–64, 81–7; James A. Tuck and William Fitzhugh, 'Palaeo-Eskimo Traditions of Newfoundland and Labrador: A Re-Appraisal,' in Canadian Archaeological Association, *Palaeo-Eskimo Cultures*, 163.
8 Tuck and Fitzhugh, 'Palaeo-Eskimo Cultures,' 161–3; Madden, 'A Late Archaic Sequence,' 88–95, 115–38.
9 Richard H. Jordan, 'Palaeo-Eskimos in Atlantic Canada: A Regional Comparison of Newfoundland and Labrador Middle Dorset,' in Canadian Archaeological Association, *Palaeo-Eskimo Cultures*, 135–50; Renouf and Murray, 'Two Winter Dwellings,' 118–31; Renouf, 'Review,' 375–416.
10 M.A.P. Renouf, 'Two Transitional Sites at Port au Choix, Northwestern Newfoundland,' in Morrison and Pilon, eds., *Threads of Arctic Prehistory*, 165–96. See also Jean-Yves Pintal, 'A Groswater Site at Blanc-Sablon, Quebec,' 145–64, and Murielle Nagy, 'A Critical Review of the Pre-Dorset/Dorset Transition,' 1–14, in the same volume; Renouf, 'Palaeoeskimo Seal Hunters,' 185–212.
11 Canadian Archaeological Association, *Palaeo-Eskimo Cultures*, 163–6; Ralph T. Pastore, 'The Spatial Distribution of Late Palaeo-Eskimo Sites on the Island of Newfoundland,' in Canadian Archaeological Association, *Palaeo-Eskimo Cultures*, 125–7; Tuck, *Prehistory*, 98–9.
12 Susan A. Kaplan, 'European Goods and Socio-Economic Change in Early Labrador Inuit Society,' in Fitzhugh, *Cultures in Contact*, 45–8; Robert McGhee, 'Peopling the Arctic,' in Harris, ed., *Historical Atlas of Canada*, 1: plate 11; James A. Tuck, 'Intermediate Indians,' Heritage Newfoundland and Labrador Heritage website, 1997.
13 Loring, 'Princes and Princesses of Ragged Fame,' 7–13, 342–408.

14 Marshall, *A History and Ethnography of the Beothuk*, 257–9; Pastore, 'Collapse of the Beothuk World,' 52–71.
15 Erwin et al., 'Form and Function,' 46–67.
16 Marshall, *Beothuk*, 257–61.
17 Ibid., 261–88.
18 Ibid., 288–93.

2: The European Encounter

1 Alan G. Macpherson, 'Pre-Columbian Discoveries and Exploration of North America,' in Allen, *North American Exploration*, 13–70; Logan, *Vikings in History*, 9–12; Lars Jørgensen, 'Political Organization and Social Life,' in Fitzhugh and Ward, *Vikings*, 72–83.
2 Alan Macpherson, 'Norse Voyages and Settlements,' in Harris, *Historical Atlas of Canada*, 1: plate 16; Birgitta Wallace, 'L'Anse aux Meadows and Vinland: An Abandoned Experiment,' in Barrett, *Contact*, 214–33.
3 Ingstad, 'Part II: Interpretation and Assessment, VIII Cultural Affinities,' in Ingstad, et al., *Norse Settlement in America*, 239–43.
4 Fitzhugh, 'Early Contacts North of Newfoundland before A.D. 1600: A Review,' in Fitzhugh, *Cultures in Contact*, 23–31; Ingstad, 'Cultural Affinities,' 242–5.
5 Macpherson, 'Norse Voyages and Settlements,' in Harris, *Historical Atlas of Canada*, 1: plate 16.
6 Macpherson, 'Pre-Columbian Discoveries,' 58–60; Quinn, 'Columbus and the North: England, Iceland, and Ireland (with new appendix)' in Quinn, *European Approaches to North America*, 18–40.
7 Quinn, 'North America: A Last Resort?' in Quinn, *European Approaches*, 221–30.
8 Pope, *Many Landfalls*, 1–16.
9 Ibid., 16–40.
10 Patrick McGrath, 'Bristol and America, 1480–1631,' in Andrews, Canny, and Hair, *The Westward Enterprise*, 81–96; A.N. Ryan, 'Bristol, the Atlantic and North America, 1480–1509,' in Hattendorf, ed., *Maritime History*, 1: 241–56; Sacks, *Widening Gate*, 19–48; Pope, *Many Landfalls*, 43–68.
11 Goertz, 'João Alvares Fagundes,' 117–28; Darlene Abreu-Ferreira, 'Portugal's Cod Fishery in the Sixteenth Century: Myths and Misconceptions,' in Candow and Corbin, eds., *How Deep Is the Ocean*, 31–44.
12 Barkham, 'French Basque "New Found Land" Entrepreneurs,' 1–43.
13 Pope, 'The Sixteenth-Century Fishing Voyage,' in Candow and Corbin, *How Deep Is the Ocean*, 15–16.
14 Innis, *The Cod Fisheries*, 11–26.
15 Pope, 'Sixteenth-Century Fishing Voyage,' 16–25.
16 Ibid., 18–24; Pope, 'Practice of Portage,' 19–41.
17 Susan A. Kaplan, 'European Goods and Socio-Economic Change in Early Labrador Inuit Society,' in Fitzhugh, *Cultures in Contact*, 50–2; Loring, 'Princes and Princesses,' 104–7.
18 Loring, 'Princes and Princesses,' 169–93.

19 Sacks, *Widening Gate*, 51–2.
20 George Best, *The First Book of the First Voyage of Martin Fobisher.* (1578), and Best, *A True Report of Such Things as happened in the Second Voyage of Captain Frobisher*, in Kenyon, *Tokens of Possession*, 40–4, 45–72. In addition to the material from Kenyon, see David Quinn, 'Frobisher in the Context of Early English Exploration'; Ann Savours, 'A Narrative of Frobisher's Arctic Voyages'; James McDermott, '"A Right Heroicall heart": Sir Martin Frobisher,' in Symons, *Meta Incognita*, 1: 7–118; Ann Savours and Sir James Watt, 'They Captured "Countrey People": Their Depiction and Medical History,' in Symons, *Meta Incognita*, 2: 553–62; Cooke, 'Frobisher, Sir Martin,' *Dictionary of Canadian Biography* (hereafter *DCB*), 1, *1000–1700*: 316–19; and Kaplan, 'European Goods,' 54–5.
21 Kaplan, 'European Goods,' 55–65.
22 Matthews, *Lectures*, 60–3.
23 Chang, 'Newfoundland in Transition,' 85–6.
24 Sacks, *Widening Gate*, 49–51.
25 Gilbert, 'Divers Places,' 147–67; Marshall, *Beothuk*, 25–31.
26 MacLean, 'Beothuk Iron,' 168–76.
27 Marshall, *Beothuk*, 31–41.

3: Migrants and Settlers: The Development of a Fishing Society, 1610–1775

1 Cell, *English Enterprise in Newfoundland*, 51–80; Sacks, *Widening Gate*, 49–51; Marshall, *Beothuk*, 31–41.
2 Cell, *Newfoundland Discovered* 12–45; Codignola, *Coldest Harbour of the Land*, 9–10; Pope, *Fish into Wine*, 194–254.
3 Chang, 'Newfoundland in Transition,' 46; Handcock, *Soe longe as there comes noe women*, 23–72.
4 Cell, *Newfoundland Discovered*, 45–59; Pope, 'Six Letters,' 16; Lahey, 'Religion in Lord Baltimore's Colonial Enterprise,' 19–48.
5 Codignola, *Coldest Harbour in the Land*, passim; Pope, *Fish into Wine*, 122–32.
6 Bannister, 'Fishing Admirals,' 166–219.
7 Matthews, 'West of England–Newfoundland Fishery,' 10–12, 65, 132–7; Pope, *Fish into Wine*, 41–4, 194–254.
8 Much of the material on the Dutch comes from Glerum-Laurentius, 'Dutch Activity in Newfoundland,' passim. On sack ships, see Pope, *Fish into Wine*, 104–16.
9 Pope, *Fish into Wine*, passim; Pope, 'Baltimore vs Kirke,' 63–98.
10 Matthews, 'West of England–Newfoundland Fishery,' 156–228; Pope, *Fish into Wine*, 161–305, 349–406; Pope, 'Outport Economics,' 153–86; Sweeny, 'What Difference Does a Mode Make?'
11 O'Flaherty, *Old Newfoundland*, 43–4; Younge, *Journal*, 55.
12 Pope, 'Scavengers and Caretakers,' 279–93.
13 Martijn, 'Early Mi'kmaq Presence,' 44–102.
14 Holly, 'Environment, History and Agency,' 20–5; Holly, 'Beothuk,' 79–90.

15 O'Flaherty, *Old Newfoundland*, 48–55.

16 Head, *Eighteenth Century Newfoundland*, 146–7.

17 Smith, *The Navy and Its Chaplains*, 160–6.

18 Hiller, 'Utrecht Revisited,' 23–40; Janzen, 'Une Grande Liaison,' 183–200; Landry, 'Lasson-Daccarrette,' 220–56.

19 Janzen, 'Illicit Trade in English Cod,' 1–7; Brière, 'The Port of Granville,' 93–107.

20 Chang, 'Newfoundland in Transition,' 36–7, 48; Mannion, 'Irish Migration and Settlement,' 257–93.

21 Chang, 'Newfoundland in Transition,' 87–89; Mannion, 'Waterford and the South of England,' 134–53.

22 Mannion, 'Waterford and the South of England,' 115–31; Smith, *Navy and Its Chaplains*, 166–7; Matthews, *Lectures*, 167–8; Melvin Baker, 'Government,' *Encyclopedia of Newfoundland and Labrador* (hereafter *ENL*), 2: 587; Murphy and Perin, *Christianity in Canada*, 110.

23 Matthews, 'West of England–Newfoundland Fishery,' 232–383; Webb, 'Leaving the State of Nature,' 156–65.

24 Matthews, *Lectures*, 96–102; Baker, 'Government,' 587–8; Bannister, *Rule of the Admirals*, passim.

25 Bannister, *Rule of the Admirals*, passim.

26 Ibid., passim.

27 O'Flaherty, *Old Newfoundland*, 76–7.

28 Head, *Newfoundland*, 87–91; O'Flaherty, *Old Newfoundland*, 77.

29 'Introduction,' in Byrne, *Gentlemen-Bishops and Faction Fighters*, 4–9.

30 O'Flaherty, *Old Newfoundland*, 78–80.

31 Bannister, 'Social Management of English Commerce.'

32 Handcock, 'Origin and Development of Trinity up to 1900,' 11–36.

33 Whiteley, 'Palliser,' 141–52; Thorpe, 'Debating Talents,' 61–83.

34 Whitely, 'Palliser,' 153–4; McEwen, 'Law of Real Property,' 58–72.

35 Byrne, *Gentlemen-Bishops and Faction Fighters*, 9.

36 Rothney, 'Case of Bayne and Brymer,' 264–75; Whitely, 'Palliser,' 155–7.

37 Patricia A. Thornton, 'The Demographic and Mercantile Bases of Initial Permanent Settlement in the Strait of Belle Isle,' in Mannion, *Peopling of Newfoundland*, 157–63; Thornton, 'The Transition from the Migratory to the Resident Fishery in the Strait of Belle Isle,' in Ommer, *Merchant Credit*, 142–44.

38 Taylor, 'The Two Worlds of Mikak,' 4–13.

39 Kleivan, *Eskimos*, 42; Whiteley, 'Moravian Mission,' 29–50.

40 Cartwright, *Labrador Journal*.

41 Murphy and Perin, *Christianity in Canada*, 111, 114, 116.

42 Parsons, 'Newfoundland Methodism,' 12–22; Murphy and Perin, *Christianity in Canada*, 129–31; Hans Rollmann, 'Laurence Coughlan and the Origins of Methodism in Newfoundland,' in Scobie and Grant, *Contribution of Methodism*, 55–67; Robinson, 'Eighteenth-Century Newfoundland Methodism,' 17–18, 31–8, 43, 47, 50, quote from 53; 'Methodism,' *ENL*, 3: 520–1.

4: Not Quite a Colony, 1775–1824

1 McDonald, 'Rivalry,' 135–50.
2 Patricia Thornton, 'The Transition from the Migratory to the Resident Fishery in the Strait of Belle Isle,' in Ommer, *Merchant Credit*, 138–66; Chang, 'Newfoundland in Transition,' 40–6; see more generally Matthews, 'West of England–Newfoundland Fishery,' and Handcock, *Soe longe as there comes noe women*.
3 A common misunderstanding about servants' preferred lien against their insolvent planter-masters' catches is that the law obliged planters' supplying merchants to pay the wages of their clients. Merchants, in fact, only had to pay wages rateably with the amount of fish and cod oil the planter traded. If, for example, a planter owed five servants £20 each in wages, but together they had caught and traded to a merchant only £50 in produce before the master became insolvent, then the merchant only had to pay the servants £10 each. The merchant was not responsible for the unpaid wage balances. On the actual application of the law see Cadigan, *Hope and Deception*, 109–11, 148–50; Cadigan, 'Merchant Capital, the State, and Labour,' 17–42.
4 C. Grant Head, Christopher Moore, and Michael Barkham, 'The Fishery in Atlantic Commerce,' in Harris, *Historical Atlas of Canada*, 1: plate 28; I use the concept of triangular trade following that of Ommer, *Outpost to Outport*, passim.
5 Janzen, 'Royal Navy,' 28–38; Head, *Newfoundland*, 146–7; Stuart R. Sutherland, 'Pringle, Robert,' *Dictionary of Canadian Biography* (hereafter *DCB*), 4, *1771–1800*: 647–8; Janzen, 'Royal Navy,' 38–48; for an expression of merchants' concerns see CO 194, vol. 33, 1776–7, B-676, ff. 130–4; Governor Montagu to Lord Germain, St. John's, 11 June 1777. This and other CO 194 citations are from Cadigan, 'Fishing Ships' Rooms Controversy.'
6 Whiteley, 'Administration of Labrador,' 92–112.
7 Hiller, 'Newfoundland Fisheries Issue,' 10–15; Innis, *Cod Fisheries*, 210.
8 Matthews, 'West of England–Newfoundland Fishery,' 453; Chang, 'Newfoundland in Transition,' 15–18; McEwen, 'Law of Real Property,' 74.
9 Janzen, 'Scottish Sack Ship,' 1–18; Janzen, 'Scottish Supercargo,' 294–302; Ommer, 'Scots in Newfoundland,' 23–24; Jeffrey A. Orr, 'Scottish Merchants in St. John's, 1780–1835,' in Macpherson, *Four Centuries*, 36–9; Mannion, 'Irish Merchants Abroad,' 127–90.
10 Chang, 'Newfoundland in Transition,' 48–65.
11 Lahey, *O'Donel*, passim; 'Introduction,' in Byrne, *Gentlemen-Bishops and Faction Fighters*, 1–9; McNally, 'A Question of Class,' 71–87.
12 Reece, 'Banditti, Part I,' 1–29; Reece, 'Banditti, Part II,' 127–41; Bannister, 'Convict Transportation,' 95–123.
13 McNally, 'Question of Class,' 87–8.
14 John Mannion, 'St. John's,' in Harris, *Historical Atlas of Canada*, 1: plate 27; Innis, *Cod Fisheries*, 289–317; Melvin Baker, 'Bowring, Benjamin,' *DCB*, 7, *1836–1850*: 101–2; Keith Matthews, *DCB*, 5, *1801–1820*: 119–20; John Mannion, 'Meagher,

Thomas,' *DCB*, 7, *1836–1850*: 597–8; English, 'Newfoundland Legal System,' 91–107.

15 Bailey, 'John Reeves,' 28–49; Bannister, 'Convict Transportation,' 106–19.

16 English, 'Newfoundland Legal System,' 91–107; J.M. Bumsted, 'Colclough, Caesar,' *DCB*, 6, *1821–1835*: 160–4.

17 McEwen, 'Real Property,' 82–5; CO 194, vol. 38, 1788–91, B-678, ff. 290–327.

18 See Innis, *Cod Fisheries*, 288–322, but more particularly Shannon Ryan, 'Fishery to Colony: A Newfoundland Watershed, 1793–1815,' in Buckner and Frank, *The Acadiensis Reader*, 1: 138–56.

19 Webber, *Fencibles*, 2–7; G.W.L. Nicholson, 'Skinner, Thomas,' *DCB*, 5, *1801–1820*: 763–4; Mannion, 'Irish Disloyalty,' 1–29.

20 Patrick O'Flaherty, 'Waldegrave, William, 1st Baron Radstock,' *DCB*, 6, *1821–1835*: 796.

21 Byrne, 'Ireland and Newfoundland,' 4–8; Webber, *Fencibles*, 37–70.

22 McNally, 'Question of Class,' 88–9.

23 C. Grant Head, 'Gower, Sir Erasmus,' *DCB*, 5, *1801–1820*: 359–61.

24 Ryan, 'Fishery to Colony,' 134–48.

25 Cadigan, *Hope and Deception*, 37–43.

26 Frederic F. Thompson, 'Holloway, John,' *DCB*, 6, *1821–1835*: 323–4. McEwen, 'Real Property,' 91–8; Keith Matthews, 'MacBraire, James,' *DCB*, 6, *1821–1835*: 417–20; Bumsted and Matthews, 'Tremlett (Trimlett), Thomas,' *DCB*, 6, *1821–1835*: 784–5. On the Society of Merchants' antagonism to Tremlett see O'Flaherty, 'Seeds of Reform,' 45.

27 Smith, 'Beothuks and Methodists,' 119–20; Marshall, *Beothuk*, 134–51, 426–7.

28 CO 194, vol. 52, 1812, B-684, ff. 86–109; Whiteley, *Duckworth's Newfoundland*, 46–50; McEwen, 'Law of Real Property,' 106–8.

29 CO 194, vol. 57, 1816, B-686, ff. 36–7, 137; vol. 38, 1788–91, B-678, ff. 290–324. William H. Whitely, *Duckworth's Newfoundland* (St John's, 1985), 15–19. Frederick Jones and G.M. Story, 'Anspach, Lewis Amadeus,' *DCB*, 6, *1821–1835*: 9–11. W. Gordon Handcock, 'Bland, John,' *DCB*, 6, *1821–1835*: 70–1.

30 Raymond J. Lahey, 'Power, John,' *DCB*, 6, *1821–1835*: 613–14.

31 Lahey, 'Scallan, Thomas,' *DCB*, 6, *1821–1835*: 690–4.

32 Cadigan, *Hope and Deception*, 56–9; Cadigan, 'Artisans in a Merchant Town,' 95–119.

33 Hiller, 'Newfoundland Fisheries Issue,' 15–16; Innis, *Cod Fisheries*, 224–5; Balcom, *Lunenburg Fishing Industry*, 5–7; Vickers, *Farmers and Fishermen*, 145–52, 264–88.

34 Ryan, *Ice Hunters*, 65–105.

35 On Conception Bay, see Cadigan, *Hope and Deception*, 65–8; for supporting evidence, see Krista L. Simon, 'Women in the Courts of Placentia District, 1757–1823,' in English, *Essays*, 272–99.

36 Cadigan, *Hope and Deception*, 64–80; Willeen Keough, '"Now You Vagabond [W]hore I Have You": Plebeian Women, Assault Cases, and Gender and Class Relations on the Southern Avalon, 1750–1860,' in English, *Essays*, 237–71; Keough, *Slender Thread*, passim.

37 Sean Cadigan, 'Whipping Them into Shape: State Refinement of Patriarchy among Conception Bay Fishing Families, 1787–1825,' in McGrath, Neis, and Porter, eds, *Their Lives and Times*, 48–59.

38 Marshall, *Beothuk*, 185–221

39 On Forbes's rulings on property rights see Bruce Kercher and Jodie Young, 'Formal and Informal Law in Two New Lands: Land Law in Newfoundland and New South Wales under Francis Forbes,' in English, *Essays*, 147–91.

40 Cadigan, *Hope and Deception*, 93–9; Patrick O'Flaherty, 'Lundrigan (Landergan, Landrigan, Lanergan), James,' *DCB*, 6, *1821–1835*: 409–11; O'Flaherty, 'Forbes, Sir Francis,' *DCB*, 7, *1836–1850*: 301–4; Phillip Buckner, 'Hamilton, Sir Charles,' *DCB*, 7, *1836–1850*: 376–7.

41 Orr, 'Scottish Merchants,' 43–9; Baker, 'Government of St. John's,' 4–23, and 'Absentee Landlordism.'

5: A Colonial State, 1824–1855

1 Frederic F. Thompson, 'Cochrane, Sir Thomas John,' *Dictionary of Canadian Biography* (hereafter *DCB*), 10, *1871–1880*: 178–80; Leslie Harris and P.G. Cornell, 'Tucker, Richard Alexander,' in *DCB*, 9, *1861–1870*: 794; J.B. Cahill, 'Brenton, Edward Brabazon,' and William Kirwin, 'Buchan, David,' in *DCB*, 7, *1836–1850*: 104–5, 114–15.

2 Goudie, 'Down North;' Bill Rompkey, *Labrador*, 40–9; Budgel and Staveley, *Labrador Boundary*, 3–5.

3 Plaice, *Native Game*, 27–30.

4 John Mannion and Gordon Handcock, 'Origins of the Newfoundland Population, 1836.' In Gentilcore, *Historical Atlas of Canada*, 2: plate 8; Cadigan, *Hope and Deception*, 123–4.

5 Cadigan, *Hope and Deception*, 92–3.

6 Handcock, *Soe longe as there comes noe women*, 106; Michael Staveley, 'Population Dynamics in Newfoundland: The Regional Patterns,' in Mannion, *Peopling of Newfoundland*, 49–76; Patricia A. Thornton, 'The Transition from the Migratory to the Resident Fishery in the Strait of Belle Isle,' in Ommer, *Merchant Credit*, 138–66; Thornton, 'Frontier Demographic Experience,' 141–62.

7 Ryan, *Ice Hunters*, 121–9.

8 Cadigan, 'Artisans in a Merchant Town,' 95–119; James K. Hiller, 'Bennett, Charles James Fox,' *DCB*, 11, *1881–1890*: 65–6.

9 PANL, GN2/2, Box 2, 1827, John Moore to W.A. Clarke, St John's, 17, 18 May 1827; Magistrate John Broom to W.A. Clarke, St John's, 19 May 1827; William Warner and Edward Keilley to the magistrates, St John's, 17 May 1827; George W. Busted to W.A. Clarke, St John's, 27 July 1827; William Carson to the magistrates, St John's, 1 August 1827; J. Shea to the magistrates, St John's, 1 August 1827; Edward Kielley to the magistrates, St John's, 3 August 1827; William Warner to the magistrates, 3 August 1827; M.A. Fleming to the colonial secretary, St John's, 13 August 1827.

10 'Unions,' *Encyclopedia of Newfoundland and Labrador* (hereafter *ENL*), 5: 453.
11 Gillespie, *A Class Act*, 17–18.
12 MacKinnon, 'Farming the Rock,' 32–61; Cadigan, 'Artisans in a Merchant Town,' 116–17; Hornsby, *Cape Breton*, 59–62.
13 Cadigan, *Hope and Deception*, 141–60.
14 Bannister, 'The Campaign for Representative Government,' 19–40.
15 Keith Matthews, 'The Class of '32: St. John's Reformers on the Eve of Representative Government,' in Buckner and Frank, *Acadiensis Reader*, 1: 212–26; O'Flaherty, 'Seeds of Reform,' 39–59.
16 Rosemary E. Ommer, 'The 1830s: Adapting Their Institutions to Their Desires,' in Buckner and Reid, *Atlantic Region*, 284–306.
17 Cadigan, *Hope and Deception*, 123–8.
18 Cadigan, 'Chilling Neglect.'
19 Matthews, 'West of England–Newfoundland Fishery,' 174–9; Handcock, *Soe longe as there comes noe women*, 233; Rosemary E. Ommer, 'Introduction,' in Ommer, *Merchant Credit*, 9–15; Cadigan, *Hope and Deception*, 102.
20 Cadigan, *Hope and Deception*, 116–17; Little, 'Collective Action,' 25–31.
21 Cadigan, *Hope and Deception*, 127; Frederic F. Thompson, 'Cochrane, Sir Thomas John,' *DCB*, 10, *1871–1880*: 178–80.
22 Noel, *Politics in Newfoundland*, 1–10. This is only a precursory sketch of a complex political history. For greater detail see Gunn, *Political History*, 3–128.
23 Cadigan, 'Chilling Neglect.'
24 O'Flaherty, *Old Newfoundland*, 148–50.
25 Fitzgerald, 'Fleming and Ultramontanism,' 27–44; O'Flaherty, *Old Newfoundland*, 153–5.
26 Raymond Lahey, 'Fleming, Michael Anthony,' *DCB*, 7, *1836–1850*: 292–9; Philip McCann, 'Bishop Fleming and the Politicization of the Irish Roman Catholics in Newfoundland, 1830–1850,' in Murphy and Byrne, *Religion and Identity*, 81–98.
27 Cadigan, *Hope and Deception*, 141–50.
28 Hereward and Elinor Senior, 'Boulton, Henry John,' *DCB*, 9, *1861–1870*: 69–72; O'Flaherty, *Old Newfoundland*, 160–1; Little, 'Collective Action,' 12–13.
29 Cadigan, *Hope and Deception*, 147–50.
30 Gunn, *Political History*, 44, 204–5; O'Flaherty, *Old Newfoundland*, 161–3; Little, 'Collective Action,' 16–17; Cadigan, *Hope and Deception*, 150–6.
31 Budden, 'Newfoundland Natives Society,' 11–52; J.K. Hiller, 'Shea, Sir Ambrose,' *DCB*, 13, *1901–1910*: 942–3; Cadigan, *Hope and Deception*, 157–9.
32 Gunn, *Political History*, 89–94.
33 Philip Buckner, 'Harvey, Sir John,' *DCB*, 8, *1851–1860*: 374–84; McCann, 'Invention of Tradition,' 86–103; Fitzgerald, 'Fleming and Ultramontanism,' 40–4.
34 Cadigan, *Hope and Deception*, 128–31.
35 Cadigan, 'Chilling Neglect'; Cadigan, *Hope and Deception*, 131–3.
36 Hollett, 'Resistance to Feild,' passim; Hollett, 'Evangelicals vs. Tractarians,' 245–78; Johnson, 'Marriage Law,' 282–97; Winsor, 'Methodism,' 58–9, 118–20; 'Methodism,' *ENL*, 3: 522–3.

37 Cadigan, *Hope and Deception*, 133–40.
38 Trudi Johnson, 'Defining Property for Inheritance: The Chattels Real Act of 1834,' in English, *Essays*, 192–216; Cadigan, *Hope and Deception*, 64–80, 83; Barbara Neis, 'Familial and Social Patriarchy in the Newfoundland Fishing Industry,' in Newell and Ommer, *Fishing Places, Fishing People*, 32–54.
39 Cadigan, *Hope and Deception*, 115–16.
40 The preceding paragraphs are based on Cadigan, *Hope and Deception*, chap. 6.
41 Cadigan, *Hope and Deception*, 46, 59, 132; 'Cozens, Charles,' *ENL*, 1: 554.
42 Judith Fingard, 'The Poor in Winter: Seasonality and Society in Pre-Industrial Canada,' in Cross and Kealey, *Pre-industrial Canada*, 62–78; Fingard, 'The Relief of the Unemployed Poor in Saint John, Halifax and St. John's, 1815–1860,' in Buckner and Frank, *Acadiensis Reader*, 1: 198–219.
43 Cadigan, 'The Moral Economy of the Commons,' 9–42.
44 Cadigan, *Hope and Deception*, 158–9.
45 Hiller, 'Bennett,' 66.
46 Gunn, *Political History of Newfoundland*, 120–7.
47 Cadigan, 'Chilling Neglect.'
48 Robert M. Lewis, 'The Survival of the Planters' Fishery in Nineteenth and Twentieth Century Newfoundland,' in Ommer, *Merchant Credit*, 110–11.

6: Responsible Government and Landward Industrialization, 1855–1895

1 Gunn, *Political History*, 143–4. The standard account of colonial frustration with imperial foreign relations is Thompson, *French Shore Problem*. See also Cadigan, 'A Shift in Economic Culture.'
2 Gunn, *Political History*, 149–51; Cadigan, 'Shift in Economic Culture.'
3 James K. Hiller, 'Shea, Sir Ambrose,' *Dictionary of Canadian Biography* (hereafter *DCB*), 13, *1901–1910*: 942–4; Gunn, *Political History*, 152–5; 'Mullock, John Thomas,' *Encyclopedia of Newfoundland and Labrador* (hereafter *ENL*), 3: 646–7.
4 Cadigan, 'The sea was common,' passim.
5 Gunn, *Political History*, 155–75; Moulton, 'Constitutional Crisis,' 251–72.
6 Sean Cadigan, 'Failed Proposals,' in Newell and Ommer, *Fishing Places, Fishing People*, 147–69.
7 Hiller, 'Shea,' 943–4; Cadigan, 'Shift in Economic Culture.'
8 James Hiller, 'Confederation Defeated: The Newfoundland Election of 1869,' in Hiller and Neary, *Newfoundland in the Nineteenth and Twentieth Centuries*, 67–70.
9 Murphy and Perin, *Christianity in Canada*, 295; Jones, 'Religion,' 64–76; Philip McCann, 'The Politics of Denominational Education in the Nineteenth Century in Newfoundland,' in McKim, *The Vexed Question*, 30–59; G.M. Story, 'Mummers in Newfoundland History: A Survey of the Printed Record,' in Halpert and Story, *Christmas Mumming*, 178–9.
10 Cadigan, 'Shift in Economic Culture'; James K. Hiller, 'Confederation Defeated,' 67–89.
11 James K. Hiller, 'Bennett, Charles James Fox,' *DCB*, 11, *1881–1890*: 67–8.

12 James Hiller, 'The Railway and Local Politics in Newfoundland, 1870–1901,' in Hiller and Neary, *Newfoundland in the Nineteenth and Twentieth Centuries*, 123–9; Hiller, 'Bennett,' 68; Hiller, 'Shea,' 944.

13 Hiller, 'Bennett,' 68; Hiller, 'Pulp and Paper Industry,' 42–68; Cadigan, 'Community Regulation.'

14 Rosemary E. Ommer, 'Highland Scots Migration to Southwestern Newfoundland: A Study of Kinship,' and John J. Mannion, 'Settlers and Traders in Western Newfoundland,' in Mannion, *Peopling of Newfoundland*, 212–33, 234–75; Butler, 'L'Acadie,' 180–207; Bartels and Janzen, 'Micmac Migration,' 71–96.

15 Mailhot, *Sheshatshit*, 14–23; Plaice, *Native Game*, 31–5; Ryan, 'Innu Settlement,' 4–5; Bill Rompkey, *Labrador*, 42–3; Kennedy, *People of the Bays and Headlands*, 47–126.

16 Hiller, 'Carter,' 164, *DCB*, 12, *1891–1900*; Thompson, *French Shore*, 43–5; 'Lobster,' *ENL*, 3: 352.

17 Hiller, 'Carter,' 164; Peter Neary, 'The French and American Shore Questions as Factors in Newfoundland History,' in Hiller and Neary, *Newfoundland in the Nineteenth and Twentieth Centuries*, 114–5; Reeves, 'Fortune Bay Dispute.'

18 Sean Cadigan, 'Failed Proposals,' 147–69.

19 Sanger, 'Dundee–St. John's Connection,' 1.

20 Ryan, *Ice Hunters*, 117.

21 Fizzard, *Unto the Sea*, 108–11; Winsor, 'Newfoundland Bank Fishery,' 1–44; Balcom, *Lunenburg Fishing Industry*, 30–1.

22 Reeves, 'Fortune Bay Dispute,' passim.

23 J.K. Hiller, 'History of Newfoundland,' 39; Hewitt, 'Fisheries Commission, 1888–1893,' 58–80.

24 J.K. Hiller, 'The Railway and Local Politics in Newfoundland, 1870–1901,' in Hiller and Neary, *Newfoundland in the Nineteenth and Twentieth Centuries*, 130.

25 Cadigan, 'Smoke in the Woods.'

26 'Foxtrap,' *ENL*, 2: 368.

27 'Elections,' *ENL*, 1: 694–5.

28 'Manufacturing and Refining,' *ENL*, 3: 443–5; 'Benevolent Irish Association,' *ENL*, 1: 174–5; 'Loyal Orange Association,' *ENL*, 3: 381–4; 'Fishermen, Society of United (SUF),' *ENL*, 2: 177–8; 'Star of the Sea Association,' *ENL*, 5: 292–3.

29 Morgan, 'Class and Congregation,' 46–147.

30 Joy, 'Trades and Manufacturing,' 1, 20, 37–8, 70–1, 120; Gillespie, *Class Act*, 20–2; Bassler, *Vikings to U-Boats*, 100.

31 Moyles, *Salvation Army*, 5–48; Dunton, 'Origins and Growth,' 35, 53, 59–63, 73–87.

32 Hewitt, 'Fisheries Commission.'

33 Dickinson and Sanger, *Shore-Station Whaling*, 42–4.

34 'French Shore,' *ENL*, 2: 412–15; Mannion, 'Settlers and Traders,' 251–2.

35 R.E. Ommer, 'Ships and Shipping, 1863–1914,' and C.G. Head, R.E. Ommer, and P.A. Thornton, 'Canadian Fisheries, 1850–1900', in Gentilcore, *Historical Atlas of Canada*, 2: plates 37, 39; E.W. Sager and J.J. Mannion, 'Sea and Livelihood in

Atlantic Canada,' in Kerr and Holdsworth, *Historical Atlas of Canada*, 3: plate 23; Sager, *Seafaring Labour*, 67–73; Sager with Panting, *Maritime Capital*, 91–125.

36 J.K. Hiller, 'A History of Newfoundland'; 'Morine, Alfred Bishop,' *ENL*, 3: 618–19.

37 Sean Cadigan and Jeffrey Hutchings, 'Nineteenth-Century Expansion of the Newfoundland Fishery for Atlantic Cod: An Exploration of Underlying Causes,' in Holm, Smith, and Starkey, *Exploited Seas*, 31–65.

38 Ibid.; Ryan, *Fish Out of Water*, 44–6, 247.

39 Ommer, 'Merchant Credit,' 167–89.

40 Ryan, *Fish Out of Water*, 58–69; McDonald, *To Each His Own*, 1–15; David G. Alexander, 'Development and Dependence in Newfoundland, 1880–1970,' in Alexander, *Atlantic Canada*, 3–31; Ommer, 'Merchant Credit,' 167–89; Sweeny, with Bradley and Hong, 'Movement, Options and Costs,' 111–21; Robert C.H. Sweeny, 'The Social Trap: Technological Change and the Newfoundland Inshore Fishery,' in Vickers, *Marine Resources*, 295–310; Sweeny, 'Accounting for Change: Understanding Merchant Credit Strategies in Outport Newfoundland,' in Candow and Corbin, *How Deep Is the Ocean*, 121–38.

41 Baker and Neary, 'Sir Robert Bond,' 12; 'Bank Crash,' *ENL*, 1: 120–3; 'Confederation,' *ENL*, 1: 498–9.

42 Ommer, 'One Hundred Years of Fishery Crises,' 5–20.

7: Twilight of the National Policy, 1897–1908

1 Pope, *Many Landfalls*, 73–5, 91–125; Smrz, 'Cabot 400,' 16–31.

2 Hiller, 'History of Newfoundland,' 209–24; 'Chamberlain-Bayard Treaty,' *Encyclopedia of Newfoundland and Labrador* (hereafter *ENL*), 1: 396.

3 'Reid Newfoundland Company,' *ENL*, 4: 564–5.

4 The preceding discussion of railway development in Newfoundland is based on Hiller, 'The Railway and Local Politics,' and Hiller, 'The Political Career of Robert Bond,' in Hiller and Neary, *Twentieth-Century Newfoundland*, 11–46; see also 'Morris, Edward Patrick,' *ENL*, 3: 622, and Hiller, 'Bond and the Pink,' 113–33.

5 'Judiciary,' *ENL*, 2: 145–6; Hiller, 'Anglo-French Newfoundland Convention,' 82–98; Hiller, 'Bond, Bait, and Bounties: The Newfoundland Government and the Negotiation of the Entente Cordiale,' in Hiller and English, *Newfoundland and the Entente Cordiale*, 77–94.

6 Wheaton, 'R.G. Dun & Company,' 120–37.

7 Joy, 'Trades and Manufacturing,' passim.

8 Gillespie, *Class Act*, 22–4.

9 Chisholm, 'Organizing on the Waterfront,' 37–59.

10 Eric W .Sager, 'The Merchants of Water Street and Capital Investment in Newfoundland's Traditional Economy,' in Fischer and Sager, *Enterprising Canadians*, 75–96; David Alexander, 'Development and Dependence in Newfoundland, 1880–1970,' in Alexander, *Atlantic Canada*, 3–32.

11 Martin, *Once Upon a Mine*, 10–54; 'Notre Dame Bay,' *ENL*, 4: 122.

12 Cadigan, 'Recognizing the Commons,' 209–34.
13 Ibid.
14 Hiller, 'Origins of the Pulp and Paper Industry,' 42–68.
15 Joy, 'Trades and Manufacturing,' 37–100.
16 Ommer, 'What's Wrong with Canadian Fish,' 122–42.
17 Bassler, *Sanctuary Denied*, 44–57; Hong, 'Newfoundland's Chinese Immigration Act of 1906,' 5, 59, 64; Kahn, *Listen*, 17–27; McGrath, *Saltfish and Shmattes*, 36–66.
18 Carol Brice-Bennett, 'Missionaries as Traders: Moravians and the Inuit, 1771–1860,' in Ommer, *Merchant Credit*, 223–46; Bassler, *Vikings to U-Boats*, 32–60; Nowak, 'Eskimo Language,' 173–97; Loring, 'Archaeology,' 53–76; Bill Rompkey, *Labrador*, 43–4.
19 Hubbard, *Woman Who Mapped Labrador*, 18–27; 'Hubbard, Leonidas, Jr,' *ENL*, 3: 1–2; 'Innu,' *ENL*, 3: 47–50.
20 Ronald Rompkey, *Grenfell*, passim.
21 James K. Hiller, 'The Newfoundland Credit System: An Interpretation,' in Ommer, *Merchant Credit*, 86–101; Alexander, 'Development and Dependence in Newfoundland'; David Alexander, 'Newfoundland's Traditional Economy and Development to 1934,' in Hiller and Neary, *Newfoundland in the Nineteenth and Twentieth Centuries*, 17–39.
22 Sager, 'Merchants of Water Street,' 75–96.
23 Busch, 'Sealers' Strike of 1902,' 73–101.
24 Ryan, *Ice Hunters*, 213–71.
25 Ryan, *Fish Out of Water*, 55–6; David A. Macdonald, 'They Cannot Pay Us in Money: Newman and Company and the Supplying System in the Newfoundland Fishery, 1850–1884,' in Ommer, *Merchant Credit*, 114–28.
26 Reeves, 'Alexander's Conundrum,' 1–39.
27 Ibid., 22–31; Reeves, 'Aping the "American Type,"' 44–72.

8: The Politics of Hope and Demoralization, 1908–1934

1 The case for class distinctions is made in Sweeney, with Bradley and Hong, 'Movement, Options and Costs,' 111–21; Sweeney, 'The Social Trap: Technological Change and the Newfoundland Inshore Fishery,' in Vickers, *Marine Resources and Human Societies*, 295–310. Sager, *Seafaring Labour*, 24, 73, 114, 122–3, 228–9.
2 Winsor, 'Newfoundland Bank Fishery,' 45–9; David A. Macdonald, 'They Cannot Pay Us in Money: Newman and Company and the Supplying System in the Newfoundland Fishery, 1850–1884,' in Ommer, *Merchant Credit*, 114–28; Raoul Anderson, '"Chance" and Contract: Lessons from a Newfoundland Banks Fisherman's Anecdote,' in the same volume, 167–182.
3 Neis, 'A Sociological Analysis,' passim. See also 'Fishermen's Protective Union (F.P.U.),' *Encyclopedia of Newfoundland and Labrador* (hereafter *ENL*), 2: 180–6; Winsor, 'Newfoundland Bank Fishery,' 65.
4 McDonald, *To Each His Own*, 15–17; Gerald Panting, '"The People" in Politics,' in Cuff, *Coaker Anthology*, 71–8.

5 Sweeney, Social Trap,' 302–5; McDonald, *To Each His Own*, 25–33; 'Port Union,' *ENL*, 4: 401–2.
6 Hong, 'Newfoundland Board of Trade,' 20–49.
7 Ibid., 80–139; Hiller, 'History,' 175; McDonald, *To Each His Own*, 33–6; Cadigan, 'Recognizing the Commons,' 209–34; Snell, 'Newfoundland Old Age Pension,' 86–94.
8 The preceding discussion of the FPU in politics is based largely on McDonald, *To Each His Own*, 34–47. For more on Bond's rancour towards Coaker see Baker and Neary, 'Sir Robert Bond,' 22–6.
9 Ryan, *The Ice Hunters*, 306–17; 'Kean, Abram, Jr,' *ENL*, 3: 155–6, 166; Kean, *Old and Young Ahead*; Brown, *Death on the Ice*.
10 O'Brien, 'Newfoundland Patriotic Association,' passim; Sharpe, 'Race of Honour,' 27–56; Martin, 'Absolute Disloyalty,' 17–19.
11 Facey-Crowther, *Lieutenant Steele*, 193–200; Lackenbauer, 'Newfoundland Regiment,' 176–214; 'Beaumont Hamel,' *ENL*, 1: 161–5; 'Gallipoli,' *ENL*, 2: 462–3.
12 Harding, 'Beaumont Hamel,' 4.
13 Hiller, 'Bond and the Pink,' 127–8.
14 O'Brien, 'Newfoundland Patriotic Association,' 235–75.
15 'Regiment, Royal Newfoundland,' *ENL*, 4: 552–61.
16 Kahn, *Listen*, 25; Bassler, *Vikings to U-Boats*, 141–67; 'Shiwak, John, Jr,' *ENL*, 5: 177; Rompkey, *Labrador*, 65.
17 Rompkey, *Labrador*, 43–4, 62–7; Plaice, *Native Game*, 37–40.
18 McInnis, 'All Solid along the Line,' 61–84; Cuff, 'Quill and Hammer.'
19 Except where otherwise cited, the preceding discussion of the FPU and the First World War is based on McDonald, *To Each His Own*, 54–85.
20 McInnis, 'All Solid along the Line,' 83–4.
21 Alexander, *Decay of Trade*, 20–7; McDonald, *To Each His Own*, 86–105.
22 McDonald, *To Each His Own*, 106–25; Noel, *Politics in Newfoundland*, 151–8; Hiller, 'Politics of Newsprint,' 3–19.
23 R.M. Elliott, 'Newfoundland Politics in the 1920s: The Genesis and Significance of the Hollis Walker Enquiry,' in Hiller and Neary, *Newfoundland in the Nineteenth and Twentieth Centuries*, 181–204.
24 'Monroe, Walter Stanley,' *ENL*, 3: 599–601.
25 O'Brien, 'Newfoundland Patriotic Association,' 53–4; Margot Iris Duly, '"The Radius of Her Influence for Good": The Rise and Triumph of the Women's Suffrage Movement in Newfoundland, 1909–1925,' in Kealey, *Pursuing Equality*, 66–162; 'Earle, Julia Salter,' *ENL*, 1: 663; Snell, 'Old Age Pension,' 95; 'Nursing and Industrial Association, Newfoundland Outport (NONIA),' *ENL*, 4: 136–8.
26 Forestell, 'Times Were Hard,' 147–66.
27 Budgel and Staveley, *Labrador Boundary*, 5–7.
28 Henriksen, *Hunters*, 1–16; Tanner, 'Loin des Yeux, Loin du Coeur,' 19–31.
29 McDonald, *To Each His Own*, 131–4.
30 Hanrahan, *Tsunami*, 156–96; Ruffman and Hann, 'Newfoundland Tsunami,' 97–148.

31 Article 10, 21 Sept. 1932 and 'Notes of a Visit to Greece, 1932' in *Past, Present and Future*, n.p.; Alexander, *Decay of Trade*, 22–4.

32 *Daily News*, St John's, 1 February 1922; Crawley, 'Off to Sydney,' 27–51; David Frank, 'The 1920s: Class and Region, Resistance and Accommodation,' in Forbes and Muise, *Atlantic Provinces*, 233–71; the link between Newfoundland and more international trends was first made by Kealey in 'Canadian Labour Revolt,' 34.

33 *Daily News*, St John's, 1, 10 May 1926.

34 *Daily News*, 6 September, 7 December 1926. Weir, *Miners of Wabana*. The *Daily News* articles cited in the preceding notes are from research in Cadigan, 'Nova Scotian in Newfoundland.'

35 Facey-Crowther, 'War and Remembrance'; Overton, 'Economic Crisis,' 85–124; Bassler, *Sanctuary Denied*, 84, 138.

36 Robert C.H. Sweeney, 'Accounting for Change: Understanding Merchant Credit Strategies in Outport Newfoundland,' in Candow and Corbin, *How Deep Is the Ocean*, 121–38; Cadigan, 'Battle Harbour in Transition,' 125–50; Jim Overton, 'Public Relief and Social Unrest in Newfoundland in the 1930s: An Evaluation of the Ideas of Piven and Cloward,' in G. Kealey, *Class, Gender, and Region*, 153–66.

37 James Overton, 'Riots, Raids, and Relief, Police, Prisons and Parsimony: The Political Economy of Public Order in Newfoundland in the 1930s,' in Leyton, O'Grady, and Overton, *Violence*, 209–30; 'McGrath, James J.,' *ENL*, 3: 409.

38 Hiller, *Confederation*, 3–4; Overton, 'Riots, Raids, and Relief,' 236–65; Budgel and Staveley, *Labrador*, 11.

39 Neary, *Newfoundland*, 15–43; Great Britain, *Newfoundland Royal Commission 1933: Report* (Amulree Report), 77–81, 84, 209–14.

9: Commission, Depression, and War, 1934–1945

1 Sutherland, 'Newfoundland Loggers,' 83–101; Neary, 'The Bradley Report,' 193–232.

2 The Hope Simpsons letters have been collected and edited in Neary, *White Tie and Decorations*, 47, 52–4, 60, 109, 112, 118–20.

3 Tuck, 'Newfoundland Ranger Force,' 1–83.

4 Rompkey, *Labrador*, 86–9.

5 Gordon Handcock, 'The Commission of Government's Land Settlement Scheme in Newfoundland,' in Hiller and Neary, *Twentieth-Century Newfoundland*, 123–52; Neary, *Newfoundland*, 12–108; McCann, 'Educational Policy,' 201–16; Overton, 'Adult Education and Land Settlement,' 250–82.

6 Rennie, 'Industrial Disaster,' 107–16.

7 Quote from Kathryn Welbourn, 'Pierce Power and the Riot of 1935,' in Writers' Alliance, *Desperate Measures*; James Overton, 'Riots, Raids and Relief: Police, Prisons, and Parsimony: The Politics of Public Order in Newfoundland in the 1930s,' in Leyton, O'Grady, and Overton, *Violence and Public Anxiety*, 276–302.

8 Sutherland, 'Newfoundland Loggers,' 101–15.

9 Candow, *Lomond*, 31–2; White, 'Creating Community,' 45–58.

10 Botting, 'Getting a Grand Falls Job,' passim; see also Morrison, 'Female Work-force Participation in a Milltown.'
11 Howard and Howard, *Early Glimpses*, 2–3; Berends, 'Divided Harvest,' 16; Janes, *History of the Pentecostal Assemblies*, 87–94, 158, 183–95; Pinsent, 'Institutionaliza-tion of Experiential Religion,' 48, 54–9, 76–7, 83–8; Hattie-Longmire, 'Sit down, brother,' 10–18, 20–30, 67–76.
12 Gillespie, *Class Act*, 53–78.
13 Saunders, *Doctor Olds*, 71–107, 229–36; Neary, *Newfoundland*, 52–3, 'Tuberculo-sis,' *Encyclopedia of Newfoundland and Labrador* (hereafter *ENL*), 5: 432; 'Health,' *ENL*, 2: 872; Overton, 'Brown Flour and Beriberi,' 12–21.
14 Snell, 'Old Age Pension,' 96–103.
15 Bassler, *Sanctuary Denied*, 93–118, 131–57; Rompkey, *Labrador*, 84–9, 114.
16 Baird, *Report on Agricultural Conditions*, 1–16; Banks, *Schemes*, 3–46; Gorvin, *Re-port on Land Settlements*, 2–16; Neary, *Newfoundland*, 95–127. Gorvin, *Papers*, 2–16, 22; Jamieson, *No Place for Fools*, 25.
17 Neary, *Newfoundland*, 63–84, 104–5.
18 Webb, 'Origins of Public Broadcasting,' 88–106; Alexander, *Decay of Trade*, 28–32.
19 Melvin Baker and Shannon Ryan, 'The Newfoundland Fishery Research Com-mission, 1930–34,' in Candow and Corbin, *How Deep Is the Ocean*, 160–70.
20 Neary, *Newfoundland*, 84–94; Baker and Pitt, *Prudent Measures*, 11–45; White, 'Creating Community,' 45–85; Cadigan, 'Restructuring the Woods: Timber Rights, Power, and Agency in White Bay, Newfoundland, 1897–1959,' in Sinclair and Ommer, *Power*, 56–65.
21 Quote from Neary, 'Future of Newfoundland,' 29; Neary, *Newfoundland*, 114–21; 'World War II,' *ENL*, 5: 628–31.
22 Neary, 'Goose Bay Agreement,' 39–62; MacKenzie, *Atlantic Triangle*, 67–86, 92–126; Ransom, 'Canada's "Newfyjohn" Tenancy,' 45–71.
23 Neary, *Newfoundland*, 144–82; High, 'Outport to Outport Base,' 84–113.
24 Rompkey, *Labrador*, 92–6.
25 Kennedy, *People of the Bays and Headlands*, 175–9.
26 Lewis and Shrimpton, 'Policymaking in Newfoundland,' 209–39.
27 Sara Flaherty, '"Out of Date in a Good Many Respects": Newfoundland's Fight for Judicial Separation and Divorce in the 1940s,' in Cullum, McGrath, and Porter, *Weather's Edge*, 222–33; Haywood, 'Delinquent Females,' passim; Neary, 'Grave Problem,' 79–103.
28 Neary, '"A Mortgaged Property": The Impact of the United States on New-foundland, 1940–49,' in Hiller and Neary, *Twentieth-Century Newfoundland*, 183–5; High, 'Outport to Outport Base,' 84–113; High, 'Working for Uncle Sam,' 84–107.
29 Rennie, 'Industrial Disaster,' 117–36; Brown, *Standing into Danger*, passim.
30 Gillespie, *Class Act*, 81–3.
31 Tuck, 'Newfoundland Ranger Force,' 84–91.
32 Alexander, *Decay of Trade*, 34–98.
33 Sinclair, *State Intervention*, 32–4.

34 Alexander, *Decay of Trade*, 1–18, 128–65.
35 Webb, 'Constructing Community,' 239–58; Baker and Overton, 'Smallwood on Liberalism,' 75–126.
36 Gillespie, *Class Act*, 85–90; Strong, *Union Organizer*, 14–15; 'Power, Gregory J.,' *ENL*, 4: 432–3; 'Fogwill, W. Irving,' *ENL*, 2: 242.
37 MacKenzie, *Atlantic Triangle*, 126–63; Hiller, *Confederation*, 5–12.

10: The Land of Milk and Honey, 1946–1972

1 Pottle, *Newfoundland, Dawn without Light*, 13.
2 Horwood, *Joey*, 60–72; Gwyn, *Smallwood*, 62–75; Webb, 'Constructing Community,' 170–4.
3 Hiller, 'Career of Bradley,' 163–80; Hiller, *Confederation*, 18–20, 27; Horwood, *Joey*, 74–5; 'Fogwill, W. Irving,' *Encyclopedia of Newfoundland and Labrador* (hereafter *ENL*), 2: 242; 'Power, Gregory J.,' *ENL*, 4: 432–3.
4 Hiller, *Confederation*, 22–37; Blake, *Canadians at Last*, 146–70.
5 Webb, 'Responsible Government League,' 203–20; 'Fogwill, Frank D.,' *ENL*, 2: 242.
6 Quote from Chafe, *Railroad*, 94; Fitzgerald, 'Roche,' 33; Fitzgerald, 'True Father of Confederation,' 188–219; Jamieson, *No Place for Fools*, 121–3; Hiller, *Confederation*, 50.
7 Mackenzie, 'Terms of Union,' 234.
8 Webb, 'Responsible Government,' 218; Keough, 'Huckster Shop,' 73–93, 102–8; Williams, 'Fisher–Merchant Relationships,' 161–5; O'Brien, 'Trade Fields,' 59–61.
9 Snell, 'Newfoundland Old Age Pension Programme,' 104–9; Browne, *Newfoundlander*, 357–9; Sinclair, *State Intervention*, 32–4.
10 The Smallwood government's views and plans are succinctly stated in Newfoundland, *Report of the Royal Commission on Agriculture, 1955*, 1: 54–5, 95, 124–32.
11 Horwood, *Joey*, 58–60; Letto, *Chocolate Bars*, ix–xiii, 4–7, 97–100; Blake, *Canadians at Last*, 94–114.
12 Bassler, *Valdmanis*, passim; Dunn, 'Quest for Accountability,' 192–3.
13 PANL, GN 31/2, box 61, file 194/2, I, folio 20, 21–2, 32; Ricketts to Smallwood, Westport, White Bay, 11 April 1952, cited in Cadigan, 'Restructuring the Woods,' 69.
14 Horwood, *Joey*, 153, 173–4; Gwyn, *Smallwood*, 131–3; Rowe, *Into the Breach*, 125–7; Sutherland, 'We are only loggers,' 4–5.
15 H. Landon Ladd, 'The Newfoundland Loggers' Strike of 1959,' in Cherwinski and Kealey, *Lectures*, 149–64; Gwyn, *Smallwood*, 199–222; Paine, 'Mastery of Smallwood,' 191–212; Lembcke and Tattam, *One Union*, 155–76.
16 Gillespie, *Class Act*, 107–18; Horwood, *Joey*, 252–3.
17 Margaret Conrad, 'The 1950s: The Decade of Development,' in Forbes and Muise, *The Atlantic Provinces in Confederation*, 401–7; MacEachern, *Natural Selections*, 20, 127–51.
18 Wright, *Fishery*, 117–49; Wright, 'Fishing in the Cold War,' 239–58.

19 Peter Neary, 'Party Politics in Newfoundland, 1949–71: A Survey and Analysis,' in Hiller and Neary, *Newfoundland in the Nineteenth and Twentieth Centuries*, 204–45; Matthews, *Creation of Regional Dependency*, 169–93; Rowe, *Smallwood Era*, 87–128; Baker, 'Rural Electrification,' 190–209.

20 Iverson and Matthews, *Communities in Decline*, 121–28; Blake, *Canadians at Last*, 146–76; Matthews, *Regional Dependency*, 169–93; Alexander, *Decay of Trade*, 1–18, 128–65; Cadigan, 'The Role of Agriculture in Outport Self-Sufficiency,' in Ommer, *Resilient Outport*, 241–62; David Alexander, 'Economic Growth in the Atlantic Region, 1880 to 1940,' in Alexander, *Atlantic Canada*, 64; Peter Neary, 'Party Politics in Newfoundland, 1949–71: A Survey and Analysis,' in Hiller and Neary, *Newfoundland in the Nineteenth and Twentieth Centuries*, 204–45.

21 Gwyn, *Smallwood*, 240–66; Rompkey, *Labrador*, 120–9.

22 Tanner, 'Aboriginal Peoples,' 246–8; Peter Penashue, 'Healing the Past, Meeting the Future,' in Scott, *Aboriginal Autonomy*, 21–2.

23 Ryan, 'Innu Settlement,' 5–18.

24 Plaice, *Native Game*, 58–123.

25 Press, 'Davis Inlet,' 189–98; Hardin, 'Rescaling,' 3–14.

26 Rennie, 'And there's nothing,' 264–93. For more on the social impact of industrial diseases from mining in St Lawrence see Leyton, *Dying Hard*, passim.

27 Jim Overton, 'Coming Home: Nostalgia and Tourism in Newfoundland,' in Buckner and Frank, *The Acadiensis Reader*, 2: 418–31; Overton, *World of Difference*, 1–32.

28 Miriam Wright, 'Women, Men and the Modern Fishery: Images of Gender in Government Plans for the Canadian Atlantic Fisheries,' in McGrath, Neis, and Porter, *Their Lives and Times*, 129–43; Wright, 'Young Men and Technology,' 143–59.

29 'Horwood, Harold Andrew,' *ENL*, 2: 1038; Horwood, *Joey*, 252–4; 'Guy, Ray,' *ENL*, 2: 768; O'Flaherty, *Rock Observed*, 161–76; Fowler, 'Distinct Society,' 1–5; Overton, 'Cultural Revolution,' 166–204.

30 'Electric Reduction Company of Canada Industries Limited (ERCO),' *ENL*, 1: 749–52; 'Linerboard Limited, Labrador,' *ENL*, 3: 306; Baker, 'Rural Electrification,' 201–5; Michelle McBride, Gregory S. Kealey, and Sean Cadigan, 'Jobs at Any Cost: The Political Economy of Development in Twentieth-Century Newfoundland,' in Ommer, *Resilient Outport*, 271–4, Horwood, *Joey*, 306–7.

31 Gwyn, *Smallwood*, 282–302; Crosbie, *No Holds Barred*, 65–84.

32 Churchill, 'Pragmatic Federalism,' 215–46; Plaice, *Native Game*, 36; Armitage and Ashini, 'Partners in the Present,' 37.

33 'Teachers' Association, Newfoundland and Labrador,' *ENL*, 5: 344–5; Gwyn, *Smallwood*, 324.

34 Gwyn, *Smallwood*, 303–9; Inglis, *More than Just a Union*, 143–239.

35 'Fogo Island,' *ENL*, 2: 240–1; Bonnie J. McCay, 'Fish Guts, Hair Nets and Unemployment Stamps: Women and Work in Co-operative Fish Plants,' in Sinclair, *Question of Survival*, 105–32; Roger Carter, 'Co-operatives in Rural Newfoundland and Labrador: An Alternative?' in Sinclair, *Question of Survival*, 207–19.

36 Martin, *Once upon a Mine*; Narvaez, 'Protest Songs,' passim; Rennie, 'And there's nothing,' 378–444.
37 Gillespie, *Class Act*, 121–6, Hoy, *Wells*, 298.
38 Gwyn, *Smallwood*, 323–52.

<h2>11: The Limits of Neo-nationalism, 1972–2003</h2>

1 Paine, *Ayatollahs and Turkey Trots*, 1–9.
2 Herbert Halpert, 'Preface,' and Gerald Thomas and J.D.A. Widdowson, 'Introduction,' in Thomas and Widdowson, *Studies in Newfoundland Folklore*, xi–xxiii; J.D. House, 'Does Community Really Matter in Newfoundland and Labrador? The Need for Supportive Capacity in the New Regional Economic Development,' in Byron, *Retrenchment and Regeneration*, 228–9.
3 Usmiani, *Second Stage*, 91–101; Cook, 'National Cultures and Popular Theatre,' 4–82, 110–14; Fowler, 'Distinct Society,' 6–7, 229–318; quotes from Brookes, *A Public Nuisance*, 11, 105, 170.
4 Devine, 'Necessary Evils,' 113; Walsh is quoted in Clarke, *Stand and Deliver*, 227; the other quotes are from Brookes, *Public Nuisance*, 163. See also Cook, 'National Cultures and Popular Theatre,' 83–5, 113–14.
5 Payne, *Ayatollahs and Turkey Trots*, 9–18.
6 Peter R. Sinclair, 'The State Encloses the Commons: Fisheries Management from the 200-Mile Limit to Factory Freezer Trawlers,' and J. Douglas House, 'Canadian Fisheries Policies and Troubled Newfoundland Communities,' in Sinclair, *Question of Survival*, 157–77, 178–202.
7 Harter, 'Greenpeace Canada,' 83–119; Bulliet, *Hunters, Herders, and Hamburgers*, 1–35; Candow, *Of Men and Seals*, 129–37; 'Codpeace Foundation,' *Encyclopedia of Newfoundland and Labrador* (hereafter *ENL*), 1: 470–1.
8 'Baker's Brook,' *ENL*, 1: 117–18; 'Belldown's Point,' *ENL*, 1: 170–1; 'Cow Head,' *ENL*, 1: 551–3; 'Green Point,' *ENL*, 2: 721–2; 'Lobster Cove,' *ENL*, 3: 353–4; 'Norris Point,' *ENL*, 4: 99–100; 'Rocky Harbour,' *ENL*, 4: 616–17; 'Sally's Cove,' *ENL*, 5: 61–2; 'Woody Point,' *ENL*, 5: 622–3; Overton, 'Critical Examination,' 34–47; MacEachern, *Natural Selections*, 238; Brookes, *A Public Nuisance*, 78–96.
9 Payne, *Ayatollahs and Turkey Trots*, 18–59; quote from House, 'Premier Peckford,' 12–31, 20.
10 Peckford, *Past in the Present*, vi; other quotes from 29.
11 Pocius, 'Mummers Song,' 57–86.
12 Peckford, 'Discussion Paper on Fisheries Issues,' 2–5; House, 'Premier Peckford,' 19; 'Flags,' *ENL*, 2: 195–9.
13 House, *Challenge of Oil*, 43–74.
14 Royal Commission on the Ocean Ranger, *Report*, 151–2; Chiles, *Inviting Disaster*, 19–35; Nishman, 'Through the Portlights,' 157–68; O'Neill, 'Mobil and the Canadian Offshore,' 71–104; House, *But Who Cares Now*, 49.
15 Jeffrey A. Hutchings and Ransom A. Myers, 'The Biological Collapse of Atlantic

Cod off Newfoundland and Labrador: An Exploration of Historical Changes in Exploitation, Harvesting Technology, and Management,' in Arnason and Felt, *North Atlantic Fisheries*, 37–94; Bonnie J. McCay, 'Fish Guts, Hair Nets and Unemployment Stamps: Women and Work in Co-operative Fish Plants,' in Sinclair, *Question of Survival* 46; Bonnie J. McCay, '"Fish Is Scarce": Fisheries Modernization on Fogo Island, Newfoundland,' in Anderson, *North Atlantic Maritime Cultures*,155–88; Sinclair, *From Traps to Draggers*, 47–8; Lawrence F. Felt and L.W. Locke, '"It Were Well to Live Mainly off Fish": The Collapse of Newfoundland's Fishery and Beyond,' in Arnason and Felt, *North Atlantic Fisheries*, 197–236; Neis, 'From "Shipped Girls" to "Brides of the State,"' 185–202; Sean Cadigan, 'The Role of Agriculture in Outport Self-Sufficiency,' in Ommer, *Resilient Outport*, 241–62; Schrank, 'Bureaucracy, Politics, Economics,' 1–11.

16 D.R. Matthews, *Controlling Common Property*, 38–65; Inglis, *More Than Just a Union*; Close, 'Unconventional Militance,' 3–11.

17 Sinclair, 'State Encloses the Commons,' 157–76; Power, *What Do They Call a Fisherman?* 39–40; 'Young, Victor Leyland,' *ENL*, 5: 646.

18 Summers, *Regime Change*, 195; 'Mining,' *ENL*, 3: 578–9.

19 House, *Challenge of Oil*, 303–12; House, 'Don Quixote,' 171–88.

20 English, 'Intervention,' 20–34; Kealey, *Newfoundland Labour Movement*, 202–9; Norcliffe, *Global Game*, 97–104.

21 Overton, 'A Newfoundland Culture?' 5–22.

22 Newfoundland and Labrador, *Building on Our Strengths*, 17–36, 445–60; House, 'Does Community Really Matter?' 230–3.

23 Government of Newfoundland and Labrador, 'Enquiry into Sprung,' 127–5.

24 Peckford, 'Statement'; Ferre, 'Once upon a Train,' 77–110.

25 The discussion of Meech Lake is based on Webber, *Reimagining Canada*, 121–75; Coyne, *Roll of the Dice*, passim; Hoy, *Wells*, 150–207.

26 Hughes, *Steering the Course*, 247–64; Harris, *Unholy Orders*, passim.

27 Lawton, 'Development, Dependency,' 25–41.

28 Hoy, *Wells*, 297–314.

29 Tomblin, 'Newfoundland and Labrador,' 100–3.

30 House, 'New Regional Development,' 11–31; House, 'Does Community Really Matter?' 233–46; House, *Against the Tide*, 150–75; Overton, 'Academic Populists,' 1–54.

31 Finlayson, *Fishing for Truth*, 156–75; Donald Harold Steele and Raoul Anderson, 'The Commercial Annihilation of Northern Cod: The Fate of the 1986 and 1987 Year-Classes,' in Candow and Corbin, *How Deep Is the Ocean*, 261–7; see NIFA president Cabot Martin's regular observations on the developing fisheries crisis in a weekly newspaper, later reprinted in Martin, *No Fish and Our Lives*, passim. On the relationship between science and fishers see Neis, 'Fishers' Ecological Knowledge,' 155–78.

32 Craig T. Palmer, 'The Troubled Fishery: Conflicts, Decisions, and Fishery Policy,' in Felt and Sinclair, *Living on the Edge*, 57–76.

33 Williams, *Our Lives Are at Stake*; Roberts and Robbins, 'Gathering Voices,' 7;
an excellent analysis of the ongoing gender dimensions of the fisheries crisis is
Power, *What Do They Call a Fisherman?*

34 Sinclair and Felt, 'Coming Back,' 1–25; Peter R. Sinclair, with Heather Squires
and Lynn Downton, 'A Future without Fish? Constructing Social Life on Newfoundland's Bonavista Peninsula after the Cod Moratorium,' in Newell and Ommer, *Fishing Places*, 321–39; Sinclair, 'Industrialization and Rural Development,'
55–78.

35 Great Big Sea, *Great Big Sea*, track 5; Pierson, 'Ray Guy's Journalism: "A humane
sense of proportion,"' 'Two Newfoundland Poets (Des Walsh and Mary Dalton),' and 'Medieval Survivals: Reflections on Ron Hyne's *Cryer's Paradise*,' in
Pierson, *Hard-Headed and Big-Hearted*, 81–91, 120–8, 197–215.

36 Henriksen, *Hunters*, 14–45; Henriksen, *Life and Death*, 3–9; Press, 'Davis Inlet,'
193–203.

37 Hardin, 'Rescaling of the Innu,' 26–35; Landry, 'Re/locating the Mushuau Innu,'
52–3, 131–42; Wadden, *Nitassinan*, passim; Tanner, 'The Double-Bind of Aboriginal Self-Government,' in Scott, *Aboriginal Autonomy*, 405–8; see also Samson, *Way
of Life*, passim.

38 Clark, *Stand and Deliver*, 227–32.

39 Quote from House, 'Does Community Really Matter?' 260–1; see also House,
Against the Tide, passim. House argues that the Tobin government did its best to
obliterate memory of the ERC and its related agencies. Tobin, *All in Good Time*
offers nothing on the subject. See also Tomblin, 'Newfoundland and Labrador,'
103.

40 Hood and Baikie, 'Mineral Resource Development,' 7–29; Armitage and Ashini,
'Partners in the Present,' 31–40; McAleese, 'Reinternment,' 41–52; Goldie, *Inco*,
38–9, 146–62, 182–6, 186, 302–3; Tobin, *All in Good Time*, 206–17; Rompkey, *Labrador*, 155–65.

41 'Schools,' *ENL*, 5: 100–6; Tobin, *All in Good Time*, 182–94.

42 Boswell, 'Vanishing Report,' 279–89.

Conclusion: Not a Nation

1 House, 'Change from Within,' 480. I have touched on themes outlined in this
conclusion in 'Missed Opportunity,' 6–7, and 'Regional Politics,' 163–8.

2 Newfoundland and Labrador, 'Population Projections,' 1; Newfoundland and
Labrador, *Economic Review*, 11; Statistics Canada, 'Newfoundland and Labrador.'

3 Hiller, 'Bond and the Pink,' 113–33; Bannister, 'Making History,' 175–94.

4 House, *But Who Cares Now?* 28.

5 Wadden, *Nitassinan*, 47.

6 Innu Nation, *Gathering Voices*, 43.

7 Archibald and Crnkovich, *If Gender Mattered*, 10–14.

8 Bannister, *Politics of Cultural Memory*, 141–3.

9 *The Independent* (St John's), 15 August 2004, http://www.theindependent.ca/article.asp?AID=298&ATID=2 (accessed 3 May 2004).
10 'UN Body Says Danny Williams' Government Must Act,' National Union of Public and General Employees, http://www.nupge.ca/news_2005/n28jn05.htm (accessed 27 June 2007).

Bibliography

While I have read widely in the literature about Newfoundland and Labrador, I have appended only a list of the specific works I have cited in the text. Readers may also wish to consult the Newfoundland and Labrador Heritage website, http://www.heritage.nf.ca/, which began under the direction of James K. Hiller. Olaf U. Janzen compiles and updates regularly a very useful 'Reader's Guide to the History of Newfoundland and Labrador to 1869,' which is available at http://www.swgc.mun.ca/nfld_history/index.htm. The most important resource for anyone interested in reading further on any aspect of Newfoundland and Labrador is the Centre for Newfoundland Studies Queen Elizabeth II Library, at Memorial University. Readers may search its catalogue and periodical article bibliography at http://www.library.mun.ca/qeii/cns/index.php.

Primary Sources

Canada. 'Newfoundland and Labrador: Biggest Net Loss in Two Decades to Migration.' Ottawa: Statistics Canada, 2007. http://www12.statcan.ca/english/census01/Products/Analytic/companion/mob/nf.cfm (accessed 31 December 2007).

– *Eastern Newfoundland Settlement Survey, 1953 (Preliminary report) Bonavista.* Ottawa: Queen's Printer, 1953.

Gorvin, J.H. *Papers Relating to a Long Range Reconstruction Policy,* vol. 1. St John's: Government of Newfoundland, 1938.

– *Report on Land Settlements in Newfoundland.* St John's: Government of Newfoundland, 1938.

Great Britain. *Newfoundland Royal Commission Report, 1933.* London: HMSO, 1933.

Great Britain. Colonial Office Records, 1775–1855. CO 194. Microfilm copies on deposit at the Centre for Newfoundland Studies Queen Elizabeth II Library, Memorial University of Newfoundland.

McDonald, R. et al. *Report of Agricultural Commissioners Appointed by the Government to Enquire into Agriculture and Industries*. St John's: Government of Newfoundland, 1889.

Newfoundland and Labrador. *Economic Review 2007*. St John's: Economics and Statistics Branch (Economic Research and Analysis Division), Department of Finance, 2007.

– 'Population Projections Newfoundland and Labrador.' St John's: Economics and Statistics Branch (Economic Research and Analysis Division), Department of Finance, 2007. http://www.economics.gov.nl.ca/pdf/high/popbyagehigh.pdf (accessed 31 December 2007).

– 'Royal Commission of Enquiry into the Involvement of the Government of Newfoundland and Labrador and Any of its Agencies or Corporations with Sprung Sales Limited, or Sprung Environmental Space Enclosures Limited or Newfoundland Enviroponics Limited.' St John's: Government of Newfoundland, 1992.

– *Building on Our Strengths: Summary Report of the Royal Commission on Employment and Unemployment*. St John's: Government of Newfoundland, 1986.

– *Report of the Royal Commission on Agriculture, 1955*, vol. 1. St John's: Government of Newfoundland, 1955.

Provincial Archives of Newfoundland and Labrador. Newfoundland. Incoming Correspondence of the Colonial Secretary's Office, 1826–55. GN2/2.

Past, Present and Future: Being a Series of Articles Contributed to the Fishermen's Advocate, 1932. By Sir W.F. Coaker, K.B.E. Together with Notes of a trip to Greece 1932 And a Foreword by J.H. Scammell, n.d., n.p.

Peckford, A. Brian. 'Statement by Honourable A. Brian Peckford, Premier of Newfoundland and Labrador on the "Newfoundland Transportation Initiative."' St John's, 1988.

Peckford, A. Brian. 'Discussion Paper on Fisheries Issues Presented ... to The Honourable James McGrath, Minister of Fisheries and Oceans.' St John's, 1979.

Royal Commission on the Ocean Ranger Marine Disaster. *Report*, vol. 1. St John's: The Commission, 1984–1985.

Books

Alexander, David. *Atlantic Canada and Confederation: Essays in Canadian Political Economy*. Compiled by Eric W. Sager, Lewis R. Fischer, and Stuart O. Pierson. Toronto: University of Toronto Press, 1983.

– *The Decay of Trade: An Economic History of the Newfoundland Salt Fish Trade, 1935–1965*. St John's: Institute of Social and Economic Research, 1977.

Allen, John Logan, ed. *North American Exploration*, vol. 1: *A New World Disclosed*. Lincoln and London: University of Nebraska Press, 1997.

Anderson, Raoul, ed., *North Atlantic Maritime Cultures*. The Hague: Mouton, 1979.

Andrews, K.R., N.P. Canny, and P.E.H. Hair, eds. *The Westward Enterprise: English Activities in Ireland, the Atlantic, and America 1480–1650*. Liverpool: Liverpool University Press, 1978.

Archibald, Linda, and Linda Crnkovich. *If Gender Mattered: A Case Study of Inuit Women, Land Claims and the Voisey's Bay Nickel Project*. Ottawa: Status of Women Canada, 1999.

Arnason, Ragnar, and L. Felt, eds. *The North Atlantic Fisheries: Successes, Failures and Challenges*. Charlottetown: Institute of Island Studies 1995.

Baird, W.W. *Report on Agricultural Conditions and Possibilities of Development Thereof in Newfoundland*. St John's: Government of Newfoundland, 1934.

Baker, Melvin, and Janice Miller Pitt. *By Wise and Prudent Measures: The Development of Forestry on the Salmonier Line*. St John's: Government of Newfoundland and Labrador, 1998.

Balcom, B.A. *History of the Lunenburg Fishing Industry*. Lunenburg, NS: Lunenburg Marine Museum Society, 1977.

Banks, A.B. *Schemes for the Encouragement of Agriculture and Stock Raising*. St John's: Government of Newfoundland, 1939.

Bannister, Jerry. *The Politics of Cultural Memory: Themes in the History of Newfoundland and Labrador in Canada, 1972–2003*. Report Commissioned by the Royal Commission on Renewing and Strengthening Our Place in Canada. St John's, 2003.

Bannister, Jerry. *The Rule of the Admirals: Law, Custom, and Naval Government in Newfoundland, 1699–1832*. Toronto: University of Toronto Press, 2003.

Barrett, James H., ed. *Contact, Continuity, and Collapse: The Norse Colonization of the North Atlantic*. Turnhout, Belgium: Brepols, 2003.

Bassler, Gerhard. *Vikings to U-Boats: The German Experience in Newfoundland and Labrador*. Montreal and Kingston: McGill–Queen's University Press, 2006.

– *Alfred Valdmanis and the Politics of Survival*. Toronto: University of Toronto Press, 2000.

– *Sanctuary Denied: Refugees from the Third Reich and Newfoundland Immigration Policy, 1906–1949*. St John's: Institute of Social and Economic Research, 1992.

Blake, Raymond B. *Canadians at Last: Canada Integrates Newfoundland as a Province*. Toronto: University of Toronto Press, 1994.

Brookes, Chris. *A Public Nuisance: A History of the Mummers Troupe*. St John's: Institute of Social and Economic Research, 1988.

Brown, Cassie. *Standing into Danger: The True Story of a Wartime Disaster*. St John's: Flanker Press, 1985.

Brown, Cassie, with Harold Horwood. *Death on the Ice*. Toronto: Doubleday, 1974.

Browne, William J. *Eighty-Four Years a Newfoundlander*. St John's: Dicks and Company, 1981.

Buckner, P.A., and David Frank, eds. *The Acadiensis Reader*, vol. 1: *Atlantic Canada before Confederation*. Fredericton: Acadiensis Press, 1990.

– *The Acadiensis Reader*, vol. 2: *Atlantic Canada after Confederation*, 2nd ed. Fredericton: Acadiensis Press, 1988.

Buckner, Phillip A., and John G. Reid, eds. *The Atlantic Region to Confederation: A History*. Toronto and Fredericton: University of Toronto Press and Acadiensis Press, 1994.

Budgel, Richard, and Michael Staveley. *The Labrador Boundary*. Happy Valley–Goose Bay: Labrador Institute of Northern Studies Memorial University of Newfoundland, 1987.

Bulgin, Iona Bulgin, ed. *Cabot and His World Symposium, June 1997: Papers and Presentations*. St John's: Newfoundland Historical Society, 1997.

Bulliet, Richard W. *Hunters, Herders, and Hamburgers: The Past and Future of Human–Animal Relationships*. New York: Columbia University Press, 2005.

Busch, Briton Cooper. *The War against the Seals: A History of the North American Seal Fishery*. Montreal and Kingston: McGill–Queen's University Press, 1985.

Butler, Victor. *Sposin' I Dies in D' Dory*. St John's: Jesperson, 1977.

Byrne, Cyril J., ed. *Gentlemen-Bishops and Faction Fighters: The Letters of Bishops O'Donel, Lambert, Scallan and Other Irish Missionaries*. St John's: Jesperson, 1984.

Byron, Reginald, ed. *Retrenchment and Regeneration in Rural Newfoundland*. Toronto: University of Toronto Press, 2003.

Cadigan, Sean T. *Hope and Deception in Conception Bay: Merchant–Settler Relations in Newfoundland, 1785–1855*. Toronto: University Of Toronto Press, 1995.

Canadian Archaeological Association. *Palaeo-Eskimo Cultures in Newfoundland, Labrador and Ungava*. St John's: Memorial University of Newfoundland, 1986.

Candow, James E., and Carol Corbin, eds. *Lomond: The Life and Death of a Woods Town*. St John's: Harry Cuff Publications, 1998.

– *How Deep Is the Ocean? Historical Essays on Canada's Atlantic Fishery*. Sydney: University College of Cape Breton Press, 1997.

– *Of Men and Seals: A History of the Newfoundland Seal Hunt*. Ottawa: Environment Canada, Canadian Parks Service, 1989.

Cartwright, George. *Captain George Cartwright and His Labrador Journal*. Edited by C.W. Townsend. Boston 1911.

Cell, Gillian. *Newfoundland Discovered: English Attempts at Colonization 1610–1630*. London: Hakluyt Society, 1982.

– *English Enterprise in Newfoundland 1577–1660*. Toronto: University of Toronto Press, 1969.

Chafe, W.J. *I've Been Working on the Railroad: Memories of a Railwayman, 1911–1962*. St John's: Harry Cuff Publications, 1987.

Cherwinski, W.J.C., and Gregory S. Kealey, eds. *Lectures in Canadian Labour and Working-Class History*. St John's: Committee on Canadian Labour History, 1985.

Chiles, James R. *Inviting Disaster: Lessons from the Edge of Technology: An Inside Look at Catastrophes and Why They Happen*. New York: Harper Business, 2001.

Clark, Andrew. *Stand and Deliver: Inside Canadian Comedy*. Toronto: Doubleday, 1998.

Codignola, Luca. *The Coldest Harbour of the Land: Simon Stock and Lord Baltimore's Colony in Newfoundland, 1621–1649*. Translated by Anita Weston. Montreal and Kingston: McGill–Queen's University Press, 1988.

Coyne, Deborah. *Roll of the Dice: Working with Clyde Wells during the Meech Lake Negotiations*. Toronto: James Lorimer, 1992.

Crellin, John K. *Home Medicine: The Newfoundland Experience*. Montreal and Kingston: McGill–Queen's University Press, 1994.

Crosbie, John C. *No Holds Barred: My Life in Politics*. Toronto: McClelland and Stewart, 1997.

Cross, Michael S. and Gregory S. Kealey, eds. *Pre-industrial Canada, 1760–1849: Readings in Canadian Social History*, vol. 2.Toronto: McClelland and Stewart, 1982.

Cuff, Robert H., ed. *A Coaker Anthology*. St John's: Creative, 1986.

Cullum, Linda, Carmelita McGrath, and Marilyn Porter, eds. *Weather's Edge: Women in Newfoundland and Labrador, A Compendium*. St John's: Killick Press, 2006.

Dickinson, Anthony B., and Chesley W. Sanger. *Twentieth-Century Shore-Station Whaling in Newfoundland and Labrador*. Montreal and Kingston: McGill–Queen's University Press, 2005.

Dictionary of Canadian Biography (DCB). Volumes 1, 4–13. Toronto: University of Toronto Press, 1966, 1972, 1976, 1979, 1982, 1983, 1985, 1987, 1988, 1990, 1994.

Encyclopedia of Newfoundland and Labrador. (ENL). Volumes 1–5. St John's: Newfoundland Book Publishers, 1981, 1984, 1991, 1993, 1994.

English, Christopher, ed. *Essays in the History of Canadian Law*, vol. 9: *Two Islands: Newfoundland and Prince Edward Island*. Toronto: University of Toronto Press, 2005.

Facey-Crowther, David R., ed. *Lieutenant Owen William Steele of the Newfoundland Regiment: Diary and Letters*. Montreal and Kingston: McGill–Queen's University Press, 2002.

Felt, Lawrence, and Peter R. Sinclair. *Living on the Edge: The Great Northern Peninsula of Newfoundland*. St John's: Institute of Social and Economic Research, 1995.

Finlayson, Alan Christopher. *Fishing for Truth: A Sociological Analysis of Northern Cod Assessments from 1977–1990*. St John's: Institute of Social and Economic Research, 1994.

Fischer, Lewis R., and Eric W. Sager. *The Enterprising Canadians: Entrepreneurs and Economic Development in Eastern Canada, 1820–1914*. St John's: Maritime History Group, Memorial University of Newfoundland, 1979.

Fitzhugh, William W., ed. *Cultures in Contact: The Impact of European Contacts on Native American Cultural Institutions A.D. 1000–1800*. Washington and London: Smithsonian Institute Press, 1985.

Fitzhugh, William W., and Elisabeth I. Ward, eds. *Vikings: The North Atlantic Saga*. Washington and London: Smithsonian Institution Press/National Museum of Natural History, 2000.

Fizzard, Garfield. *Unto the Sea: A History of Grand Bank*. Grand Bank, NL: Grand Bank Heritage Society, 1987.

Forbes, E.R., and D.A. Muise, eds. *The Atlantic Provinces in Confederation*. Fredericton and Toronto: Acadiensis Press and University of Toronto Press, 1993.

Gentilcore, R. Louis, ed. *Historical Atlas of Canada*, vol. 2: *The Land Transformed, 1800–1891*. Toronto: University of Toronto Press, 1993.

Gillespie, Bill. *A Class Act: An Illustrated History of the Labour Movement in Newfoundland and Labrador*. St John's: Creative, 1986.

Goldie, Raymond. *Inco Comes to Labrador*. St John's: Flanker Press, 2005.

Gunn, Gertrude E. *The Political History of Newfoundland, 1832–1864*. Toronto: University of Toronto Press, 1966.

Gwyn, Richard. *Smallwood: The Unlikely Revolutionary*. Toronto: McClelland and Stewart, 1962, 1972.

Halpert, Herbert, and G.M. Story, eds. *Christmas Mumming in Newfoundland*. Toronto: University of Toronto Press, 1969, 1990.

Handcock, W. Gordon. *Soe longe as there comes noe women: Origins of English Settlement in Newfoundland*. St John's: Breakwater, 1989.

Hanrahan, Maura. *Tsunami: The Newfoundland Tidal Wave Disaster*. St John's: Flanker Press, 2004.

Harris, Michael. *Unholy Orders: Tragedy at Mount Cashel*. Toronto: Penguin, 1991.

Harris, R. Cole, ed. *Historical Atlas of Canada*, vol. 1: *From the Beginning to 1800*. Toronto: University of Toronto Press, 1987.

Hattendorf, John B., ed. *Maritime History*, vol. 1: *The Age of Discovery*. Malabar, FL: Kreiger, 1996.

Head, C. Grant. *Eighteenth Century Newfoundland*. Toronto: McClelland and Stewart, 1976.

Henriksen, Georg. *Life and Death among the Mushuau Innu of Northern Labrador*. St John's: Institute of Social and Economic Research, 1993.

– *Hunters in the Barrens: The Naskapi on the Edge of the White Man's World*. St John's: Institute of Social and Economic Research, 1973, 1997.

Hiller, James K. *Confederation, Deciding Newfoundland's Future, 1934 to 1949*. St John's: Newfoundland Historical Society, 1998.

Hiller, James K., and Christopher J.B. English, eds. *Newfoundland and the Entente Cordiale, 1904–2004*. St John's: Newfoundland and Labrador Studies 2007.

Hiller, James K., and Michael F. Harrington, eds. *The Newfoundland National Convention 1946–1948*, vol. 1: *Debates*. Montreal and Kingston: McGill–Queen's University Press, 1995.

Hiller, James, and Peter Neary, eds. *Confederation: Deciding Newfoundland's Future, 1934 to 1949*. St John's: Newfoundland Historical Society, 1998.

– *Twentieth-Century Newfoundland: Explorations*. St John's: Breakwater, 1994.

– *Newfoundland in the Nineteenth and Twentieth Centuries*. Toronto: University of Toronto Press, 1980.

Holm, Paul, Tim D. Smith, and David J. Starkey, eds. *The Exploited Seas: New Directions for Marine Environmental History*. St John's: International Maritime Economic History Association, 2001.

Hornsby, Stephen J. *Nineteenth-Century Cape Breton: A Historical Geography*. Montreal and Kingston: McGill–Queen's University Press, 1992.

Horwood, Harold. *Joey: The Life and Times of Joey Smallwood*. Toronto: Stoddart, 1989.

House, J.D. *Against the Tide: Battling for Economic Renewal in Newfoundland and Labrador*. Toronto: University of Toronto Press, 1999.

– *But Who Cares Now? The Tragedy of the Ocean Ranger*. Edited by Cle Newhook. St John's: Breakwater, 1987.

– *The Challenge of Oil: Newfoundland's Quest for Controlled Development*. St John's: Institute of Social and Economic Research, 1985.

Howard, Douglas C., and Muriel B. Howard. *Early Glimpses of Pioneering in Newfoundland and Labrador*. Canada: (no publisher), between 1987 and 2004).

Hoy, Claire. *Clyde Wells: A Political Biography*. Toronto: Stoddart, 1992.

Hubbard, Mina. *The Woman Who Mapped Labrador: The Life and Expedition Diary of Mina Hubbard*. Edited by Roberta Buchanan and Bryan Greene. Biography by Anne Hart. Montreal and Kingston: McGill–Queen's University Press, 2005.

Hughes, Sam. *Steering the Course: A Memoir*. Montreal and Kingston: McGill–Queen's University Press, 2000.

Inglis, Gordon. *More Than Just a Union: The Story of the NFFAWU*. St John's: Jesperson, 1985.

Ingstad, Anne Stine, with contributions by Charles J. Bareis, et al. *The Discovery of a Norse Settlement in America*. Oslo, Bergen, Tromsø: Univesrititsfurlaget, 1977.

Innis, Harold A. *The Cod Fisheries: The History of an International Economy* (1940). Toronto: University of Toronto Press, rev. ed., 1954.

Innu Nation and the Mushuau Innu Band Council. *Gathering Voices: Finding Strength to Help Our Children/Mamunitau staianimuanu: ntuapatetau tshetshi uitshiakuts stuassiminuts*. Edited by Camille Fouillard. Vancouver: Douglas and McIntyre, 1995.

Iverson, Noel, and D. Ralph Matthews. *Communities in Decline: An Examination of Household Resettlement in Newfoundland*. St John's: Institute of Social and Economic Research, 1968, 1979.

Jamieson, Don. *No Place for Fools: The Political Memoirs of Don Jamieson*. St John's: Breakwater, 1989.

Janes, Burton K. *History of the Pentecostal Assemblies of Newfoundland*. St John's: Pentecostal Assemblies of Newfoundland and Labrador, 1996.

Kahn, Alison J. *Listen While I Tell You: A Story of the Jews of St John's*. St John's: Institute of Social and Economic Research, 1987.

Kealey, Gregory S., ed. *Class, Gender, and Region: Essays in Canadian Historical Sociology*. St John's: Committee on Canadian Labour and Working-Class History, 1988.

– *The History and Structure of the Newfoundland Labour Movement*. St John's: Royal Commission on Employment and Unemployment, Newfoundland and Labrador, 1986.

Kealey, Linda, ed. *Pursuing Equality: Historical Perspectives on Women in Newfoundland and Labrador*. St John's: Creative, 1993.

Kean, Abram. *Old and Young Ahead* (1935). Edited by Shannon Ryan. St John's: Flanker Press, 2000.

Kennedy, John C. *People of the Bays and Headlands: Anthropological History and the Fate of Communities in the Unknown Labrador*. Toronto: University of Toronto Press, 1995.

Kenyon, W.A., ed. *Tokens of Possession: The Northern Voyages of Martin Frobisher*. Toronto: Royal Ontario Museum, 1975.

Keough, Willeen. *The Slender Thread: Irish Women on the Southern Avalon, 1750–1860*. New York: Columbia University Press, 2006. www.gutenberg-e.org/keough.

Kerr, D., and D.W. Holdsworth, eds. *Historical Atlas of Canada*, vol. 3: *Addressing the Twentieth Century*. Toronto: University of Toronto Press, 1990.

Kleivan, Helge. *The Eskimos of Northeast Labrador: A History of Eskimo–White Relations, 1771–1955*. Oslo: Norsk Polarinstitutt, 1966.

Lahey, Raymond J. *James O'Donel in Newfoundland, 1784–1807*. St John's: Newfoundland Historical Society Pamphlet #8, 1984.

Lembcke, Jerry, and William M. Tattam. *One Union in Wood: A Political History of the International Woodworkers of America*. New York: International Publishers, 1984.

Letto, Douglas M. *Chocolate Bars and Rubber Boots: The Smallwood Industrialization Plan*. Paradise, NL: Blue Hill Publishing, 1998.

Leyton, Elliott. *Dying Hard: The Ravages of Industrial Carnage*. Toronto: McClelland and Stewart, 1975.

Leyton, Elliott, William O'Grady, and James Overton. *Violence and Public Anxiety: A Canadian Case*. St John's: Institute of Social and Economic Research, 1992.

Logan, F. Donald. *The Vikings in History*. 3rd ed. New York and London: Routledge, 2005.

MacEachern, Alan. *Natural Selections: National Parks in Atlantic Canada, 1935–1970*. Montreal and Kingston: McGill–Queen's University Press, 2001.

MacKenzie, David. *Inside the Atlantic Triangle: Canada and the Entrance of Newfoundland into Confederation, 1939–1949*. Toronto: University of Toronto Press, 1986.

Macpherson, Alan G., ed. *Four Centuries and the City: Perspectives on the Historical Geography of St John's*. St John's: Department of Geography, Memorial University of Newfoundland, 2005.

Macpherson, Alan G., and Joyce Brown Macpherson, eds. *The Natural Environment of Newfoundland, Past and Present*. St John's: Department of Geography, Memorial University of Newfoundland, 1981.

Mailhot, José. *The People of Sheshatshit: In the Land of the Innu*. Translated by Axel Harvey. St John's: Institute of Social and Economic Research, 1997.

Mannion, John J. ed. *The Peopling of Newfoundland: Essays in Historical Geography*. St John's: Institute of Social and Economic Research, 1977.

Marshall, Ingeborg. *A History and Ethnography of the Beothuk*. Montreal and Kingston: McGill–Queen's University Press, 1996.

Martin, Cabot. *No Fish and Our Lives: Some Survival Notes for Newfoundland*. St John's: Creative Press 1992.

Martin, Wendy. *Once Upon a Mine: The Story of Pre-Confederation Mines on the Island of Newfoundland*. Montreal: Canadian Institute of Mining and Metallurgy, 1983.

Matthews, David Ralph. *Controlling Common Property: Regulating Canada's East Coast Fishery*. Toronto: University of Toronto Press, 1993.

– *The Creation of Regional Dependency*. Toronto: University of Toronto Press, 1983.

Matthews, Keith. *Lectures on the History of Newfoundland, 1500–1830*. St John's: Breakwater, 1988.

McDonald, Ian D.H. *'To Each His Own': William Coaker and the Fishermen's Protective Union in Newfoundland Politics, 1980–1925*. Edited by J.K. Hiller. St John's: Institute of Social and Economic Research, 1987.

McGrath, Carmelita, Barbara Neis, and Marilyn Porter, eds. *Their Lives and Times: Women in Newfoundland and Labrador, a Collage*. St John's: Killick Press, 1995.

McGrath, Robin. *Salt Fish and Shmattes: The History of Jews in Newfoundland and Labrador from 1770*. St John's: Creative, 2006.

McKim, William A., ed. *The Vexed Question: Denominational Education in a Secular Age*. St John's: Breakwater, 1988.

McManus, Gary E., and Clifford H. Wood. *Atlas of Newfoundland and Labrador*. St John's: Breakwater, 1991.

Morrison, David, and Jean-Luc Pilon, eds. *Threads of Arctic Prehistory: Papers in Honour of William E. Taylor, Jr*. Ottawa: Canadian Museum of Civilization, 1994.

Moyles, R.G. *The Salvation Army in Newfoundland: Its History and Essence*. St John's: Salvation Army of Canada and Bermuda, 1997.

Murphy, Terrence, and Roberto Perin. *A Concise History of Christianity in Canada*. Toronto: Oxford University Press, 1996.

Murphy, Terrence, and Cyril J. Byrne, eds. *Religion and Identity: The Experience of Irish and Scottish Catholics in Atlantic Canada*. St John's: Jesperson, 1987.

Neary, Peter, ed. *White Tie and Decorations: Sir John and Lady Hope Simpson in Newfoundland, 1934–1936*. Toronto: University of Toronto Press, 1996.

– *Newfoundland in the North Atlantic World, 1929–1949*. Montreal and Kingston: McGill–Queen's University Press, 1988.

Newell, Dianne, and Rosemary Ommer, eds. *Fishing Places, Fishing People: Issues in Canadian Small-Scale Fisheries*. Toronto: University of Toronto Press, 1999.

Noel, S.J.R. *Politics in Newfoundland*. Toronto: University of Toronto Press, 1971.

Norcliffe, Glen. *Global Game, Local Arena: Restructuring in Corner Brook, Newfoundland*. St John's: Institute of Social and Economic Research, 2005.

O'Flaherty, Patrick. *The Rock Observed: Studies in the Literature of Newfoundland*. Toronto: St John's, 1979.

– *Old Newfoundland: A History to 1843*. St John's: Long Beach Press, 1999.

Ommer, Rosemary E. *From Outpost to Outport: A Structural Analysis of the Jersey-Gaspé Cod Fishery, 1767–1886*. Montreal and Kingston: McGill–Queen's University Press, 1991.

– ed. *The Resilient Outport: Ecology, Economy, and Society in Rural Newfoundland*. St John's: Institute of Social and Economic Research, 2002.

– ed. *Merchant Credit and Labour Strategies in Historical Perspective*. Fredericton, NB: Acadiensis Press, 1990.

Ommer, Rosemary E., with the Coasts Under Stress Research Project Team. *Coasts Under Stress: Restructuring and Social-Ecological Health*. Montreal and Kingston: McGill–Queen's University Press, 2007.

Overton, James. *Making a World of Difference: Essays on Tourism, Culture and Development in Newfoundland*. St John's: Institute of Social and Economic Research, 1996.

Paine, Robert, with Cynthia Lamson. *Ayatollahs and Turkey Trots: Political Rhetoric in the New Newfoundland: Crosbie, Jamieson and Peckford*. St John's: Institute of Social and Economic Research, 1981.

Peckford, A. Brian. *The Past in the Present: A Personal Perspective on Newfoundland's Future*. St John's: Harry Cuff Publications, 1983.

Pierson, Stuart. *Hard-Headed and Big-Hearted: Writing Newfoundland*. Edited by Stan Dragland. St John's: Pennywell Books, 2006.

Plaice, Evelyn. *The Native Game: Settler Perceptions of Indian/Settler Relations in Central Labrador*. St John's: Institute of Social and Economic Research, 1990.

Pope, Peter E. *Fish into Wine: The Newfoundland Plantation in the Seventeenth Century*. Chapel Hill and London: University of North Carolina Press, 2004.

– *The Many Landfalls of John Cabot*. Toronto: University of Toronto Press, 1997.

Pottle, Herbert L. *Newfoundland, Dawn without Light: Politics, Power and the People in the Smallwood Era*. St John's: Breakwater, 1979.

Power, Nicole G. *What Do They Call a Fisherman? Men, Gender, and Restructuring in the Newfoundland Fishery*. St John's: Institute of Economic and Social Research, 2005.

Prowse, D.W. *A History of Newfoundland* (1895). Portugal Cove–St Philip's, NL: Boulder Press, 2002.

Quinn, David B., ed. *European Approaches to North America, 1450–1640*. Aldershot, England: Ashgate, 1998.

Reeves, John. *History of the Government of the Island of Newfoundland* (1793). Wakefield, England: S.R. Publishers, 1967.

Renouf, M.A.P. *Ancient Cultures, Bountiful Seas: The Story of Port au Choix*. St John's: Historic Sites Association of Newfoundland and Labrador, 1999.

Rompkey, Bill. *The Story of Labrador*. Montreal and Kingston: McGill–Queen's University Press, 2003.

Rompkey, Ronald. *Grenfell of Labrador: A Biography*. Toronto: University of Toronto Press, 1991.

Rose, George A. *Cod: The Ecological History of the North Atlantic Fisheries*. St John's: Breakwater, 2007.

Rowe, Frederick W. *Into the Breach: Memoirs of a Newfoundland Senator*. Toronto: McGraw-Hill Ryerson, 1988.

– *The Smallwood Era*. Toronto: McGraw-Hill Ryerson, 1985

Ryan, Shannon. *The Ice Hunters: A History of Newfoundland Sealing to 1914*. St John's: Breakwater, 1994.

– *Fish Out of Water: The Newfoundland Saltfish Trade 1814–1914*. St John's: Breakwater, 1986.

Sacks, David Harris. *The Widening Gate: Bristol and the Atlantic Economy, 1450–1700*. Berkeley and Los Angeles: University of California Press, 1991.

Sager, Eric W. *Seafaring Labour: The Merchant Marine of Atlantic Canada, 1820–1914*. Montreal and Kingston: McGill–Queen's University Press, 1989.

– with Gerald E. Panting. *Maritime Capital: The Shipping Industry in Atlantic Canada, 1820–1914*. Montreal and Kingston: McGill–Queen's University Press, 1990.

Samson, Colin. *A Way of Life That Does Not Exist: Canada and the Extinguishment of the Innu*. St John's: Institute of Social and Economic Research, 2003.

Saunders, Gary L. *Doctor Olds of Twillingate: Portrait of an American Surgeon in Newfoundland*. St John's: Breakwater, 1994.

Scobie, Charles H.H., and John Webster Grant, eds. *The Contribution of Methodism to Atlantic Canada*. Montreal and Kingston: McGill–Queen's University Press, 1992.

Scott, Colin H. *Aboriginal Autonomy and Development in Northern Quebec–Labrador.* Vancouver: University of British Columbia Press, 2001.

Sinclair, Peter, ed. *A Question of Survival: The Fisheries and Newfoundland Society.* St John's: Institute of Social and Economic Research 1988.

– *State Intervention and the Newfoundland Fisheries: Essays on Fisheries Policy and Social Structure.* Aldershot, England: Ashgate, 1987.

– *From Traps to Draggers: Domestic Commodity Production in Northwest Newfoundland, 1850–1982.* St John's: Institute of Social and Economic Research 1985.

Sinclair, Peter, and Rosemary Ommer, eds. *Power and Restructuring: Shaping Coastal Society and Environment.* St John's: Institute of Social and Economic Research, 2006.

Smith, Waldo E.L. *The Navy and Its Chaplains in the Days of Sail.* Toronto: Ryerson Press, 1961.

Sparkes, R.F. *The Winds Softly Sigh.* St John's: Breakwater, 1981.

Strong, Cyril W. *My Life as a Newfoundland Union Organizer: The Memoirs of Cyril W. Strong.* Edited by Gregory S. Kealey. St John's: Committee on Canadian Labour History, 1987.

Summers, Valerie. *Regime Change in a Resource Economy: The Politics of Underdevelopment in Newfoundland since 1825.* St John's: Breakwater, 1994.

Symons, Thomas H.B., ed. *Meta Incognita: A Discourse of Discovery, Martin Frobisher's Arctic Expeditions, 1576–1578,* vols 1–2. Hull, PQ: Canadian Museum of Civilization, 1999.

Thomas, Gerald, and J.D.A. Widdowson, eds. *Studies in Newfoundland Folklore: Community and Process.* St John's: Breakwater, 1991.

Thompson, Frederic F. *The French Shore Problem in Newfoundland: An Imperial Study.* Toronto: University of Toronto Press, 1961.

Tizzard, Aubrey M. *On Sloping Ground: Reminiscences of Outport Life in Notre Dame Bay, Newfoundland.* St John's: Breakwater, 1984.

Tobin, Brian, with John L. Reynolds. *All in Good Time.* Toronto: Penguin Canada, 2002.

Tuck, James A. *Ancient People of Port au Choix: The Excavation of an Archaic Indian Cemetery in Newfoundland.* St John's: Institute of Social and Economic Research, 1976.

– *Newfoundland and Labrador Prehistory.* Toronto: Van Nostrand, 1976.

Usmiani, Renate. *Second Stage: The Alternative Theatre Movement in Canada.* Vancouver: University of British Columbia Press, 1983.

Vickers, Daniel, ed. *Marine Resources and Human Societies in the North Atlantic since 1500.* ISER Conference Paper Number 5. St John's: Institute of Social and Economic Research, 1996.

– *Farmers and Fishermen: Two Centuries of Work in Essex County, 1630–1830.* Chapel Hill and London: University of North Carolina Press, 1994.

Wadden, Marie. *Nitassinan: The Innu Struggle to Reclaim Their Homeland.* Rev. ed. Vancouver: Douglas and McIntyre, 2001.

Webber, David A. *Skinner's Fencibles: The Royal Newfoundland Regiment 1795–1802.* St John's: Newfoundland Naval and Military Museum, 1964.

Webber, Jeremy. *Reimagining Canada: Language, Culture, Community, and the Canadian Constitution*. Montreal and Kingston: McGill–Queen's University Press, 1994.

Weir, Gail. *The Miners of Wabana*. St John's: Breakwater, 1989.

Whitely, William H. *Duckworth's Newfoundland*. St John's: Cuff Publications, 1985.

Williams, Susan. *Our Lives Are at Stake: Women and the Fishery Crisis in Newfoundland and Labrador*. St John's: Institute of Social and Economic Research, 1996.

Wright, Miriam. *A Fishery for Modern Times: The State and the Industrialization of the Newfoundland Fishery, 1934–1968*. Don Mills: Oxford University Press, 2001.

Writers' Alliance of Newfoundland and Labrador. *Desperate Measures: The Great Depression in Newfoundland and Labrador*. St John's: Writers' Alliance of Newfoundland and Labrador, 1996. http://www.nald.ca/CLR/social/book4/book4.pdf (accessed 18 May 2007).

Younge, James. *The Journal of James Younge, 1647–1721, Plymouth Surgeon*. Edited by F.N.L. Poynter. London: Longmans 1963.

Articles

Armitage, Peter, and Daniel Ashini. 'Partners in the Present to Safeguard the Past: Building Cooperative Relations between the Innu and Archaeologists Regarding Archaeological Research in Innu Territory.' *Études Inuit Studies* 22, 2 (1998): 31–40.

Bailey, Mark W. 'John Reeves, Esq. Newfoundland's First Chief Justice: English Law and Politics in the Eighteenth Century.' *Newfoundland Studies* 14, 1 (1998): 28–49.

Baker, Melvin. 'Rural Electrification in Newfoundland in the 1950s and the Origins of the Newfoundland Power Commission.' *Newfoundland Studies* 6, 2 (1990): 190–209.

Baker, Melvin, and Peter Neary. 'Sir Robert Bond (1857–1927): A Biographical Sketch.' *Newfoundland Studies* 15, 1 (1999): 1–54.

Baker, Melvin, and James Overton. 'J.R. Smallwood on Liberalism in 1926.' *Newfoundland Studies* 11, 1 (1995): 75–126.

Bannister, Jerry. 'Making History: Cultural Memory in Twentieth-Century Newfoundland.' *Newfoundland Studies* 18, 2 (2002): 175–94.

– 'The Fishing Admirals in Eighteenth-Century Newfoundland.' *Newfoundland Studies* 17, 2 (2001): 166–219.

– 'Convict Transportation and the Colonial State in Newfoundland, 1789.' *Acadiensis* 27, 2 (1998): 95–123.

– 'The Campaign for Representative Government.' *Journal of the Canadian Historical Association*, new series, 5 (1994): 19–40.

Barkham, Michael M. 'French Basque "New Found Land" Entrepreneurs and the Import of Codfish and Whale Oil to Northern Spain, c. 1580 to c. 1620: The Case of Adam de Chibau, Burgess of Saint-Jean-de-Luz and Sieur de S. Julien.' *Newfoundland Studies* 10, 1 (Spring 1994): 1–43.

Bartels, Dennis A., and Olaf U. Janzen. 'Micmac Migration to Western Newfoundland.' *Canadian Journal of Native Studies* 10, 1 (1990): 71–96.

Boswell, Peter G. 'The Vanishing Report: A Political Analysis of the Newfoundland and Labrador Royal Commission on Renewing and Strengthening Our Place in Canada.' *Newfoundland Studies* 18, 2 (2002): 279–89.

Brière, Jean-François. 'The Port of Granville and the North American Fisheries in the 18th Century.' *Acadiensis* 14, 2 (1985): 93–107.

Busch, Briton Cooper. 'The Newfoundland Sealers' Strike of 1902.' *Labour/Le Travail* 14 (1984): 73–101.

Butler, Gary R. 'L'Acadie et la France se recontrent: le peuplement franco-acadien de la baie St-Georges, Terre-Neuve.' *Newfoundland Studies* 10, 2 (1994): 180–207.

Cadigan, Sean T. 'Recognizing the Commons in Coastal Forests: The Three-Mile Limit in Newfoundland, 1875–1939.' *Newfoundland and Labrador Studies* 21, 2 (2006): 209–34.

– 'Regional Politics Are Class Politics: A Newfoundland and Labrador Perspective on Regions.' *Acadiensis* 35, 2 (2006): 163–8.

– 'The Moral Economy of the Commons: Ecology and Equity in the Newfoundland Cod Fishery, 1815–1855.' *Labour/Le Travail* 43 (Spring 1999): 9–42.

– 'Missed Opportunity: The Rock at Fifty.' *Beaver* 79 (1999): 6–7.

– 'Artisans in a Merchant Town: St John's, Newfoundland, 1775–1816.' *Journal of the Canadian Historical Association/Revue de la Société historique du Canada*, new series, 4 (1993): 95–119.

– 'Merchant Capital, the State, and Labour in a British Colony: Servant–Master Relations and Capital Accumulation in Newfoundland's Northeast-Coast Fishery, 1775–1799.' *Journal of the Canadian Historical Association/Revue de la Société historique du Canada*, new series, 2 (1991): 17–42.

– 'Battle Harbour in Transition: Merchants, Fishermen, and the State in the Struggle for Relief in a Labrador Fishing Community during the 1930s.' *Labour/Le Travail* 26 (Fall 1990): 125–50.

Chisholm, Jessie. 'Organizing on the Waterfront: The St John's Longshoremen's Protective Union (LSPU), 1890–1914.' *Labour/Le Travail* 26 (1990): 37–59.

Churchill, Jason. 'Pragmatic Federalism: The Politics Behind the 1969 Churchill Falls Contract.' *Newfoundland Studies* 15, 2 (1999): 215–46.

Close, David. 'Unconventional Militance: Union Organized Fish Sales in Newfoundland.' *Journal of Canadian Studies* 17, 2 (1982): 3–11.

Crawley, Ron. 'Off to Sydney: Newfoundlanders Emigrate to Industrial Cape Breton, 1890–1914.' *Acadiensis* 17, 2 (1988): 27–51.

Dunn, Christopher. 'The Quest for Accountability in Newfoundland and Labrador.' *Canadian Public Administration* 47, 2 (2004): 184–206.

English, Christopher. 'The Development of the Newfoundland Legal System to 1815.' *Acadiensis* 20 (Autumn, 1990): 91–107.

Erwin, John C., et al. 'Form and Function of Projectile Points and the Trajectory of Newfoundland Prehistory.' *Canadian Journal of Archaeology* 29 (2005): 46–67.

Fitzgerald, John Edward. 'Archbishop E.P. Roche, J.R. Smallwood, and Denominational Rights in Newfoundland Education, 1948.' *CCHA Historical Studies* 65 (1999): 28–49.

4.

34 Bibliography

- 'Michael Anthony Fleming and Ultramontanism in Irish-Newfoundland Catholicism, 1829–1850.' *CCHA Historical Studies* 64 (1998): 27–44.
- '"The True Father of Confederation" Archbishop E.P. Roche, Term 17, and Newfoundland's Union with Canada.' *Newfoundland Studies* 14, 2 (1998): 188–219.

Forestell, Nancy M. 'Times Were Hard: The Pattern of Women's Paid Labour in St John's between the Two World Wars.' *Labour/Le Travail* 24 (1989): 147–66.

Gilbert, William. '"Divers Places": The Beothuk Indians and John Guy's Voyage into Trinity Bay in 1612.' *Newfoundland Studies* 6, 2 (1990): 147–67.

Goertz, Richard. 'João Alvares Fagundes, Capitão de Terra Nova [1521].' *Canadian Ethnic Studies* 33, 2 (1991): 117–28.

Goudie, Nina Jane. 'Down North on the Labrador Circuit: The Court of Civil Jurisdiction 1826 to 1833.' Silk Robes and Sou-westers: History of the Law and the Courts, Newfoundland and Labrador Heritage website. http://www.heritage.nf.ca/lawfoundation/essay2/default.html (accessed 22 May 2007).

Harding, Robert J. 'Glorious Tragedy: Newfoundland's Cultural Memory of the Attack at Beaumont Hamel, 1916–1925.' *Newfoundland and Labrador Studies* 21, 1 (2006): 3–40.

Harter, John-Henry. 'Environmental Justice for Whom? Class, New Social Movements, and the Environment: A Case Study of Greenpeace Canada, 1971–2000.' *Labour/Le Travail* 54 (2004): 83–119.

Hewitt, Keith W. 'The Newfoundland Fishery and State Intervention in the Nineteenth Century: The Fisheries Commission, 1888–1893.' *Newfoundland Studies* 9, 1 (1993): 58–80.

High, Steven. 'Working for Uncle Sam: The "Comings" and "Goings" of Newfoundland Base Construction Labour, 1940–1945.' *Acadiensis* 32, 2 (2003): 84–107.

- 'From Outport to Outport Base: The American Occupation of Stephenville, 1940–1945.' *Newfoundland Studies* 18, 1 (2002): 84–113.

Hiller, James K. 'Robert Bond and the Pink, White and Green: Newfoundland Nationalism in Perspective.' *Acadiensis* 36, 2 (2007): 113–33.

- 'The Newfoundland Fisheries Issue in Anglo-French Treaties, 1713–1904.' *Journal of Imperial and Commonwealth History* 24, 1 (1996): 1–23.

- 'The 1904 Anglo-French Newfoundland Fisheries Convention: Another Look.' *Acadiensis* 25, 1 (1995): 82–98.

- 'Utrecht Revisited: The Origins of French Fishing Rights in Newfoundland Waters.' *Newfoundland Studies* 7, 1 (1991): 23–39.

- 'The Politics of Newsprint: The Newfoundland Pulp and Paper Industry, 1915–1939.' *Acadiensis* 19, 2 (1990): 3–39.

- 'The Career of F. Gordon Bradley.' *Newfoundland Studies* 4, 1 (1988): 163–80.

- 'The Origins of the Pulp and Paper Industry in Newfoundland.' *Acadiensis* 11, 2 (1982): 42–68.

Hollett, Calvin. 'Evangelicals vs. Tractarians, Resistance to Bishop Field at Harbour Buffett, Placentia Bay, 1849–1854.' *Newfoundland Studies* 18, 2 (2002): 245–78.

Holly, Donald H. 'The Beothuk on the Eve of Their Extinction.' *Arctic Anthropology* 37, 1 (2000): 79–95.

- 'Environment, History, and Agency in Storage Adaptation: On the Beothuk in the 18th Century.' *Canadian Journal of Archaeology* 22, 1 (1998): 101–22.

Hood, Bryan C. 'The Maritime Archaic Indians of Labrador: Investigating Prehistorical Social Organization.' *Newfoundland Studies* 9, 2 (1993): 163–84.

Hood, Bryan C., and Gary Baikie. 'Mineral Resource Development, Archaeology and Aboriginal Rights in Northern Labrador.' *Études Inuit Studies* 22, 2 (1998): 7–29.

House, J.D. 'Change from Within the Corridors of Power: A Reflective Essay of a Sociologist in Government.' *Canadian Journal of Sociology* 30, 4 (2005): 471–90.

- 'The New Regional Development: Is Rural Development a Viable Option for Newfoundland and Labrador?' *Newfoundland Studies* 17, 1 (2001): 11–32.

- 'The Don Quixote of Canadian Politics? Power in and Power over Newfoundland Society.' *Canadian Journal of Sociology* 10, 2 (1985): 171–88.

- 'Premier Peckford, Petroleum Policy, and Popular Politics in Newfoundland and Labrador.' *Journal of Canadian Studies* 17, 2 (1982): 12–31.

Janzen, Olaf. '"They are not such great Rogues as some of their Neighbours": A Scottish Supercargo in the Newfoundland Fish Trade, 1726.' *Newfoundland Studies* 17, 2 (2001): 294–309.

- 'A Scottish Sack Ship in the Newfoundland Trade 1726–27.' *Scottish Economic and Social History* 18, 1 (1998): 1–18.

- 'The Illicit Trade in English Cod into Spain, 1739–1748.' *International Journal of Maritime History* 8, 1 (1996): 1–22.

- '"Une Grande Liaison": French Fishermen from Île Royale on the Coast of Southwestern Newfoundland, 1714–1766 – A Preliminary Survey.' *Newfoundland Studies* 3, 2 (1987): 183–200.

- 'The Royal Navy and the Defence of Newfoundland during the American Revolution.' *Acadiensis* 14, 1 (1984): 28–48.

Johnson, Trudi. '"A Matter of Custom and Convenience": Marriage Law in Nineteenth-Century Newfoundland.' *Newfoundland Studies* 19, 2 (2003): 282–96.

Jones, F. 'Religion, Education and Politics in Newfoundland, 1836–1875.' *Journal of the Canadian Church Historical Society* 12 (1970): 64–76.

Kealey, G.S. '1919: The Canadian Labour Revolt.' *Labour/Le Travail* 13 (1984): 11–44.

Lackenbauer, P. Whitney. 'War, Memory, and the Newfoundland Regiment at Gallipoli.' *Newfoundland Studies* 15, 2 (1999): 176–214.

Lahey, Raymond J. 'The Role of Religion in Lord Baltimore's Colonial Enterprise' *Avalon Chronicles* 3 (1998): 19–48.

Landry, Nicolas. '"Qu'il serra fait droit à qui il appartiendra": la société de Lasson-Daccarrette à Plaisaance, 1700–1715.' *Newfoundland Studies* 17, 2 (2001): 220–56.

Lawton, William. 'Development, Dependency and the Role of Government: An Analysis of Newfoundland's Political Discourse in 1990.' *British Journal of Canadian Studies* 11, 1 (1996): 24–51.

Lewis, Jane, and Mark Shrimpton. 'Policymaking in Newfoundland during the 1940s: The Case of the St John's Housing Corporation.' *Canadian Historical Association* 65, 2 (1984): 209–38.

Little, Linda. 'Collective Action in Outport Newfoundland: A Case Study from the 1830s.' *Labour/Le Travail* 26 (Fall 1990): 7–35.

Loring, Stephen. 'The Archaeology of Eskimo Hutte (IKDB-2): Inuit Sovereignty in the Torngat.' *Études Inuit Studies* 22, 2 (1998): 53–76.

Mackenzie, David. 'The Terms of Union in Historical Perspective.' *Newfoundland Studies* 14, 2 (1998): 220–37.

MacKinnon, Robert. 'Farming the Rock: The Evolution of Commercial Agriculture around St John's, Newfoundland, to 1945.' *Acadiensis* 20, 2 (Spring 1991): 32–61.

MacLean, Laurie. 'Beothuk Iron – Evidence for European Trade?' *Newfoundland Studies* 6, 2 (1990): 168–76.

Mannion, John. 'Irish Migration and Settlement in Newfoundland: The Formative Phase, 1697–1732.' *Newfoundland Studies* 17, 2 (2001): 257–93.

– '"... Notoriously disaffected to the Government ...": British Allegations of Irish Disloyalty in Eighteenth-Century Newfoundland.' *Newfoundland Studies* 16, 1 (2000): 1–29.

– 'Waterford and the South of England: Spatial Patterns in Shipping Commerce, 1766–1777.' *International Journal of Maritime History* 6, 2 (1994): 115–31.

– 'Irish Merchants Abroad: The Newfoundland Experience, 1750–1850.' *Newfoundland Studies* 2, 2 (1986): 127–90.

Martijn, Charles A. 'Early Mi'kmaq Presence in Southern Newfoundland: An Ethno-historical Perspective, c. 1500–1763.' *Newfoundland Studies* 19, 1 (2003): 44–102.

– 'Review Article: *A History and Ethnography of the Beothuk* by Ingeborg Marshall.' *Newfoundland Studies* 12, 2 (1996): 105–31.

McAleese, Kevin. 'The Reinternment of Thule Inuit Burials and Associated Arte-facts: IDRC-14 Rose Island, Saglek Bay, Labrador.' *Études Inuit Studies* 22, 2 (1998): 41–52.

McCann, Philip. 'Culture, State Formation and the Invention of Tradition: New-foundland, 1832–1855.' *Journal of Canadian Studies* 23 (1988): 86–103.

– 'The Educational Policy of the Commission of Government.' *Newfoundland Studies* 3, 2 (1987): 201–16.

McDonald, Terry. '"I Had Better Be without Him": Rivalry, Deception and Social Status within the Poole–Newfoundland Trade.' *Newfoundland Studies* 16, 2 (2000): 135–50.

McInnis, Peter. '"All Solid along the Line": The Reid Newfoundland Strike of 1918.' *Labour/Le Travail* 26 (1990): 61–84.

McNally, Vincent J. 'A Question of Class? Relations between Bishops and Lay Lead-ers in Ireland and Newfoundland 1783–1807.' *CCHA, Historical Studies* 64 (1998): 71–87.

Moulton, E.C. 'Constitutional Crisis and Civil Strife in Newfoundland, February to November 1861.' *Canadian Historical Review* 48, 3 (1967): 251–72.

Neary, Peter. '"A Grave Problem Which Needs Immediate Attention': An American Report on Venereal Disease and Other Health Problems in Newfoundland, 1942.' *Newfoundland Studies* 15, 1 (1999): 79–103.

– 'The Diplomatic Background to the Canada–Newfoundland Goose Bay Agree-ment of October 10, 1944.' *Newfoundland Studies* 2, 1 (1986): 39–62.

- 'Great Britain and the Future of Newfoundland, 1939–45.' *Newfoundland Studies* 1, 1 (1985): 29–56.
- 'The Bradley Report on Logging Operations in Newfoundland, 1934: A Suppressed Document.' *Labour/Le Travail* 16 (1985): 193–232.
Neis, Barbara. 'From "Shipped Girls" to "Brides of the State": The Transition from Familial to Social Patriarchy in the Newfoundland Fishing Industry.' *Canadian Journal of Regional Science* 16, 2 (1993): 185–202.
- 'Fishers' Ecological Knowledge and Stock Assessment in Newfoundland.' *Newfoundland Studies* 8, 2 (1992): 155–78.
Nowak, Elke. 'The "Eskimo Language" of Labrador: Moravian Missionaries and the Description of Labrador Inuttut, 1733–1891.' *Études Inuit Studies* 23, 1–2 (1999): 173–97.
O'Flaherty, Patrick . 'The Seeds of Reform: Newfoundland, 1800–18.' *Journal of Canadian Studies* 23 (Fall 1988): 39–59.
O'Neill, Brian. 'Mobil and the Canadian Offshore: A Study of Context and Purpose.' *Newfoundland Studies* 3, 1 (1987): 71–104.
Ommer, Rosemary E. 'One Hundred Years of Fishery Crises in Newfoundland.' *Acadiensis* 23, 2 (Spring 1994): 5–20.
- 'Merchant Credit and the Informal Economy: Newfoundland, 1919–1929.' *Historical Papers, 1989*. Quebec City: Canadian Historical Association, 167–89.
- 'What's Wrong with Canadian Fish?' *Journal of Canadian Studies* 20, 2 (1985): 122–42.
- 'The Scots in Newfoundland.' *Newfoundland Quarterly* 77, 4 (1982): 23–31.
Overton, James. 'Academic Populists, the Informal Economy and Those Benevolent Merchants: Politics and Income Security Reform in Newfoundland.' *Journal of Peasant Studies* 28, 1 (2000): 1–54.
- 'Sparking a Cultural Revolution: Joey Smallwood, Farley Mowat, Harold Horwood and Newfoundland's Cultural Renaissance.' *Newfoundland Studies* 16, 2 (2000): 166–204.
- 'Brown Flour and Beriberi: The Politics of Dietary and Health Reform in Newfoundland in the First Half of the Twentieth Century,' *Newfoundland Studies* 14, 1 (1998): 1–27.
- 'Moral Education of the Poor: Adult Education and Land Settlement Schemes in Newfoundland in the 1930s.' *Newfoundland Studies* 11, 2 (1995): 250–83.
- 'Economic Crisis and the End of Democracy: Politics in Newfoundland during the Great Depression.' *Labour/Le Travail* 26 (1990): 85–124.
- 'A Newfoundland Culture?' *Journal of Canadian Studies* 23, 1–2 (1988): 5–22.
- 'A Critical Examination of the Establishment of National Parks and Tourism in Underdeveloped Areas: Gros Morne National Park in Newfoundland.' *Antipode* 11, 2 (1979): 34–47.
Paine, Robert. 'The Mastery of Smallwood and Interlocutory Rhetoric.' *Newfoundland Studies* 2, 2 (1986): 191–212.
Pastore, Ralph. 'The Collapse of the Beothuk World.' *Acadiensis* 19, 1 (1989): 52–71.
Pocius, Gerald L. 'The Mummers Song in Newfoundland: Intellectuals, Revivalists, and Cultural Nativism.' *Newfoundland Studies* 4, 1 (1988): 57–86.

Pope, Peter. 'Outport Economics: Culture and Agriculture in Later Seventeenth-Century Newfoundland.' *Newfoundland Studies* 19, 1 (2003): 153–86.
– 'Baltimore vs Kirke: Newfoundland Evidence in an Interregnum Lawsuit.' *Avalon Chronicles*, 3 (1998): 63–98.
– 'Six Letters from the Early Colony of Avalon.' *Avalon Chronicles*, 1 (1996): 1–20.
– 'The Practice of Portage in the Early Modern North Atlantic: Introduction to an Issue in Maritime Historical Anthropology.' *Journal of the Canadian Historical Association*, new series, 6 (1995): 19–41.
– 'Scavengers and Caretakers: Beothuk/European Settlement Dynamics in Seventeenth Century Newfoundland.' *Newfoundland Studies* 9, 2 (Fall 1993): 279–93.
Porter, Marilyn. '"She Was Skipper of the Shore Crew": Notes on the Sexual Division of Labour in Newfoundland.' *Labour/Le Travail* 15 (1985): 105–23.
Press, Harold. 'Davis Inlet in Crisis: Will the Lessons Ever Be Learned?' *Canadian Journal of Native Studies* 15, 2 (1995): 187–209.
Ransom, Bernard. 'Canada's "Newfyjohn" Tenancy: The Royal Canadian Navy in St John's, 1941–1945.' *Acadiensis* 23, 2 (1994): 45–71.
Reece, Bob. '"Such a Banditti": Irish Convicts in Newfoundland, 1789. Part I.' *Newfoundland Studies* 13, 1 (1997): 1–29.
– '"Such a Banditti": Irish Convicts in Newfoundland, 1789. Part II.' *Newfoundland Studies* 13, 2 (1997): 127–41.
Reeves, William G. 'Alexander's Conundrum Reconsidered: The American Dimension in Newfoundland Resource Development, 1898–1910.' *Newfoundland Studies* 5, 1 (1989): 1–37.
– 'Aping the "American Type": The Politics of Development in Newfoundland, 1900–1908.' *Newfoundland Studies* 10, 1 (1994): 44–72.
Rennie, Richard. 'The Historical Origins of an Industrial Disaster: Occupational Health and Labour Relations at the Fluorspar Mines, St Lawrence, Newfoundland, 1933–1945.' *Labour/Le Travail* 55 (Spring 2005): 107–42.
Renouf, M.A. 'A Review of Palaeoeskimo Dwelling Structures in Newfoundland and Labrador.' *Études Inuit Studies* 27, 1–2 (2003): 375–416.
– 'Palaeoeskimo Seal Hunters at Port au Choix, Northwestern Newfoundland.' *Newfoundland Studies* 9, 2 (1993): 185–212.
Renouf, M.A.P. and Maribeth S. Murray. 'Two Winter Dwellings at Phillip's Garden, a Dorset Site in Northwest Newfoundland.' *Arctic Anthropology* 36, 1–2 (1999): 118–32.
Rothney, Gordon O. 'The Case of Bayne and Brymer: An Incident in the Early History of Labrador.' *Canadian Historical Review* 15, 3 (September 1934): 264–75.
Ruffman, Alan and Violet Hann. 'The Newfoundland Tsunami of November 18, 1929: An Examination of the Twenty-Eight Deaths of the "South Coast Disaster."' *Newfoundland and Labrador Studies* 21, 1 (2006): 97–148.
Ryan, James J. 'Economic Development and Innu Settlement: The Establishment of Sheshatshit.' *Canadian Journal of Native Studies* 8, 1 (1988): 1–25.
Sanger, C.W. 'The Dundee–St John's Connection: Nineteenth Century Interlinkages between Scottish Arctic Whaling and the Newfoundland Seal Fishery.' *Newfoundland Studies* 4, 1 (1988): 1–26.

Sharpe, Christopher A. 'The "Race of Honour": An Analysis of Enlistments and Casualties in the Armed Forces of Newfoundland: 1914–1918.' *Newfoundland Studies* 4, 1 (1988): 27–56.

Sinclair, Peter R. 'Industrialization and Rural Development: Contrasting Labour Markets and Perceptions of the Future on the Bonavista Peninsula and Isthmus of Avalon, Newfoundland.' *Newfoundland Studies* 15, 1 (1999): 55–78.

Sinclair, Peter R., and Lawrence F. Felt. 'Coming Back: Return Migration to Newfoundland's Great Northern Peninsula.' *Newfoundland Studies* 9, 1 (1993): 1–25.

Smith, Philip E.L. 'Beothuks and Methodists.' *Acadiensis* 16, 1 (1996): 118–35.

Smrz, Jirí. 'Cabot 400: The 1897 St John's Celebrations.' *Newfoundland Studies* 12, 1 (1996): 16–31.

Snell, James G. 'The Newfoundland Old Age Pension Programme, 1911–1949.' *Acadiensis* 23, 1 (1993): 86–94.

Sutherland, Dufferin. 'Newfoundland Loggers Respond to the Great Depression.' *Labour/Le Travail* 29 (1992): 83–101.

Sweeny, Robert C. H. 'What Difference Does a Mode Make? A Comparison of Two Seventeenth-Century Colonies: Canada and Newfoundland.' *The William and Mary Quarterly* (April 2006). http://www.historycooperative.org/journals/wm/63.2/sweeny.html (accessed 7 May 2006).

– with David Bradley and Robert Hong. 'Movement, Options and Costs: Indexes as Historical Evidence, a Newfoundland Example.' *Acadiensis* 22, 1 (Autumn 1992): 111–21.

Tanner, Adrian. 'The Aboriginal Peoples of Newfoundland and Labrador and Confederation.' *Newfoundland Studies* 14, 2 (1998): 238–52.

– 'Loin des Yeux, Loin du Coeur: Terre-Neuve et l'Administration des Innus du Labrador.' *Recherches Amerindiennes au Quebec* 27, 1 (1997): 19–31.

Taylor, J. Garth. 'The Two Worlds of Mikak.' Part One. *The Beaver* 314, 3 (1983): 4–13.

Thornton, Patricia A. 'Newfoundland's Frontier Demographic Experience: The World We Have Not Lost.' *Newfoundland Studies* 1, 2 (1985): 141–62.

Thorpe, Frederick J. 'The Debating Talents of the First Governor of Saint-Pierre and Miquelon, François-Gabriel d'Angeac, 1764–1769.' *Newfoundland Studies* 18, 1 (2002): 61–83.

Tomblin, Stephen. 'Newfoundland and Labrador at the Crossroads: Reform or Lack of Reform in a New Era?' *Journal of Canadian Studies* 37, 1 (2002): 89–108.

Webb, Jeff A. 'Constructing Community and Consumers: Joseph R. Smallwood's *Barrelman* Radio Programme.' *Journal of the Canadian Historical Association*, new series, 8 (1997): 239–58.

– 'The Origins of Public Broadcasting: The Commission of Government and the Creation of the Broadcasting Corporation of Newfoundland.' *Acadiensis* 24, 1 (1994): 88–106.

– 'Leaving the State of Nature: A Locke-Inspired Political Community in St John's, Newfoundland, 1723.' *Acadiensis* 21, 1 (1991): 156–65.

– 'The Responsible Government League and the Confederation campaigns of 1948.' *Newfoundland Studies* 5, 2 (1989): 203–20.

Wheaton, Carla. '"The Trade in the Place Is in a Very Critical State": R.G. Dun and

Company and the St John's Business Community, 1855–1874.' *Acadiensis* 29, 2 (2000): 120–37.

White, Neil. 'Creating Community: Industrial Paternalism and Town Planning in Corner Brook, Newfoundland, 1923–1955.' *Urban History Review* 32, 2 (2004): 45–58.

Whiteley, W.H. 'Newfoundland, Quebec, and the Administration of the Coast of Labrador, 1774–1783.' *Acadiensis* 6, 1 (Autumn 1976): 92–112.

– 'Governor Hugh Palliser and the Newfoundland and Labrador Fishery, 1764–1768.' *Canadian Historical Review* 50, 2 (June 1969): 141–52.

– 'The Establishment of the Moravian Mission in Labrador and British Policy, 1763–83.' *Canadian Historical Review* 45, 1 (March 1964): 29–50.

Wright, Miriam. 'Young Men and Technology: Government Attempts to Create a "Modern" Fisheries Workforce in Newfoundland, 1949–1970.' *Labour/Le Travail* 42 (Fall 1998): 143–59.

– 'Fishing in the Cold War: Canada, Newfoundland and the International Politics of the Twelve-Mile Fishing Limit, 1958–1969.' *Journal of the Canadian Historical Association*, new series, 8 (1997): 239–58.

Theses, Dissertations, Unpublished Papers, Recordings

Baker, Melvin. 'Absentee Landlordism and Municipal Government in Nineteenth Century St John's.' Paper presented to the Canadian Historical Association, Guelph, June 1984.

– 'The Government of St John's, Newfoundland 1800–1921.' PhD thesis, University of Western Ontario, 1980.

Bannister, Jerry. 'The Social Management of English Commerce: Benjamin Lester's Empire in Trinity and Poole, 1755–1775.' Paper presented to the Sixth Annual Conference of the Omohundro Institute of Early American History and Culture, University of Toronto, June 2000.

Berends, Kurt O. 'A Divided Harvest: Alice Belle Garrigus, Joel Adams Wright, and Early New England Pentecostalism.' Master of Theology, Wheaton College Graduate School, 1993.

Botting, Ingrid. '"Getting a Grand Falls Job": Migration, Labour Markets, and Paid Domestic Work in the Pulp and Paper Mill Town of Grand Falls, Newfoundland, 1905–1939.' PhD thesis, Memorial University of Newfoundland, 2000.

Budden, Geoff. 'The Role of the Newfoundland Natives Society in the Political Crisis of 1840–1842.' BA honours dissertation, Memorial University of Newfoundland, 1983.

Byrne, Cyril J. 'Ireland and Newfoundland: The United Irish Rising of 1798 and the Fencible's Mutiny in St John's, 1799.' Lecture presented to the Newfoundland Historical Society, St John's, 9 November 1977.

Cadigan, Sean T. 'A Nova Scotian in Newfoundland: Harry Crowe, Progressive Capitalism, and Common Property Rights in the Coastal Communities of White Bay, 1923–28.' St John's, Memorial University of Newfoundland, 2005.

– 'Community Regulation of Coastal Forests in Newfoundland, 1875–1945.' Paper presented to the Atlantic Canada Studies Conference 13, Halifax, May 2000.

– 'A Smoke in the Woods: The Moral Economy of Forest Fires in Outport Newfoundland, 1875–1946.' Paper presented to the Canadian Historical Association, Sherbrooke, June 1999.

– '"The sea was common, and every man had a right to fish in it": Failed Proposals for Fisheries Management and Conservation in Newfoundland, 1855–1880.' Occasional Paper, Eco-Research Project, Memorial University of Newfoundland, 1996.

– 'A Shift in Economic Culture: The Impact of Enclave Industrialization on Newfoundland, 1855–1880.' Paper presented to the Atlantic Canada Studies Conference, Moncton, 1996.

– 'A "Chilling Neglect": The British Empire and Colonial Policy on the Newfoundland Bank Fishery, 1815–1855.' Paper presented to the Canadian Historical Association Annual Meeting, Montreal, 1995.

– 'The Role of the Fishing Ships' Rooms Controversy in the Rise of a Local Bourgeoisie: St John's, Newfoundland, 1775–1812.' Paper presented to the Atlantic Canada Studies Conference, St John's, Newfoundland, May 1992.

Chang, Margaret A. 'Newfoundland in Transition: The Newfoundland Trade and Robert Newman and Company 1780–1805.' MA thesis, Memorial University of Newfoundland, 1974.

Cook, Patricia Margaret Anne de Gruchy. 'National Cultures and Popular Theatre: Four Collective Companies in Quebec and Newfoundland.' MA thesis, Carleton University, 1986.

Cuff, Robert H. 'Quill and Hammer: Class and Labour Activism in Newfoundland and Nova Scotia, 1919–1925.' BA dissertation, Memorial University of Newfoundland, 1980.

Devine, Michael L. 'Necessary Evils: Strangers, Outsiders and Outports in Newfoundland Drama.' PhD thesis, University of Toronto, 2007.

Dunton, Jefferson D. 'The Origins and Growth of the Salvation Army in Newfoundland, 1885–1901.' MA thesis, Memorial University of Newfoundland, 1996.

English, Christopher. 'Intervention by Invitation: The ILO in Canada 1983–1985.' St John's, 1989.

Facey-Crowther, David R. 'War and Remembrance: Newfoundland and the Great War.' Paper on deposit at the Center for Newfoundland Studies Memorial University of Newfoundland, 1996.

Ferre, Sandrine. 'Once Upon a Train: A Study of the Railway in Newfoundland: Reality of the Past, Legend of the Present.' Mémoire pour la Maîtrise de Lettres, l'Université de l'Ouest, 1992.

Fitzgerald, John Edward. 'Conflict and Culture in Irish-Newfoundland Roman Catholicism, 1829–1850.' PhD thesis, University of Ottawa, 1997.

Fowler, Adrian. 'Distinct Society: Cultural Identity in Twentieth-Century Newfoundland Literature.' PhD thesis, University of Ottawa, 2002.

Glerum-Laurentius, Dickey. 'A History of Dutch Activity in the Newfoundland Fish

Trade from about 1590 till 1680.' MA thesis, Memorial University of Newfoundland, 1960.

Great Big Sea. *Great Big Sea*. CD 10088. Compact disc. St John's, NL: NRA Produc-
tions, 1993.

Handcock, W. Gordon. 'The Origin and Development of Trinity up to 1900.' Ms.,
Memorial University of Newfoundland, 1981 [copy deposited at the Centre for
Newfoundland Studies Queen Elizabeth II Library, Memorial University of New-
foundland].

Hardin, Janice M. 'The Rescaling of the Innu.' MA thesis, West Virginia University,
2003.

Hattie-Longmire, Brenda. '"Sit down, brother!": Alice B. Garrigus and the Pentecostal Assemblies of Newfoundland. MA thesis, Mount Saint Vincent University,
2001.

Haywood, Ruth. '"Delinquent, Disorderly and Diseased Females": Regulating Sexu-
ality in Second World War St John's, Newfoundland.' MA thesis, Memorial University of Newfoundland, 2002.

Hiller, J.K. 'A History of Newfoundland, 1874–1901.' PhD thesis, University of Cam-
bridge, 1971.

Hollett, Calvin. 'Resistance to Bishop Edward Feild in Newfoundland 1845–1857,
Harbour Buffett: A Case Study.' MA thesis, Memorial University of Newfoundland, 2002.

Hong, Robert G. '"An Agency for the Common Weal": The Newfoundland Board of
Trade, 1909–1915.' MA thesis, Memorial University of Newfoundland, 1998.

– '"To take action without delay": Newfoundland's Chinese Immigration Act of
1906.' BA honours dissertation, Memorial University of Newfoundland, 1987.

Jelsma, Johan. 'A Bed of Ochre: Mortuary Practices and Social Structure of a Maritime Archaic Indian Society at Port au Choix, Newfoundland.' PhD thesis, Rijksu-
niversiteit Groningen, 2000.

Joy, John L. 'The Growth and Development of Trades and Manufacturing in St
John's, 1870–1914.' MA thesis, Memorial University of Newfoundland, 1977.

Keough, Brian M. 'Huckster Shop to Superette: An Ethno-historical Analysis of the
Development of the Outport Shop on the Sotuhern Avalon Peninsula (Nfld.).' MA
thesis, Memorial University of Newfoundland, 1975.

Knowling, William Ronald. '"Ignorant, Dirty, and Poor": The Perception of Tuberculosis in Newfoundland, 1908–1912.' MA thesis, Memorial University of Newfoundland, 1996.

Landry, Deborah D. 'Re/locating the Mushuau Innu of Utshimassits in the Canadian Press 1993–2002.' MA thesis, Acadian University, 2003.

Loring, Stephen G. 'Princes and Princesses of Ragged Fame: Innu Archaeology and
Ethnohistory in Labrador.' PhD thesis, University of Massachusetts, 1992.

Madden, Marcie M. 'A Late Archaic Sequence in Southern Labrador.' MA thesis,
Memorial University of Newfoundland, 1976.

Martin, Chris. 'Absolute Disloyalty? Perceptions of Recruitment in Outport
Newfoundland, 1914–1918.' Paper prepared for HIST 6075, Advanced Studies

in Labour and Working-Class History.' Memorial University of Newfoundland, 2007.

Matthews, Keith. 'History of the West of England–Newfoundland Fishery.' PhD thesis, Oxford University, 1968.

McEwen, Alexander Campbell. 'Newfoundland Law of Real Property: The Origin and Development of Land Ownership.' PhD thesis, University of London, 1978.

Morgan, Laura Bonnie Colleen. 'Class and Congregation: Social Relations in Two St John's, Newfoundland, Anglican Parishes, 1877–1909.' MA thesis, Memorial University of Newfoundland, 1996.

Morrison, Colleen. 'Female Workforce Participation in a Milltown: The Effect of the Paper Mill on Female Labour Force Opportunities.' Paper prepared for HIST 6075, Advanced Studies in Labour and Working-Class History.' Memorial University of Newfoundland, 2003.

Narvaez, Peter. 'Protest Songs of a Labour Union on Strike.' PhD thesis, Indiana University, 1986.

Neis, Barbara. 'A Sociological Analysis of the Factors Responsible for the Regional Distribution of the Fishermen's Protective Union of Newfoundland.' MA thesis, Memorial University of Newfoundland, 1980.

Nishman, Rob. 'Through the Portlights of the Ocean Ranger: Federalism, Energy, and the American Development of the Canadian Eastern Offshore, 1955–1985.' MA thesis, Queen's University, 1991.

O'Brien, Lawrence J. 'The Trade Fields of a Newfoundland Outport Mercantile Firm in 1951.' MA thesis, Memorial University of Newfoundland, 1987.

O'Brien, Patricia R. 'The Newfoundland Patriotic Association: The Administration of the War Effort, 1914–1918.' MA thesis, Memorial University of Newfoundland, 1981.

Parsons, Jacob. 'The Origins and Growth of Newfoundland Methodism, 1765–1855.' MA thesis, Memorial University of Newfoundland, 1964.

Pinsent, William P. 'The Institutionalization of Experiential Religion: A Study of Newfoundland Pentecostalism.' MA thesis, Memorial University of Newfoundland, 1998.

Reeves, W.G. 'The Fortune Bay Dispute: Newfoundland's Place in Imperial Treaty Relations under the Washington Treaty, 1871–1885.' MA thesis, Memorial University of Newfoundland, 1971.

Rennie, Richard Charles. '"And there's nothing goes wrong": Industry, Labour, and Health and Safety at the Fluospar Mines, St Lawrence, Newfoundland, 1933–1978.' PhD thesis, Memorial University of Newfoundland, 2001.

Roberts, Joanne, and Nancy Robbins. 'Gathering Voices: Women of Fishing Communities Speak.' St John's: Women's Enterprise Bureau, 1995.

Robinson, Mary Angela. 'Eighteenth-Century Newfoundland Methodism as a Revitalization Movement.' MA thesis, Memorial University of Newfoundland, 1996.

Schrank, William E. 'Bureaucracy, Politics, Economics: The Pathology of Fisheries, Newfoundland 1976–1981.' Paper prepared for delivery at the IIFET 2000 Conference, Cornwallis, Oregon, July 2000.

Sutherland, Duff. '"We are only loggers": Loggers and the Struggle for Development in Newfoundland, 1929–1959.' PhD thesis, Simon Fraser University, 1995.

Tuck, Marilyn. 'The Newfoundland Ranger Force, 1935–1950.' MA thesis, Memorial University of Newfoundland, 1983.

'UN Body Says Danny Williams' Government Must Act.' National Union of Public and General Employees website. http://www.nupge.ca/news_2005/n28jn05.htm (accessed 27 June 2007).

Williams, Brian G. 'An Ethnohistorical Study of Fisher–Merchant Relationships in Burin, Newfoundland.' MA thesis, Memorial University of Newfoundland, 1994.

Winsor, Fred. 'The Newfoundland Bank Fishery: Government Policies and the Struggle to Improve Bank Fishing Crews' Working, Health, and Safety Conditions, 1876–1920.' PhD thesis, Memorial University of Newfoundland, 1996.

Winsor, Naboth. 'Methodism in Newfoundland, 1855–1884.' MA thesis, Memorial University of Newfoundland, 1970.

Index

Acadians, 65, 134, 239
Act for the Defence of Newfoundland (1939), 224
Act to Facilitate the Economic Development of Special Areas of Newfoundland (1940), 221
Acts of Trade and Navigation, 50
Admiralty Court, 82
Advisory Committee to the Cabinet on Demobilization and Economic Readjustment, 229
Advocate Mines, 273
A.E. Reed pulp company, 164
Agricultural and Rural Development Act, 246
agriculture, 7, 27, 46, 51, 64, 78, 80, 92, 100–2, 104–8, 118–23, 127, 128, 129, 131, 133, 140, 142, 147, 148, 162, 212, 213, 289, 290
Alberta, 268, 275
Alderdice, Frederick, 207, 208, 221
Aliens Act (1906), 166
Allardyce, Elsie, 200
amalgamated legislature, 117
American Embargo Act, 84
American Revolution, 71–3, 75, 77, 97
American Smelting and Refining Company, 257

Amulree, Lord, 207
Amulree Commission, 208, 209, 211, 222, 236
Anglo-American Convention of 1818, 90, 140, 173
Anglo-American tribunal, 1874–77, 137
Anglo-French Commission, 127
Anglo-Newfoundland Development Company, 164, 196, 197, 199, 210, 211, 215, 216, 223, 247
Anspach, Lewis, 88
anti–seal hunt protests, 264–5
Aquafort, 46
Arctic Basin, 5
Argentia, 225, 232, 284, 285
Armstrong, Whitworth and Company, 196
artisans, 69, 75, 80, 84, 103, 104, 144, 289
Atlantic Accord, 272, 286
Atlantic Charter, 225
Atlantic Groundfish Adjustment Program, 280
Atlantic Groundfish Strategy, 280
Attuiock, 69
Avalon, colony of, 47
Avalon Peninsula, 8, 41, 42, 46, 53, 57, 61, 73, 79, 101, 138, 141, 143, 158, 177, 223, 238, 290